Archaeology of Precolumbian Florida

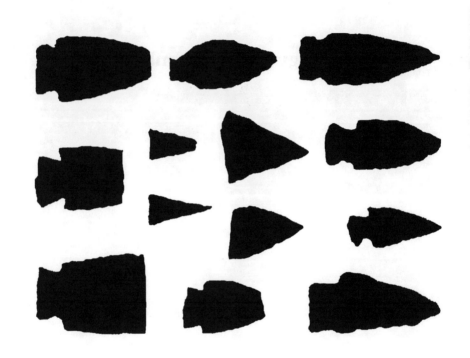

ARCHAEOLOGY

of Precolumbian Florida

Jerald T. Milanich

University Press of Florida

Gainesville Tallahassee Tampa Boca Raton Pensacola Orlando Miami Jacksonville

Library of Congress Cataloging-in-
Publication Data

Milanich, Jerald T.
    Archaeology of Precolumbian Florida/Jerald T. Milanich
        p. cm.
    Includes bibliographical references and index.
    ISBN 0-8130-1272-4 (cloth: acid-free paper).—ISBN
0-8130-1273-2 (paper: acid-free paper)
        1. Indians of North America—Florida—Antiquities. 2. Florida—
Antiquities. I. Title
    E78.F6M545   1994   93-36888
    975.9'01—dc20   CIP

The University Press of Florida is the schol-
arly publishing agency for the State
University System of Florida, comprised of
Florida A&M University, Florida Atlantic
University, Florida International
University, Florida State University,
University of Central Florida, University of
Florida, University of North Florida,
University of South Florida, and University
of West Florida.

University Press of Florida
15 Northwest 15th Street
Gainesville, FL 32611

CONTENTS

 **ILLUSTRATIONS**

Tables

Pensacola

Apalachicola

Tallahassee

Aucilla R.

River

Suwannee

Jacksonville

St. Johns River

Withlacoochee R.

Orlando

Tampa

Kissimmee R.

Lake
Okeechobee

Caloosahatchee

Fort Myers

Miami

0   100
miles

Modern Florida

PREFACE

Today the mounds and villages of the precolumbian native American Indians who once lived in Florida are still very much in evidence. In parks like Lake Jackson in the panhandle, Turtle Mound on the Atlantic coast, and Crystal River on the Gulf coast, modern Floridians can visit archaeological sites—shell and earthen middens and mounds—left by the native inhabitants of Florida. Remnants of thousands of other sites exist, although countless others have vanished under the onslaught of roads, buildings, and parking lots that are built each year in Florida to accommodate a continually growing population. Where Jacksonville, Tampa, Miami, and Disney World exist today, precolumbian populations once flourished.

Who were these native Florida Indians? How long were they here? How did they live? These are questions that we can answer using information gathered from a century or more of archaeological investigations.

From such research we know that at least several hundred thousand people, possibly more, were living in Florida in the late fifteenth or early sixteenth century when Europeans first sighted the peninsula's coasts. Ancestors of those native Floridians had been here for 12,000 years. Over the millennia many different cultures had developed, adjusting to different environments and dealing with the problems and challenges presented by increasing populations, new ideas, and innovations. In 1492, at the time of Christopher Columbus's first voyage, thousands of native villages were occupied between the Florida Keys and the western end of the panhandle.

The European conquest of Florida was catastrophic for these native peoples. Two hundred and fifty years after the conquistadors invaded, the indigenous populations had been decimated. They could not maintain their numbers in the face of diseases brought to North America from Europe and, perhaps, Africa. No descendants of the native American Indians who had lived here since people first migrated into the land we now call Florida survived the European conquest.

Florida would not remain empty of native peoples, however. During the first half of the eighteenth century Creek Indians moved southward into Florida, often occupying lands previously inhabited by the Apalachee and Timucuan peoples. These Creeks were the ancestors of the modern Seminole and Miccosukee peoples.

This book relates the story of the native Florida Indians before the coming of the Europeans. Using information gleaned from archaeological excavations we will look back though time and examine the precolumbian cultures, cultures that were ancestral to the many societies living in Florida in the early sixteenth century. Theirs is an intriguing story, one that is an important part of our heritage.

A future volume will tell the story of the native peoples of Florida after the coming of the Europeans. In this book—with a few exceptions—I deliberately have not cited archaeological or documentary evidence from the colonial period as clues to understanding precolumbian Florida. Instead, those sources will be used to recount the stories of the colonial-period Indians and the impact of the European presence in the sixteenth and seventeenth centuries.

It would be possible to write an entire book about each of Florida's precolumbian native cultures. Indeed, books have been written about some of them. The goal here is a more modest one: to provide an introduction, albeit a thorough one, to the various precolumbian groups. This book is written for anyone—scholar, student, resident, or visitor—interested in the history of those native peoples.

There is a story behind the development of this book. Just as the native peoples living here at the time the Europeans invaded could trace their ancestry back to earlier societies and populations, so can this volume trace its genesis back to an earlier book, *Florida Archae-*

ology, first published in 1980. That volume had its beginning in September 1972 when Charles Fairbanks and I signed a contract to write it. The contract called for delivery of a completed manuscript in March 1974. We did not make it. Not until late June 1979 was the manuscript finally submitted to the publisher. *Florida Archaeology* appeared in print in September 1980, eight years after its inception.

After more than a decade that volume became dated, the result of the huge number of archaeological research projects undertaken in Florida since 1980. It grew clear that we needed a new book recounting what we have learned.

This volume begins with a history of archaeology in Florida, followed by ten chapters divided into three parts, each with an introduction. My intent has been to create a readable overview, but I also have tried to provide extensive citations so that readers who wish to do so can consult the original publications and reports.

The first part of the book describes the earliest aboriginal cultures in Florida, those we call Paleoindian and Archaic. These peoples were hunter-gatherers, although by 2000 B.C. Archaic villagers must have been using a variety of local plants, some of which they may have cultivated, or, at least, encouraged to grow in proximity to settlements. The nature of these horticultural practices was quite different from the farming done by some later peoples.

By 500 B.C. a number of distinctive cultures were inhabiting the environmental zones of Florida. Although such regional cultures probably were present in the Archaic period, we have trouble recognizing them in the archaeological record. It is only after about 500 B.C., when distinctive styles of pottery were made in different parts of the state, that we can begin to talk about regional cultures with some certainty. These regional cultures, each correlating with different geographical and environmental zones, are the focus of part II.

Sometime between A.D. 800 and 1000 farming societies with social and political institutions more complex than those present earlier first appeared in the eastern portion of northwest Florida. One new culture, Fort Walton, was similar to the agricultural societies developed elsewhere in the interior of the southeastern United States during the same period. Archaeologists call these Mississippian cultures, deriving the name from the Mississippi River Valley where such cultures have been studied.

Though true Mississippian societies were not found outside of northwest Florida, there is no doubt that other Florida societies were influenced by Fort Walton and, perhaps, Mississippian cultures north and west of the state. Part 3 discusses the Fort Walton culture and contemporary cultures of the late precolumbian period.

Because many among the audience for which this book is written are not archaeologists, I have tried to keep the archaeological jargon to a minimum. For instance, radiocarbon dates are not presented in radiocarbon years, nor have they been corrected using bristlecone pine corrections, nor are the standard deviations given. Readers will immediately recognize that last sentence as a fine example of the type of jargon I hope to avoid. But they should be aware that radiocarbon dates are not exact calendar dates and that various corrections are necessary to turn them into exact dates or, more correctly, into a probable calendar date range (for a complete discussion of radiocarbon dating, see Thomas 1989:292–307). The radiocarbon dates presented here are only guides. For the earlier cultures in Florida's history (the peoples described in chapters 2 and 3) the radiocarbon dates are several hundred years or more younger (nearer the present) than the corresponding calendar date. As dates get closer to the present, the difference between radiocarbon date and true calendar date grows less.

Much debate surrounds the interpretation of radiocarbon dates, and research on their calibrations continues. Even so, radiocarbon dating is a powerful tool for archaeology. Its widespread use beginning in the 1950s has revolutionized archaeological dating and provided uncontroverted evidence for the age of human cultures in the Americas and the evolution of those cultures over time.

A note concerning terminology is needed. Throughout the book, I use culture and geographical terms to refer to specific regions of the state, especially in parts II and III. The terms—for example, north Florida, north-central Florida, southwest Florida—designate specific regions and are more precise than the more general, less well defined geographical indicators such as northern Florida and southern Florida. At various times the area occupied by a regional culture may be the same as a geographical region, and both terms are used interchangeably—for instance, the southwest region is the same as the Caloosahatchee region.

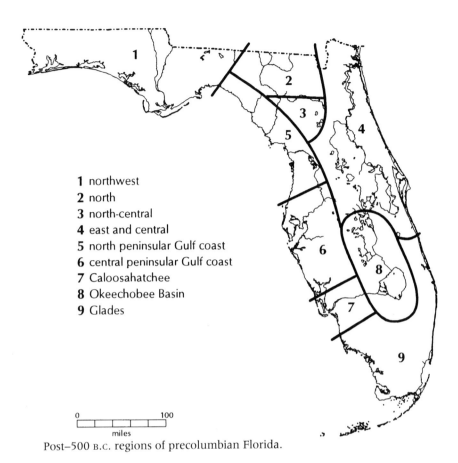

1 northwest
2 north
3 north-central
4 east and central
5 north peninsular Gulf coast
6 central peninsular Gulf coast
7 Caloosahatchee
8 Okeechobee Basin
9 Glades

0   100
miles

Post–500 B.C. regions of precolumbian Florida.

The illustrations in this volume include something old, something new, and a lot borrowed. My intention is to show some of the past and present people involved in Florida archaeology while giving some sense of the history of archaeological research. The way research was carried out in the 1930s or even in the 1950s is different from its interdisciplinary nature today. I also have provided illustrations of the stone artifacts and potsherds that typify what archaeologists usually find in sites, interspersing them with illustrations of less common but more spectacular examples of precolumbian crafts, such as Weeden Island pottery vessels.

Last, our information about the precolumbian peoples of Florida is uneven across the state. We know more about some regions and cultures and times, less about others. That is the nature of archaeological enquiry. And the more known about a culture, the more sophisticated the research questions posed in subsequent research.

The next time you order an ice cream cone at River Walk in Jacksonville, dine at a bayfront restaurant in Tampa, stay at a hotel on the Miami River, or dance to country tunes at Church Street Station in Orlando, squint a bit and visualize how things must have been hundreds and even thousands of years ago when native American Indians walked in the places you are walking. As much as the English settlers at Jamestown or the Spanish missions of California, the history of those native American Indians is a part of our heritage. I hope this book provides an opportunity to understand that heritage better and to heed the voices of the people who lived in precolumbian Florida.

In writing this book I have relied on reports, articles, books, and monographs written by a number of archaeologists. They are too numerous to mention, but I thank them all. James B. Griffin, Nancy Marie White, and J. Raymond Williams were kind enough to read complete drafts of *Archaeology of Precolumbian Florida*. Their comments—sometimes humorous, sometimes critical, and always worthwhile—were a tremendous help in the final crafting of the manuscript. David Brose also read a draft and provided commentary. I also received critical support from Judith Bense, Brinnen Carter, Glen Doran, Albert Goodyear, John Griffin, Kenneth Johnson, Timothy Kohler, George Luer, William Marquardt, Jeffrey Mitchem, Claudine Payne, Michael Russo, and David Webb. All read and commented on various chapters. Many of this group of seventeen scientists also provided access to unpublished data and ideas. They certainly have my thanks for their contributions.

Thanks are also due the editors and staff of the University Press of Florida. Walda Metcalf and the rest of the crew who work in the funny houses behind the Krystal fast-food restaurant always are supportive of my endeavors. They also are an excellent publishing house, and I have enjoyed working with them. My maps were drafted by Jan Coyne, one of the new breed of computer cartographers. Her skills sure made my life easier.

Last, I wish to acknowledge the students who wrote sections of the Florida Comprehensive Historic Preservation Plan (the Compplan). These students helped me to realize the need for a new overview of

Florida archaeology, and they provided a valuable introduction to new literature and new ideas related to Florida archaeology. They are George Avery, Nina T. Borremans, Kathleen Hoffman, William Johnson, Laura Kozuch, Jeffrey Mitchem, Claudine Payne, Michael Russo, Rebecca Saunders, and Karen Jo Walker. Five of these ten have gone on to receive their doctoral degrees, writing dissertations on topics related to their Compplan contributions. A sixth has completed her master's thesis, and the other four are in the final stages of dissertation writing, most on subjects related to their Compplan topics. Our Compplan project was supported, funded, and guided by James Miller, chief of the Bureau of Archaeological Research, an agency of the Florida Division of Historical Resources. It was also critiqued by numerous Florida archaeologists, who provided valuable insights.

I hope that it is clear from these acknowledgments that archaeologists no longer work alone. Uncovering what happened hundreds and thousands of years ago is a complicated process, one that must involve many people working together. In Florida we are lucky to have a competent group of archaeologists willing to collaborate to understand the past. It is my sincere hope that this volume has done justice to their contributions.

A Brief History of
Archaeology in Florida

1 The growth of archaeological research in Florida since the 1960s has been phenomenal. Today the Florida Archaeological Council, an organization of professional archaeologists who work in the state, numbers more than seventy individuals. In 1980 the organization did not exist. Significantly, most archaeologists are not employed in universities or museums; the majority work for government agencies, like the Florida Bureau of Archaeological Research or the National Park Service, or they are employed by private companies. Their employment is due in part to federal and state laws and regulations, as well as county and city laws, that recognize the importance of managing our archaeological resources. Just as we have laws regulating and protecting our natural resources, so do we now have legislation managing our archaeological resources, laws that have stimulated an unprecedented amount of archaeological research.

Archaeological legislation results from increased public interest in the past, an interest reflected in the numerous newspaper accounts that continue to appear across the state. That interest also has led to a greater role for archaeology in public and private universities, and to the growth of private sector archaeology. Significant research is being done by faculty and a large number of graduate students, as well as by archaeological consultants. This legal and public surge of support for archaeology has brought about a boom in research in Florida. New publications and reports about the archaeology of Florida appear in

1

print almost daily. Our knowledge is increasing exponentially, making it almost impossible for one individual to digest it all.

Early Observers

The present success enjoyed by archaeology was not always the case. With a few notable exceptions, archaeological research in Florida dates only from the federal relief programs of the 1930s, when a handful of archaeologists practiced their profession. Even into the 1970s, relatively few practiced in the state. The archaeological boom began after 1970 and has been expanding ever since.

Before the 1930s, there were archaeological observations and projects carried out in Florida, several quite important, providing at least some information about the precolumbian peoples. The early European explorers and colonists certainly observed native peoples and must have seen earlier sites, remains left behind by precolumbian Indians. Some of the archaeological sites they saw are the ones being excavated today. For example, the French Huguenots in the mid-1560s observed the Timucua Indians of northeast Florida, perhaps the Saturiwa, interring their dead in mounds (Lorant 1946:115). Such mounds, probably associated with the St. Johns archaeological culture, have been excavated by archaeologists (e.g., Hemmings and Deagan 1973).

Another example is provided by the same French colony. René de Laudonnière, its leader, mentions a long causeway, probably a linear earthwork, at the native village of Edelano, located on an island in the St. Johns River (Laudonnière 1975:115, 131). The island is probably Murphy Island just south of Palatka, where such earthworks have been noted by archaeologists (Goggin 1952c:131).

Later in the sixteenth century the Spanish governor of St. Augustine, Pedro Menéndez de Avilés, also saw native cultural features that today are important archaeological sites. He and his men visited temples and the house of a chief built on top of large mounds at the Calusa Indian town of Calos located on Mound Key south of Fort Myers (Rogel in Zubillaga 1946). More than one hundred years later, Franciscan missionary priests who visited the same town provided intriguing firsthand observations about one of these mounds and the building on it (Hann 1991:159–169). Recently archaeologists have reconnoitered the same mounds.

Other early travelers in Florida also described archaeological sites. The naturalists John and William Bartram noted many Indian remains, some of which can be identified and have been investigated in the twentieth century. One notable site is Mount Royal, a large St. Johns culture mound just north of Lake George in western Putnam County. William Bartram twice visited the site (in 1765 and 1774) and described it:

> At about fifty yards distance . . . stands a magnificent Indian mount. About fifteen years ago I visited this place, at which time there were no settlements of white people, but all appeared wild and savage; yet in that uncultivated state it possessed an almost inexpressible air of grandeur. . . . But what greatly contributed towards completing the magnificence of the scene, was a noble Indian highway, which led from the great mount, on a straight line, three quarters of a mile, first through a point or wing of the orange grove, and continuing thence through an awful forest of live oaks, it was terminated by palms and laurel magnolias, on the verge of an oblong lake, which was on the edge of an extensive green level savanna. This grand highway was about fifty yards wide, sunk a little below the common level, and the earth thrown up on each side, making a bank of about two feet high. (Bartram 1928:101–102)

The large mound and "highway" still exist today.

First Excavations

These early observers were not archaeologists, and they did not excavate any of the sites they saw. The first actual digging should probably not be called archaeology but rather antiquarianism. It seems to have been undertaken by a New Hampshire physician, John Durkee, who had come to Jacksonville for his health. In 1834 he dug in a mound on the St. Johns River below Jacksonville and wrote his brother of his observations; it was nearly a century and a half before they were published (Hoole 1974). During the Second Seminole War in the late 1830s, another physician, Samuel Forry, excavated a mound near Fort Taylor (west of Lake Poinsett in northeast Osceola County) during a lull in his duties as a military surgeon (Forry 1928:98–99).

None of these or other early nineteenth-century excavations contributed much to our knowledge of Florida's past. Until the middle of the nineteenth century, archaeology in the United States was in what

Gordon Willey and Jeremy Sabloff (1974:21–41) have called the Speculative Period. These early students of both archaeology and native American Indians were content to weave speculative fabrics on a minimum of actual data in order to satisfy their own interests in ancient humans. Some excavations were conducted, but generally without much purpose except to find things.

In 1859, Daniel G. Brinton published a book about the Florida peninsula in which he summarized his own travels and the little coherent information available at that time (Brinton 1859). Henry R. Schoolcraft, in a monumental work on native American Indians, devoted a brief summary to the elaborate Gulf coast aboriginal pottery that we now classify as Weeden Island (Schoolcraft 1854:75–82). But these scattered descriptions probably did not yield much reliable information about the native people in Florida's past.

Somewhat better work was stimulated by the publication in 1851 of an English translation of A. von Morlot's work on kitchen middens, now more commonly called shell middens (Morlot 1861:284–343). This Danish archaeologist demonstrated that in Scandinavia highly significant information could be recovered from these trash piles deposited by early inhabitants. Earlier speculation had alternated between considering them intentionally constructed mounds or platforms and viewing them as the natural result of hurricanes. Morlot set a fashion in archaeology that has continued intermittently to the present, and his contribution cannot be ignored.

Perhaps the first person to follow Morlot's lead and to dig in Florida shell middens was Jeffries Wyman, the first curator of the Peabody Museum at Harvard University. He first dug in shell middens along the St. Johns River in 1867 and continued more excavations in 1869, 1871, and 1874 (Wyman 1868, 1875). Wyman, a scientifically trained observer in the natural sciences, concluded that the shell mounds were indeed made by native American Indians, thus offering a final answer to the debate that had spanned several decades. He was able to demonstrate that the mounds dated from the precolumbian period and that they were stratigraphically deposited, with older artifacts below younger ones.

Wyman's pioneering work was followed by a series of excavations by S. T. Walker, perhaps the most important of which was at Cedar Key on the Gulf coast. There he observed stratigraphy and applied an evolutionary framework to his data (Walker 1880, 1883, 1885). At that time the Smithsonian Institution and the associated Bureau of American Ethnology were engaged in a survey of aboriginal sites in the United States. Their interest, in contrast to that of Wyman and Walker, was largely in the "monuments," or mounds. The bureau's field agent, J. P. Rogan, dug two mounds in Alachua County and located a number of others that were listed and briefly described in a catalogue published by Cyrus Thomas (1894). Rogan's excavations leave much to be desired by modern standards, and Thomas's summary does little but list the mounds. The descriptions are so vague that it is often impossible to determine the exact location or cultural content of the sites. The work of Rogan and Thomas did, however, focus attention on the numerous and potentially informative archaeological sites and artifacts in Florida.

The closing decade of the nineteenth century marked the beginning of the extensive archaeological work of Clarence B. Moore, a wealthy Philadelphian who had traveled widely and had made his first visit to Florida in 1875. Moore equipped himself with a coal-fired, steam-powered houseboat, the *Gopher*, in which he traveled to archaeological sites in the southeastern United States during the winter season. His first Florida excavations took place along the St. Johns River in 1892 (Moore 1892–94). During subsequent winters—he continued to excavate sites until nearly 1920—Moore worked his way around the entire peninsula and also visited sites in the panhandle. He excavated readily accessible burial mounds and dug in many middens that were within reach of waters navigable by the *Gopher*.

In the light of modern archaeological techniques and methods, it is easy to criticize the work of this energetic individual. Indeed, many of his mound excavations completely demolished the object of his investigations, leaving only a donut-shaped deposit of spoil for the modern archaeologist. But he did excavate carefully, and he kept respectable notes, which are available today (Davis 1987). He was also an astute observer, noting differences in types of mounds as well as the artifacts in the mounds he excavated. Moore was also careful to contribute many of the objects he unearthed—especially ceramic vessels—to museums, where they can be restudied today.

It is easy to lament Moore's destruction of so many sites—perhaps hundreds—but had he not excavated them, some other persons might have, resulting in the loss of all of the information. Moore also was prompt in publishing reports on his excavations, including an abundance of illustrations. Comparison of his field notes with his publications shows that he did little actual analysis beyond putting in print what are in effect illustrated field notes. However, not all of the information in his field notes found its way into print. Modern students of archaeology who use his data should always consult the original field notes from his excavations, which are catalogued and curated at the Huntington Free Library in New York. The largest number of the ceramic vessels he excavated from Florida sites are curated at the New York branch of the National Museum of the American Indian, formerly the Museum of the American Indian.

Modern archaeologists have a peculiar love-hate relationship with Clarence Moore—hate for excavating all of those sites but love for saving so much information that otherwise might have been lost. As Gordon Willey (1949a) has amply demonstrated, it is possible to fit much of Moore's work into modern classifications, and his reports are the starting point for research in much of the state, especially east Florida and the Gulf coast and panhandle regions.

Around the turn of the century, the number of winter visitors to Florida began to increase and to include some with an avocational interest in the past and in archaeology. These visitors occasionally dug in archaeological sites. With a few exceptions (e.g., Featherstonhaugh 1897, 1899), most of the information they might have produced was never recorded. Local residents also excavated in mounds, sometimes as part of Sunday afternoon outings (e.g., Bell 1883). Again, details on such work were either not recorded or were superficial.

One extraordinary late nineteenth-century project was the Pepper-Hearst expedition to Key Marco on the southwest Florida coast, directed by Frank H. Cushing (Cushing 1897; Gilliland 1975, 1989). Cushing's discovery of elaborate and varied wooden and fiber objects preserved in muck has never been duplicated. These materials—objects normally not preserved in archaeological deposits—provide a unique glimpse of the material culture of the native peoples who lived on that coast.

Cushing felt that the artifacts in the muck represented refuse collected under pile dwellings, such as those suggested by mid-nineteenth-century reports from the Upper Rhineland and Switzerland

Sites and locales visited or investigated prior to the 1940s.

(Cushing 1897). His accounts of the discoveries created a stir at the time, although his imaginative reconstructions of the culture of Key Marco have been largely revised.

Cushing, like Moore, did much to focus public attention on the range and abundance of archaeological materials in the peninsula. Today the artifacts from Key Marco remain an unsurpassed study collection for information about the maritime native cultures of Florida (see Gilliland 1975).

While World War I occupied the attention of many, there was a hiatus in the serious study of archaeology in Florida. One major exception was the work in 1917 of Nels C. Nelson at the Oak Hill site in Volusia County (Mitchem 1990). But one archaeological incident would create great controversy. During the war years, a drainage development near Vero on the east coast uncovered a human skeleton in presumed association with the remains of mammoth and other Pleistocene animals. The opinions of contemporary experts differed on whether this and a similar find at Melbourne a few years later could be taken as valid evidence of the presence of humans in the New World during glacial times. Aleš Hrdlička, prominent physical anthropologist at the United States National Museum (a division of the Smithsonian Institution), argued that the Vero and Melbourne finds were intrusive to the Melbourne geological formation, and few people were prepared to counter his opinion. More recent examination of the crania has suggested that they may indeed belong to the Paleoindian period (Stewart 1946). A final resolution of the cultural affiliation(s) of these two collections of human skeletal remains probably will never be reached.

The 1920s and 1930s

All these varied activities meant that by 1920 the archaeological study of Florida Indians was at least started, but by modern standards little problem-oriented research had been done. It was recognized that the state had many differing archaeological sites within its varied geographic areas, but no synthesis or taxonomy of those sites and the cultures they represented had been attempted. There was no cogent program of archaeological research, and no agency or institution within the state was engaged in archaeological research or teaching. As elsewhere in the country, both field and analytical techniques were either in their infancy or were ignored by the few people working sporadically in the region.

The land boom of the early 1920s brought an influx of residents, many of whom were informed about and interested in archaeology. Florida also drew the interest of archaeologists and other scientists eager to experience the state's charms. In 1923–1924 a major excavation was undertaken at the large, complex site of Weeden Island on the western shore of Old Tampa Bay. Under the auspices of the Smithsonian Institution, fieldwork was supervised by Matthew W. Stirling under the general direction of Jesse W. Fewkes (Fewkes 1924). Because Fewkes and Stirling were professionally trained, this can be considered the first truly scientific archaeological project in the state. Nearly a century after Dr. Durkee's digging professional archaeology was under way. The excavations established the type site for the Weeden Island culture, providing basic definitive data on which future studies would rely. For the first time there was an accurate description of one of the burial mounds found throughout much of west peninsular and northern Florida and associated with the spectacular pottery that had been described by Holmes two decades earlier. More important, the Weeden Island excavations established an interest in the area by the Bureau of American Ethnology and the Smithsonian Institution.

When the Civil Works Administration was organized in 1933 as part of Franklin Roosevelt's scheme to combat the depression, Matthew Stirling realized that Florida and archaeology were admirably suited. Archaeologists needed a great deal of hand labor and thus could employ large numbers of workers. They did not compete with private businesses, and Florida's mild climate meant that work could be carried out year-round. As a result, nine federal projects were established in Florida, all sponsored by the Federal Emergency Relief Administration. Stirling also apparently realized that the large numbers of people assigned to the projects meant that excavations could be undertaken at large sites that might not otherwise be investigated.

For the next seven years the various federal relief agency projects were to contribute a great fund of information on the archaeology of Florida and to develop chronologies and classifications for the state. Much of what was learned would be put to use in the years to come.

The nine federally sponsored projects were at six Florida locations: Perico Island and three sites on the Little Manatee River in Manatee County (including Thomas Mound), the Englewood Mound in Sarasota County, the large Belle Glade site group near Lake Okeechobee in Palm Beach County, the Ormond Beach Mound in Volusia County, and two sites on Canaveral peninsula in Brevard County. Trained archaeologists were the field directors. Unfortunately no provision was made in the Civil Works Administration or the succeeding Works Project Administration for postexcavation analysis and the writing of reports on these projects. A few smaller excavations were reported in rather cursory fashion (e.g., Stirling 1935). Later, Gordon Willey (1949a) was able to analyze the data from the sites on the Gulf coast and to use the material in his pioneering Gulf coast study. And still later Jesse Jennings, Gordon Willey, and Marshall Newman (1957) reported on the Ormond Beach Mound, leaving only the Canaveral sites largely unreported. The notes from the sites as well as the collections themselves were catalogued in the National Museum of Natural History of the Smithsonian Institution, where they are still available to students of archaeology.

While the primary goal of the emergency relief archaeological projects was to provide employment and thus stimulate the economy, they did set the pattern for large-scale publicly supported excavations. And the excavations produced information that is fundamental to our understanding of the archaeology of precolumbian and colonial period Florida.

During the depression, an additional, and more prolonged, effort in archaeology was the work conducted by the Civilian Conservation Corps in the Ocala National Forest. Some of the project leaders conducted site surveys and limited excavations in the forest during their free time. Reports of their findings, which were solely descriptive and published in a limited mimeographed format, provide site locations and typological information on which later work could build (Abshire et al. 1935; Potter and Taylor 1937; Anonymous n.d.).

The result of all this early work, especially that undertaken under the auspices of the various federal agencies, was to make Florida's public more aware of the state's archaeological resources and of what should be done about them. The Florida Historical Society formed a committee on archaeology that published an inventory of known sites. For a brief period, Florida even had a state archaeologist (Vernon Lamme), who excavated several sites, including several in Jefferson County. Soon the Florida Geological Survey began an archaeological survey conducted by Clarence Simpson, who located a large number of sites and carried out excavations in Hillsborough County in 1935–1938, some in conjunction with federal relief projects. With members of his family, Clarence Simpson also excavated in a number of northern Florida sites. Artifacts from these latter investigations, as well as some field notes, are curated at the Florida Museum of Natural History.

The formation of the Southeastern Archaeological Conference in 1938 (in which persons working in Florida were not directly involved, probably because of lack of institutional affiliation) served as a means of developing regional chronologies for the southeast region of the

A federal relief program archaeological field crew in 1937 or early 1938 at Thomas Mound on the Little Manatee River in Hillsborough County. The photograph was taken by Clarence Simpson (courtesy Florida Museum of Natural History).

United States. When institutional archaeology did begin, it could find a ready placement for Florida chronologies (see Stirling 1936) in the framework of the entire Southeast.

The Modern Era

At the time archaeological work was halted by World War II, there was a generally understood chronology for the Southeast (including Florida), some valuable excavations at sites that were to become type sites (e.g., Weeden Island and Belle Glade), recognition of the St. Johns area and the Gulf coast as specific culture areas, and a beginning of a local chronology. A significant project was a survey of the panhandle coast by Gordon Willey and Richard B. Woodbury; the two published a chronology for the region in 1942.

Immediately after the war, archaeology seemed to spring to life with a number of developments that have persisted to the present. In 1946 the Florida Park Service established a program of archaeology directed by John W. Griffin with headquarters in Sebring. Griffin, aided by Hale G. Smith and, after 1948, by Ripley Bullen, investigated a number of precolumbian and colonial period sites. Under Griffin's leadership, a file of known sites was established. Park Service records show more than 560 sites were recorded, many visited by Griffin and his assistants. Early on, Griffin integrated history and archaeology in studies of the mission system, other colonial sites, and sites of the plantation period. Mark Boyd was the Park Service historian at the time and collaborated with Griffin in these studies.

The names of sites that Griffin and his team investigated read like a who's who of Florida archaeological sites. Park Service investigations resulted in a large number of scientific publications by Griffin, Smith, Boyd, and Bullen (e.g., Boyd, Smith, and Griffin 1951; Bullen 1949, 1951b, 1952b; Griffin 1946, 1947, 1948a, b, 1949b, 1950; Griffin and Bullen 1950; Griffin and Smith 1948, 1949, 1954). All are frequently cited classics in Florida archaeology.

Griffin also promoted archaeology in the state through an active program of public lectures and a number of popular articles, many published in the *Florida Highways* magazine. The latter, well illustrated and with titles like "Digging Up Florida's Past," "History along Florida's Roads," and "Early Hunters of Florida," were reprinted and distributed by the Park Service. These activities and media coverage of ongoing excavations did much to bring archaeology to the public eye.

In 1948 the office of Park Service archaeologist was moved to Gainesville to the Florida State Museum on the campus of the University of Florida. When the Park Service ceased archaeological activities in 1953, its collections and records, along with Ripley Bullen, were transferred to the museum. Today the records and collections are still curated there and are used regularly. Perhaps more than any other single activity, the Florida Park Service's archaeology initiative was the birth of modern archaeology in the state. It is safe to say that the Park Service archaeology program led to the inclusion of archaeology as a discipline at both the University of Florida and Florida State University, as well as at the Florida State Museum. It is a tribute to John Griffin that so much was accomplished in so short a time. And Griffin did it all on a shoestring: the Park Service's budget for archaeology for the 1947–48 fiscal year, including all salaries, was $11,277.50!

One Florida Park Service activity was the organization of a small working conference on Florida archaeology, held at Daytona Beach in 1947. Those in attendance included Mark Boyd, Winston Ehrmann (a University of Florida faculty member who chaired the Organizing

John Griffin in 1948 at his Florida Park Service office in the Florida State
Museum on the campus of the University of Florida. A recent furniture
survey of the anthropology range at the museum left the staff flabbergasted.
Griffin's desk, identified by marks in the lower, open drawer, is still being
used in the historical archaeological laboratory.

Committee of the Florida Anthropological Society), Charles Fairbanks,
John Goggin, John Griffin, Wesley Hurt, Albert Manucy, Hale Smith,
Antonio Waring, and Gordon Willey. A second, larger conference was
held at Rollins College in 1949, and its proceedings of the latter were
edited by John Griffin (Griffin 1949). These formal and informal con-
ferences involved people from neighboring states and served to define
the immediate goals of the discipline in the state.

Upon the withdrawal of the Park Service from archaeology, the Florida State Museum (now the Florida Museum of Natural History), a unit of the University of Florida, became active in archaeology. Its staff began a broad program of excavation, concentrated more in the northern half of the state. Reports appeared regularly and included a museum monograph series. Ripley Bullen and William H. Sears staffed the museum's Florida archaeology program from the 1950s into the early 1960s. Throughout his career in archaeology at the museum, Bullen, who died in 1976, was assisted by his wife, Adelaide Kendall Bullen. She participated in many excavations and published a number of articles with him (often as senior author). Trained as a physical anthropologist, she maintained an office and laboratory at the Florida State Museum and provided osteological expertise for numerous archaeological projects, despite being unsalaried.

Another important curator at the museum has been Elizabeth S. Wing, who has helped to pioneer zooarchaeological research in the United States. The comparative collections she has assembled and the analysis done by her and several generations of students (as well as visiting scientists who regularly use her laboratory) have provided new vistas on the subsistence systems, diets, and environments of pre-columbian Floridians. The numerous publications of these museum curators—Adelaide and Ripley Bullen, William Sears (who moved to Florida Atlantic University in 1963), and Elizabeth Wing—are classics in the field, and many are cited in this book.

Two years after the Park Service archaeologists began work, John M. Goggin was appointed archaeologist in the Department of Sociology at the University of Florida. Beginning with the 1949–1950 academic year, a separate department of anthropology was established. One course offered was APY 400 Field Session in Archeology (du Toit 1986: 29–31). The next year graduate courses were taught.

During the Park Service days, Goggin often collaborated and interacted with Griffin, helping to expand the state site files and exchanging information. Goggin's level of archaeological research nearly matched that of the Park Service (Goggin 1948, 1949a, b, 1950a, b, 1951, 1952a, b, c, 1953).

Following Goggin's death in 1963, Charles H. Fairbanks became chair and continued the program of research and student training. The department received permission to grant doctoral degrees in 1967. The first Ph.D. degree was granted to Barbara Purdy in 1971. Purdy later

Attendees at the 1947 conference sponsored by the Florida Park Service were (*left to right*) John Goggin, Charles Brookfield (National Audubon Society), Albert Manucy (National Park Service), John Griffin, Hale Smith, Wesley Hurt (Alabama Museum of Natural History), Charles Fairbanks, Antonio Waring, Jr. (of Savannah), and Gordon Willey. Other attendees were Mark Boyd, W. W. Ehrmann (University of Florida), and Lewis Scoggin (Florida Park Service). In his annual report for 1947–48, Griffin wrote, "This was the first conference to be held on Florida archaeology, and the discussions proved to be of great value, particularly since so much of the recent research material is unpublished."

Ripley Bullen in the field on the Chattahoochee River–Jim Woodruff Reservoir project in 1953. It was his first major project after joining the faculty of the Florida State Museum, today the Florida Museum of Natural History (courtesy Florida Museum of Natural History).

joined the University of Florida faculty, carrying out important research at a number of Archaic lithic sites in northern Florida before
turning her attention to wet sites archaeology.

Florida State University also organized an archaeology program
early on. In 1948, Hale Smith joined the faculty on a part-time basis
while completing his doctoral degree at the University of Michigan. In
1951 he returned full-time to FSU as chair of the anthropology department and undertook numerous projects in the northern part of the
state. Smith was soon joined by Charles Fairbanks, who was a member
of the FSU faculty for nearly a decade before replacing Goggin at the
University of Florida. By the mid-1950s Adelaide and Ripley Bullen,
Charles Fairbanks, John Goggin, John Griffin, William Sears, and Hale
Smith all were doing archaeology in Florida, and students in anthropology at FSU and anthropology/sociology at UF were producing
theses on archaeological topics.

Several other archaeology programs in the state deserve comment.
In 1948 the Florida Anthropological Society was established, and its
journal, *Florida Anthropologist*, continues to be published. This society is
one of the oldest state societies in the country and continues to provide a forum for interaction between professional and avocational
archaeologists. While the bulk of its publications have been on archaeological subjects, it still remains a society dedicated to the whole discipline of anthropology, and it receives support from persons with a
broad range of backgrounds and interests.

The statewide archaeological site file, begun by the Park Service and
supported early on by other archaeologists, such as Goggin, is a major source of information as well as a tool for managing archaeological resources within the state. Under the curation of the Bureau of
Archaeological Research in Tallahassee, the computerized inventory
continues to grow. Presently more than 13,000 sites are recorded in it.
It is an extraordinary database with information on the location and
cultural affiliation of each site, as well as other data, such as setting,
distance to water, and relevant collections.

In addition to his contributions to anthropology at the University of
Florida, John Goggin is largely responsible for several other initiatives
important to Florida archaeology. Among these were the definition of
cultural subareas of the state and the chronological stages found in each.
He also developed the concept of cultural tradition beyond what was

Charles Fairbanks and Kathleen Deagan in 1979 at a plantation site, St. Simons Island, Georgia. Deagan and her Florida State University field school students from St. Augustine were visiting Fairbanks's University of Florida archaeological field school. Such visits—a form of intellectual as well as social cross-fertilization—have a long tradition in Florida (courtesy Kathleen Deagan).

then in current usage. Goggin's approach focused attention on the persistence through time of distinctive ways of behavior that characterize a specific human group (Goggin 1949b). Many of the regional cultures recognized today in Florida were Goggin's taxonomic contructs.

Because Willey's *Archeology of the Florida Gulf Coast*, published in 1949, focused on the cultures of that region, Goggin initially concentrated his research on the northeast part of the state, and he published a definitive study (Goggin 1952c) of the northern St. Johns River area.

He also worked a great deal in south Florida, although his major monograph on that region was never published (Goggin n.d.).

Historical Archaeology

Even though C. B. Moore and others had discovered European objects in some sites and had demonstrated that native peoples continued to use mounds to inter their dead for at least a short time after the French and Spanish first were in Florida, it was not until 1939 that specifically historical archaeology was undertaken. In that year, W. J. Winter began a series of excavations in St. Augustine under the sponsorship of the National Park Service and the St. Augustine Historical Preservation Association. This work was to serve as a valuable foundation for future work in the city and eventually to develop into a full-scale problem-oriented program of historical archaeology.

During the period of Florida Park Service archaeology, Boyd, Smith, and Griffin (1951) had excavated in Spanish-Indian mission sites in the Tallahassee area, and the Park Service had carried out limited additional historical work elsewhere. Griffin recommended a number of historic sites for acquisition by the state, and, undoubtedly, had the Park Service continued archaeology, much more historical archaeology would have been done.

Goggin, at the University of Florida, embarked on a study of the colonial and postcolonial era, especially the Spanish colonial period. He was particularly interested in the native peoples of the mission system and the use of Spanish artifacts to date sites. His work resulted in a highly valuable study of Spanish olive jars (Goggin 1960) and, posthumously, in a definitive study of Spanish majolica (Goggin 1968). Goggin's investigations of Spanish sites also took him to the Caribbean, Mexico, and Panama, but his major interest remained the Spanish-Indian mission system.

At about the same time that Goggin was achieving breakthroughs in the identification and dating of Spanish artifacts, more work was beginning in sites of the colonial period. By the early 1950s, Hale Smith, at Florida State University, was actively engaged in Spanish–native American Indian archaeological research in the state.

With the approach of the quadricentennial of Florida's founding—1965, the 400th anniversary of St. Augustine—the Historic St. Augustine Preservation Commission (later designated the St. Augustine

Preservation Board) was established. Along with the St. Augustine Historical Society and the St. Augustine Restoration Foundation, the board undertook a series of excavations in the historic city designed to collect data on specific buildings that could be developed as historic houses to draw tourists.

In the decade following the quadricentennial, a continuing program of colonial archaeology was developed in St. Augustine through the cooperative action of the Historic St. Augustine Preservation Board, the University of Florida, Florida State University, and the Society of Colonial Dames (cf. Deagan 1974, 1983). The program approached research problems from the newly emphasized concept of processual archaeology, which encouraged seeking specific explanations of cultural process rather than simply digging because the sites were there. Since 1974 Kathleen Deagan and a host of Florida State University and University of Florida archaeological field schools have done much in St. Augustine to illuminate the Spanish colonial process. Today, Preservation Board and city archaeologists also are involved in excavations in St. Augustine.

During the same time, investigations began at sites pertaining to black history, initially at the slave cabins of the Kingsley Plantation on Ft.

Participants in a 1980 Florida State University archaeological field school in St. Augustine directed by Kathleen Deagan (*back row, right*). Generations of students have learned archaeology at field schools, which also provide graduate students with data for theses and dissertations. Reports resulting from nearly fifty years of field courses are a font of information on precolumbian and colonial-period Florida (courtesy Kathleen Deagan).

George Island north of Jacksonville (Fairbanks 1974). The development of historical, particularly colonial and plantation period, archaeology in Florida somewhat preceded similar developments in nearby states.

The historical archaeology begun by Griffin and others, especially the investigation of Spanish-Indian missions, continues to the present. Of particular note is the long-term project of the Florida Bureau of Archaeological Research at the late seventeenth-century Apalachee Indian–Spanish mission and town of San Luís in Tallahassee. That project, originally under the direction of Gary Shapiro and now headed by Bonnie McEwan, provides a model for other site-oriented projects that combine research and public education.

Underwater Archaeology

To some extent research into European and African traditions was concurrent with the development of underwater archaeology in the state. The first known underwater work occurred in 1952 during the attempt by the National Park Service to find some evidence of the French Huguenot fort at Fort Caroline on the St. Johns River east of Jacksonville. Later, Goggin did much to develop a strong program for the instruction of students and for research in underwater sites. His work at Oven Hill, a Seminole site on the Suwannee River, provided a solid foundation for the definition of the cultural remains of that tribal group (see Gluckman and Peebles 1974).

Of course, underwater archaeology was not confined to historic sites. Especially in the underwater caves in the northern karst (limestone-underlain) region of the state, Goggin did much pioneering work. At Devil's Den, he found human skeletal material with the same fluoride content as extinct mammals. Gradually, a series of finds, largely in the Ichetucknee, Santa Fe, Aucilla, and other rivers of northern Florida, showed a relatively dense scatter of Paleoindian stone points, frequently in the same localities as bones of extinct mammals. Reexamination of the mammal bones disclosed that a small percentage showed cut marks, evidently the result of butchering by humans (Bullen, Webb, and Waller 1970). Today evidence from the rivers leaves no doubt that Paleoindians and Pleistocene fauna coexisted in Florida (Webb et al. 1984), and important research on underwater Paleoindian and early Archaic period sites in the Aucilla River is

One of the pioneers of underwater archaeology as well as the first archaeologist on the faculty of the University of Florida, John Goggin, dives at Oven Hill, a site on the Suwannee River in Dixie County. He is holding a Seminole vessel recovered from the river. Investigation of the site took place intermittently from 1958 to 1962 (courtesy Margaret Knox Goggin). The inset is a museum inventory record of the same vessel (courtesy Florida Museum of Natural History).

continuing under the direction of S. David Webb of the Florida Museum of Natural History.

   Although the underwater archaeology program at the University of Florida was abandoned after Goggin's death, underwater archaeology is still thriving in Florida. One important facet is concerned with

Above-water operations at the Page-Ladson underwater site in the Aucilla River. Members of the excavation team used a floating pump system *(left)* to screen deposits from the river bottom. A field workstation is in operation on the shore (courtesy Brinnen Carter).

submerged shipwrecks off Florida's coasts, largely the east coast and the Florida Keys where colonial-period Spanish ships laden with treasure were lost to summer and fall hurricanes. After 1964 the program of state-supervised salvage of these wrecks increased substantially. Until 1967 the recovered materials comprising the state's share of salvaged material were conserved in the laboratory at the Department of Anthropology at the University of Florida. The proper cleaning and preservation of materials recovered from marine sites is even more important than that for land remains, since sea salts cause severe deterioration even after artifacts have been removed from the ocean. That laboratory probably was the first program of conservation and preservation of underwater artifacts in any state. Since 1967 the state's conservation program has been located in Tallahassee at the Division of Historical Resources (formerly the Division of Archives, History, and Records Management). The conservation laboratory still operates, although licensed salvage companies in the state are now responsible for the conservation of the materials their diving operations recover.

Another underwater focus is the investigation of Paleoindian, Archaic, and later period sites that lie off the present Gulf of Mexico and Atlantic coasts (Ruppé 1980; Stright 1987; Dunbar, Webb, Faught et al. 1989; Murphy 1990). Such research may someday revise much of what is known about early human settlements in Florida.

The Division of Historical Resources

The emergence of the Division of Historical Resources within the Florida Department of State was the result of a series of federal and state legislative and administrative initiatives that began in the middle 1960s. Enacting legislation also provided for protection of archaeological sites on state lands. Originally established as the Division of Archives, History, and Records Management, a name later changed to Division of Historical Resources, the agency has been a major governmental supporter of archaeology. Within the division, L. Ross Morrell was designated the first state archaeologist, and he soon assembled a staff that made the office the largest single employer of professional archaeologists in the state.

Today the division and its Bureau of Archaeological Research, the latter headed by James J. Miller, is one of the finest state archaeological agencies in the country. Over the years division and bureau archaeologists have published on a wide variety of topics—especially the aboriginal cultures and the Spanish missions of northwest Florida—and made major contributions to our understanding of the past.

The bureau, in conjunction with other sections of the division, also serves as liaison with various state and federal agencies, promulgates regulations in accordance with state laws, and reviews archaeological surveys and other research carried out by private firms in the state. And, as mentioned, the bureau curates the archaeological site files. In addition, the director of the division, as state historic preservation officer, is the liaison for nominations to the National Register of Historic Places and is charged with nominating historic or archaeological sites. The bureau and the division, its parental agency, are legally, literally, and figuratively guardians of Florida's archaeological resources. The agencies and their staffs deserve accolades for their activities in support of Florida archaeology.

The 1980s and Beyond

The period following 1980 has been a time of expansion. There continue to be significant state projects (sponsored by the Division of Historical Resources) and federal projects (sponsored by the National Park Service and the USDA Forestry Service). There is emphasis on archaeology in the anthropology departments at Florida Atlantic University, the Florida Museum of Natural History, Florida State University, Rollins College, the University of Central Florida, the University of Florida, the University of South Florida, and the University of West Florida. Although having no separate anthropology departments, the University of North Florida has an archaeologist on the faculty working in Florida, and the University of Miami has also sponsored archaeological research. Archaeology graduate students at several of these universities—FAU, FSU, UF, and USF—continue to carry out a large portion of the archaeology done in university settings. Theses and dissertations produced by graduate student archaeologists in Florida number in the hundreds. Some cities and counties also have archaeologists on staff, as does the Archaeological and Historical Conservancy, Inc., whose offices are housed in south Florida.

State funds (most often administered through the Division of Historical Resources) and various federal grants (notably the National Science Foundation and the National Endowment for the Humanities) provide resources for a great deal of research in the state. Other grants come from private foundations and organizations, such as the National Geographical Society, Colonial Dames, and Wentworth Foundation, as well as private corporations. Local and county governments also fund research in accordance with state and federal regulations, as do private companies. Most of this work is done by nongovermental archaeological consultants and firms. It is likely that most archaeological projects in Florida are being carried out in response to government-mandated regulations.

The Florida Anthropological Society continues to support archaeology and to provide a forum for cooperation between avocational and professional archaeologists. At times some of its members and regional chapters participate in field projects. Professional archaeologists have organized the Florida Archaeological Council and have become an effective voice for archaeology in the state.

The result of this growth in archaeology in Florida since 1980 is an explosion of new knowledge. New approaches, new field and analytical techniques, and an emphasis on interdisciplinary research have resulted not only in larger quantities of knowledge but in new types of information gathered within an increasingly more sophisticated and scientific milieu. Just as important is the presence of university, governmental, and agency archaeological programs in every part of the state. Such programs serve as centers from which long-term investigations of specific sites and regions can be carried out. The result is organized, high-quality research and new information on every part of the state, from Dade County and southeast Florida to Pensacola and the western panhandle.

Recent archaeological projects represent every time period from earliest to most recent. Some notable projects in southern Florida are the Granada site in Miami (Griffin et al. 1985), the Fort Center site in the Lake Okeechobee Basin (Sears 1982), and John Griffin's synthesis of the archaeology of Everglades National Park (Griffin 1988). Other large south Florida projects include the National Park Service's survey of the Big Cypress National Preserve, supervised by John Erenhardt and resulting in a number of reports from 1978 to 1980, and the work by William Marquardt and his students and associates on the southwest Florida coast (Russo 1991; Marquardt 1992). The growth of archaeology in southern Florida perhaps has been greater than in any other part of the state.

A host of archaeologists have been involved in projects around the greater Tampa Bay region in both coastal and inland locales. Projects associated with the excavation of archaeological sites impacted by the construction of Interstate 75 around Tampa Bay resulted in a particularly large number of significant studies, many initiated by University of South Florida archaeologists and their past or present students. Sites of almost every period have been investigated in the region—from Paleoindian to the Mississippian period—and the results have had a great influence on our interpretations not only of the native cultures of greater Tampa Bay but of the rest of the state as well (Luer and Almy 1982; Daniel and Wisenbaker 1987; Mitchem 1989; for a listing of the I-75 reports, see Daniel and Wisenbaker 1987:1–4).

On the opposite side of the state, Glen Doran and David Dickel of Florida State University directed the Windover Pond project, the excavation of 7,000-year-old artifacts and human burials, some with preserved brains and other tissue (Doran and Dickel 1988a, b; Doran 1992). Because of the specialized kinds of analyses that have been

William Marquardt at the Useppa Island site in southwest Florida. He and his field crews have sought the involvement of local people, successfully combining research with public education (courtesy Lindsey Williams).

applied to the unique collections from the site, Windover Pond may turn out to be one of the most significant archaeological sites ever excavated. Its importance, as well as a reflection of how far archaeology has come in Florida, is underlined by Glen Doran's being named Floridian of the Year by the *Orlando Sentinel* newspaper in 1987. Barbara Purdy's investigations and overviews of archaeological wet sites in Florida have also garnered public attention as well as producing important new information, especially on plant remains (Purdy 1987a, b, 1991).

The post-1980 era saw completion of the McKeithen Weeden Island study in northern Florida (Milanich, Cordell et al. 1984). That region has been the focus of a number of excavations and surveys focusing on the late precolumbian and colonial-period cultures (Johnson 1991; Weisman 1992). Studies of the various societies of the colonial period and their interaction with the Spaniards in Florida—especially the Franciscan–Indian missions—have blossomed across northern Florida from St. Augustine west to Tallahassee. Kathleen Deagan has published on St. Augustine and colonial Spanish material culture in general (Deagan 1983, 1987), and she and many others are continuing studies of material culture.

In addition to Brent Weisman's work at the Fig Springs mission site in north Florida, a number of other mission projects are under way, including the long-term research at San Luís in Tallahassee supervised by Bonnie McEwan (Marrinan 1985; McEwan 1991; Hoshower 1992; Weisman 1992). In Florida these mission studies, as well as studies of colonial-period native groups, have been informed by and carried out in conjunction with excellent historical research (Hann 1988, 1990, 1991; Worth 1992).

The Tallahassee region and all of northwest Florida have been the focus of a great deal of significant archaeological enquiry. Two precolumbian cultures in that region, Fort Walton and Weeden Island, have been investigated by numerous archaeologists (White 1982; Scarry 1984a). The excavations by David Brose and his students at Case Western Reserve University were especially important. A number of significant surveys also have been undertaken in the region (Tesar 1980; White 1981b). Farther west in the panhandle, in Pensacola, Judith Bense has successful merged archaeological enquiry with public education and public involvement, resulting in a model project of how to build support for research and for the preservation of archaeological sites (Bense 1985). That theme—building public support through public education—is becoming increasingly prevalent in Florida archaeology in the 1990s.

The archaeology of the Seminole and Miccosukee peoples also has received attention. The National Park Service surveys in Big Cypress

Top, Ann Cordell, archaeologist and ceramic technology specialist, in the field at Mound C at the McKeithen site in 1977; *bottom*, Cordell in her laboratory at the Florida Museum of Natural History analyzing the mineralogical constituents of the McKeithen ceramics. Increasingly, the interdisciplinary nature of archaeological inquiry requires the participation of scientists who combine field collecting of data with laboratory analysis (courtesy Florida Museum of Natural History).

Preserve, directed by John Erenhardt, and excavations in the northern part of the state, home of the Seminole until they were forced into southern Florida after the Second Seminole War, have built on the early work of John Goggin to open new anthropological vistas on these native peoples (Dickinson and Wayne 1985; Weisman 1989).

Florida archaeology has come a long way in the century and a half since John Durkee first dug in a mound on the bank of the St. Johns River. The explorations of Clarence Moore did more than any other early work to bring to public attention the varied archaeological resources of the state. Many modern projects still use Moore's excavations as a baseline for research. The federal relief agency excavations of the early 1930s were important, but while they did large-scale work for virtually the first time in the state, publication was delayed, and they contributed less to our contemporary knowledge than a lot of other work. The research of Gordon Willey and his milestone publication on the Gulf coast (Willey 1949a) helps to make the 1940s the real beginning of scientific reporting in the state.

Beginning in the same period John Griffin, Hale Smith, John Goggin, and Adelaide and Ripley Bullen all made significant contributions to archaeology in Florida and our knowledge of the native groups that lived in the state in the past. Following their lead, archaeologists continue to investigate almost every imaginable topic and period. Aided by an array of specialists—geologists, zooarchaeologists, archaeobotanists, soil scientists, and others—these archaeologists are literally uncovering new information at a record pace.

Perhaps just as important, archaeologists are making their information available to the public. Now more than ever before, the story of the native American Indians who lived in Florida in the past is becoming a part of the heritage that we share and of which we are all aware. Perhaps books such as this one will help in that educational process.

Early Hunters, Gatherers, and Fishers

 **PART I**

Many generations of students from the University of Florida in Gainesville have escaped the oppressive heat of summer by tubing down the Ichetucknee River. Mounting automobile and even tractor tire inner tubes at the river's head spring, relief-seeking tubers enjoy a two-hour refreshing soak drifting along with the current before arriving at the landing place by the U.S. Highway 27 bridge. The river continues past the bridge for a half mile before emptying into the Santa Fe River, which in turn joins the Suwannee River flowing to the Gulf of Mexico. Canoeists, aficionados of Florida's natural beauty, occasionally make the entire journey from the Ichetucknee River to the Gulf.

A person attemping this same journey 12,000 years ago would not have gotten very far. The Ichetucknee River was not a flowing river, nor was the Santa Fe. Neither would have existed in its present form. At that time, the end of the Pleistocene epoch—the great Ice Age—Florida was much drier than at present. Rather than flowing rivers, the limestone-bottomed Ichetucknee and Santa Fe rivers were probably a series of small watering holes that drew animals seeking water and humans seeking animals. In many respects the water holes were like the watering holes found today in the savannas of Africa. The paucity of surface water was the result of different rainfall patterns and a greatly lowered water table.

As might be expected, a drier environment meant a different array of plants and animals in addition to different land forms. If there is one thing we have learned about the archaeology of precolumbian peoples, it is that to understand them, we must understand their environment. That is not an easy task.

Were there actually people in Florida 12,000 years ago to paddle a canoe down the Ichetucknee River to the Gulf had there been water on which to do so? In the 1920s, when river traffic was practically nonexistent and the river had not yet suffered the indignity of having hundreds of thousands of pairs of feet dragged along its bottom, at least one family of north Florida visitors to the Ichetucknee did what no one else had apparently done. Instead of looking up while in the river, they looked down. The Simpson family of High Springs, one son of which was the same Clarence Simpson who served as archaeologist for the Florida Geological Survey in the 1930s, collected thousands of artifacts from the bed of the river. They installed glass bottoms in buckets, which could then be lowered into the water like giant swim masks, enabling them to get a better view of artifacts on the river bottom (Simpson 1935). They later went so far as to invent a glass-bottomed rowboat in which one could float and see the river bottom.

The Simpsons' collection includes artifacts from a cross-section of the native cultures who inhabited north Florida from Seminole times back well into the precolumbian era. One artifact aroused considerable scientific excitement. Two sections of a broken, beveled ivory point fit together in the shape of a tool identical to a beveled ivory point found at the famous Blackwater Draw archaeological site near Clovis, New Mexico. It was at Blackwater Draw that artifacts first had been found in undeniable association with the bones of now-extinct species of Pleistocene animals (Jenks and Simpson 1941). Here was strong evidence that humans lived in Florida as long ago as they did in the southwest United States, a region where only recently it had been shown that people had lived sufficiently long ago to have hunted Ice Age animals.

Today we know that the beveled ivory tool was a foreshaft, part of a composite harpoonlike spear point, and that it was made from the ivory tusk of a Pleistocene-age mammoth. Such ivory tools and the stone lanceolate points they held are excellent evidence of the presence of early humans. Many such tools have now been found in

Florida in other inundated archaeological sites. As we shall see in chapter 2, people indeed lived in Florida 12,000 years ago.

Today we can begin to describe and interpret the lifeways of these people to whom the name Paleoindians is given, the same name given to contemporaneous cultures elsewhere in the United States. Our information about these early Floridians is increasing almost daily. Much of this new knowledge comes from a better understanding of the Florida environment of the Paleoindians. Work by people like James Dunbar, Melanie Stright, S. David Webb, and their associates is demonstrating that there is great potential for learning even more about the Florida Paleoindians, and that such information is going to influence Paleoindian studies throughout the hemisphere.

Paleoindians lived in Florida relatively unchanged for several thousand years. Two phenomena probably account for the gradual development after about 7500 B.C.—9,500 years ago—of new lifeways and the onset of what archaeologists call the Archaic period. First is the end of the Pleistocene—the Ice Age—and the onset of the Holocene epoch—modern times. As the glaciers in colder climes around the world melted, sea levels rose and wetter conditions appeared. Some of the Pleistocene animals hunted by Paleoindians disappeared, the victims of native hunters, new environmental conditions, or both. Along the coasts and in the rivers new resources were available for the taking, and Archaic populations quickly took advantage of them. Fish and shellfish were probably added to a wide variety of plants and animals that had long been a part of the human diet.

Changes in settlements and social structure probably also occurred as a result of the second factor: population increase. People make more people, especially under favorable environmental and economic conditions. After 7500 B.C. northern Florida, the home of most Paleoindians, became more densely populated, a result of both more people and the fact that Florida was literally shrinking. As sea levels rose, inundating large expanses of coastal lands, the area of Florida was eventually reduced by roughly half. With wetter conditions, some portions of Florida previously inhospitable or only lightly populated during Paleoindian times became the home of expanding Archaic populations. More surface water supported more people.

The Archaic peoples, like their Paleoindian predecessors, knew the land and how to live on it. Over the next thousands of years they would inhabit almost all, if not all, areas of the state, taking advantage of the resources of the coasts, the interior rivers and lakes, and the expanses of interior hardwood forests.

That Archaic populations were larger than Paleoindian populations is difficult at the present time to prove. If we begin to compare the number of Paleoindian sites to the number of Archaic sites, however, compensating for the longer duration of the Archaic period (about twice the Paleoindian period), it seems obvious that populations were significantly larger in the Archaic period. Not only are there more sites, there also are larger sites, reflecting larger populations, repetitive occupations, or both. As a consequence, there are many more Archaic artifacts in archaeological collections than Paleoindian artifacts.

For instance, from the Ichetucknee River we have handfuls of Paleoindian projectile points and tools, while from the same locale we have hundreds and perhaps thousands of Archaic artifacts. All of the available evidence points to larger human populations in Florida during the Archaic period.

It should be emphasized that although the relative amount of Paleoindian artifacts is many orders of magnitude less than Archaic artifacts, the total amount of Paleoindian artifacts from Florida is quite large when compared with quantities from other locations in the eastern United States. So there were significant Paleoindian populations in the state, but there were even larger Archaic populations.

The cultures of the Archaic period were not a single entity, static in time. Fluctuating environmental conditions and cultural changes characterize the period from 7500 B.C. to 500 B.C. Archaic cultures and the environment of Florida in 7500 B.C. were quite different than the cultures and environment of 500 B.C. The style of life during the early Archaic period, until about 5000 B.C., probably was more similar to that of the Paleoindians than it was to those of later cultures. After 5000 B.C., middle Archaic societies sharing similar lithic assemblages were living in a wide variety of environmental zones—riverine and inland, wetland and forest areas. Some sites are quite large. By 3000 B.C., the time of the appearance of late Archaic cultures, essentially modern environmental conditions were reached. After that time coastal Archaic occupations became more numerous; the remains of late Archaic cultures are especially noteworthy along the southwest

Florida coast and the salt marsh–barrier island regions of northeast Florida, two relatively propitious coastal locales important to later peoples as well. By the end of the late Archaic period we can begin to see the regionalization that characterized the many cultures of later times.

Earlier Archaic populations also may have lived along the coasts, but as yet remains comparable to those of the late period have not been found. This could be a result of the inundation of those earlier sites, such as in the Tampa Bay locale, where dredging has uncovered extensive inundated shell middens.

Exactly when to end the Archaic period is a topic of taxonomic debate. The appearance of fired clay pottery in coastal sites after about 2000 B.C. or slightly earlier provides a convenient marker, causing some chronologies to terminate the late Archaic period at that point. In such chronologies the late Archaic period is followed by the Orange period, 2000–1000 B.C., and the Transitional period, 1200–500 B.C., two divisions that fill the temporal gap to the time of regional cultures (Bullen 1975:6). But evidence from excavated sites increasingly indicates that late Archaic lifeways continue unchanged to 1000 or 500 B.C. in most regions of the state, especially in riverine and coastal locales. An alternative taxonomic scheme, the one used in this book, is to extend the late Archaic period to 500 B.C., recognizing that there are at least several discernible geographic varieties of late Archaic cultures in Florida and that those cultures are transitional to the better-defined regional cultures present after 500 B.C. Taxonomies are heuristic devices that help to organize data; as additional data are collected and new conclusions reached, taxonomies should be revised.

In the chapter that follows we will examine the archaeological evidence for Paleoindians in Florida and the interpretations archaeologists have made from those data. Chapter 3 looks at the Archaic cultures in Florida and the nature of the adaptations those people made to the different environmental zones and resources within the state over time. By 500 B.C. the development of regional cultural adaptations resulted in a host of distinct cultures that can be described and studied by modern archaeologists. The descendants of those regional cultures—people called the Calusa and Apalachee and Potano—lived in Florida in the early sixteenth century. It was their ancestors who were there 12,000 years ago in places like the Ichetucknee River.

The Paleoindians

2

Paleoindians, the first people to live in Florida, were the descendants of human populations who entered North America from eastern Asia during the later portion of the Pleistocene. The exact timing of this migration from Asia is much debated, as is whether there were multiple migrations (Fagan 1987). What is certain is that during the last glaciation, a time when sea levels were as much as 320–380 feet lower than they are today due to the huge amounts of water frozen in glaciers, people walked from easternmost Asia into Alaska across a dry "land bridge" that was at least 1,000 miles wide. The concept of a "bridge" is a poor one, for the dry landmass that extended across what is now the Bering Strait was no narrow strip of land. It was an arctic savanna as wide as the distance from Orlando to New York City, and people not only crossed it, they probably lived on it for many generations (see Hoffecker, Powers, and Goebel 1993).

Descendants of these people of Asian ancestry moved southward, most likely down an ice-free corridor west of the McKenzie River in Canada. Within a relatively short time, perhaps only hundreds of years, groups of humans moved into large parts of South and North America, including, by at least 12,000 years ago, Florida. There is no archaeological evidence of human populations in Florida before the Paleoindians, as has been suggested for some other regions of the United States (see Fagan 1987, for a discussion of the evidence).

The first inhabitants of the Americas were once thought to be nomadic populations who roamed tracts of land hunting large animals, most species of which were driven to extinction at the end of the Pleistocene. Elephants, horses, camels, a larger species of bison—a menagerie of Pleistocene fauna—were hunted with lanceolate stone points and butchered with unifacial stone tools. This big game hunting model of Paleoindians, derived largely from sites in the western United States, dominated interpretations and even influenced our view of Paleoindians in Florida. Today, thanks to a great deal more evidence from sites outside of the western United States, including Florida, we are beginning to understand better that the cultural adaptations of Paleoindians included many settlement and subsistence traits beyond hunting big game. Let us travel into Florida with the Paleoindians who first came here some 12,000 years ago.

Florida at that time would likely not be recognizable to a modern resident. For one thing, it was much larger than at present. Today the distance from Clearwater on the Gulf coast east-northeast across the width of Florida to Cocoa on the Atlantic coast is 145 miles. With the level of the sea 160 feet lower than at present, the distance from Gulf to Atlantic on this same line was about 280 miles; the Gulf coast was 40–70 miles farther west than it is today. About half of the land exposed 12,000 years ago is now inundated continental shelf.

With greatly lowered sea levels in early Paleoindian times, today's well-watered inland environments were arid uplands interspersed with more hospitable river drainage systems. For instance, the Ichetucknee River, which today is 50 miles from the Gulf coast, was about 120 miles from the Gulf shoreline and at a much higher elevation above mean sea level. And the groundwater table, which today gushes out of the limestone basin of the Ichetucknee, was many yards lower when Paleoindians camped nearby. The many springs that feed the river today did not exist 12,000 years ago.

The scenario upon which most students of late Pleistocene environments agree is that the inland rivers, lakes, springs, and other extensive surface water features such as marshes and wet prairies were virtually nonexistent when humans first lived in Florida (Dunbar 1991: 185–192; a review of various lines of evidence for the Paleoindian climate can be found in Daniel and Wisenbaker 1987:152–161; also see Watts and Hansen 1988). In the interior of the state potable water

Approximate extent of Florida's shoreline during the Paleoindian period with sea levels 130–165 feet below today's.

was found in what were then limestone-bottomed catchments lined with marly deposits—that is, in water holes, lakes, and prairies fed by rainfall—and in very deep sinkholes that were fed at least occasionally by groundwater from springs. At times the shallower catchments went dry.

Such catchments—sinkholes and the like—were most prevalent in those areas of the state characterized by Tertiary limestone deposits. Such karstic conditions are found from Tampa Bay north through the western half of peninsular Florida into the panhandle to the tri-state region around the Chipola River and extending into southeast

Alabama and southwest Georgia. Karst topography also extends well west of modern north peninsular Florida and is a part of the present-day continental shelf.

As would be expected, the lack of surface water in interior Florida resulted in different plant communities than are present today in the state's reasonably well-watered landscape. In general during the late Pleistocene, Florida was much drier and cooler than today. But the climate did fluctuate, with some periods of slightly wetter relative conditions—for example, a one-thousand-year wetter period near 11,000 B.C. (Watts and Hansen 1988). But even these less arid periods, such as the one that ended about 12,000 years ago, were significantly drier than modern conditions.

Following that time, and extending to about 9,500–9,000 years ago, a period of more arid conditions again prevailed. Although some localized catchment areas could at times support moderately moist vegetation, most of Florida was typified by xerophytic—dry—species of plants, with scrub oaks, pine, open grassy prairies, and savannas most common. Possibly these arid surface conditions were ameliorated in inland regions where ground water was higher relative to the land surface and where thicker clayey deposits provided more effective perched water tables. Under any of these conditions, the Paleoindian sites that are likely to have been present are inundated today.

In summary, it is certain that during the Paleoindian period, 10,000 B.C.–7500 B.C., Florida was cooler and drier than at present and water was in shorter supply at inland locations. The best sources of water apparently were watering holes, especially very deep springs that reached down to the water table and other perched, still-water retention basins. Both kinds of sites are likely to be inundated in present-day Florida.

Settlement and Sites—The Oasis Model

The supposition that such watering holes existed is crucial to the most widely accepted explanation of Paleoindian settlement patterning. That model, called the oasis hypothesis by James S. Dunbar and S. David Webb (Dunbar 1983, 1991; Webb et al. 1984; Dunbar, Webb, and Cring 1989), was originally set forth by Wilfred T. Neill (1964;

Neill called sites watering holes, rather than oases). The oasis model suggests the water holes were crucial to the animals that depended on them to secure drinking water in the arid environment, especially under the most arid conditions when sources of water were in short supply. Watering holes, gathering places for animals, also must have provided good hunting for carnivores. In addition to drawing animals, the water sources would have been important to the Paleoindians, who also needed water and who could hunt and eat the animals who frequented the locales.

If this model is accurate, then evidence of Paleoindian camps and hunting and butchering activities—artifacts and, perhaps, the bones of animals hunted and eaten by humans—should be found at former water holes and other perched water sources, including shallow lakes and prairies, and at deep sinks in the karstic, Tertiary limestone regions of Florida where such features existed in the past. This is exactly the correlation that has been demonstrated by Dunbar, Webb, and their associates (Dunbar and Waller 1983; Dunbar, Webb, and Cring 1989:474–475). These researchers also have found that some sites occur in areas just outside of the Tertiary karst regions. In these marginal areas, such as the present-day St. Johns River and Hillsborough River drainages, limestone deposits are deeply buried. In Paleoindian times, such marginal locales could have provided perched water sources in flat-bottomed peneplain lakes and prairies. Let us look at the evidence for the presence of Paleoindians in such locations.

As early as the 1940s the finds of the Simpson family had shown that Paleoindian artifacts and the bones of extinct animals were found together in the rivers within the karstic region of northern Florida (Jenks and Simpson 1941; Simpson 1948). Later, many sport divers collected hundreds of Paleoindian points and other artifacts, as well as fossilized bones of animals, from the beds of north Florida rivers. Some of these bones display dramatic evidence of the hunting and butchering activities of Paleoindians. One of the first to be studied was a vertebral spine of a mammoth recovered from the Santa Fe River that shows distinct butchering marks (Bullen, Webb, and Waller 1970). A more recent find is a partial skeleton of a *Bison antiquus*, an extinct species of bison, which was found in the Wacissa River with a broken stone projectile point still lodged in its skull (Webb et al. 1984).

Extent of the karstic and marginal regions (based on Dunbar 1991).

How could the presence of these materials in the rivers be explained? The most accepted theory in the 1970s was articulated by Benjamin Waller, a sport diver and later an associate of Dunbar, who hypothesized that Paleoindians ambushed game at river crossings (Waller 1970). Gradually, the game-crossing explanation evolved into the oasis hypothesis. The restatement of that model grew from early attempts by Waller and Dunbar (1977; Dunbar and Waller 1983) to map the distribution of Paleoindian points in Florida. To accomplish this they needed to examine the collections of sport divers. Their results were impressive, showing what most of the divers already knew: Paleoindian materials were almost entirely restricted to the regions of Tertiary limestone formations. Building on these data and stimulated by his earlier hydrological research at the Fowler Bridge

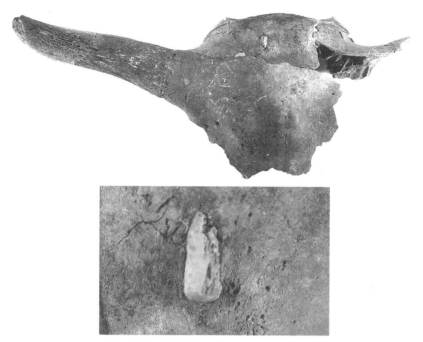

Bison antiquus skull with a broken chert point sticking in it (*top*); enlarged view (*bottom*). When killed, the mature female probably measured 3 feet across at the horn tips. Only the horn cores (shown here) were present when the skull was recovered by Roger Alexon in the Wacissa River. The distance between the horn cores is 25 inches (Webb et al. 1984; courtesy Vertebrate Paleontology Range, Florida Museum of Natural History).

mastodon site in Hillsborough County (Dunbar 1981), Dunbar offered the revised oasis model as an explanation for the distribution of Paleoindian sites across the Florida landscape (Dunbar 1983).

New information on Paleoindians in Florida continues to surface, and all of it supports the oasis model. The most recent distribution maps of Paleoindian points in Florida show that 92 percent of Clovis and Suwannee projectile points—diagnostic Paleoindian artifacts—are found in the region of Tertiary limestone features (Dunbar 1991). This region, extending from Tampa Bay north into the panhandle, includes the Santa Fe River–Ichetucknee River basin, where the largest numbers of points have been found; the Aucilla River–Wacissa River basin; the Steinhatchee River; the Oklawaha River–Silver River system; the

Withlacoochee River (in west central Florida); the Hillsborough River; the Chipola River; and, to a lesser extent, the St. Johns River (Dunbar, Webb, and Cring 1989:475; Dunbar 1991).

It has now been shown that archaeological sites, some of them Paleoindian in age, also are found near what would have been former water sources in the karstic formations that extend under the Gulf of Mexico off the present Florida Gulf coast. Underwater surveys in Apalachee Bay have located six inundated sites 0.6 to 6 miles offshore at depths of 1.5 to 17 feet. Probable sites have been located even farther out in the Gulf, but they have not yet been studied (Faught 1988; Dunbar, Webb, Faught et al. 1989:27–28; Dunbar, Webb, and Faught 1991). One other possible offshore site, perhaps from the early Archaic period, was located 20 miles offshore in 38 feet of water. These extraordinary data suggest that someday scientists may be able to show that as much as one-half of Florida's Paleoindian sites are under the Gulf of Mexico and that they have been inundated by the rise in sea level that has occurred since Paleoindians lived here. Attempts are underway to exactly map the shoreline of Paleoindian times, an exercise that will greatly aid future attempts to locate inundated sites (Stright 1987; Faught 1988; Dunbar, Webb, Faught et al. 1989; Garrison 1991).

Deep springs and other water sources were not restricted to northern Florida. Research at several sites in southern peninsular Florida suggests that the limited water sources in that region also drew Paleoindians. Two sources in Sarasota County are deep sinkholes that in Paleoindian times would have provided access to the lowered water table. Warm Mineral Spring and Little Salt Spring have produced important data on Paleoindian lifeways. Another early southern peninsular Florida site is the Cutler Fossil site in Dade County (Carr 1986). We would expect archaeologists to continue to find Paleoindian materials in southern Florida, especially at locations where a geological feature, such as a deep sinkhole, would have provided a water source. The numbers of such sites will be much less than for northern Florida, however, where underwater surveys in the Half-Mile Rise section of the Aucilla River and two other locales in the same river already have led to the recording of twenty-six Paleoindian sites, more inundated Paleoindian sites than were known in all of Florida previously (Dunbar, Webb, and Cring 1989:476; their work has been carried out with the cooperation of sport divers).

Rivers, off-shore locales, and sites associated with Paleoindian archaeological assemblages.

Dating and Subsistence

One of the best reported of these underwater Paleoindian sites is Page/Ladson in Jefferson County (Dunbar, Faught, and Webb 1988; Dunbar, Webb, and Cring 1989). The site, one of the twenty-six in the Half Mile Rise section of the Aucilla River, is described by its excavators as "an arroyo-like feature" cutting into the underlying limestone. The limestone river bottom at that point is relatively shallow and flat, six to thirteen feet deep, but with occasional much deeper sinkholes extending down into the limestone to depths of 25 to 95 feet. These sinks and the perched ponds that existed at various times in what is now the river bottom were the sources of water that drew animals and Paleoindians.

Underwater excavations have allowed the field team to interpret the depositional history of the site and to radiocarbon date strata associated with its human occupations. Excavations show that although upper strata (nearer the surface) included materials that had been redeposited by river action—including Paleoindian artifacts, animal bones, and more recent human artifacts—there are lower strata of quiet-water (nonfluvial) deposits of peat and clay-marl. Those deposits date from the Paleoindian period and are sealed undisturbed below the later, redeposited strata.

The exciting information recovered from the Page/Ladson site shows the great potential of underwater sites to produce extraordinary data on Paleoindians. Like the sinkhole sites in Sarasota County, the Page/Ladson site and other riverine sites provide the opportunity for recovering artifacts that would ordinarily not be preserved at dry-land sites. Ivory, bone, wood, and even plant remains deposited in wet locales, subsequently sealed below later deposits and rising waters, are preserved at such sites. Such locales contain organic materials and afford a unique glimpse at the diets and artifacts of these early peoples. One extraordinary discovery from the Page/Ladson site is a deposit of mastodon digesta, which has been radiocarbon dated to 12,500 B.C. (Webb, Dunbar, and Newsom 1992). Not only can we learn what animals Paleoindians ate, but we can study the diets of the animals as well.

At the Page/Ladson site radiocarbon dates from the deposits containing Paleoindian artifacts range from at least 10,000 to 7500 B.C. These undisturbed strata are sealed under younger, Archaic-period strata dated to 2000 B.C. and more recent strata. Evidence for alternating periods of greater and lesser wetness are recorded in the strata, as would be expected for a perched watering hole.

The radiocarbon dates from the site strongly support other dates obtained from Florida Paleoindian sites. The Wacissa River *Bison antiquus* skull with the broken stone point has been dated to more than 10,000 years ago, and a humerus of the same animal found several feet away was dated 11,170 years ago. Similar dates have come from Paleoindian materials and bones recovered by Carl J. Clausen from the Little Salt Spring sinkhole in Sarasota County. At that site an extinct giant land tortoise and a pointed wooden stake possibly driven through the animal were dated to 13,450 and 12,030 years ago. Two wooden stakes, perhaps anchors pounded into the side of the sink to aid people in lowering themselves to the level of the water, yielded dates of 9,645 and 9,500 years ago, while charcoal from a small hearth was dated to 10,190 years ago (Clausen et al. 1979:611). The stakes' late Paleoindian or early Archaic dates are comparable to a series of dates obtained from Warm Mineral Spring, another deep sinkhole in Sarasota County (Clausen, Brooks, and Wesolowsky 1975:9). Occupations of those springs at that time, about 7500 B.C., may correlate with the less arid conditions that began about 10,000 years ago.

The Page/Ladson site and several other inundated paleontological and archaeological locales provide evidence of the animal species that were available to Paleoindians for food. Bones of these animals are preserved at the inundated sites but are not found at dry-land Paleoindian sites in Florida. The list of animals includes both modern species and species that became extinct at the end of the Pleistocene, about the end of Paleoindian times or slightly later. In some instances, we have direct evidence that such animals were butchered and eaten, such as the mammoth from the Santa Fe River, the bison from the Wacissa River, and possibly the giant land tortoise from Little Salt Spring believed to have been impaled with a wooden stake.

Other animals associated with Paleoindian sites such as Little Salt Spring (Clausen et al. 1979:610) and the Aucilla River sites (data provided by S. David Webb; also see Dunbar, Webb, and Cring 1989) include both extinct and extant species. Many of the extinct forms were large mammals: sloth, tapir, horse, camelids, and mammoth. Smaller animals, now extinct, were also eaten, including a species of box turtle. The most important extant forms were deer, fish, turtles, and shellfish; others were gopher tortoise, diamondback rattlesnake, raccoon, opossum, rabbit, muskrat, and wood ibis.

From Warm Mineral Spring (Cockrell and Murphy 1978:6) other extant animals have been identified, including panthers and frogs. All could have been eaten by Paleoindian peoples.

These data indicate that Paleoindians certainly hunted large game such as mammoth and mastodon as well as other now-extinct species. But they also hunted and trapped many other animals found in Florida at that time, from deer to muskrat, raccoon, and opossum. They used these not only for food but also for furs, ligaments, antlers, and bones for tools. Most likely, when all the evidence is in, we will have learned that the early hunter-gatherers hunted and gathered almost everything that was edible or usable, including a variety of plants. It will also be interesting to discover whether coastal resources, such as shellfish, and fish were a part of their diet. Research at inundated Paleoindian sites has the potential to provide such evidence, including plant remains. What might well prove to be inundated Paleoindian shell middens are reasonably accessible in Tampa Bay (Goodyear and Warren 1972; Goodyear, Upchurch, and Brooks 1980; Goodyear et al. 1983).

The Tool Kit

With what did the Paleoindians hunt and butcher these animals? What kinds of tools did they have to fashion clothing and shelter? The Paleoindian tool kit is more limited in its variety than are the tool assemblages of later Florida native peoples. That is to be expected for people who probably did not remain long in one place but continually moved among different camps and water sources to take advantage of concentrations of game.

Archaeologists have noted great uniformity in Paleoindian artifacts ranging from sites in Florida to those of the semiarid parts of the western United States. Except for expertly fashioned bifacial points, many of the tools made from stone are unifacial and probably served several purposes. It perhaps was easier to carry a few tools to do many jobs than to carry a larger number of specialized tools. In Florida, thanks once again to the special preservative nature of inundated sites, ivory, bone, and even wooden Paleoindian objects have been recovered, providing a more complete view of Paleoindian technology than that derived from other states.

The most widely recognized Paleoindian tool in Florida is the Suwannee point, which Ripley Bullen (1975:55) has described as "slightly waisted . . . with concave base, basal ears, and basal grinding of bottom and waisted parts of sides."

Excavations at the Harney Flats site in the Hillsborough River drainage, a marginal locale adjacent to the Tertiary limestone region immediately to the north, have provided information on the manufacturing process of Suwannee points (Daniel and Wisenbaker 1987:44–53). The first step was the striking of a large blade from a chert core. This blank was then worked bifacially into a preform, and

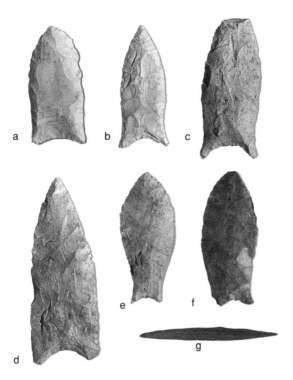

Paleoindian tools: *a*, fluted Clovis point 2⅜ inches long that appears to have been reworked after having the tip broken; *b–d*, Suwannee points; *e–f*, Simpson points; *g*, small ivory shaft with roughened end for hafting. Note the basal ears and basal grinding (thinning) on the points.

then further knapped bifacially into the finished product. Hundreds of these Suwannee points have come from springs and rivers in northern Florida, inundated Paleoindian camps (Dunbar and Waller 1983).

Some, if not all, of these and other Paleoindian lanceolate points were hafted by attaching them to an ivory foreshaft, in turn attached to a wooden spear shaft. The foreshaft, round in cross section, was manufactured from mammoth ivory (two possibly of mastodon ivory are known). One end was beveled and roughened to provide a better haft for the stone point that was attached to it with pitch and sinew. The other end was pointed to fit in the wooden shaft. It was one of these ivory foreshafts that the Simpson family recovered from the Ichetucknee River. More than three dozen have now been found in Florida, all from sites in the karstic region (Dunbar 1991:193).

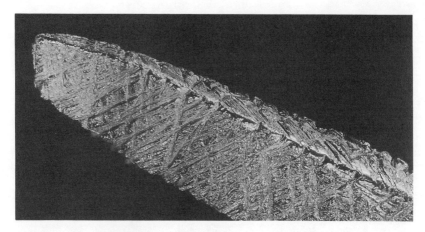

Roughened end of a beveled ivory shaft just over one-half inch in diameter from the Sloth Hole site on the Aucilla River, Jefferson County (photograph by Ronald Wolff, University of Florida Department of Zoology; courtesy Vertebrate Paleontology Range, Florida Museum of Natural History, Richard Ohmes Collection).

Another stone point found in Paleoindian contexts in Florida is the Simpson point (Bullen 1975:56), which is very similar to the Suwannee point but with a narrower base. Simpson points are possibly Suwannee points that were snapped at the waist, either in the manufacturing process or in use, and then reworked. Because the new base—what had been the narrow-waisted portion of the old point—was smaller across, the Simpson point was shorter and with a narrower base than the Suwannee point from which it was made.

Clovis points, fluted lanceolate Paleoindian points, also occur in Florida, comprising about 10 percent of the Paleoindian points recorded from the Santa Fe River drainage and 39 percent of the sample from the Aucilla River basin (Dunbar, Webb, and Cring 1989:475). These figures may reflect chronological differences in the history of Paleoindian settlement of the two regions. They might also suggest an initial settlement of Florida by Paleoindians who made Clovis points. The fluted base of the Clovis point appears especially well suited to the beveled end of the ivory foreshaft, and the distributions of these two tools are similar.

Although the stone points and ivory foreshafts are the most distinctive and most easily identified of the Paleoindian artifacts, other tools are known from the Harney Flats site (Daniel and Wisenbaker 1987:

41–97), the Silver Springs site in Marion County (Neill 1958), also called the Paradise Park site, and other northern Florida sites (Purdy 1981:8–32). In addition to excavated specimens, many Paleoindian stone tools have been found in mixed deposits in rivers.

These Paleoindian tools tend to be unifacial and plano-convex, with steeply flaked working edges (see Purdy and Beach 1980:114–118, and Purdy 1981, for descriptions of Paleoindian lithic technology). Some are little more than flakes or blades that were struck from cores, used, and discarded. (But do not discount the sharpness of such blades; modern surgeons have used obsidian blades as scalpels, finding them sharper than steel because of less microscopic pitting along the cutting surface.) Unifacial scrapers—including endscrapers, discoidal scrapers, and oblong scrapers—adzes, and various retouched flake and blade tools, including spokeshaves, were found at the Harney Flats site (Daniel and Wisenbaker 1987:62–81, 86–87). An adze also was recovered from a Paleoindian stratum at the Page/Ladson site. Unifacial tools like those from Harney Flats are found among the artifacts from many of the riverine Paleoindian sites in northern Florida, often in mixed collections of redeposited materials.

Other Paleoindian stone tools from Harney Flats and elsewhere include cores and bifacial knives (some may be scrapers), which generally have flat bases with rounded corners and measure 4–6 inches in length. Another type of knife, the Waller knife or hafted flake knife, is more limited in distribution and is most common in and around the Santa Fe River (Waller 1971). The knives appear to be made from flakes; one side displays flake scars while the other, the side that came off the core, is smooth and slightly convex or concave. Two side notches near one end were apparently used to haft the tool. Most are just over an inch in length and less than an inch and one-half wide, and all are unifacially retouched on the edges.

Another item in the tool kit is oval ground stone weights the shape and size of eggs with one end flattened (Neill 1971; Purdy 1981:30). Most likely these are bolas; the stone weights were attached by thongs and thrown to bring down water birds and other game. One such stone was recovered from the Page/Ladson site from a stratum dated 12,330 years ago (Dunbar, Webb, and Cring 1989:479).

A common bone tool found at Paleoindian sites is the double-pointed point. Made from ground splinters of bone, these tools are

Paleoindian tools: *a*, bifacial knife 4⁵⁄₁₆ inches long; *b–d, f–g,* unifacial blade and flake knives; *e,* bola weight.

sharpened on both ends and generally are round in cross section, about four inches long. More than a hundred of these have been found at the Priscilla mastodon site in the Aucilla River. Waller (1976) has suggested these points are actually pins used to hold back tissue while animals were butchered. Thousands have been found in northern Florida rivers, including many at the Page/Ladson site.

Underwater excavations at Warm Mineral Spring (Cockrell and Murphy 1978:figs. 4, 5) have also produced bone and shell tools from Paleoindian strata, several of which indicate use of the spear-thrower. One is a shell spur or "trigger"; these fitted over the end of the throwing stick and provided a surface for the base of the shaft or dart to butt against. A possible throwing-stick weight also was recovered. Other tools from that site include a worked fossil shark tooth; a bone, eyed needle; a socketed antler point; and a socketed bone handle (Cockrell and Murphy 1978:fig. 5).

From Little Salt Spring, Clausen (Clausen et al. 1979:611, fig. 2) recovered a similar socketed antler projectile point and a portion of what appears to be a carved oak log mortar, perhaps used to grind seeds or nuts. One of the more extraordinary artifacts from that site is the head of a nonreturnable wooden boomerang. Carved from oak, the tool is similar to boomerangs used by the Australian aborigines.

During late Paleoindian times, post–8000 B.C., wetter conditions characterized Florida (relative to the arid period of the previous 2,000 years). Late Paleoindian hunter-gatherers probably had a larger number of water sources and to alter their hunting and foraging strategies, using greater areas of the state. Certainly late Paleoindian stone points are much more widely distributed than earlier varieties.

One change in the tool kit that occurred during this late portion of the Paleoindian period is the disappearance of the large lanceolate points—Suwannee and Simpson—and the appearance of smaller points. Some of the latter are still lanceolate-shaped with concave bases and usually with waisting and basal grinding. Such points include Tallahassee, Santa Fe, and Beaver Lake types (Bullen 1975:45–47; Bullen's chronology is not strictly adhered to here). Other points, some with side notching, also are believed to date from this period: Dalton, Gilchrist, Greenbriar, Hardaway Side-Notched, and Bolen (Plain and Beveled) (Bullen 1975:44, 49–53; also see Warren and Bullen 1965; Purdy 1981:24–26). These types appear to be stylistically transitional from Paleoindian to Archaic points. A Bolen Beveled point came from a stratum at the Page/Ladson site dated 9,730 years ago, and a Bolen Plain point came from a lower stratum (Dunbar, Webb, and Cring 1989:479, 483). Both Bolen Beveled and Bolen Plain points were recovered from Harney Flats (Daniel and Wisenbaker 1987:55), and Bolen and Greenbriar points have been recovered from an inundated site in Boca Ciega Bay near St. Petersburg (Goodyear, Upchurch, and Brooks 1980) and from a large land site, 8Hi450(D), inland from Tampa Bay in Hillsborough County (Daniel and Wisenbaker 1981). Bolen points also have been excavated from another site northeast of Tampa Bay, the Deerstand site in the Hillsborough River drainage (Daniel 1982). Both latter sites contained a variety of lithic artifacts.

Site 8Hi450(D) might have been the location of a substantial late Paleoindian occupation, and Deerstand seems to have been a workshop for bifacial tools.

There is an ongoing discussion among specialists over the exact temporal placement of the notched points such as Bolens. Some have argued that notched varieties taxonomically are early Archaic, while others have argued for a separate, late Paleoindian provenance for the Dalton and related points. Still others argue for a temporal separation of the smaller lanceolate forms and the notched types. Presently there are too few excavated data to resolve all the issues. Bolen points do occur in Paleoindian contexts, however, and at Harney Flats they are found with Suwannee and Simpson points. Two radiocarbon dates from the Bolen surface at the Page/Ladson site, other data from that site, and the data from Harney Flats offer evidence that Bolen points are from the late Paleoindian period and that, rather than replacing the larger lanceolate varieties, they may have been contemporaneous with them for a time.

Specialists also have questioned whether Bolen and other notched points are points at all or, instead, hafted knives. Indeed, the beveling so apparent on Bolen Beveled points apparently results from continued resharpening. The turning over of the tool to pressure-flake and sharpen each edge results in beveled surfaces. Edge resharpening is probably more typical of a knife than of a point. Over time, as a result of resharpening, Bolen Plain tools become Bolen Beveled tools. Eventually the beveled tools were resharpened down to a nub and were discarded. Similar short, stubby tools that are not beveled are not found. Analysis of one hundred Bolen Beveled tools in the Florida Museum of Natural History showed 97 percent had a right-hand-made bevel and 3 percent a left-hand-made bevel, possibly reflecting handedness among the tools' users.

Other Paleoindian notched point varieties also may have been knives. Different types could represent different stages in the use cycle of knives, which were resharpened or reworked to extend their utility.

Antler flakers may be another late Paleoindian tool. Two antler-flaking tools, probably used to pressure-flake stone points or other tools, were found in the Bolen strata at the Page/Ladson site (Dunbar, Webb, and Cring 1989). Similar flakers have come from mixed

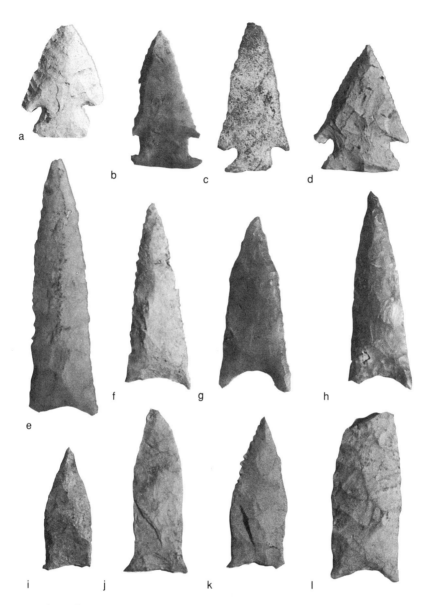

Late Paleoindian points: *a, b–d,* Bolen Beveled (*a* is 1½ inches long); *c,* Bolen Plain; *e–h,* Santa Fe; *i–j,* Beaver Lake; *k–l,* Tallahassee. All are basally thinned and *e–k* appear to exhibit reworking.

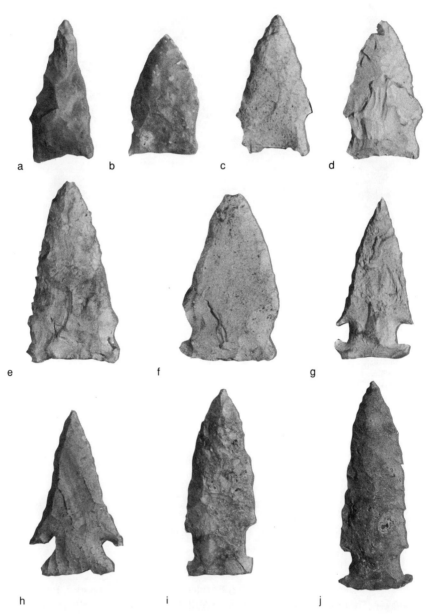

Late Paleoindian points: *a–b*, Nuckolls variety of Dalton (*a* is 1⅞ inches long); *c–d*, Colbert variety of Dalton; *e–f*, Greenbriar; *g–h*, Bolen Beveled; *i–j*, Bolen Plain (both exhibit edge use).

Microliths from the Nalcrest site: *a–b,* expended cores (*a* is 1 inch wide); *c–d,* drills; *e–g,* thumbnail scrapers; *h–j,* flake knives; *k–m,* end scrapers.

deposits in the Ichetucknee River and are included in the Simpson Collection at the Florida Museum of Natural History.

One remarkable site in central Florida—Nalcrest—has yielded a variety of what are possibly late Paleoindian microlithic tools similar to those associated with Dalton point assemblages elsewhere in the Southeast. A few microcores—though no microlithic assemblage—were recovered at Harney Flats (Daniel and Wisenbaker 1987:83–84), and microliths have been found elsewhere in Florida, but in nothing like the quantity found at the Nalcrest site on Lake Weohyakapka in Polk County. Bullen and Beilman (1973) reported on the Nalcrest microlithic tool complex, which was collected underwater around the edge of the lake. Although the largest number of projectile points from the Nalcrest site are of Archaic types, the similarity of the microlith complex to late Paleoindian microlith assemblages elsewhere seems to place it in that time period. Certainly the tools were used and deposited during a period of greater aridity than is present today.

The Nalcrest site is unique in Florida; no other single site has produced such a large number and variety of microliths, although single or multiple specimens are found. Bullen and Beilman's analysis involved only a portion of the large collection now housed at the Florida Museum of Natural History. The microlith assemblage, the tools of which measure from 0.4 to 1.75 inches in length, includes tiny stemmed points or knives and a variety of scrapers, drills, and other knives (Bullen and Beilman 1973:4–9, figs. 2, 3, 6–10). The Nalcrest tools might have been used to scrape, perforate, and cut up leather or to work plant fibers for cordage or basketry. Although not yet found at Paleoindian sites in Florida, fiber and cordage have come from early Archaic sites, and there is no reason to think the Paleoindians did not have such items, so necessary for everyday life.

In the last two decades, stimulated by new data from inundated archaeological sites like Page/Ladson, Little Salt Spring, and Warm Mineral Spring and by excavations at Harney Flats, our knowledge about Paleoindians in Florida has taken a giant step forward. We have new models of settlement and new understanding of the environment in which Paleoindians lived. We know the Paleoindian way of life came to an end about 9,500 years ago. The combined effects of climatic change, higher water tables, and the loss of the largest game animals necessitated changes in the adaptations of human populations in Florida. New lifeways developed. Those new Archaic-period cultures, which developed after 7500 B.C., are the subject of chapter 3. As we shall see, wet sites play a major role in providing information about those peoples as well.

Archaic Cultures

3

The Archaic period has traditionally been divided into three temporal divisions—early, middle, and late—based largely on projectile-point typologies (Bullen 1975; Milanich and Fairbanks 1980:chap. 3). Unfortunately, the quantity of excavated data used to establish these typologies and taxonomic schemes was not as great as one might have desired. Early knowledge of Archaic populations came largely from upland sites in interior Florida, sites most often characterized by lithic artifacts collected from surface surveys rather than from excavations. Coastal Archaic-period populations were poorly represented.

Beginning in the 1970s, the underwater archaeological work at Little Salt Spring (Clausen et al. 1979), terrestrial excavations on the southwest Florida coast (Division of Archives 1970; Cockrell 1970; Widmer 1974; McMichael 1982; Milanich, Chapman et al. 1984), and new understanding of Holocene climatic and environmental changes in Florida laid the groundwork for a reassessment of the Archaic period. Informed by additional excavations on the southwest coast (Russo 1991), research at the Windover Pond site in Brevard County (Doran and Dickel 1988a, b), work in east and northeast Florida (Russo 1992a), and excavations at Harney Flats, Page/Ladson, and other sites, this reassessment calls into question previous models of Archaic cultures (Ste. Claire 1990; Russo et al. 1992). As for so much of Florida's past, multidisciplinary archaeological research projects are

1   8AI356
2   8Le484
3   Bay West
4   Canton Street
5   Culbreath Bayou
6   Dixie Lime Cave No. 1
7   Gauthier
8   Harney Flats
9   Horr's Island
10 Johnson Lake
11 Kanapaha
12 Little Salt Spring
13 Meig's Pasture
14 Mount Taylor
15 Page/Ladson
16 Republic Grove
17 Sen. Edwards
18 Tick Island
19 Timucua Preserve sites
20 Trilisa Pond
21 Useppa Island
22 Warm Mineral Spring
23 Windover Pond

Archaic-period archaeological sites.

providing new understanding of the nature and complexity of Archaic cultures.

It no longer is reasonable to use only projectile points to subdivide the Archaic period temporally or its cultures spatially. New environmental and climatic data and increased knowledge of artifact assemblages and site types form the basis for dividing the Archaic period. These data allow a much fuller picture of the Archaic cultures than was possible previously.

The environment did not change quickly during the Archaic period. Although the beginning or end of a wetter or drier period is assigned a specific date, that date is a convenient marker approximating the start or end of a gradual trend. After 8000 B.C., as less arid conditions began to prevail, the late Paleoindian peoples did not wake up one day, note it was wetter, and decide to shift settlement patterns and develop new tool assemblages. Over many generations climatic fluctuations, a rise in sea levels, and increasing populations resulted in the changes that are visible in the archaeological record.

Early Archaic Period

Cultural changes began after about 8000 B.C. in late Paleoindian times with the onset of less arid conditions. As we saw in chapter 2, that date correlates with changes in projectile-point types, specifically a transition from lanceolate to stemmed varieties. Beginning about 7500 B.C. the Paleoindian points and knives were no longer made. They were replaced by a variety of stemmed tools, such as the Kirk, Wacissa, Hamilton, and Arredondo types. Kirk points or knives, and the related Wacissa type, may be earliest. At Harney Flats, Daniel and Wisenbaker (1987:33–34) found a Kirk strata overlying Paleoindian deposits and underlying middle Archaic–period deposits.

Kirk points or knives and other early Archaic diagnostic tools often are found at the same sites as Paleoindian assemblages, suggesting that, at least initially, early Archaic peoples and Paleoindians shared similar lifeways. But with the wetter conditions that began about 8000 B.C. (a period of greater aridity would begin again in about 6000 B.C.) and the extinction of some of the Pleistocene animal species that had helped sustain earlier populations, the Paleoindian subsistence regime was no longer an efficient adaptation to the Florida environment. Sufficient changes in artifact assemblages had occurred by 7500 B.C. for modern archaeologists to recognize a new culture, that of the early Archaic period.

Because these changes did not occur overnight, we would expect an overlap between Paleoindian site locales and early Archaic site locations. As early Archaic cultures adjusted to new environmental conditions, we should find other early Archaic sites in different locations from Paleoindian sites, locales that were suitable for occupation for the first time because of increased surface water. Early Archaic peoples were less constrained by the availability of water than their Paleoindian ancestors and could hunt and collect from old and new site locations. Early Archaic peoples might be viewed as a population changing from the nomadic Paleoindian subsistence pattern to the more settled coastal- and riverine-associated regimes of the middle Archaic period.

Archaeological evidence for this model does exist. Early Archaic materials are found at the same sites as Paleoindian artifacts; Page/Ladson, Harney Flats, Little Salt Spring, and Warm Mineral Spring are examples. Also, the distribution of early Archaic artifacts is greater than that of Paleoindian materials, and more land sites, rather than inundated sites, are known. Around the extensive perched water sources of northern Florida, such as Paynes Prairie and Orange Lake, large quantities of Arredondo, Hamilton, and Kirk points have been surface collected, while Paleoindian points are found only in very small quantities. Early Archaic points also are found in smaller numbers at upland sites in northern Florida where Paleoindian artifacts are not present, such as at Trilisa Pond where Arredondo points were recovered (Neill 1964). Although this pattern is based largely on documented collections from Alachua and Marion counties, there is no reason to think the pattern is different elsewhere in interior northern Florida.

To date, no early Archaic sites have been well documented in coastal or riverine settings that are associated with extensive shellfish middens. But such sites probably do exist, today either inundated beneath the Gulf of Mexico or buried under more recent, middle Archaic middens.

Because of a lack of excavated collections, our knowledge of the full range of the early Archaic lithic and bone tool assemblages is uncertain. According to Ripley Bullen's typology of Florida projectile points, points include Kirk, Hamilton, Arredondo, and Wacissa—probably the earliest—and Florida Spike, Thonotosassa, Hardee Beveled, Savannah River, Florida Morrow Mountain, and Sumter (Bullen 1975:33–41). Use roughening along the edges of many of these points suggests they were used as knives.

With few exceptions (e.g., Trilisa Pond in Marion County), most other stone tools believed to be early Archaic have been surface collected with early Archaic projectile points rather than excavated from good contexts. Such tools have been collected around Paynes Prairie and at other north Florida sites where Paleoindian points are rare. These early Archaic tools are quite different from the Paleoindian lithic assemblage, reflecting the cultural adjustments made after 7500 B.C. as native populations successfully coped with the conditions of the early

Early Archaic points (or knives): *a–c*, Arredondo (*a* is 2 ⅞ inches long); *d–f*, Hamilton.

Holocene. Because there are no chronological controls for these sur-face-collected tools, the listing here should be considered tentative.

Probable early Archaic stone tools are percussion flaked; some are cores or large flakes that received only enough shaping to make them usable. Tools used for more than one purpose (e.g., both scraping and

Early Archaic points (or knives): *a,* Florida Morrow Mountain, 3 ¾ inches
long; *b,* Florida Spike; *c,* Savannah River; *d–e,* Kirk Serrated; *f,* Sumter.

chopping) also seem to be common, as do the large core and flake
tools, some weighing several pounds. There also are many more types
of tools than in the Paleoindian assemblage, implying that the users of
the tools were performing many tasks. Some of the large choppers
might have been used in working wood. Large flake and core tools
show use as planes and hammerstones; other tools are bifacial

scrapers, bifacial knives, unifacial scrapers, end scrapers, flake knives, flake scrapers, and choppers, as well as composite tools (see Purdy and Beach 1980; Purdy 1981). Hafted-end scrapers, some knapped intentionally and others probably reworked broken projectile points or knives, are known, along with expanded-base drills and hafted drills.

Undoubtedly many tools were made from bone, but because of the acid nature of Florida soils, none have been preserved in land sites. Large numbers of bone tools have been recovered, however, from Florida rivers, especially the Ichetucknee River, thanks again to the Simpson family of High Springs. These bone tools cannot absolutely be attributed to the early Archaic period, but the large numbers of Archaic-period projectile points found with them strongly suggest that such tools were used throughout the early and middle Archaic periods.

The variety of bone artifacts preserved in the Ichetucknee River almost equals that of the stone tools. Double-pointed points made from bone splinters, flat or lenticular in cross section, are similar to bone tools from the Paleoindian period. Very common, the points may have been used as spear tips, or several may have been hafted together on a shaft to make a fishing gig. One such point with a small bone barb attached to the tip with pitch has been found by divers in the Oklawaha River. Carved barbed points—some with multiple barbs—and bone pins are less common, and socketed antler points are rarer still. Barbara Purdy's (1973) summary of the distributional data relating to these bone tools also suggests they were used throughout the Archaic periods.

Other bone tools from the Ichetucknee River in the Simpson Collection are fish hooks, throwing-stick weights, socketed antler handles, throwing-stick triggers, splinter awls, deer-ulna awls, beaver teeth showing evidence of hafting, and antler punches. It should be stressed again that these same tool types probably were used over thousands of years.

The early Archaic populations, like their Paleoindian ancestors, established camps around water sources. But because such water sources were much more numerous and larger than in earlier times, the early Archaic peoples could sustain larger populations, occupy sites for longer periods, and perform activities that required longer occupation at a specific locale. Archaeologically this development is

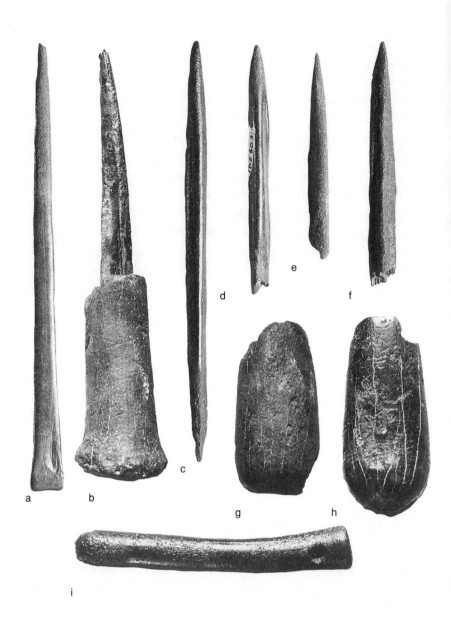

Archaic bone tools from the Ichetucknee River. Some are types also used in the Paleoindian period: *a*, bone pin, 6 inches long; *b*, splinter awl placed in a hollowed antler handle; *c–f*, bone points, awls, or parts of fish spears; *g–h*, hollowed antler handles; *i*, flaker with perforation.

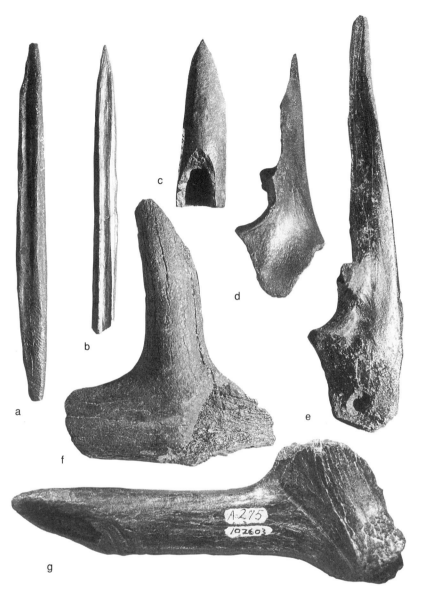

Archaic bone tools from the Ichetucknee River. Some are types also used in the Paleoindian period: *a*, fish spear, 4 ¾ inches long, made from bone splinter with roughening for hafting on the base; *b*, splinter point, awl, or fish spear; *c*, hollowed antler point; *d–e*, deer ulna awls; *f–g*, deer antler punches.

reflected in more sites, sites in more locales, larger sites, a greater range of tools, and sites with significant numbers of burials, compared to the Paleoindians.

Dugout canoes dating to the early Archaic period have not yet been found in Florida. The association of people and waterways, however, makes it likely that canoes were in use in the early Archaic period. One Florida dugout canoe has been radiocarbon dated to 5,120 years ago, and others are known from the late Archaic period and later periods in precolumbian Florida (Newsom and Purdy 1990).

Windover Pond

Were it not for one extraordinary site in Brevard County, our picture of early Archaic people would stop here. The excavation of the Windover Pond site by Glen H. Doran and David N. Dickel of Florida State University has provided unprecedented and dramatic information on the people at that site 7,000 to 8,000 years ago.

Early Archaic peoples used the Windover Pond site when the climate in Florida was again drier, though less arid than at the end of the Pleistocene. Because of higher sea levels, groundwater was higher and there were more water habitats, including Windover Pond, which after about 8000–9000 B.C. held water continuously.

Windover was first discovered in 1982 when a backhoe operator was digging peat from a small pond—about a quarter of an acre of surface area—so it could be filled in and a road constructed across it. A bucketload of peat scooped from the pond included human bones. Archaeologists were summoned, and it soon became evident that under the quiet waters of Windover Pond lay a scientific treasure of immeasurable importance.

Doran and his team of archaeologists and other scientists began investigating the pond in 1984, excavating the early Archaic–period people buried in peat deposits at what was now the bottom of the pond. Excavations would continue into 1986.

The site is one of the most important found anywhere in the world, and it is providing types of information, such as changes in human genetic diversity through time, previously unobtainable. It is fortunate that the site was discovered at a time when multidisciplinary research was the norm and medical and biochemical research had developed to the point where scientists could undertake study of the 7,000-year-old

Glen Doran (*left*, in hat) and David
Dickel (*right*, in hat) helping to drop
a wellpoint into the water-saturated
peat deposits at the Windover Pond
site. Attached to pumps, the well-
points lowered the water table at
the site, allowing excavation (courtesy Department of Anthropology,
Florida State University).

Excavations in the northern part of the Windover Pond site, which has been
pumped almost dry (courtesy Department of Anthropology, Florida State
University).

human tissues preserved in the peat. It also is fortunate that Doran recognized the potential of the site and was the project director. In conjunction with David N. Dickel, Doran has coordinated the interdisciplinary analysis of the artifacts and recovered data (Doran et al. 1986; Doran and Dickel 1988a, b; Stone, Dickel, and Doran 1990). Nearly half the pond and its contents remain unexcavated, left for future archaeologists with even more sophisticated recovery and analytical techniques than we have at present.

Windover Pond, on the edge of the Atlantic coastal ridge five miles from Cape Canaveral, is fed by rainfall and groundwater. Ten to eleven thousand years ago the pond collected only rainwater or surface runoff. Little water would have seeped into the pond because of lowered groundwater tables. At that time plant materials, water lilies and the like, began to accumulate in the bottom of the pond, apparently in some quantities, forming a loosely consolidated peat. Peat formation has continued to the present. Doran and his field team recognized five peat strata, some of which today have the consistency of dense chocolate mousse. Differences in peat composition reflect fluctuations in deposition and water conditions. When excavated the thickest peat was in the center of the pond under about six feet of water.

About 8,000 years ago early Archaic peoples began visiting the pond, at that time a woody marsh, to bury their dead in the peat deposits. The peat was less thick than it is today, and it was covered with less water. Why they chose that particular pond or why they interred people in the peat is a mystery. Each body was wrapped in fabric, which was then staked to the soft peat in or on the bottom of the pond, apparently to keep the body submerged (Doran and Dickel 1988a:273, 276). We know that each individual was buried within forty-eight hours after death because brain and other soft tissues, as well as proteins and mitochondrial DNA, are preserved.

The stratum containing the burials today is the middle peat deposit. This peat stratum with its human interments was subsequently covered by two more peat layers.

The peat also preserved artifacts and a large sample of plant and animal remains that found their way accidentally into the pond or were placed with burials. The artifacts include textiles, stone and bone tools, and wooden objects. Some of the plant and animal remains were collected from the stomach areas of bodies and represent the remains of the last meals eaten by those individuals. Others are foods or raw materials brought to the pond, and still others are species that entered the pond through natural processes. They provide information on plants and animals that were available to the early Archaic peoples and that came from the area immediately around the pond.

Use of the pond for interments continued for at least a thousand years, until about 7,000 years ago. Multiple radiocarbon dates from human bone and tissue, wooden stakes found with burials, and peat deposits around, under, and above the burial stratum pinpoint the period of site use (Doran and Dickel 1988a:266). Perhaps after 5000 B.C., wetter local conditions filled the pond with enough water to make it too difficult to bury people in the peat in the pond bottom, and interments were halted.

Although interments were made over a relatively long period, the clustering of bodies suggests that burials were deposited in the pond during at least five or six discrete episodes of short duration within the millennium of use. During each episode bodies apparently were placed in a single cluster. Ongoing radiocarbon dating of the individuals in each cluster will establish the sequence and absolute dates of each burial episode. If this spatial-temporal pattern proves to be true, it suggests that for several years a single social group used the pond to bury their dead, placing bodies in one small area of the pond that was somehow marked or recorded in memory. Later another group, presumably the descendants of that same group, again used the pond for burial.

The possibility that a single, genetically related population used the pond over a millennium is exciting. The genetic materials being identified from tissues of individuals and groups can be compared and insights gained regarding how chromosomes and genes change through time. No other collection of genetic material in the world spans such a time range. The potential for learning about human evolution, genetically related health problems, and other changes in genetic characteristics makes Windover Pond a priceless treasure of unique scientific information. The 168 bodies (Stone, Dickel, and Doran 1990:177), including 91 preserved brains (Doran et al. 1986:804–805), are providing unprecedented data relating to the native peoples of the

Western hemisphere and humankind in general (Hauswirth, Dickel, Doran, et al. 1988; Lawlor, Dicket, Hauswirth, et al. 1991). Voices from the past can indeed tell us much that is useful today.

The animals identified from Windover Pond that probably lived in the immediate area include river otter, three species of indigenous rats, squirrel, rabbit, opossum, thrush, American coot, geese or ducks, great blue heron and other wading birds, double-crested great cormorant, pied-billed grebe, alligator, soft-shelled turtle, pond turtle, eastern box turtle, mud and musk turtles, snapping turtle, indigo snake, several species of water snake, siren, greater siren, two-toed amphiuma, frog, largemouth bass, red-eared sunfish, bowfin, catfish, and Florida gar (Doran and Dickel 1988a:282). A variety of plants also were identified, including a prickly pear pad (*Opuntia*) placed with a burial and a gourd (*Lagenaria siceria*), probably used as a container (Doran and Dickel 1988b:368). It is likely that the gourd was a wild plant native to Florida.

The number of stone artifacts recovered from the site was remarkably small: five bifacial tools, one of which was broken, and several chert flakes (Doran and Dickel 1988a:281). Three of the tools are stemmed points or knives that resemble early Archaic–period Florida Spike or Thonotosassa forms (Bullen 1975:40–41). Pitch, still apparent, was used to attach them to hafts or handles.

Wooden and bone objects found with burials were more numerous than lithic items. A number of wooden stakes, some with the bark removed, had been fire sharpened (Doran and Dickel 1988b:368). Shark teeth and dog or wolf teeth were hafted with pitch for use as tools (Doran and Dickel 1988b:368–369). Other tools were made from mammal bone and deer antler, as well as from manatee, bird, and panther or bobcat bone. They include incised tubes fashioned from bird bone, pins, barbed pins, awls, and throwing-stick weights made from deer antler (Doran and Dickel 1988a:275, 279–280). Shell tools and beads made from Sabal palm berries, shell, and seeds also were found. The range and types of bone and antler artifacts, including pieces of antler found in various stages of tool manufacture, closely resemble the bone tool assemblage from the Ichetucknee River.

Early Archaic peoples who visited Windover Pond to bury their dead also had a well-developed and sophisticated array of cordage and fabric. The unique preservation of such artifacts in Windover Pond provides us with the earliest examples of these materials in Florida. Doran and Dickel (1988a:274) report seven twining or weaving styles that used fibers taken from Sabal palms, saw palmettos, and other plants. Styles include a finely woven 25-strand-per-inch fabric, perhaps used to fashion tunic-like inner garments. Other coarser and more durable fabrics were identified, along with an open-twined bag, matting, and other fabrics.

The early Archaic peoples at Windover and elsewhere in Florida had a material culture that allowed them to sustain their way of life, but by our standards it could not have been an easy one. Water was in shorter supply than at present, and groups had to move between water sources to find game. The early Archaic people had to hunt or collect everything they ate and gather all of the raw materials they needed to make clothing, tools, and fabrics. They had to carry many of their personal possessions with them as they moved to take advantage of game, water, and other resources. Survival was not assured. One sixteen-year-old buried at Windover died from a combination of poor health factors that included spina bifida, with a loss of sensory perception to the lower leg, and osteomyelitis, which ultimately resulted in the loss of one foot due to infection and bone deterioration (Doran and Dickel 1988a:277). Other pathological conditions also were observed in the burial population (Dickel and Doran 1989).

That children may have been valued in the relatively harsh setting of the early Archaic period may be reflected in the observation at Windover Pond that more artifacts were found with subadult than with adult burials (Doran and Dickel 1988a:274). The importance of water to the early Archaic people may be exhibited in their returning their dead to a pond for final burial.

Middle Archaic Period

The drier-than-present conditions that began during the latter part of the early Archaic period continued after 5000 B.C. But compared to earlier times in Florida, during the middle Archaic period more and larger surface water sources were available. Throughout that period environmental and climatic conditions would ameliorate, becoming progressively more like modern conditions, which appeared by about 3000 B.C.

Middle Archaic sites are found in a variety of locations, including, for the first time, freshwater shell middens along the St. Johns River and the Atlantic lagoon. Middle Archaic peoples also lived in the Hillsborough River drainage northeast of Tampa Bay, along the southwest Florida coast (where marine shell middens are found), and in south Florida locales such as Little Salt Spring in Sarasota County. In addition, middle Archaic sites occur throughout the forests of the interior of northern Florida. One of the largest known middle Archaic sites (8A1356) is located on the northern side of Paynes Prairie (Clausen 1964). Another large site is found on what today is an island in the St. Johns River in southern St. Johns County. As more archaeological surveys are performed in wetland locales, more locales of intensive middle Archaic occupation undoubtedly will be discovered.

Radiocarbon dates from a number of sites help to establish the chronological parameters for this period and its distinctive stemmed projectile points, including the Newnan point (Bullen 1975:31). The dates, all from sites where Newnan points have been excavated, include two dates averaging about 4000 B.C. from site 8A1356 in Alachua County (in Clausen, Brooks, and Wesolowsky 1975:28), several dates averaging about 4000 B.C. from Little Salt Spring (Clausen et al. 1979:611), and three dates averaging about 3460 B.C. from the Tick Island site in Volusia County (Jahn and Bullen 1978:22, n.1). Similar dates have come from several other middle Archaic sites, all of which are pond cemeteries.

At the Harney Flats site Daniel and Wisenbaker (1987:33–34) isolated a middle Archaic component with Newnan points above the early Archaic component, further verifying the relative temporal position of Newnan points. At that site, the archaeologists found increased amounts of silicified coral in the middle Archaic stratum and an increased amount of heat-treated lithic material. Heat treating—thermal alteration—leaves the stone a reddish color and makes it more glasslike and easier to chip (Purdy 1971).

The middle Archaic artifact assemblage is characterized by several varieties of stemmed, broad-blade projectile points. The Newnan point (Clausen 1964:8–11; Bullen 1975:31) is the most distinctive and widespread. One variety of the Newnan point is the Hillsborough point. Other middle Archaic stemmed points, sometimes found in association with Newnan, are Putnam, Levy, Marion, and Alachua (Bullen 1975:32). A single radiocarbon date of 3000 B.C. has come from an

Middle Archaic points: *a–c, g* Newnan (*a* is 3 ¾ inches long); *d–f,* Hillsborough.

inundated offshore site in the Econfina Channel in Apalachee Bay where a Putnam or Marion point was recovered (Dunbar, Webb, and Faught 1991: 134–135). Recently, more of these points have been found by Michael Faught, along with other lithic tools.

A number of middle Archaic sites have been excavated and an even larger number located and collected or tested as a result of surveys in the interior forested highlands of northwest and northern peninsular Florida and in the region around Tampa Bay, especially in the Hillsborough River drainage. Small special-use sites predominate, although larger sites also are found. These small, camp-size sites appear as scatters of lithic artifacts and probably were used for hunting and for collecting, perhaps on a seasonal basis. Other sites, such as Wetherington Island in northeast Hillsborough County, were quarry sites where chert was mined and roughly shaped before being taken to other locations for working into tools (Chance 1981, 1982). Special-use camps are characterized by lithic debitage (waste flakes) and tools, including points, knives, scrapers, and a few larger chopping or hammering tools. Because of soil conditions, preserved faunal or floral remains are rarely found at these sites. Often these small sites contain components that pre- or postdate the middle Archaic occupation, making it difficult to definitively separate middle Archaic lithic assemblages from earlier or later materials.

Reports documenting such relatively small (in terms of materials found) special-use sites include studies of the Kanapaha area in Alachua County (Hemmings and Kohler 1974), sites in Leon County (Tesar 1980), and several sites in the Hillsborough River drainage in northeast Hillsborough County. The latter include site 8Hi450(D) (Daniel and Wisenbaker 1981), site 8Hi483(B) (Gagel 1981), the Deerstand site (Daniel 1982), and the Ranch House site (Estabrook and Newman 1984).

Larger sites believed to be central-base settlements occupied by larger groups of people are also known. These may cover several acres or more and contain tens of thousands of pieces of chert debitage and tools (e.g., the Senator Edwards site in Marion County; see Purdy 1975; Purdy and Beach 1980). Amounts of lithic debris and tools found on these larger sites contrast sharply with the smaller quantities at special-use sites.

Tools other than points collected from these larger interior sites include most, if not all, of the types discussed for the early Archaic period and more, such as blades and a greater variety of unifacial and bifacial tools. One implication is that if the middle Archaic peoples were performing the same types of activities at their villages and camps as their early Archaic ancestors, they must have been using a much greater variety of tools to do them. A more sedentary way of life may have led to the acquiring of more specialized tools. At least some of the tools, perhaps those used for woodworking, are quite large and would not have been easily transportable in any numbers. Their appearance may signal woodworking connected with building more permanent houses.

As yet we do not have a good comparative analysis between lithic collections from small, presumed special-use sites and large central-base sites. However, several lithic analyses from special-use sites in Hillsborough County provide firm ground for such comparative studies (Daniel and Wisenbaker 1981; Gagel 1981; Chance 1981, 1982; Daniel 1982; Estabrook and Newman 1984).

Quarry sites have been identified as occurring in the middle Archaic period, both large sites in localities of major chert outcroppings and small sites near smaller outcroppings. Chert deposits often outcrop along rivers or around lakes as erosion cuts through the soil to the underlying limestone. An excellent example of a large quarry-tool manufacturing site is the Senator Edwards site in Marion County (Purdy 1975) dating from the early and middle Archaic periods. Limited excavation of the site yielded more than 500 tools, 50,000 flakes, 4,600 utilized flakes, and 6,000 blades. Other large workshop sites that possibly also functioned as central-base settlements are the Johnson Lake site in Marion County (Bullen and Dolan 1959), site 8Le484 (Tesar 1980:794–842), and the Haufler site (8Al28).

Caves are a type of site known only from a very few examples in northern Florida. Excavations in Dixie Lime Cave No. 1 (Bullen and Benson 1964) produced a modest assortment of points, other tools, and bones of animals, which suggests that the cave served as a camp for hunting deer and opossum. The game could have been brought back to the cave and butchered. Deer hides might also have been tanned there, because scraping tools were a common artifact.

Several other excavated sites help to provide some understanding of the range of middle Archaic activities. One is the type site for the Newnan point, site 8A1356, which was investigated in the 1960s. Information from that site led to the recognition of the assemblage associated with that point at north Florida interior sites (Clausen 1964). The site, located just east of Gainesville on the high ground separating Newnan's Lake from Paynes Prairie, covers more than several acres.

Of the 186 middle Archaic–period stemmed projectile points recovered, 95 percent were Newnan points. Other tools, found in smaller quantities, were ovate blanks (probably brought from quarry sites and used to make the points), bifacial knives with rounded or squared bases, sandstone hones, hammerstones, and cruciform drills. The most numerous artifacts were blades, flakes, and cores associated with a well-developed blade industry. Many blades were also used as cutting tools. Although blades are found occasionally at other middle Archaic sites, 8A1356 is unique in the quantity of blades recovered, especially considering that only a small portion of the site was excavated.

Evidence of the activities associated with the blades is not preserved in the archaeological record. Were the points and blades used to hunt and butcher animals that roamed nearby Paynes Prairie? Or was the prairie a lake at that time? Were the blades used to clean fish?

Another site providing information on the range of middle Archaic activities is Little Salt Spring in Sarasota County (Clausen et al. 1979). As noted in chapter 2, the spring first was occupied during Paleoindian times. Middle Archaic peoples apparently also found the spring a convenient source of water. During the time they used the spring, ground water would have been nearer the surface and the water level in the sink would have been much higher than during earlier times, providing easier access.

Carl Clausen's investigations at the site revealed an as yet largely unexplored village area fifteen to thirty acres in extent. The village borders a slough that drains into the sinkhole containing the spring. Human burials were placed in the wet muck in the slough bottom and in the sinkhole itself, similar to the burial pattern at Windover Pond. Clausen estimates that the slough burial area may hold more than 1,000 people (Clausen et al. 1979). Bodies, extended and on their backs, were placed on branches or biers of wax myrtle in graves dug into the muck. Bodies and biers were wrapped in grass.

As at Windover Pond, preservation of organic remains at Little Salt Spring was excellent. Some burials contained brain and other tissue (Clausen et al. 1979:612).

An oak digging stick sharpened on one end was placed with one person. Another individual buried in the now-inundated spring basin was accompanied by a wooden tablet with a bird carved on it. The tablet is similar in shape to ones found at the Key Marco site in Collier

County, which dates several thousand years after Little Salt Spring. Newnan points were recovered from the spring itself as well as from the village and the slough.

Underwater interments have been noted at two other south Florida sites radiocarbon dated to the middle Archaic period—Bay West and Republic Grove. (They also have been found at Warm Mineral Spring, where burials containing brain tissue were first found in Florida [Royal and Clark 1960]). Bay West in Collier County (Beriault et al. 1981) was discovered when peat was being dredged from a pond. Unfortunately, the peat-mining operation severely disturbed the site, destroying valuable evidence and leaving the archaeologists to salvage whatever information they could. In addition, no pumping system was available to remove water covering the stratum containing the human interments. Without proper pumps, excavating a wet site is impossible. Despite these handicaps important data were gathered that suggest an overall burial pattern—interments in the bottom of a shallow pond—similar to that at both the Windover Pond and the Little Salt Spring sites. Apparently early and middle Archaic peoples throughout peninsular Florida used aquatic environments for burial.

The salvage investigations at Bay West produced a series of radiocarbon dates between 4900 and 4000 B.C. (Beriault et al. 1981:50). As would be expected from a site dating to that time period, Newnan and other middle Archaic points were found. Like the Windover Pond site, the Bay West site was located about six miles from the coast with a midden immediately adjacent to the burial area. Middle Archaic points also were recovered from the midden.

Thirty-five to forty people had been interred in the Bay West pond (Beriault et al. 1981:50), at least some of whom had been placed on leafy biers, perhaps on branches laid down in graves dug into the peat. Short, fire-sharpened wooden stakes were associated with the burials, similar to the stakes found with burials at the Windover Pond and the Little Salt Spring sites. Possibly they were used to help hold interred bodies below the level of pond water, as suggested by Glen Doran for the burials in Windover Pond.

Artifacts recovered by Beriault and his team include small wooden sticks, possibly used as bow drills for starting fires; antler tools with wooden hafts that appear to be sections of throwing sticks; two throwing-stick triggers; and bone points or pins.

Republic Grove, a third middle Archaic pond burial site with an adjacent land site, was found in Hardee County in 1968 (Wharton, Ballo, and Hope 1981). Middle Archaic points and three wooden stakes with radiocarbon dates ranging from about 3750 to 4530 B.C. confirm the temporal placement of the site. A fourth date of about 500 B.C. may be in error.

At least 37 people were interred in the muck at Republic Grove, several of whom exhibited various pathologies, such as arthritis (Saunders 1972). As at the other pond burial sites, individual burials were associated with wooden stakes and were accompanied by artifacts, including cordage and matting. Also found were throwing-stick triggers made from antler, awls made from mammal ulnae and deer metapodials, a bone deflesher, scrapers made from deer scapulae, and bone pins and knives. In addition, shark teeth, tubular stone beads, and several antler ornaments were excavated, as were stone drills made from Archaic points, flake scrapers and knives, and a flake chopping-tool (Wharton, Ballo, and Hope 1981).

Together, the Little Salt Spring, Bay West, and Republic Grove sites provide a rare glimpse of the range of objects used by the middle Archaic peoples, especially the wooden, antler, and bone tools not preserved on land sites. As demonstrated by the Windover Pond site, these cemeteries have the potential to provide extraordinary information about native peoples. The challenge in the future will be to find pond cemeteries before they are disturbed, excavate them, and analyze their contents with state-of-the-art methods. As Barbara Purdy and her colleagues have demonstrated (Purdy 1988, 1991), the importance of archeological wet sites should not be underestimated.

Not all middle Archaic peoples interred their dead in pond or slough cemeteries. Excavations by Ripley Bullen (1962) at the Tick Island site located in the St. Johns River drainage just west of Lake Woodruff revealed 175 middle Archaic burials. One individual had a Newnan point sticking in a vertebra, and two others each were found with a Newnan point in close association, graphic evidence of violence.

Tick Island interments seem to have been made in small clusters in separate episodes, as at the Windover Pond site. The burial ritual began with the scraping of a shallow depression in the top of an existing freshwater shell midden. Bodies, each probably wrapped in a flexed position, were placed in the depression in a cluster and covered with a mound of sand. Some of the sand appears to have been impregnated with charcoal. Over time, this process was repeated as other groups were interred. Later, post–middle Archaic peoples reused the site, depositing many feet of shell refuse on top of the burial area. Radiocarbon dates associated with the middle Archaic burials were 3080, 3370, and 3500 B.C. (A.K. Bullen 1972:166; Jahn and Bullen 1978).

The bones of the burial population from Tick Island show several pathological conditions, including nonvenereal, syphilitic-like osteopathologies (probably an early form of treponemal infection); healed bone fractures; and periostitis (A. K. Bullen 1972).

Tick Island contains one of a number of Archaic-period freshwater shell midden sites in the central St. Johns River drainage. There is great continuity in site selection, subsistence, and artifacts between these middle Archaic sites and those of the late Archaic period in this section of the St. Johns River.

Another burial area dating to the middle Archaic period, and probably the late Archaic period as well, was excavated by B. Calvin Jones of the Florida Bureau of Archaeological Research. The Gauthier site in Brevard County contained as many as 110 individuals. Another 40–50 are estimated to have been destroyed by a dragline (Carr and Jones 1981). Like the other Archaic cemeteries (except Republic Grove), the Gauthier site is near the coast, about six miles inland.

The Gauthier site interments seem to have been made by scraping a shallow depression in the soil (rather than in shell, as at Tick Island) and laying bodies in it, at times on top of one another. Five clusters of burials were apparent. Jones was unable to obtain radiocarbon dates from most of the skeletal remains because they were highly mineralized, probably as a result of the limestone strata directly under the burials. One radiocarbon date, 2390 B.C., was obtained, however (Maples 1987). Along with this date, Newnan, Culbreath (a late Archaic marker), and other points found in the cemetery place the burials in the middle to late Archaic period, suggesting that the site is later than the Little Salt Spring and Bay West sites.

Artifacts found with the flexed burials included limestone throwing-stick weights, antler triggers from throwing sticks, projectile points, other stone tools, tubular *Busycon* shell beads, tools and ornaments of bone, and worked shark teeth that probably had been hafted and used as knives or scrapers.

One individual had been interred wearing two hair ornaments or parts of a headdress, each consisting of a piece of incised antler four to five inches long with a small hole drilled in it through which a lock of hair could be partially pulled. A raccoon baculum (penis bone) was then used to secure the hair in the hole (Carr and Jones 1981:86–87). The person wearing these ornaments was accompanied by a number of other artifacts, suggesting special social status.

Although the Tick Island and Gauthier cemeteries contrast with the pond-muck-peat cemeteries, the artifacts associated with the Archaic burials at all of the sites fit comfortably into a single assemblage. It is tempting to suggest, however, that the Tick Island and the Gauthier sites, the latter being the most recent of the Archaic-period cemeteries, represent a burial pattern that roughly correlates with the end of the middle Archaic period. At that time pond burials fell into disuse and were replaced by a new burial pattern.

Pollen evidence from Florida and south central Georgia (Watts 1969, 1971; Watts and Hansen 1988) indicates that increasingly moist conditions appeared during the middle Archaic period after about 4000 B.C., and that a gradual change in forest cover took place, with oaks in some regions giving way to pines or mixed forests. The resulting vegetation communities after 3000 B.C. are essentially little different from those found in colonial times before widespread nineteenth- and twentieth-century land alterations. The vegetative changes that culminated by 3000 B.C. may be related to shifts in settlement locations that occurred toward the end of the middle Archaic period, including extensive occupation by Archaic peoples of what is now the Atlantic coastal lagoon in St. Johns County and the St. Johns River valley. The large shell middens that accumulated after 4000 B.C., especially along the St. Johns River in Volusia County, suggest that significant numbers of people were using the resources of the river and its adjacent forests. This pattern would continue for the next 6,000 years, into the colonial period.

During the middle Archaic period people also lived along the Gulf coast; at least we can first document their presence there at this time. A shell midden on Useppa Island in Lee County and a midden stratum on Horr's Island in Collier County have been radiocarbon dated to about 3330 B.C. and 4200 B.C., respectively (Milanich, Chapman et al. 1984:270; Russo 1991:423). It is likely that other middle Archaic shell middens and perhaps even earlier shell middens existed along the Gulf coast (e.g., Warren 1964, 1970; Goodyear and Warren 1972; Goodyear, Upchurch, and Brooks 1980), but they have been inundated or obliterated by the rising sea. Shell middens at both the Useppa Island and the Horr's Island sites accumulated in Pleistocene dunes, accounting for their presence today.

After 3000 B.C., a period in which sea-level rise was less than in earlier times, the evidence for coastal populations in Florida is much more definitive. Late Archaic shell middens are preserved in many locales along the coast and along the St. Johns River. In the next section we will examine some of the late Archaic cultures associated with these middens.

Late Archaic Period

In the late Archaic period in Florida, beginning in 3000 B.C., regionalization of cultures occurred as human populations elaborated lifeways well adapted to specific environmental zones. Cultures once subject to various long-term environmental and climatic changes and fluctuations (e.g., periods of aridity characterized by scarce surface water) no longer faced those challenges. With the arrival of essentially modern environmental conditions by 3000 B.C. (Watts and Hansen 1988:310), shellfish, fish, and other food resources from bountiful freshwater and coastal wetlands were important to increasingly larger native populations. Extensive late Archaic middens are found in several locations: (1) along the northeast coast and inland waterway from Flagler County north; (2) along the coast of southwest Florida from Charlotte Harbor south into the Ten Thousand Islands; and (3) in the braided river-marsh system of the central St. Johns River, especially below Lake George. The importance of the wetlands in these regions to aboriginal settlement was probably duplicated in other coastal regions, especially the Tampa Bay–central peninsular Gulf coast and the northwest coast, but the archaeological evidence is not yet convincing. In the Tampa Bay area many of the late Archaic sites are inundated, and in other regions late Archaic sites probably also are inundated, or they remain unexcavated. One such site, radiocarbon dated to 2800 B.C., has been found in 15–20 feet of water 200 yards off the beach in St. Lucie County on the Atlantic coast (Murphy 1990). The trend, however, is for late Archaic sites to be found in every wetland locale where extensive surveys or excavations are carried out.

During the late Archaic period, by about 2000 B.C. or slightly earlier, the firing of clay pottery was either invented in Florida or the technique diffused here from coastal Georgia and South Carolina, where early dates for pottery have been obtained. At one time it was thought that the earliest pottery-manufacturing culture in Florida was the Orange culture of the St. Johns region in northeast Florida. But additional evidence from southwest Florida (e.g., Division of Archives 1970; Cockrell 1970; Widmer 1974; McMichael 1982; Russo 1991) indicates fired clay pottery just as early in that region. Indeed, some dates on early pottery from northeast and southwest Florida are comparable to the early dates from sites in Georgia and South Carolina.

Pottery is an easily recognizable artifact, and the earliest ceramics in Florida were tempered with plant fibers—palmetto fiber or Spanish moss—making this ware even more distinctive. Because the first use of pottery is well dated to the period from 2000 B.C. or slightly before to 1000 B.C. or slightly after, fiber-tempered pottery serves as a convenient horizon across the state.

The earliest (ca. 2000–1650 B.C.) fiber-tempered pottery was undecorated. After 1650 B.C. geometric designs and punctations were used as surface decoration, providing an important tool for differentiating earlier and later sites of the 2000–1000 B.C. period.

The available evidence suggests few if any differences in late Archaic lifeways before and after the appearance of fiber-tempered pottery. In fact, there appears to be great uniformity in local settlement patterns and artifact assemblages—except for the absence or presence of fiber-tempered pottery—wherever late Archaic sites are found. With the onset of the late Archaic period by 3000 B.C., several regional cultural adaptations were established that changed little over the next several thousand years. Where intensive agriculture never took hold, such as in most of southern Florida and many coastal areas, the general subsistence patterns of the late Archaic period continued largely unchanged into the colonial period.

There are changes apparent in the archaeological record of the late Archaic period, however, that serve to distinguish it from the middle Archaic period. But these changes are related to demography rather than changes in basic lifeways. Most noticeable is an increase in the number and density of sites. Sites containing fiber-tempered pottery are found throughout the state. In those wetland areas cited earlier, sites are both large and densely clustered and certainly were associated with sedentary populations. Moreover, in every region where the larger and densely distributed sites are found, preceramic late Archaic sites also have been found, suggesting that demographic and settlement changes began at least by the onset of the late Archaic period at 3000 B.C. In Florida, cultural regionalization first began to occur at least by the late Archaic period.

Relatively large numbers of late Archaic peoples lived in some regions of the state and not in others. At least this is the conclusion that we must draw from the evidence at hand. For instance, large late Archaic sites are relatively uncommon in the interior highland forests of northwest Florida and northern peninsular Florida, regions where earlier middle Archaic sites are known. When late Archaic occupations are recognized, largely because of the presence of fiber-tempered pottery, they are either small artifact scatters or components in sites containing debris from several different periods. The lack of sites in the interior forests suggests that nonwetland locales either were not inhabited on a year-round basis or were inhabited by only small populations.

Why was this so? One explanation is that, with the environmental conditions present by 3000 B.C., coastal and riverine wetland settings could most easily support increasing populations. It was much less difficult to harvest fish and mollusks than to maintain a hunting-gathering way of life in the interior forests. We can guess that from the end of the middle Archaic period on, populations on the coasts and in the St. Johns River drainage continued to increase and expand until eventually those environments could support no more people. At that point, shortly after A.D. 100, sedentary villages and large populations are found in the interior forests (see chapter 4).

East Florida

Can we identify some of these regional late Archaic cultures living in wetland locales? In east Florida—consisting of the St. Johns River drainage, the coastal lagoon system, and the coastal salt marsh–tidal stream–barrier island system—archaeologists have defined both a preceramic middle and late Archaic–period culture, Mount Taylor; and a late Archaic–period culture associated with fiber-tempered pottery, the Orange culture. The exact date for the beginning of the Mount Taylor culture is uncertain, but it must be sometime in the middle Archaic period. Should middle Archaic sites found in the St. Johns drainage, such as Tick Island, be included in the rubric Mount Taylor, emphasizing the continuity between middle and late Archaic–period shell mound–dwelling peoples of that region? Probably they should. Are there differences between the Mount Taylor archaeological assemblage and the assemblage associated with later Orange period sites? Other than the presence in the latter of fiber-tempered pottery, no differences have yet been articulated. At this time the best solution seems to be to use Mount Taylor to refer to the preceramic period that dates from the middle into the late Archaic period (from 5000 to 2000 B.C.) and to use Orange to refer to the late Archaic period after 2000 B.C. when fiber-tempered pottery was made.

The situation is muddied by the occasional use of the term *Transitional* to refer to the period from 1200 or 1000 to 500 B.C., said to be a time characterized by the use of fiber-tempered pottery and pottery tempered with a mixture of sand and fiber (semi-fiber-tempered pottery). As George Shannon (1986) and Michael Russo (in Russo, Cordell, and Ruhl 1992) have pointed out, however, semi-fiber-tempered pottery may not be the chronological marker it was once thought to be. And although the Transitional may refer to changes in ceramic manufacturing techniques, the period 1200 or 1000 to 500 B.C. may not be a cultural transition in eastern Florida. As James Miller (1991:161–163) has shown, when one tries to isolate Transitional-period sites in the St. Johns River drainage, not many can be found, in part because it is difficult to decide exactly what constitutes a Transitional ceramic assemblage versus a ceramic assemblage that can be assigned to either the Orange period or to the following St. Johns I period. At this time, it seems best to discard the term *Transitional period* (see Bullen 1959 for another view).

The name Mount Taylor culture was originated by John Goggin, who derived it from the Mount Taylor site in Volusia County, a preceramic middle and late Archaic shell midden excavated by C. B. Moore (1893:12–13, 113–115) in the late nineteenth century. Our knowledge of the archaeology of the Mount Taylor and Orange periods is based on the work of Goggin (1952b); several important excavations carried out by Bullen (1955c, 1962, 1969), Bullen and Bryant (1965), and others (e.g., Cumbaa and Gouchnour 1970) at sites in the central St. Johns River drainage; excavations on the coastal lagoon in Volusia and St. Johns counties (Griffin and Smith 1954; Bullen and Bullen 1961a; Miller 1980; Bond 1992); a survey of the Guana marsh-lagoon tract in St. Johns County north of St. Augustine (Newman and Weisman 1992); and a program of archaeological survey and testing directed by Michael Russo in the Timucuan Ecological and Historic Preserve on the northeast coast (Russo 1992b; Russo, Cordell, and Ruhl 1992).

These excavations, spanning four decades, make it obvious that Orange-period sites will be found almost everywhere archaeologists look in east Florida, especially in coastal settings or on the St. Johns or Oklawaha rivers. The largest sites are located where wetland resources are most productive. This is probably true for fiber-tempered pottery occupations throughout Florida.

Russo's work in northeast Florida has established the presence of both Mount Taylor–period and Orange-period coastal middens in that locale. Russo located a number of shell middens in the coastal salt marsh—e.g., McGundo Islands, Oxeye Islands (twelve separate small middens), Pepper Island, and Rollins Bird Sanctuary—and obtained radiocarbon dates between 3200 and 1800 B.C. from their Mount Taylor components. Orange-period sites yielded dates from about 1900 B.C. to 1400 B.C.

Russo also verified the presence of extensive Orange-period shell middens—middens 10 feet high and extending for more than 425 yards, encircling what could be a central plaza or residential area—on Fort George Island. Other large Orange-period shell sites, some ring-shaped, are known from the Guana Tract, a coastal, barrier island–salt marsh locale in St. Johns County (Newman and Weisman 1992:168).

Analysis of several fish and mollusk species from these late Archaic sites leaves no doubt that late Archaic peoples were living full-time along the northeast Florida coast, utilizing the resources of the coastal marshes and adjacent hardwood forests (Russo 1992b). Looking at the overall pattern of settlement, Russo suggests that the extensive Orange-period middens on Fort George Island may have been a "centralized village which articulated with outlying habitation areas," and the small salt marsh island middens may be the remains of "simple

In the early 1950s the Bluffton site in the central St. Johns River valley in
Volusia County was commercially mined for shell. A large number of late
Archaic artifacts were collected when the shell was washed before being sold
(photograph by John Griffin; courtesy Florida Museum of Natural History).

shellfish and fish processing stations," or what is left of formerly large,
now partially inundated, sites (Russo 1992b:198).

Today, with sea levels about five feet higher than during the late
Archaic period, many late Archaic sites are probably inundated or
buried under salt marshes (see Miller 1992 for a discussion of coastal
sea rise and its effect on the St. Johns drainage). The only ones left for
modern archaeologists to observe are either middens originally deposited on higher ground—e.g., the modern barrier islands, such as
Fort George Island—or middens that have been surrounded by the
encroaching salt marsh as it moves inland with the rising sea. As with
Paleoindian and early and middle Archaic–period coastal sites in
Florida, the rise in sea level has hidden a portion of the archaeological
record of the late Archaic period.

Zooarchaeological analyses by Stephen Cumbaa (1976) and Russo
(in Russo, Cordell, and Ruhl 1992) provide information on the diet of
the late Archaic peoples living near the coast and in the central St.
Johns River drainage, respectively. Cumbaa's pioneering analysis of a
Mount Taylor midden focused on the importance of freshwater shell-

Michael Russo excavating a late Archaic coastal shell midden in northeast
Duval County in 1992 (courtesy Southeast Archeological Center, National
Park Service).

fish in the diet. He noted that the riverine Mount Taylor shell middens
were, by volume, 98–99 percent pond snail. At specific sites, the sizes
of the snails in the middens decreased through time, suggesting that
the rate of harvesting snails was greater than the snails' rates of repro-
duction and growth.

Cumbaa suggests that the snails, so prominent in late Archaic middens on the St. Johns and Oklawaha rivers (cf. Bullen 1969; Cumbaa
and Gouchnour 1970), were an easily collected resource that drew
people to certain riverine locales. When the snails were overharvested,
the people moved and harvested snails at other locales. Snails could be
collected simply by picking them off the sandy river bottom and
putting them in net carry-bags or in baskets. Freshwater mussels also
were an important resource and, at least at some late Archaic riverine
locales, were the primary molluscan food.

In the northeast Florida coastal sector Russo (Russo 1992; Russo,
Cordell, and Ruhl 1992) found oyster as well as oyster and coquina
shell middens for the Mount Taylor and Orange periods. Other mollusk species were included in the middens, but only the dwarf surf
clam (*Mulinia lateralis*) made up more than 1 percent of mollusk shells

in any midden. Careful recovery and analysis revealed shrimp and crab remains and more than twenty species of marine fish. The most important fish were Menhaden (*Brevoortia* spp.) and Atlantic croaker (*Micropogonias undulatus*). Sharks and rays also were eaten, as were snakes, turtles, lizards, salamanders, siren, rodents, and deer.

From other east Florida sites we have evidence that bear, wildcat, otter, opossum, rabbit, and turtle were hunted and collected; at times even dogs were eaten. Two coastal sites have produced remains of the now-extinct great auk. Other birds that were taken include loon, common murre, and gannet. Porpoise bones also have been identified from coastal middens.

Although a wide variety of both vertebrate and invertebrate animal species have been identified, marine resources—fish and mollusks— were the most important sources of meat for the Archaic-period coastal populations, as they probably were for all later coastal dwellers. Fish and mollusks were probably the most important meat sources for the late Archaic riverine dwellers as well. Wetlands—whether coastal marsh–tidal stream systems or riverine-marsh systems—presented precolumbian peoples with relatively easily collectable foods. Of all natural ecosystems, shallow water and tidal marsh systems trap the most energy that is easily convertible to food (that is, edible animals).

Few artifacts have been identified from Mount Taylor– and Orange-period coastal shell middens, largely because extensive excavations have not been undertaken or discreet cultural deposits from those periods could not be isolated. More have come from the riverine middens, which have been more extensively investigated and collected. From what has been found we can infer aspects of subsistence technology, such as the throwing stick, whose use is suggested by steatite throwing-stick weights and stemmed projectile points. No doubt traps, snares, and fish traps also were in use. Russo (1992:198) suggests that along the coast fine-mesh nets were used to take fish from the estuarine tidal creeks.

Impressions of woven basketry, fabrics, and matting have been found on the bottoms of a number of fiber-tempered vessels (Benson 1959). Most common are varieties of twilling, but plaited and twined weaves also are present. The impressions were made when the as yet unfired vessels were either intentionally or unintentionally pushed down on the mat or fabric.

Fiber-tempered pottery from the Bluffton site: *a, d,* Orange Incised (*a* is 2½ inches high); *b,* Tick Island Incised; *c,* Orange Plain rim with node (courtesy Florida Museum of Natural History).

Picks and hammers made of shell and points and pins made of bone are the most common tools found in the shell middens. *Strombus* celts have also been found; *Busycon* hammers, seemingly rarer at Mount Taylor sites, are more common at Orange sites, as are shell picks. *Busycon* cups, often displaying burned bottoms, which suggests they were used in cooking, have been found at a number of late Archaic sites (e.g., Bond 1992:157). Some bone pins are incised with the same designs found on the Orange fiber-tempered pottery vessels.

Other bone tools include splinter awls and awls round in cross section, which might have been useful in shellfish processing. A very few peg-topped bone pins, some engraved, are present along with small chert-flake scrapers. Size and wear patterns of the latter suggest they could have been used to scrape basket splints. Other artifacts, all rare, include stemmed projectile points (some very large and possibly used as knives), drilled and incised turtle carapaces used as decorative items, hollowed antler sockets for holding tools, and bone fishhooks.

Orange Period Ceramic Chronology

Period	Dates (B.C.)	Ceramic attributes
Orange 5	1000–500	Chalky St. Johns ware appears late; some quartz sand temper mixed with fiber in paste; some coiling; bowls most common; some late pottery with incising, triangular punctations, and/or side lugs.
Orange 4	1250–1000	Some mixed quartz sand and fiber temper; some early coiled pottery; simple incised decorative motifs.
Orange 3	1450–1250	Large, straight-sided and round-mouthed vessels with flat bottoms; some square or rectangular vessels, ca. 10 cm deep; walls 4–13 mm thick; lips simple rounded or flattened; some side lugs below rims; some vessels resemble steatite vessels in shape; incised straight lines, some parallel and slanting; some punctations or ticks; no Tick Island types.
Orange 2	1650–1450	Vessel shapes same as Orange 1; decorations include incised concentric vertical diamonds with horizontal lines; Tick Island styles—incised spirals with background punctations (rare); plain pottery common.
Orange 1	2000[a]–1650	Pottery hand molded and fiber tempered; thin walls 6–7 mm; simple rounded lips; shallow, flat-based, and straight-sided bowls; rectangular containers, 10 by 20 by 10 cm, some with luglike appendages; no decorations.

Source: Based on Bullen (1955c, 1972).

[a] Or slightly earlier.

Of all the artifacts found in Orange-period sites, the most common is pottery. Bullen has presented detailed descriptions of changes in fiber-tempered pottery through time (Bullen 1955c, 1972). Documenting these changes is useful for establishing subperiods within the Orange period. A summary of these changes in decorative and manufacturing techniques is presented in the table opposite (Orange Period Ceramic Chronology).

Northwest Florida

Many late Archaic sites in northwest Florida probably have been drowned by the Gulf of Mexico. Surveys have located small late Archaic occupations away from the coast in the interior forests (e.g., in the Torreya Ravines in Gadsden and Liberty counties, Percy and Jones 1976:113–114). Larger sites are present in wetland locales, such as those near the Jim Woodruff Reservoir (Bullen 1958; White 1981a) and in the Apalachicola River valley near the coast (Meadows and White 1992). Along the western coastal zone, especially around Choctawhatchee Bay, are a number of late Archaic sites dated to 2000 to 600 B.C. The archaeological assemblage associated with those sites is the Elliott's Point complex (Lazarus 1958; Thomas and Campbell 1991), which extends east to the lower Apalachicola valley (Meadows and White 1992). That complex apparently represents "a localized expression" of the Poverty Point culture, which is centered in the lower Mississippi River valley (Thomas and Campbell 1991:103).

Louis Tesar's intensive survey of selected portions of Leon County located late Archaic sites that he describes as "generally small, less than one acre extractive sites" (Tesar 1980:585–587). The number of sites was the same as the number of middle Archaic sites, but much less than the number of sites of the post–500 B.C. period. It seems certain that as more surveys and excavations are carried out in wetland areas of northwest Florida, many more late Archaic sites will be found.

Fiber-tempered pottery found in northwest Florida has been assigned to the Norwood series and differentiated from the Orange series of east Florida (Phelps 1965). But it is not certain that these are separate ceramic series. Surfaces of Norwood Simple Stamped vessels display stick impressions, a decorative treatment quite distinct from the incised motifs on Orange vessels. However, fiber-tempered pottery with Orange-style decorations is also present. No technological anal-

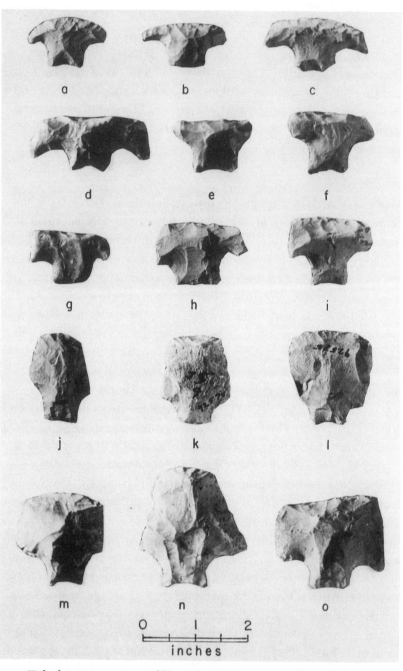

Hafted scrapers excavated by Ripley Bullen from a late Archaic/early Deptford component at site 8Ja5 in Jackson County. This illustration was first used in his report (Bullen 1958: plate 67; courtesy Florida Museum of Natural History).

yses of Norwood and Orange wares have been performed to determine if manufacturing techniques can be used to further distinguish these two fiber-tempered series.

Some archaeologists have tried to differentiate Norwood from Orange by stating that Norwood pottery has quartz inclusions (sand) added to the paste, while Orange pottery does not. But this is not always true. Not all Norwood fiber-tempered pottery contains quartz inclusions and some Orange fiber-tempered pottery does. It seems best at this time to treat these types as variants of the same ware, at least until detailed ceramic studies are done.

Extensive coastal shell middens dating to the late Archaic period in northwest Florida are less rare than previously thought. Although sites probably have been inundated by the sea, surveys continue to locate more and more middens. One that has been studied is the Meig's Pasture site in Okaloosa County. Associated with the Elliott's Point complex, the site has been investigated by several archaeological teams (Curren 1987:11–15). The site, a horseshoe-shaped midden about 320 feet across at the open end, is 820 yards from the present coastline on a freshwater spring. This location may account for the site not being inundated by the rising Gulf.

Three closely grouped radiocarbon dates from the site average about 1700 B.C. No fiber-tempered pottery was found, suggesting that the site was occupied just before the introduction of fiber-tempered pottery to the late Archaic artifact assemblage. Within the site a number of large, trenchlike cooking pits were found. Some were as large as thirteen feet long, and up to three feet wide and three feet deep. After use, they were filled with refuse that included faunal remains, mainly shell and bone. The relative amounts of animal species present often varied widely between pit deposits, perhaps reflecting the collecting habits of the native peoples. Sometimes oysters and deer might be eaten, at other times sea catfish and marsh clams.

Caleb Curren's 1987 report on Meig's Pasture is augmented by detailed archaeobotanical and zooarchaeological studies. Michael Russo's analysis of animal remains indicates that more than twenty species of shellfish were collected (in Curren 1987). The most important were oysters, *Mercenaria* clams, marsh clams (*Rangia*), and marsh periwinkle. Fish, especially sea catfish, jack crevalle, and Atlantic croaker, were common; eagle rays, ladyfish, shad, menhaden, herring, anchovies, gafftopsail catfish, pinfish, porgies, silver perch, spot, and mullet also were eaten. Freshwater and land turtles were a part of the diet, as were rabbit, eastern gray squirrel, river otter, and deer. Besides fish and shellfish, deer were an important source of meat. One grape seed (*Vitis* sp.), hickory nut shells, and a possible cabbage palm seed were present, as were lumps of resinous material that probably is pine resin (Newsom in Curren 1987).

The lithic artifact assemblage from the site is remarkably small, just eight objects: three small pieces of sandstone, perhaps grinding tools; a quartzite hammerstone; two flake tools of Tallahatta quartzite; and two heavily used stemmed points or knives made of chert. The source of the Tallahatta quartzite and the chert was probably southeast Alabama (Curren 1987:74).

Nine clay objects, probably broken cooking balls, were also found, similar to objects found in a variety of sizes and shapes in other parts of the lower Southeast during this time period that are believed to have been used for cooking. The size of tennis balls, they were first heated in a fire and then transferred to an "oven" or pit where their heat could bake food. Such clay balls are much more common in northwest Florida than elsewhere in Florida (Thomas and Campbell 1991).

Another important late Archaic Elliott's Point complex site is Buck Bayou Mound, a large semicircular shell midden located on Choctawhatchee Bay in Walton County (Fairbanks 1959; Thomas and Campbell 1991). Prentice Thomas and L. Janice Campbell, archaeologists with New World Research, Inc., have suggested that the Buck Bayou Mound site is a regional center associated with outlying, smaller settlements. The Meig's Pasture site may be a similar, but smaller, center.

In addition to the clay balls and other types of artifacts from Meig's Pasture, other Elliott's Point complex sites also contain microliths, often used as perforators, and stemmed projectile points. Shell beads, bone pins and needles, and bowls and other items of steatite also have been found, along with Norwood fiber-tempered pottery (Thomas and Campbell 1991).

Excavations in northwest Florida, especially research centered on the Elliott's Point complex, suggest that the coastal late Archaic peoples of that region were sedentary, like the contemporaneous late Archaic people in the northeast. In both regions, wetland resources in

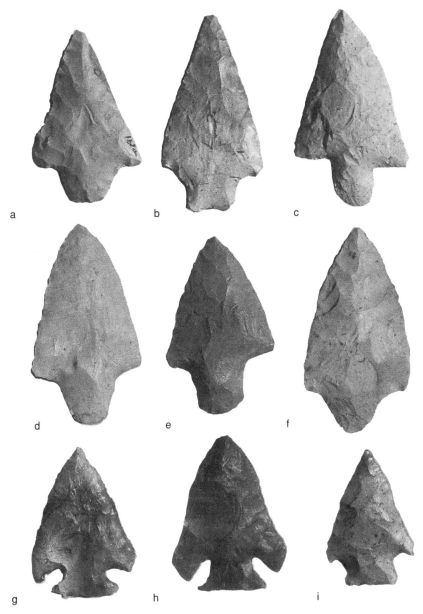

Middle and late Archaic points: *a–b*, Levy (*a* is 2 ⅜ inches long); *c–e*, Marion; *f*, Putnum; *g,i*, Lafayette; *h*, Clay.

combination with hunting and collecting of adjacent forests provided the livelihood for the native peoples. In the next section we will look at still another coastal late Archaic culture, one centered on Tampa Bay and the central Gulf coast.

Greater Tampa Bay

Late Archaic–period sites—middens adjacent to the Gulf and smaller sites back from the coast proper—have been identified in the Tampa Bay–central Gulf coast region. Both preceramic sites and sites associated with fiber-tempered pottery are present. The culture associated with these sites is unnamed. An apt name might be Culbreath Bayou, derived from the Culbreath Bayou site, a preceramic late Archaic shell midden adjacent to Tampa Bay (Warren, Thompson, and Bullen 1967).

The Interstate 75 archaeological project located several sites with late Archaic components in the wetlands of the Hillsborough River drainage. One, Wetherington Island, is a reused quarry first used in earlier Archaic times (Chance 1981, 1982). Other inland sites include Deerstand, Ranch House, and Marita (Daniel 1982; Estabrook and Newman 1984). Coastal shell middens are also known around Tampa Bay and to the south in Sarasota County (see Hill Cottage Midden, Bullen and Bullen 1976).

The Culbreath Bayou site contained a preceramic late Archaic component. Excavations showed the most common projectile-point types were Culbreath (most common), Clay, and Lafayette, all of which are stemmed and corner-notched varieties (Bullen 1975:26–28). Some were asymmetrical, resharpened on one edge of the blade, suggesting use as hafted knives. Other tools were hafted scrapers, end scrapers, and ovate and trianguloid knives.

Warren (1968) has reported on materials dredged from Apollo Beach, another site on Tampa Bay that produced large numbers of late Archaic points and associated tools. Unlike Culbreath Bayou, the Apollo Beach collection apparently was not associated with a shell midden.

Other areas in the Tampa Bay area, such as the Canton Street site (Bullen, Askew et al. 1978), appear to have been first occupied by people who made fiber-tempered pottery. Many of those same locales continued to be occupied into the post–500 B.C. period. At such sites Culbreath points are found in fewer quantities, and Lafayette points are more common. Hernando and Citrus points, popular in later times in northwest Florida, also are found at these sites (Bullen 1975: 24–25), as are crudely knapped stemmed points or knives. Other artifacts include steatite ornaments; sandstone and steatite sherds (suggesting some vessels were made from stone rather than clay); an imitation carnivore jaw made of slate; bone awls; *Busycon* shell hammers and picks; and stone cleavers, perhaps used as scrapers.

The fiber-tempered pottery found at some late Archaic sites around Tampa Bay, like that from northwest Florida, includes both Orange plain and decorated pottery and Norwood pottery with stick impressions (e.g., Daniel 1982:121–122). The range of the practice of stick-impressing fiber-tempered pottery seems to be along the Gulf coast from the panhandle to Tampa Bay.

Many late Archaic sites in the Tampa Bay region probably either are inundated or were destroyed around the turn of the century. Formerly so numerous, shell middens of all periods were used to provide road materials for towns like Bradenton and Tampa. As ludicrous as it seems, this practice still goes on today in parts of Florida.

Southwest Coast

In addition to east and northwest Florida and Tampa Bay, extensive late Archaic shell middens are present in southwest Florida. Test excavations in the early 1980s on Useppa Island (Milanich, Chapman et al. 1984) and on Horr's Island (McMichael 1982) located late Archaic-period preceramic shell middens in Pleistocene dune settings. Some of these sites are quite large: the Horr's Island midden is sixteen feet deep in some places. Previous research on the south end of Marco Island (Division of Archives 1970; Cockrell 1970; Widmer 1974) had determined that at least some of the extensive shell middens on the dunes in that locale were associated with fiber-tempered pottery and also dated from the late Archaic period.

Because the shell middens at all of these sites were originally deposited on dunes well above the level of the Gulf of Mexico, they have not been inundated by post-2000 B.C. rises in sea level. Fiber-tempered pottery also has been observed in small amounts at other coastal sites in the region (Griffin 1949b). More late Archaic coastal sites probably exist in as yet unsurveyed dune settings or in locales back from the coast. Many more sites probably have been inundated.

Additional excavations at the Useppa Island Archaic site tested by Jefferson Chapman and his research team (Milanich, Chapman et al. 1984) have been undertaken by Corbett Torrence as a part of the Florida Museum of Natural History's Southwest Florida Project, directed by William Marquardt. A number of shell tools have been identified, including a manufacturing sequence in which the columella from *Busycon* shells were shaped into tools.

The large preceramic midden on Horr's Island found during a survey and testing project (McMichael 1982) has now been the focus of extensive testing, and a great deal of additional information has been collected (Russo 1991). Tall sand dunes on the west and north ends of Horr's Island, an inverted T-shaped island, form two sides of a U-shaped parabolic dune whose northern side is now on the southern end of Marco Island. The large parabolic dune apparently formed during the Pleistocene around a lagoon, which today is Barfield Bay.

McMichael's original survey of Horr's Island located four shell mounds in addition to the extensive shell midden, all deposited on dunes. Radiocarbon dates place the midden in the period 3000–2000 B.C. Similar dates were obtained from the shell mounds, but it was thought that the mounds had been made by later peoples building with late Archaic–period shell midden. Russo's investigations showed this was not the case (Russo 1991). His careful excavations and analysis produced persuasive evidence that the four mounds, one of which was nearly 20 feet high, and the large, late Archaic shell midden—measuring more than 300 by 600 yards—were contemporary and associated with villagers who resided on the coast year-round. In the midden were numerous small hearths and post molds suggesting circular to oval houses, 13 by 15 feet in diameter. The presence of substantial houses supports Russo's model of a sedentary lifeway, as do seasonality data obtained from several fish and mollusk species.

Excavations in the four shell mounds (labeled A–D) indicate that two of them, Mounds B and C, were intentionally constructed of discarded primary shell refuse. They were not built by redepositing debris from an older midden. This construction method was a labor-saving technique: shell refuse needed only be carried once. Mound B contained a flexed human burial. The excavations in the two mounds were limited, and other burials might have been present.

Mounds A and D were constructed in similar fashion, but each also contained sand mound-fill strata. Mound A, the largest, contained two human interments. If the mounds can be said to be burial mounds, they are the earliest known in the southeastern United States. Along with the archaeological evidence gathered from other late Archaic sites in Florida, the Horr's Island data provide a picture of a sedentary lifeway well before the appearance of post–500 B.C. regional cultures, which are well documented in Florida.

The tool kit of the Horr's Island villagers was centered on shell tools rather than stone tools. Most likely they also had many wooden tools, but such tools have not been preserved in the terrestrial site. Russo (1991) and his research team identified *Busycon* dippers and spoons made from the outer portion of the shell; columella hammers and cutting tools, such as adzes and chisels; and hammers and cutting tools made from whole shells. Quahog clams were used as anvils, digging tools, scrapers, and spokeshaves. Other shell tools were *Melongena* hammers and *Macrocallista* knives. The shell tool assemblage is like those from the Archaic site on Useppa Island and the Hill Cottage Midden at the Palmer site in Sarasota County. This southern Gulf coast assemblage is quite different from the shell tools found in east and northwest Florida, however, which are many fewer in number.

Limestone blocks from the Horr's Island late Archaic midden were used as platforms on which shell tools could be ground; the blocks were also used to grind bola stones, four of which were found. The blocks could also have been used to grind Setaria seeds (a panicoid grass), which were found in some quantity in the midden (Russo 1991:370). Other stone artifacts were extremely scarce: a Newnan point, perhaps salvaged from an earlier site, and a few chert flakes.

From their location on Barfield Bay the late Archaic villagers had easy access to the same marine resources that would continue to support coastal populations in the region for the next 5,000 years. Russo (1991:80–145) identified eighty-eight separate animal species that were eaten, seventy-four of which are animals living in estuarine habitats. Marine resources, especially oysters and hardhead catfish (*Ariopsis felis*) provided much of the meat diet at the site. Of lesser importance were clams, lightning whelks, pinfish, threadfin herring, and mojarra. The total species list is a veritable compendium of the mollusks and fish that can be collected along the coast. Terrestrial and freshwater animals were also eaten, but in much lesser quantities.

The late Archaic villagers, like the people that followed them, apparently ate nearly everything that was available along the coast. The ease with which food could be collected allowed populations to establish sedentary settlements and to further elaborate their cultural systems. By or shortly after 3000 B.C. coastal and riverine cultures were characterized by greater cultural complexity, sedentism, and regionalization. As more research is completed and differences among the late Archaic cultures in Florida are recognized, it seems certain that specific regional manifestations and adaptations will be defined. Those cultures will be more closely linked to the post–500 B.C. regional cultures that are the focus of Part II.

Development of Regional Cultures

 **PART II**

In Part I we traced the evolution of precolumbian Florida from the early hunters, gatherers, and fishers of the Paleoindian period through the late Archaic populations living along the coasts and within the central portion of the St. Johns River drainage. At about 2000 B.C., or slightly before, the people living in those areas had learned to fire clay to make ceramic containers. From that time onward, all of Florida's native peoples manufactured pottery. Broken fragments of ceramic vessels—potsherds—are almost indestructible in the archaeological record. They provide archaeologists with an important tool to help distinguish the temporal and geographical ranges of precolumbian cultures.

Ceramics are an important chronological marker because specific styles are known to have been manufactured during specific periods. At a single point in time, a culture may manufacture several types of pottery, each in a specific relative amount or percentage. Comparing percentages over time allows archaeologists to calculate the relative date when the types were made. In addition, certain styles or types of ceramics are associated only with individual cultures. An archaeologist presented with a large enough sample of pottery from a site—about 200 potsherds including various decorated types—can determine that the pottery is from, for example, an Alachua culture site in north-central Florida dating to about A.D. 1200. Because potsherds offer this facility of interpretation, our taxonomy of precolumbian cultures in Florida after 500 B.C. is at least partially a taxonomy of ceramic assemblages composed of individual types of pottery and of groups of types.

In chapter 3 several of the major regional cultures that manufactured fiber-tempered pottery were described. Those cultures were not the only ones who manufactured fiber-tempered pottery during the period 2000 to 500 B.C. Sites with fiber-tempered pottery are found throughout the state. As we have seen, however, coastal and riverine sites are most extensive. The noncoastal and nonriverine sites are relatively small, and they are not densely distributed compared to sites in regions such as the St. Johns River drainage or southwest Florida.

There are several ways to interpret these distributional data. The distributions may reflect reality; in other words, during the later Archaic period the largest and densest populations were in the regions where the largest and densest shell middens are found. Another interpretation is that our distributional data are skewed because late Archaic sites in forested areas do not contain large amounts of shell refuse and are not as apparent as shell midden sites.

The former explanation seems more likely. Indeed, if it is correct that in some coastal regions late Archaic sites have been inundated and others have not yet been found, we might guess that significant populations lived in other coastal locales beyond those mentioned in chapter 3. Estuarine and riverine settings where shellfish and fish could easily be taken are especially productive, and we would expect late Archaic populations to have lived in all such locales. This would include the entire Gulf of Mexico coast, large parts of the Atlantic coastal lagoon system and the adjacent coast where salt marsh–tidal stream systems were present, and the upper St. Johns River.

Our view of what settlement patterns were like in that 2,500-year period before 500 B.C. may indeed be hidden by the sea. That this is probably the case seems obvious when we look at the distribution of cultures in Florida after 500 B.C. People were living almost everywhere: along the coasts, in the interior river valleys and marsh systems, in the Lake Okeechobee Basin, and elsewhere in the interior of southern Florida. Less intensively occupied were the interior forested highlands of northern Florida, although that would change after about A.D. 100 or so.

At 500 B.C. populations did not suddenly flock to new sections of the coast or other locales. Late Archaic–period populations must have already been occupying those locales; what we see after 500 B.C. may in part be the result of population growth. But it also may be the nature of the archaeological record, including the appearance of regional ceramic assemblages that make it easier for us to recognize and study specific regional cultures. Ancestral, late Archaic–period regional cultures may have been in those same locations before 500 B.C., but after that time the archaeological record is clearer.

More people and new ceramic types were not the only developments underway by 500 B.C. There is evidence that contact between Florida Indians and other native groups to the north and west of the state was ongoing. Similarities between tools and other artifacts found in Florida and non-Florida sites, the presence in Florida of exotic stone and copper artifacts that clearly were brought from more northerly places, and the presence of Gulf coast marine shells in middle and late Archaic sites in Tennessee and Kentucky (and as far away as Minnesota) provide evidence that precolumbian Florida was not isolated. Contact among the native groups of the southeastern United States, including Florida, must have been ongoing throughout their histories.

During the late Archaic period, the native people of Florida certainly had contact with contemporary people elsewhere in the Southeast, such as the Poverty Point culture that occupied the lower Mississippi River valley and some adjacent portions of Louisiana and Mississippi. Clarence Webb (1977:4–5) has reviewed the radiocarbon and thermoluminescence dates of the Poverty Point culture and suggests that the culture began about 1800 B.C. and was fully developed by 1200–1000 B.C., lasting until about 500 B.C. Artifacts associated with the culture, possibly manufactured at Poverty Point sites or at least influenced by ideas from that culture, were traded far and wide within the Southeast, reaching the Tick Island site on the St. Johns River (Jahn and Bullen 1978:figs. 21, 46, 50) and the Canton Street site in the Tampa Bay region. As we saw in chapter 3, the Elliott's Point complex of the western panhandle coastal region represents a Florida manifestation of that same Poverty Point culture (Lazarus 1958; Fairbanks 1959; Curren 1987; Thomas and Campbell 1991). Steatite potsherds also have been found at late Archaic sites in Florida. Bowls made from that stone probably were made at quarries near Atlanta or elsewhere in the Appalachian piedmont and traded south to Florida. After 500 B.C. and continuing throughout the precolumbian period, the evidence for trade and contact with non-Florida cultures grows even greater. It is a time when the precolumbian Florida cultures would share many ideas and traits with their more northerly neighbors.

After 500 B.C. the Florida native peoples, with thousands of years of knowledge about their environment and its resources, with new ideas generated from within and through contact with other societies, and with populations that continued to increase, practiced a number of lifeways, each well adapted to specific regions of the state. These cultures were not static; the same reasons that led to their development also stimulated them to continue to change and to evolve into new forms. Eventually, apparently after A.D. 750 or later, some of the northern Florida cultures began to cultivate plants, or they may have added new crops, such as corn, to the gardening activities already present. The exact nature of these economic changes is still uncertain. Some archaeologists have argued that maize—Indian corn—began to be cultivated at A.D. 600, while others argue that evidence for the more extensive agricultural practices we would expect to be associated with growing corn appear later in the archaeological record, after A.D. 1000. Less controversial is the recognition that A.D. 750 marks important changes in ceramic assemblages and other culture traits all across northern Florida. Those changes are clearly recognizable; their cause— the adoption of maize or some other stimuli—is much less certain.

In the chapters that follow we will return to the question of exactly when maize agriculture was adopted by northern Florida cultures. Presently, the earliest incontrovertible evidence in Florida for maize— the presence of charred corn cobs or kernels—is the ninth century A.D. That evidence comes from the Sycamore site in Gadsden County, a late Weeden Island site associated with the Wakulla culture (Milanich 1974; and see chapter 5).

With some major exceptions—for example, late Weeden Island–period cultures, the St. Johns II culture, and some south Florida cultures—the native Florida cultures described in part 2 all date before A.D. 750. Part 3 focuses on other cultures after A.D. 750, including ones that we know did grow corn in the late precolumbian period, after A.D.

1000. The organizational scheme is inconsistent because not all Florida cultures and regions followed the same evolutionary trajectory. Also, the present organization allows greater emphasis on both cultural continuities, (e.g., in the St. Johns region before and after A.D. 750) and discontinuities (e.g., between the north-central Florida Cades Pond and Alachua cultures, which followed one another in the same region but do not represent a developmental continuum).

Deptford, Swift Creek, and
Santa Rosa–Swift Creek Cultures

4 The Deptford culture, located along the Gulf coast of Florida and the Atlantic coast of South Carolina, Georgia, and northeast Florida, was one of the first post-Archaic regional cultures to be recognized by archaeologists (Caldwell and Waring 1939a, b, c). Deptford peoples were the descendants of the late Archaic coastal people who had lived in those same regions. As with the sites of those late Archaic populations, Deptford sites are also found away from the coast in the interior river valleys and in other locales.

One reason Deptford was the focus of archaeological attention early on is that Deptford pottery is both easily recognizable and quite distinct from earlier fiber-tempered pottery. Much of the ceramics were decorated by stamping the vessel surfaces with carved wooden paddles before the vessels were fired, imprinting distinctive groove- or check-stamped designs on them.

Deptford pottery, like that of other post–500 B.C. regional cultures, was not tempered with fibers. Instead the pastes used in making ceramic vessels contain quartz sand particles in various sizes and, occasionally, clay lumps, some intentionally added to the clay and some accidental inclusions. Deptford pottery consequently is easily distinguishable from the fiber-tempered pottery of the late Archaic period both on the basis of surface decoration and from the paste. By the early 1940s archaeologists could map the distribution of Deptford sites based on the distribution of Deptford pottery types, a practice employed for nearly all other regional cultures as well.

Coastal Deptford sites along the Gulf are more numerous than those of the late Archaic period, most likely a result of larger populations. But the distribution may also reflect the fact that fewer Deptford sites have been inundated, although at least some have been drowned by rising seas.

The Deptford culture derives its name from the Deptford site located near Savannah in the Savannah River estuary. Research by Gordon Willey and Richard Woodbury in northwest Florida (Willey and Woodbury 1942; Willey 1949a) showed that Deptford pottery also was present in that region. Subsequent work by Willey and others demonstrated that Deptford pottery is found along Florida's Gulf coast south to the Tampa Bay locale (Milanich 1973:51–52, 1980; Bense 1985; Thomas and Campbell 1985b), although sites with Deptford components are rare south of Levy County. Along the Atlantic coast Deptford sites are found from South Carolina southward at least to the mouth of the St. Johns River near Jacksonville. A few coastal sites are known from outside this distribution.

The subsistence economy of the coastal-dwelling Deptford peoples, like the late Archaic coastal societies that preceded them, was centered on the use of marine resources, especially fish and shellfish, and terrestrial resources that could be collected nearby. Judith Bense's description of the Deptford economic system in northwest Florida is an excellent statement about the entire Deptford region:

> Mollusc gathering and fishing were a major part of the economy. American oyster was the overwhelming species of choice. White-tailed deer, although not numerically abundant, have an important impact when present in the faunal assemblages. Other higher vertebrates are also occasional resources.
>
> . . . the composition of the faunal assemblages and their size classes help to describe the subsistence technology and the habitats which were exploited. Molluscs were found on the tidal flats and represent a simple gathering technology. . . . Large numbers of small schooling fishes, which inhabit the tidal creeks and shallow water zones, are indicative of mass capture techniques. They would have been acquired with fine mesh nets,

Region of the Deptford culture.

enclosures, or traps. Larger fishes may have been obtained in these catches, however, some could have been caught in the deeper parts of the estuary with hook and line, spears, nets, or enclosures. (Bense 1985:161)

Deptford sites in inland locations away from the coasts usually are small and sometimes are found under later occupations (e.g., Fradkin and Milanich 1977:170, 173; Kohler 1978:168; Tesar 1980:59, 688–726; White 1981a:625–633). Such sites may be hunting camps or some other type of special-use site. In a few wetland locales, such as in the upper Apalachicola River drainage, the size and density of inland sites is greater. Deptford-period sites with check-stamped pottery extend well up the Chattahoochee River drainage into Georgia and

Alabama. But these sites probably should be differentiated from the Florida Gulf coast region Deptford culture. Their affinities are with the inland, check-stamped pottery–making cultures of Georgia.

The exact relationships between inland and coastal Deptford sites in the Gulf region are unknown, but it is likely that before late Deptford times some of the interior special-use sites were associated with the coastal dwellers. Such Deptford sites are rarely more than thirty miles inland in the Atlantic region and sixty miles inland in the Gulf region.

This site distribution pattern—mainly coastal settlements with smaller interior sites used to gather special resources—is identical to that present in the same regions during the late Archaic period. In north-central Florida, this pattern persisted until about A.D. 100 when Deptford villages, as opposed to camps, were first established in the interior.

The temporal range of the Deptford culture has been well established through radiocarbon dates from both Atlantic and Gulf coast sites (e.g., Caldwell 1971; Milanich 1973:54–55; Bense 1985:109–110; Thomas and Campbell 1985b). Deptford pottery first appeared by about 500 B.C. In northern Florida the Deptford period persisted to about A.D. 200, with the interior sites dating to the period A.D. 100–200. In the eastern panhandle, the transition from Deptford ceramics into the Swift Creek ceramic assemblages occurred at about A.D. 250–300. Farther west in the Choctawhatchee Bay and Pensacola Bay locales, radiocarbon dates suggest that the Deptford period ended at A.D. 150 in the former and A.D. 260 in the latter (Thomas and Campbell 1990, 1993; Bense 1992; Phillips 1992). There appears to be considerable temporal overlap in northwest Florida between the Deptford ceramic assemblage and the ceramic assemblages of the later Swift Creek (east panhandle) and Santa Rosa–Swift Creek (west panhandle) cultures. Exact chronologies may differ for each estuary system in northwest Florida.

In Leon County, Louis Tesar (1980:588) has used ceramics to construct a chronology for the Deptford period in the eastern panhandle. He defines an early Deptford period characterized by fiber-tempered pottery and the Deptford ceramic series, a middle Deptford period with only Deptford series pottery types present, and a late Deptford period with Deptford pottery and Swift Creek pottery. Because ceramic series and individual types usually do not suddenly appear or disappear but rise and fall in popularity over time, archaeologists can graph relative percentages of different ceramic types or series through time, providing a simple but usable relative chronology.

On the Georgia and South Carolina coasts and in northeast Florida the Deptford ceramic series lasted until about A.D. 700, much longer than it did on the Gulf coast. This separate Deptford developmental sequence for the two coastal manifestations, as well as their geographical distance from one another, makes it taxonomically feasible to separate an Atlantic region Deptford from a Gulf region Deptford. Other archaeological evidence relevant to the Atlantic region Deptford culture, presented later in this chapter, indicates separate cultural developments in the two regions and supports this taxonomic division.

With few exceptions, individual coastal Deptford sites are neither deeply stratified nor broad in area. It hardly seems possible that the more than 1,000 years of Deptford occupation on the Atlantic coast and 600–700 years on the Gulf coast would have left so little evidence of occupation. In a few locales, however, larger and more numerous sites have been found, suggesting that in other places sites must have been destroyed or inundated by a rise in sea level since Deptford times. Research on the Georgia coast has produced evidence of such a rise in the Atlantic Ocean after approximately 1000 B.C. (DePratter and Howard 1980, 1981). In addition, local coastal dynamics, such as accretion and erosion of sections of some barrier islands, affect specific site locales. For example, some of the Deptford sites on the west side of Cumberland Island, Georgia, are being encroached upon by the salt marsh, and others have been subject to erosion. Over several thousand years, other of the Deptford sites in that region also must have been impacted.

Along the Gulf coast there also is evidence for Deptford sites being drowned or eroded. The weight of the sediments deposited by rivers flowing into the Gulf are causing the land level to fall, a condition that worsens the closer one gets to the Mississippi Delta. On the Florida peninsula coast the rate has been calculated at about 1 inch per 25 years (Fairbridge 1960). Thus, from A.D. 1 to 1990, the Gulf has risen roughly 80 inches relative to the land. Although such data are, of course, not uniform for the entire Gulf coast, archaeological evidence supports a rise in sea level relative to land level since the time of the Deptford culture. A drowned archaeological site spanning the

temporal range from the end of the Archaic period through the early
Deptford period has been located one-half mile out into the Gulf off
New Port Richey under nearly six feet of water (Lazarus 1965). Excavations by Adelaide and Ripley Bullen conducted at three Gulf coast
sites—Johns Island in Chassahowitzka Bay, Wash Island in Crystal
River, and the Battery Point site near Bayport—also confirm a post-
Deptford rise in sea level (Bullen and Bullen 1950, 1953, 1963).
Today Deptford middens on the islands off Cedar Key are being
eroded by the tide. Thus, along both the Atlantic and Gulf coasts there
is evidence for the erosion, inundation, or destruction of Deptford
sites by natural processes, both a relative rise in sea level and local
erosive conditions. As is true for earlier cultures, the coastal archaeological record for Deptford is incomplete. Coastal settlements and
economies centered on use of estuarine resources probably were
more numerous in the past than we realize today.

Settlements, Subsistence, and Social Organization

Deptford coastal sites tend to be located in live oak–magnolia hammocks immediately adjacent to salt marshes. Hammocks are present
on both the Atlantic barrier islands and the Gulf keys as well as on the
mainland proper. Other sites are located on marsh islands or larger offshore islands, but when they were occupied they were probably also in
hammocks adjacent to the marsh–tidal stream system. Today such
sites have been encroached upon by marsh accretion, or they are on
islands formed when the coastline was drowned and the land was cut
off from the mainland.

As was true for earlier coastal populations, living adjacent to both
forest and salt marsh proved an economic boon for the Deptford peoples. Acorns from oaks and palm berries from Sabal palms, common
trees in the oak-magnolia hammocks, could have been important
foods along with a host of other wild plants, including hickory nuts.
Indeed, the northern distribution of live oaks and sabal palms on the
Atlantic coast correlates with the northern distribution of Deptford
sites. Along the Gulf coast, Deptford sites tend not to be found farther
south than the northern extent of coastal mangrove forests. This distributional pattern is an example of the adaptive correlations between

regional cultures and natural environments apparent in the archaeological record after 500 B.C.

Wild foodstuffs from the forested hammocks used by the Deptford
peoples were many and varied. Although our knowledge of the plants
used by the Deptford coastal populations is limited by a lack of paleo-
botanical analyses, we can assume an analogy with later coastal native
peoples to learn some of the plants they probably used. Bones of the
animals killed and eaten by the Deptford peoples and the remains of
the shellfish they collected and ate last thousands of years in the
coastal middens, making the meat diet of the Deptford culture more
easily reconstructible.

Edible plants that have been found in the coastal hammocks and
that were probably used for food by the Deptford villagers include the
nuts and palm berries mentioned; Smilax, the roots of which are dug,
prepared, and eaten; blueberry; persimmon; wild grapes; and musca-
dine. Leaves of the yaupon holly (*Ilex vomitoria*), a large bush found in
quantities in the coastal hammocks, were used by many native peoples of the Southeast to make a sacred tea called "black drink," a caf-
feine beverage brewed from roasted leaves. Because the drink has a
long history in the Southeast, it is likely it was prepared by Deptford
peoples.

Many animal species can be observed today in the coastal hammock
areas. Deptford peoples, like their Archaic ancestors, probably hunted
or trapped nearly all of them, especially the white-tailed deer which,
in terms of meat consumed, was the most important land animal.
Animal bones from sites indicate that, in addition to deer, raccoon,
opossum, rabbit, pocket gopher, bear, bobcat, gopher tortoise, box
turtle, and Florida panther all were eaten. Bird bones found in middens are from red-breasted merganser, lesser scaup, and loon. But all
of these animals together were not as economically important as fish
and shellfish.

Although both the hammocks and the coastal marine systems
offered the Deptford people food resources and raw materials, it was
these two in combination that drew the Deptford peoples and their
Archaic predecessors to the coast. The availability of different environmental habitats, each supporting communities of potential plant and
animal food sources, made coastal locales good places to live and eat.
Within easy walking or canoe distance of the Deptford villages were a

number of such habitats—the hammock itself, beaches, salt marshes and the tidal streams that drain them, lagoons, delta areas where freshwater rivers empty into the Gulf or Atlantic, and the sea or Gulf itself. All of these habitats are distributed longitudinally along the coastal strand. The strand itself varies in width from about one mile to as much as twenty miles, the greatest width being near deltas where brackish water extends up the rivers that flow to the sea through the coastal plain. These rivers deposit silt, which spreads along the shore and causes the shallowness that is a prerequisite for marsh formation. At such locales the marsh reaches both farther inland and farther out to sea than at other places on the coast.

The marsh and tidal stream system has the greatest variety and quantity of food resources, providing the bulk of the fish and mollusk species so important to coastal dwellers. Salt marshes are composed of several species of grasses that grow only where shallow mud flats lessen the eroding force of the tides. These flats are found along the Gulf coast and the Atlantic coast north of St. Augustine. Here the sediments brought down coastal plain rivers are deposited. These rivers include, along the Gulf, the Mississippi, Mobile, Apalachicola, Ochlockonee, Suwannee, and Withlacoochee, and, on the Atlantic, the St. Marys, Altamaha, Savannah, Edisto, and Santee. There is no similar large build-up of sediments, and hence no extensive salt marshes, on much of the east coast of Florida south of St. Augustine simply because no significant rivers flow from the interior of the peninsula into the Atlantic Ocean (however, some extensive coastal marshes lie around Cape Canaveral). The salt marsh–hammock-dwelling Deptford peoples never moved south of the northernmost St. Johns River apparently in part because their economic system was not well adapted to the riverine and lagoon environments of east Florida. It is because of such environmental factors that the east and west coasts of Florida supported different aboriginal cultures. Even today, the modern settlements of the two coasts differ for this same reason; beaches and lagoons are present along the Atlantic coast south of Jacksonville Beach, while the drowned shoreline of the Gulf has its offshore keys and extensive salt marsh–tidal stream system.

Just as east Florida was not well suited to the Deptford subsistence pattern, so did the mangrove swamps of southwest Florida present a less-desirable environmental situation to peoples acquainted with the salt marsh. For this reason Tampa Bay or slightly north marks the approximate southern limit of the Gulf Deptford culture.

The salt marshes and tidal streams and the offshore shallow waters indeed proved the most important environments for the Deptford villagers. They provided huge amounts of shellfish and fish. To precolumbian peoples the coastal resources must have seemed inexhaustible. When oyster or clam beds were depleted in one locale, they could move to another, and fish were available in large quantities to be netted or trapped.

On both the Atlantic and Gulf coasts, oysters constitute about 95 percent of all shellfish found in Deptford middens, less at some Florida panhandle sites where clams comprise a high percentage. Clam middens probably also exist on the peninsular Gulf coast, but they have not yet been reported there or in the Atlantic region. Besides oysters and clams, mollusks found in middens include ribbed mussel, several species of *Tagelus*, several species of *Busycons*, *Rangia* clams, and many less important species (Bense 1985:138–147).

Along with mollusks, many species of fish can be taken from the marsh tidal streams and the adjacent waters of lagoons, sea, or Gulf. Generally, the fish netted were bottom scavengers that feed near shellfish beds or fish that could be taken from shallow waters or tidal streams. Large fish were also taken, either in traps or with nets. Bones from several species of sharks, rays, and catfish have been identified in large numbers along with drum, channel bass, sheepshead, snook, snapper, jack, trout, flounder, mullet, blowfish, and other saltwater species in lesser numbers.

Two other animals were taken from the marsh. The salt marsh terrapin (*Malaclemmys terrapin*) could be collected in some quantities, and raccoons could be hunted in salt marshes. Ordinarily nocturnal predators, raccoons hunt according to the tides in the marshes. They can be taken in relatively large numbers when the tide is out or hunted at extreme high tide when they are stranded and have to swim. With its supply of mollusks and fish and, to a lesser extent, other animals, the salt marsh–tidal stream and nearby waters were the most important habitats not only for the Deptford villagers, but for all later coastal populations.

Of much less importance was the beach habitat, never an important source of food to southeastern Indians because it harbors few species.

During the late summer months, however, large sea turtles nest on the beaches. These massive creatures, some of which can weigh nearly 500 pounds, provided a seasonal meat source, and their remains have been recovered from nearly all excavated coastal Deptford sites.

Occasionally tides deposit large numbers of small coquinas on the beach. They can be collected and boiled in water to provide a broth.

Bones from a number of freshwater turtle species also have been recovered, indicating that these amphibians were gathered from ponds and streams in the coastal hammocks. Sources of fresh water can be found on the Atlantic barrier islands and on the mainlands of both coasts. Streams that drain wetlands flow to the coast, becoming brackish as they near the tidal zone. Small ponds are kept filled by rainfall or are fed by perched groundwater tables. Freshwater fish species that might have been in these ponds also have been identified in Deptford coastal middens (Bense 1985:147). Such ponds and streams would have provided fresh water and must have been an important factor in selecting a village location.

Although the Deptford peoples occupied locales along the coasts, the presence of inland sites suggests occasional movements into the interior forests. Some Deptford populations might also have occupied inland locations year-round. As yet, however, large, dense Deptford middens that might be expected to be associated with such occupations have not been identified in Florida. Such sites are present further north in the Chattahoochee River drainage, but they are more likely to be related to Georgia cultures also characterized by check-stamped pottery, than to be inland sites associated with the Gulf Deptford culture.

Whether the small, noncoastal Deptford sites in northwest Florida were occupied during specific times of the year is unknown. The size of the inland sites relative to the coastal villages suggests short-term occupations by small groups. It is conceivable that excursions by canoe were made up the river valleys to harvest nuts, berries, and other non-marine resources during the late summer and early fall for winter use on the coast. Also in the fall deer congregate in the coastal-plain hardwood hammocks, since that is both the rutting and the acorn season. As deer are most successfully hunted at this time, the interior sites could be the remains of hunting camps.

Several of the small noncoastal Deptford sites have been investigated in north-central, north, and northwest Florida. Two of them,

Deptford, Swift Creek, and Santa Rosa–Swift Creek archaeological sites in
Florida.

Sunday Bluff and Colby, are freshwater snail and mussel middens on
the Oklawaha River in Marion County (Bullen 1969; Cumbaa and
Gouchnour 1970). Both sites were occupied at various times by Deptford and St. Johns peoples. The archaeological evidence from both
sites also indicates their use over a long period of time, from the late
Archaic period into Deptford times and even later, probably as special-
use or even seasonal sites, although this remains to be proven.

Other noncoastal Deptford sites also suggest short-term or special-
use sites. Under the Law School Mound, an Alachua culture mound in
Alachua County, a single small Deptford hearth was found. The hearth
had been lined with ferric concretions and contained charcoal and a
charred fragment of hickory nut hull. Adjacent to the hearth was a

small scatter of Deptford pottery and a unifacial chert scraping tool (Fradkin and Milanich 1977:166–178).

In Leon County, Louis Tesar tested several inland sites with Deptford components. Sites 8Le388 in the Ochlockonee drainage and 8Le463 and 8Le471 on the north shore of Lake Iamonia all contained small amounts of Deptford pottery and an array of chert cores, debitage, and unifacial and some bifacial tools (Tesar 1980:688–794). One small hearth, possibly late Deptford, was found. Tesar suggested that sites 8Le388 and 8Le463 were seasonal deer-hunting camps, probably used in the fall when hickory nuts could also be collected. The array of tools from the latter sites indicate "butchering activities, bone and/or wood working" (Tesar 1980:725, 749). A fourth site, 8Le484, probably was a quarry used during the Deptford period, as well as at other times (Tesar 1980:840).

Small inland sites with pottery, lithic cores, debitage, and unifacial and bifacial tools also have been found further west in the panhandle in the Perdido River drainage (Little, Curren, and McKenzie 1988; Little, Curren, McKenzie, and Lloyd 1988). This is the approximate western extent of sites with Deptford components.

In contrast to the small, interior Deptford sites are the sites found along the coast, most often shell heaps or shallow, horizontally distributed sheet middens, although sites with little shell but relatively dense midden deposits also are known. Some coastal sites are relatively small components of other shell middens containing potsherds, food bones, and other refuse from living activities. Circular, often overlapping, shell middens twenty to thirty feet in diameter are discernible in some locales. These separate circular piles probably represent the accumulation of refuse next to individual house locations. Over time, the number of overlapping piles increased, forming a sheet midden in which individual shell deposits can no longer be observed.

Evidence from both the Gulf and Atlantic regions suggests that other middens were communal dumps. When houses or fire pits were cleaned, or when shellfish remains were thrown away, the refuse was carried a short distance away from houses and deposited.

Surveys and excavations of Deptford sites on the Atlantic coast suggest that as many as fifteen to twenty-five separate circular shell middens may have been present at a single village. Assuming that these are associated with individual households, we can guess that villages

Judith Bense, in front of the camera at the Hawkshaw site in Pensacola, talks about the site and its significance. Her project successfully combined scientific investigations with public education (courtesy Institute of West Florida Archaeology, University of West Florida).

consisted of no more than this number of households. And because houses may have been rebuilt and new ones constructed over time, a guess of five to ten houses in any village cluster seems reasonable. This number is supported by the excellent data recovered by Judith Bense and Eloise Gadus from the Hawkshaw site in Pensacola on the Gulf coast (Bense 1985). Bense and Gadus, in the most extensive excavation of a single Deptford site undertaken thus far, uncovered seven clusters of features—refuse deposits, pits and trenchlike pits—each of which likely was associated with an individual household area. Careful cross-matching of individual potsherds among cluster features and an array of radiocarbon dates strongly suggest that five clusters of these features were contemporary—a village of five households.

The same pattern has been found on the Georgia coast, where one complete Deptford house and portions of another structure have been excavated. The two structures were of a size sufficient to house one nuclear family of five or six persons. This figure combined with the households-per-village figure yields a population of twenty-five to sixty people for a coastal settlement.

Excavation of the complete Deptford house, a presumed winter house located on Cumberland Island, Georgia, showed the structure to be oval, approximately twenty-one by thirty feet. Walls of the house were formed by placing the butt ends of posts in a trench dug for that purpose. Posts were placed side by side in the trench, the cracks between them probably caulked with brush or mud. A doorway was present in one wall. This rather substantial structure must have been occupied over a multiyear period during winter months.

One end of the house was not walled with posts. Possibly hides or reed mats were placed at that end, to be raised or lowered as weather or cooking smoke dictated. A small slot trench, which probably anchored an intrahouse partition, divided the house into two rooms, one containing a long, bathtub-shaped cooking pit or earth oven. This partition had evidently been repaired or replaced at least once during the lifetime of the house. A large post set in a trench-like post hole in the fire-pit room probably helped to support the roof. Shells were packed around the base of the wall posts and the support post to help anchor them and to counteract the acidic nature of the soil.

The center post and other large posts found at the Deptford sites on Cumberland Island were each raised into place by first digging a sloping, linear trench or slot; then the horizontal post was slid into the trench butt first, braced against the end of the trench, and raised to an upright position. Such posts must have been substantial to have required this type of procedure. The cooking-area post, for example, could have supported a considerable number of large roof beams covered with heavy roofing materials, including earth packed over grass or reeds.

Shellfish, fish, deer, and other foods were prepared for eating in the central fire pit. Refuse was dumped beside the house, forming a small, circular shell midden. The house floor was occasionally scraped clean and the refuse dumped outside the house or pushed up against the inside walls.

Trenching excavations by Bullen (1969:17–20) at the Sunday Bluff site southeast of Ocala, Florida, intersected what seems to have been the wall trench of a similar Deptford structure. If these are indeed winter houses, their presence suggests that Sunday Bluff, an inland site, was occupied at least during the winter months. Trenchlike features have also been found in northwest Florida at coastal sites (Bense 1985; Curren 1987) and could have been associated with similar houses.

A less substantial, more open type of house was excavated on Cumberland Island at a second Deptford site. The house was oval, measuring twenty by thirteen feet. Widely spaced support posts held up the roof, which was probably thatched. The floor of the house was slightly depressed; possibly the old ground surface was scraped clean before the structure was built. A small, bell-shaped storage pit had been dug in the house floor and extended down through earlier strata. No hearth was found within the confines of the house; one might have been outside.

These two types of houses may not represent all the possible structures built by the Deptford peoples. But they do suggest parameters on family and village sizes and the types of households established by the Deptford peoples. And the presence of two different types of structures, probably winter and summer houses, are what we would expect among sedentary populations living on the coast year-round.

Knowledge about how Deptford societies were organized is almost nonexistent, although hypotheses can be derived from information from other native societies. One model suggests that clusters of households—villages—were occupied by families who were interrelated, perhaps on the basis of lineage membership. When villages grew too large to be supported easily by local resources, one or more families may have left, budding off to form another village cluster elsewhere. Within a specific locale (e.g., the Horseshoe Beach area on the Gulf coast), residents of related villages would have shared kin ties, some aspects of a common history. In this fashion, over generations, people may have differentiated between themselves and people who lived in other localities.

Within a single village or related villages a religious leader may have helped to coordinate community-wide activities and ceremonies that were seen as necessary for the well-being of the group. These activities would revolve around shared beliefs that reinforced the economic and social systems. That leader or another person also may have served as a village headman to help organize economic and social activities.

The growth of ceremonialism during the late Deptford period in the Gulf region is generally viewed as indicative of more complex social organization, such as more complex inter- and intravillage ties based on shared kinship and histories. Such complexity would be expected with larger populations, relatively fewer uninhabited coastal locales into which populations could expand, and a greater sense of territory.

Judith Bense's (1985:168) summary of Deptford settlement and social systems on the panhandle coast characterizes the entire culture:

> Sites appear to be focused on fish, oyster, and nut gathering, processing, and consumption and were occupied during a few intense times. . . . [T]he settlement pattern seen in Pensacola, Choctawhatchee, and St. Andrews Bay systems is similar. All have interior and coastal sites with smaller sites inland. . . . The small size, proximity, and ease of water transport between coastal and interior Deptford site locations lead to the hypothesis that these locations within each bay system were occupied by groups of the same society, and were utilized within the seasonal round although not necessarily every year or by the same group of individuals.

Technology

Characteristic of the Deptford tool assemblage is the small number of individual tools excavated from sites both on the Atlantic and Gulf coasts. Lithic tools are extremely rare, and no detailed studies have been undertaken of the shell industry that must have existed, partly because many shell tools are so difficult to recognize. Even at a site like Hawkshaw that produced nearly 15,000 potsherds, only 80 chipped stone, 12 bone, and 12 shell artifacts were recovered. The majority of tools must have been made from wood and are not preserved in the archaeological record. Consequently, our knowledge of Deptford technology is based on supposition and a limited number of stone, bone, and shell artifacts. In addition, a few impressions of woven baskets and cordage on fired-clay ceramic vessels also have been found.

That the Deptford peoples worked wood is evident from their pottery vessels, which were stamped or malleated with carved wooden paddles (one clay paddle has been found). Most weapons and tools were probably manufactured from wood, and the full range of tools known from Archaic sites also must have been in use in the Deptford period. Medium-sized triangular projectile points have been found at Deptford sites, but whether they were used to tip the shafts of spears or arrows is uncertain. If the bow were present, and evidence for the bow and arrow is ambiguous at best, it was probably less important in food-collecting activities than were snares and nets.

Cord impressions on Deptford pottery indicate that cordage was made, and impressions of netting and woven basketry have been found on Deptford ceramics. Fiber snares could have been used to collect hammock-dwelling game and birds, and nets and weirs could have been used for fishing. Both earlier and later native peoples in Florida used such techniques. Several bannerstones—throwing-stick weights—have been recovered at village sites, suggesting that the throwing stick was in use, as it was in earlier times. Some of the large, stemmed, Christmas tree–shaped points found at Gulf sites were probably used to tip the throwing-stick darts. Bipointed bone and shell tools may have been parts of gigs for spearing fish.

The manner in which large sea mammals—seals, porpoises, and whales—were caught is not known. Nets or weirs could not have contained these agile, strong swimmers. They may have been hunted with spears. However, the very few individuals represented in archaeological sites could have been taken after being beached or injured.

As among other coastal peoples, the Deptford peoples must have used canoes, baskets, and some type of rake or similar tool to gather oysters in large quantities. Other shellfish could simply be picked off the sea bottom and put in a bag or basket. One method of opening oysters and clams and probably other mollusks was to heat or steam them over fires.

Wooden knives, scrapers, and other tools were probably used in preparing foods for eating. A few such flake, blade, and bifacial stone tools have been found at Gulf region sites, such as the Hawkshaw site and site 8Le388 (Tesar 1980; Bense 1985:11). Limestone and sandstone grinding tools were probably used to shape wooden and shell tools. Most likely, wooden pestles and mortars were used to grind seeds and acorns and other nut meats. Stone celts, hammerstones, and hones or whetstones, all present in very small quantities within the Deptford region, were employed to shape tools and perform other tasks.

Other than wood, the raw material most available on the coast was shell, which was shaped into various tools. It is often difficult, however, to separate shell tools from midden shell during an archaeological field excavation. In the past many shell tools probably have gone unnoticed. Oyster and clam shells were used as ladles or spoons, and dippers or cups were manufactured from the larger univalve species, such as *Busycons*, found in shallow waters off the Atlantic and Gulf coasts. Shell picks or adzelike tools and hammers were made by punching one or two holes in the crown of an intact whelk shell and hafting the shell on a stick. Awls or gouges were made from the shell columella, and clam shells served as scrapers.

Bone tools are rare at Deptford sites, and the only specimens known were used as points, antler flakers, pins, gouges, awls, or basket-making awls. Shark teeth were hafted and used as tools. The picture of the Deptford tool industry as one of paucity reflects our investigations, not the Deptford villagers. They must have had a diverse and efficient assemblage of tools, one that allowed them to successfully make a living in the coastal regions. We have not been able to recognize or study those tools because many probably were made of wood. In addition, only recently have we made systematic efforts to examine the shell tool industry of Florida's precolumbian coastal populations (cf. Reiger 1981; Luer 1986; Walker 1989).

A comparison of the quantity of stone tools within the two Deptford regions shows that stone was used somewhat more frequently at Gulf sites than in the Atlantic region. This is probably because chert and quartzite, from which the vast majority of stone tools was manufactured, can be quarried from outcroppings nearer the coast in southeast Alabama and northern Florida than similar outcroppings in the Atlantic region. Along the Gulf coast just north of Tampa Bay outcroppings of agatized coral also occur. In the Atlantic region lithic outcroppings are much farther inland, almost to the fall line.

Items of personal adornment were rare among the Deptford peoples. Several limestone or siltstone plummets and several shell beads made from *Oliva* shells or *Busycon* columella, bird-bone tubes or beads, a sandstone bead, a drilled black bear canine tooth, and two drilled hematite cones comprise the total known inventory of such everyday artifacts, and most of these were recovered from the Hawkshaw site.

The slender, plumb-bob-shaped plummets may actually be parts of composite fish hooks (Walker 1989).

By far the best-known Deptford artifact is fired-clay pottery. Wooden or clay paddles were used to compact the coils of clay used that built up the sides of the vessels, a technique not known in the late Archaic period when vessels were hand molded to achieve their shape. As noted, while late Archaic–period pottery contained vegetable fibers as temper, Deptford paste does not contain fiber. Present in the paste instead are sand and grit particles, many of which occur naturally in the clays of the coastal regions. Sometimes lumps of clay are present, probably clay that was not adequately dissolved and homogenized during the clay preparation process. A technological analysis of Deptford pottery completed by Ann Cordell (in Russo, Cordell, and Ruhl 1992:168–197) has shown that some Deptford pottery from northeast Florida contains sponge spicules in the paste, probably occurring naturally in the clays used for the vessels.

The use of fiber as a tempering agent died out gradually. Information from the Georgia coast indicates that fiber tempering was still used occasionally as late as about A.D. 1; on the Gulf coast, fiber-tempered pottery is relatively common in early Deptford components. On both the Atlantic and Gulf coasts, fibers are present in potsherds that were malleated with paddles with Deptford designs. Likewise, some nonfiber potsherds display Orange or Norwood styles of decoration such as punctations or stick impressions. This gradual replacement of fiber-tempered pottery by the Deptford ceramic series supports the contention of continuity between the late Archaic and Deptford peoples.

One explanation for how Deptford ceramic-making techniques were invented or adapted is that the coiling and paddle-malleating method of manufacturing was superior to the old method of hand molding and using fiber as temper. With the new technology it was possible to make large, deep, cylindrically shaped vessels that were more useful than the flatter, broader bowls or bag-shaped vessels of the late Archaic period. The Deptford vessels were more substantial, and big enough to be used for storage. They also could be used as containers for cooking over fires.

The most common Deptford vessel shape is a deep, cylindrical pot with a rounded or conoidal bottom. Some are short and somewhat stubby, though still cylindrical. Bowls occur rarely. Another character-istic of some Deptford pottery is the presence of podal supports on vessel bottoms. These supports, which allow a vessel to stand upright, also are found in contemporary Woodland cultures in the south-eastern U.S. piedmont as well as in the Tchefuncte and Bayou La Batre coastal plain cultures west of the Florida panhandle. Such similarities across large parts of the Southeast suggest common origins for innova-tions that replaced fiber-tempered pottery, continual contact among the southeastern native peoples, or both.

Surfaces of Deptford vessels either are undecorated or display mal-leated designs made by cord-wrapped or carved paddles. Brushed and punctated surfaces are present on pottery in the Savannah area and probably date from the late Deptford period. In northwest Florida, pot-tery with fabric impressions on the surface is present at Deptford sites.

Some plain vessels appear to have been malleated and then smoothed. The majority of vessels are stamped with cord-wrapped or carved wooden paddles (clay paddles might also have been used). Cord marking is present on both coasts throughout the temporal range of Deptford culture, increasing in popularity late in the Deptford period on the Atlantic coast. As a surface treatment, however, rough-ening the vessel surface with cord marking never reached the popu-larity of the carved-paddle treatment, especially the type Deptford Check Stamped.

The care with which the carved check-stamped design is applied to the pot varies from extreme precision, which produces a continuous check-stamped design over the entire surface, to random hitting, which produces a sloppy, overlapping pattern. A variant of check stamping is the ceramic type Deptford Linear Check Stamped. Gener-ally, linear check stamping as a decorative motif decreases in popu-larity through time.

Another malleated surface treatment produced by carved paddles is reflected in the type Deptford Simple Stamped, which occurs less fre-quently than linear check stamping during the early portion of the Deptford period but is found throughout the period, A variation of this motif—stick impressing—is restricted to the Gulf coast and appears to be the same as that found on Norwood fiber-tempered potsherds from the Gulf coast (Phelps 1965). The Deptford Simple Stamped paddle has

Deptford pottery: *a–f,* Deptford Check Stamped (*a* is 1¼ inches high); *g,* Deptford Simple Stamped.

Deptford pottery: *a–c,* Deptford Simple Stamped (*a* is 2 inches high); *d–h,* Deptford Linear Check Stamped.

the same long vertical grooves as the linear stamped paddle, but without the cross grooves.

Analyses of large collections of Deptford pottery from both the Gulf and Atlantic regions have been carried out by Gadus and Bense (Bense 1985) and by Chester DePratter (1979). These studies, along with the definitive studies completed in the 1930s (Caldwell and Waring 1939a, b), are basic references for anyone identifying or interpreting Deptford pottery.

The Growth of Ceremonialism

The reconstruction of religious beliefs, rituals, and religious-related social stratification from archaeological evidence is always difficult. Archaeologists can, however, derive some information from such things as earthworks, remains of special structures, burial patterns, artifacts placed with burials, and religious paraphernalia. Although these remains may provide information on only a very small portion of a society's belief and social systems, they can be used in comparative analyses to help understand the development and relationships among regional cultures.

In the case of the Deptford culture, studies of these criteria, often grouped under the term *ceremonialism,* also point up differences in the development of the Gulf and Atlantic regions. By A.D. 1 changes were occurring in the Gulf area that did not appear on the Atlantic coast. Gulf Deptford eventually evolved into the Weeden Island culture, whereas the Atlantic area cultures experienced few major cultural changes until at least A.D. 1000.

One reason for change in the Gulf region may have been its geographical location, which allowed the Deptford peoples to readily participate in the trade exchanges occurring among the western Gulf coastal plain cultures (e.g., Tchefuncte), the Woodland peoples to the north (e.g., Adena, Hopewell, Cartersville, Copena), and the cultures of southern Florida. This fortuitous position, along with increasing populations, could have been an important factor in the developments that took place in northern Florida after about 100 B.C.

We have seen that during the late Archaic period trade among the peoples of the Southeast, including the Florida natives, was ongoing. There is no reason to believe that this trade lessened during the

Deptford period. Indeed, it most likely increased, as Hopewellian societies to the north sought access to goods from Florida and vice versa. Florida marine products, especially *Busycon* shells that could be fashioned into cups, beads, and other items, and perhaps leaves of the cassina plant, could be traded for northern copper, stone, and ceramic items.

The desire for more trade goods and their associated status, coupled with a natural population increase, led to increased social interaction and complexity, reinforced by appropriate beliefs and religious practices. The same social and cultural changes taking place elsewhere in the Southeast were taking place in the Deptford region: larger populations, perhaps more complex sociopolitical organization, and new ways to establish and maintain social and economic ties among and between villages and groups of villages.

Evidence for cultural changes, increased trade and interaction, and increased populations is apparent in the archaeological record after about 100 B.C. Burial mounds perhaps associated with lineages or other social groups appear, along with individual burials accompanied by items reflecting esteem and status. Some villages with mounds probably took on special status as centers of ceremonial activity. Valued artifacts, some made by skilled artisans, were widely traded, and local craftpersons produced paraphernalia used as symbols in special religious ceremonies. Changes in social organization and ceremonial life were occurring in the Gulf Deptford region, although we can see no differences in the subsistence pattern practiced in the coastal villages.

Evidence for population increase related to economic pressure is provided by the movement of some Deptford peoples away from the coast to inland areas in northern Florida. About A.D. 100 or slightly before, the first Deptford villages are found in north-central Florida. This must have been an extraordinary transformation: coastal dweller to inland villager. We do not know how such a transition took place, but we can guess it grew out of seasonal sojourns in the interior forest and, perhaps, increased use of interior wetlands, such as those in Leon, Alachua, and Marion counties.

Ceremonial mound centers and villages are known to have been established both in north-central Florida and in the inland tri-state area of Alabama-Florida-Georgia. These new developments—population shifts and the appearance of sedentary interior villages, along with the development of new ceremonial practices—were more than sufficient for archaeologists to name new archaeological cultures, marking the end of the Gulf Deptford culture at about A.D. 100. The last century before A.D. 1 and the first century after were times of great transition among the precolumbian peoples of northern Florida. Although the coastal way of life would be continued in some post-Deptford cultures such as the Swift Creek, Santa Rosa–Swift Creek, and Weeden Island, the appearance of new cultural patterns in the interior of northern Florida would affect all future cultural developments in that region.

William Sears (1962) has described aspects of the ceremonial life associated with the post–100 B.C. late Deptford culture in the big bend area of northern Florida (the eastern panhandle and northern peninsular Gulf coast). He groups certain of these traits into an archaeologically recognizable complex called Yent, named for a site in northwest Florida. By about A.D. 100 the Yent complex had developed into the closely related Green Point complex in eastern northwest Florida. Later, Yent and Green Point elements are found in the Weeden Island ceremonial complex, and the three are closely related (Brose 1979). The exact temporal and developmental relationships between Yent and Green Point are somewhat uncertain. In general, Yent complex sites seem to be associated with late Deptford–period populations, while Green Point complex sites are associated with Swift Creek peoples. But the associations are not clearcut, and we still have much to learn about both of these ceremonial manifestations.

The Yent complex was defined by Sears (1962) on the basis of information from three Florida mounds—Crystal River in coastal Citrus County, and Yent and Pierce on the panhandle coast. Much of the information from these mounds was gathered by C. B. Moore more than seventy years ago. The artifact collections have been curated in museums where they were available to Sears for study. It is clear that the Yent ceremonial complex, like the Green Point complex, is related to the Hopewell ceremonial complex, variants of which are found across much of the eastern United States over several centuries before and after A.D. 1. Some Yent complex objects came to Florida via Hopewellian trade networks. But Yent and Green Point, like the Weeden Island ceremonial complex that followed, are Florida phenomena.

Their impetus came from local stimuli, even though some of the objects associated with them came from outside the region.

At present, the most mound sites associated with the Yent complex have been found in eastern northwest Florida; the major exception is the Crystal River site in Citrus County. The center of the later Green Point complex also was in northwest Florida. However, at least some Yent-related traits have a wide distribution on the peninsular Gulf coast, and Yent-like traits are also present in east Florida.

Items found in Yent mounds that are exotic to the Gulf region include stone, metal, ceramic, and (perhaps) some bone artifacts. Some of these resemble items found elsewhere in the Southeast during the Hopewell period. Some of the Yent nonceramic artifacts appear to be ornamental, at times elaborated forms of utilitarian artifacts (such as gorgets); perhaps they were worn or used by leaders or religious specialists. Such artifacts include copper panpipes, rectangular copper plates, and copper earspools, both single- and double-sided. Silver-plated copper earspools, one inset with a pearl on each side, were excavated from the Yent complex burial mound at the Crystal River site.

Elongate plummets and double-ended plummets, both made from copper, stone, or shell, are also represented in the Yent complex artifact inventory, as are two-hole bar gorgets of stone. Shell ornaments of various shapes and sizes, including gorgets, are common. These include many circular ornaments, some perforated, and one unique flower-shaped ornament.

Cut carnivore teeth, including puma, bear, and wolf, are present, as are shell and bone imitations of canine teeth. Several porpoise teeth have also been recovered. One cut puma jaw, perhaps part of a mask, came from Crystal River.

Some of the ceramic vessels associated with Yent mounds seem to be ceramics especially constructed or acquired through trade for ceremonial usage. Many seem to have symbolic significance, and they come in many unusual shapes and sizes. For example, there are spherical bowls, one vessel in the shape of a ram's horn, a vessel with three pouring spouts, two four-lobed pots with tetrapodal feet, and one compound jar-shaped vessel (see Sears 1962). Other vessels are of more conventional shapes: cylindrical jars, globular bowls, and deep conical vessels with flaring rims. Designs on Yent vessels include cord marking, check stamping, zoned punctations, and zoned painting. Miniature vessels, usually cylindrical pots or bowls and often with podal supports, occur in relatively large numbers in the mounds. Some are small replicas of Deptford vessels.

Similar Yent vessels are not found in the village middens of the late Deptford peoples, confirming that the vessels had special significance. Their use or deposition was evidently restricted.

Yent complex mounds are described by Sears as continual-use type—that is, the mounds were continually reused, and additional burials and other items were placed in them through time. Burials that probably motivated the mound's being built often are found near its base. Interments in Yent mounds include flexed, bundled, extended, and single-skull burials. Burial form may indicate status differences, or it may reflect the manner in which bodies of the dead were cleaned and stored.

The purpose of the ceremonial pottery associated with the Yent mounds is not certain. One explanation is that at least some of the vessels were used to serve special sacred teas or medicines. Often the vessels are found in association with *Busycon* shell drinking cups of the type known to have been used later during the Mississippian period for taking black drink. Other of the ceremonial vessels may have been used for drinking other sacred teas. Creek peoples of the eighteenth century are known to have had several separate teas, and the use of drinks for ceremonial purposes was widespread among southeastern native peoples (see Hudson 1979). It is likely that the practice of taking sacred teas was present at the time of the Yent complex, and that the Yent vessels and shell dippers were used in ceremonies similar to those of later Southeast native peoples.

Shell cups have been found at all three of the Yent complex mounds Sears used in his study. Fifty-three were taken from the mound at Crystal River, and one clay effigy of a *Busycon* shell was recovered from the Yent Mound. Cups were found in the mounds accompanying or near individual burials or in separate deposits.

Often the shell cups and the ceramic vessels were "killed" by having their bottoms knocked out. It is generally thought by some individuals that this was done to free the spirit of the pot to allow it to accompany

Pierce Zoned Red pottery vessel from Hall Mound, a Yent complex site in northwest Florida. The vessel, about 7¾ inches high, was excavated by C. B. Moore (1902: fig. 270; courtesy Smithsonian Institution).

Pierce Zoned Red vessel, about 4 inches high, excavated from Pierce Mound A by C. B. Moore (1902: fig. 155; courtesy Smithsonian Institution).

Unique ram's horn effigy about 7¾ inches high from Pierce Mound A, a Yent complex site excavated by C. B. Moore (1902: figs. 156–157; courtesy Smithsonian Institution).

the spirit of an individual buried in the mound. An alternative explanation is that the vessels were intentionally broken and placed in the mound to prevent their improper reuse.

If the shell and ceramic vessels had been used in ceremonies associated with mound burial, they may have been placed in the mounds at the same time as the human bones and bodies, which previously had been stored in a charnel house. Or individuals could have been interred with the paraphernalia that had belonged to them in life. The result of either of these practices would be caches of vessels placed with and around burials in mounds, the pattern present in Yent mounds.

Black drink and other ceremonies might also have been performed at times other than burial rituals. The shell and ceramic vessels used in those ceremonies could have been refurbished periodically. At that time the old vessels and other paraphernalia would have been placed in consecrated areas, such as mounds, which were specially prepared to receive them. This periodic purging of religious paraphernalia could have been related to seasonally determined ceremonies and also would have resulted in caches of vessels within mounds.

There is evidence that a black drink ceremony was held at the time of the construction or consecration of Yent mounds. At Pierce Mound A in Franklin County, shell cups and miniature sacred vessels were found on the old ground surface under the mound. These objects were placed around the remains of a fire, and bones of animals (remains of food?), along with teeth of a wolf and a panther, were scattered around the fire. Perhaps black drink had been brewed and drunk before beginning to build the mound. Lighting special fires and taking sacred teas on ceremonial occasions to ritually cleanse oneself and restore well-being were aspects of nearly all Southeast native cultures in the postcolumbian era.

This brief scenario of one aspect of Yent ceremonialism implies that the late Deptford people had special religious practitioners who oversaw the preparation and carrying out of ceremonies associated with mound building and the rituals surrounding the deposition of sacred objects and human interments in mounds. Charnel houses for cleaning and storage of burials and various ceremonies involving sacred medicines also might have been aspects of religious life.

Not all people were afforded mound burial, nor does it appear that all late Deptford populations were associated with the Yent complex. A few human interments have been found in Deptford villages on the Gulf coast. At the Carrabelle site in Franklin County, two cremation burials were found in the village midden with a cache of intentionally broken pottery vessels nearby. Perhaps this was a special area used for interments before mound burial was incorporated into Deptford religious and social practices. Flexed primary burials also have been found in at least one Deptford village.

On the Atlantic coast, burial mounds seem to have been a part of Deptford life early on, shortly after 400 B.C. But the complex social and ceremonial life begun during the late Deptford period on the Gulf coast and elaborated during the time of the later Swift Creek and Weeden Island cultures apparently did not take place in the Atlantic region until after about A.D. 1000.

Swift Creek Culture

The Swift Creek culture that replaced Deptford in eastern northwest Florida was first recognized in central Georgia during the late 1930s. Federal relief archaeology programs carried out near Macon at the Swift Creek site uncovered complicated-stamped pottery, which was named for that site. Soon researchers in other areas, including northwest Florida, were reporting similar complicated-stamped pottery from village sites and from mounds. Since the 1930s, when Swift Creek Complicated Stamped pottery was defined as a ceramic type, a number of related complicated-stamped pottery types have been documented as a part of the Swift Creek ceramic assemblage in northwest Florida (Willey 1949a:378–383).

In Florida, Swift Creek villages, with some exceptions (e.g., Ashley 1992), are restricted to eastern northwest Florida. The distribution of sites is from the Aucilla River in the east westward through northwest Florida. In the western panhandle, Swift Creek sites may overlie sites of the Santa Rosa–Swift Creek culture.

Swift Creek sites generally are not found in peninsular Florida (except for northern northeast Florida). To the north, they extend up the Apalachicola-Chattahoochee River drainage and into southern and central Georgia. Swift Creek sites also have been identified from the fall line in Georgia southeast to near the Atlantic coast of Georgia. That eastern distribution, which is not dense, extends southward into northeast Florida, where middens with significant amounts of Swift Creek pottery—as high as 75 percent at some sites—have been identified in the St. Johns River drainage north of Jacksonville (Ashley 1992:130–133). The implication is that the Swift Creek ceramic assemblage originated in Georgia and was adopted by late Deptford peoples in Florida.

The replacement of Deptford pottery by Swift Creek pottery in the panhandle appears to have been a gradual process, occurring over several hundred years (Bense 1992). It was during the period of the Swift Creek culture that villages were established in significant numbers in the interior forests and river valleys of the eastern panhandle. As noted in the discussion of the Deptford culture earlier in this chapter, similar settlement changes also were taking place at about the same time in north-central and north Florida.

The geographical range of Swift Creek pottery in Florida is much greater than the distribution of sites. Complicated-stamped potsherds and vessels are found as nonlocal items throughout much of the northern peninsula at sites of other cultures, including mounds along the Gulf coast and in the St. Johns region. Swift Creek pottery has also been found at sites in southern Florida, and complicated-stamped pottery types are a part of the early Weeden Island ceramic assemblage in the northwest and north regions of the state. Although the distinctive complicated-stamped wares have a wide distribution in Florida, large Swift Creek villages occur mainly in the panhandle.

Inland and coastal Swift Creek village sites in the panhandle have been investigated. In addition, many small Swift Creek sites, perhaps special-use camps, are found in inland locales, often the same as earlier Deptford inland sites (see Tesar 1980; White 1981a).

Coastal sites, probably villages, are located either immediately adjacent to the salt marsh–tidal stream system, as were Deptford sites, or farther back from the marshes in the hardwood hammocks, sometimes several miles from the Gulf. Probable village sites also are located away from the coast in the highland forests, especially in the Tallahassee Red Hills region in the upper panhandle and the Chattahoochee River valley. As noted earlier, the implication is that during

Swift Creek and Santa Rosa–Swift Creek regions.

the Swift Creek period significant native populations began to live in inland villages in northwest Florida.

Swift Creek sites are not restricted to the panhandle. A few small sites, again special-use camps, have been found east of the panhandle as far away as Columbia and Alachua counties. In the lowermost (northern) St. Johns River drainage, Swift Creek pottery is found in large and small shell middens and in sites consisting of artifact scatters. At times it is mixed with Deptford and St. Johns ceramics. One single-component (unmixed with artifacts from earlier or later cultures) Swift Creek shell midden is known in that northeast Florida area. These northeastern sites may be part of the expansion of the Swift Creek ceramic assemblage from central Georgia to the Atlantic coast of southern Georgia that occurred about A.D. 300–500 (Ashley 1992:

134–135). More research is needed to clarify this possibility and to determine if the sites are in some fashion related to demographic or economic changes.

The period of the Swift Creek culture in northwest Florida is about A.D. 150–350 or slightly later, after which time the Swift Creek ceramic assemblage developed into the Weeden Island assemblage. That and other changes allow archaeologists to define the Weeden Island cultures after about A.D. 300. The exact temporal relationships of the Deptford, Swift Creek, and early Weeden Island cultures in the panhandle remain to be clarified. Present radiocarbon dates suggest considerable overlap, especially in coastal versus interior sites, and along the coast different estuarine systems may differ from one another. It may be that the development of the Swift Creek culture in interior northwest Florida preceded the addition of Swift Creek pottery to the Deptford assemblage on the coast. In other words, the impetus for inland village life may have come from the north, rather than from coastal Deptford societies to the south (see Tesar 1980:87–108, for a discussion of temporal and spatial variations; also, White 1981a:638, for a review of radiocarbon dates suggesting that Swift Creek is earlier inland and in Georgia; and see Bense 1992).

Several Swift Creek villages have been tested or excavated and provide information on village life (Phelps 1969; Penton 1970; Fryman 1971a:3; Bense and Watson 1979). They are associated with three environmental settings. The first are the inland villages found in the river valley forests and other locales in interior northwest Florida. Soils at such locations are fertile, and gardening may have played a role in the Swift Creek economic system. Evidence of cultigens, however, is almost nil. David Phelps has identified one squash or possibly gourd seed recovered from a preserved, dessicated human fecal sample found at the coastal Refuge Fire Tower site.

These inland village sites usually are horseshoe-shaped or circular middens that presumably reflect a similarly shaped community plan. At these inland villages, burial mounds may be present.

The coastal village sites are of two main types. One resembles the inland circular or horseshoe-shaped middens. At least one of the coastal sites is described as more rectangular than round (Bense and Watson 1979). The coastal middens of this type contain marine shellfish—largely oysters—in addition to other midden materials. As at the inland village sites, a burial mound may be present adjacent to the village area. The third type of site is the coastal, linear shell midden. Generally, these middens are not extensive, and they may represent special-use sites use for collecting shellfish and for fishing.

The larger, annular middens, both those on the coast and those in the interior, probably were associated with villages. Most likely the villages were occupied year-round by sedentary populations. Villagers could have traveled to locations on the coast, however, to fish and collect shellfish. They also may have used small hunting camps, accounting for the small sites found across northwest and into north peninsular Florida. This model needs to be tested with additional data.

Swift Creek villages located adjacent to the coastal salt marsh–tidal stream system seem to have been occupied by peoples whose subsistence efforts, as one might expect, were centered on the use of resources from that environmental system. Phelps estimates that 95 percent of their meat diet came from fish and shellfish. Like their Deptford predecessors, the coastal Swift Creek villagers hunted and collected terrestrial animals. Charred hickory nuts and acorns have also been recovered from sites.

Our knowledge of the tools used by the Swift Creek people continues to expand. Penton's excavations at the Bird Hammock site indicate that bone and stone tools occur in greater numbers than they did during the preceding Deptford period. At site 8By73 several miles inland from the Gulf, Judith Bense and Thomas Watson identified a large assemblage of late Swift Creek and early Weeden Island tools. Swift Creek bone tools include awls, polished pins, flakers, and bone scrapers. Cut and polished carnivore mandibles and drilled carnivore teeth are found in the village middens, evidently objects of personal or ritual adornment. Shell tools are relatively rare, consisting of a few *Busycon* hammers, possible scrapers, ladles or cups, and columella pounders. Shell discs and pendants occur in small numbers. None of the bone and shell tools are unique; they closely resemble those found at both inland and coastal sites elsewhere in Florida from the Archaic period onward.

More distinctive is the lithic complex, especially a type of stemmed knife or projectile point that Phelps calls the Swift Creek point. The tang is only slightly narrower than the width of the blade and expands slightly toward the base. In appearance, the point closely resembles the Columbia point described by Bullen (1975:19) for the later Weeden Island period. These points likely are hafted knife blades; many exhibit resharpening. Some specimens, because of repeated sharpening, have blades only slightly longer than their stems.

Another distinctive Swift Creek lithic tool is a bifacial knife that seems to have been manufactured from a triangular blade. The width at the shoulders is always shorter than the length of the specimen, giving the finished tool a linear appearance. Bases are either flat or slightly rounded. Other stone tools include spokeshaves, hammerstones made from expended cores, flake scrapers, limestone and chert nutting stones (with one to four indentations), and sandstone abraders used to sharpen the bone awls. It is believed that nutting stones were used as platforms on which to crack nuts. One of the largest assemblages of lithic tools has come from the multicomponent Fox's Pond site, 8By73 (Bense and Watson 1979).

The ceramic inventory from the Bird Hammock site was composed almost entirely of plain and Swift Creek Complicated Stamped pottery; those types constituted 61 and 35 percent of the total ceramic inventory, respectively. Other ceramic types included check-stamped and simple-stamped pottery (Deptford types), Crooked River Complicated Stamped, St. Andrews Complicated Stamped, and cord-marked potsherds. In the Swift Creek component at Fox's Pond in Bay County, a very similar ceramic assemblage is reported: 63 percent plain, 36 percent Swift Creek Complicated Stamped, and 1 percent other, largely Weeden Island, types.

Shapes of both plain and complicated-stamped vessels are of two main types: squat bowls about 10 inches in diameter and 4 inches in height, and deep cylindrical pots with conoidal bottoms 12 to 16 inches in diameter. Rim treatments include crenelating, notching, and scalloping. All of the pottery contains quartz sand or grit in the paste.

Although it is generally assumed that Swift Creek complicated stamping was done by pressing a carved wooden paddle into the wet surface of the clay pot, at least one baked clay stamp has been found. That specimen has a complicated stamp on one side and a check-stamped impression on the other, proving rather dramatically that some Swift Creek peoples used both types of surface treatments. Examination of the complicated-stamp design on many vessels has verified, however, that most paddles were made of wood. Other distinctive

Swift Creek Complicated Stamped pottery (*a* is 2¾ inches high).

Swift Creek artifacts are small rubbing tools made from potsherds and used to smooth pottery, and baked clay or steatite equal-arm elbow pipes.

A relatively large number of baked clay figurines have been found in Swift Creek village middens. All are bare-breasted females wearing skirts with high, wide sashes around the waist. Similar figurines have been found at contemporary sites elsewhere in the Southeast and are believed to be associated with shared ideology of the general Hopewellian period (Walthall 1975).

The general picture of Swift Creek village life derived from limited excavations and surveys is of a mixed economic pattern, with some villages emphasizing riverine and forest resources and others maintaining a coastal economic orientation. On the basis of the survey data available, there seem to have been more interior villages than coastal ones. Certainly this is true when the distribution of sites in Georgia also is considered. More research is needed to determine the relationships among inland and coastal sites and to address the issues of sedentism, coastal special-use sites, and gardening. And the exact relationships between the Swift Creek and Deptford cultures remain to be determined. Was Swift Creek a culture that developed out of earlier cultures in interior Georgia—for example, the west Georgia check-stamped pottery–making culture associated with the Mandeville site—and expanded southward into northwest Florida? New lifeways certainly transformed the interior of the panhandle, even reaching to the coast, where aspects of the Deptford culture were also changed. Such influences also might have played a role in the evolution of the Deptford culture in peninsular Florida.

William Sears has organized traits from four Swift Creek mounds into the Green Point complex (Sears 1962:5–8), a ceremonial complex related to the earlier Yent complex and the later Weeden Island ceremonial complex (see Brose 1979). Like the Yent complex, the Green Point complex is a local development related to Hopewellian ceremonialism present throughout much of the interior of the southeastern United States.

Swift Creek ceremonial mounds all appear to have been constructed as repositories for human interments. Mounds are circular or oval, ranging from about 32 feet in diameter to 64 feet for the circular mounds, about 160 by 65 feet for the oval mounds. None of the mounds appears to be higher than 6 feet. Oval-shaped mounds may have originally been circular mounds to which later additions were made to receive additional interments.

The early Swift Creek mounds appear to have been built in several discrete ceremonies, each involving the deposition of burials and the placement of caches of artifacts, subsequently covered with earth to form the mound. In some mounds, additional layers of earth were added to cover additional burials and deposits. At times, each mound stratum was capped with a clay layer.

Within mounds, burials are generally flexed, although single-skull and bundled burials are known. Possibly individuals were stored in charnel houses before mound interment. The later Swift Creek mounds seem to have been constructed in a single ceremony. In such cases, a charnel house must have been used to store bodies.

Artifact caches in the mounds are composed of ceramic vessels, often of the same types as vessels found in the villages: Swift Creek Complicated Stamped, St. Andrews Complicated Stamped, Crooked River Complicated Stamped, and plain vessels. A few vessels in mounds have a zoned rocker-stamped surface treatment. Vessel shapes and decorative techniques of the ceremonial vessels, as far as can be determined from the evidence on hand, are the same as those of the utilitarian, village ceramics. This is unlike the earlier Deptford-related Yent complex and the later Weeden Island culture. Swift Creek ceremonial vessels, however, tend to have podal supports more often than do vessels in villages.

Other artifacts deposited in Swift Creek mounds include the Swift Creek knives or points, bifacial knives, and sheets of mica. Stone and fired clay elbow pipes also are occasionally found in mounds. In several Swift Creek mounds, *Busycon* shell drinking cups occur with pottery caches, as they do in Yent complex mounds. When the cups are found in mounds, they are generally accompanied by small, bowl-shaped ceremonial vessels. As suggested for the Yent complex, the caching of the cups and ceramic vessels in the mounds was probably part of a black-drink ceremony that required deposition of the vessels after they were used. At the time the mounds were constructed, temples or charnel houses containing both the bones of the deceased and certain ceremonial items might have been cleaned out (and refurbished?), and the remains and ceremonial paraphernalia deposited in

Two Swift Creek Complicated Stamped vessels excavated by C. B. Moore: *left,* from Marsh Island, *right,* from Green Point (Moore 1902:249–254, 274–281). Both are in the collections of the Smithsonian Institution; the photo was probably taken by John Goggin (courtesy Florida Museum of Natural History).

the mound. The distribution of conch shell cups with ceremonial vessels is also like that found in Yent mounds.

Santa Rosa–Swift Creek Culture

Santa Rosa is a taxonomic term often cited in the archaeological literature that presents problems for modern archaeologists. Much of the uncertainty lies in what might be called the "ceramic transition problem." Simply stated, geographical distributions of two discrete ceramic assemblages overlap where those assemblages meet. For instance, such a transition zone occurred during the Deptford period in northeast Florida. There, sites containing both Deptford and St. Johns pottery are found. Does this mean different peoples were associated with each assemblage, Deptford from the north and St. Johns from the south, and that they occupied the same sites at slightly different times? Or does the presence of the two assemblages mean that a single population was making both styles of pottery?

The western panhandle of Florida during the Swift Creek period appears to have been such a ceramic transition zone. In that region the distributions of Swift Creek pottery types and Santa Rosa pottery types

are mixed at both coastal and inland sites, which is why most archaeologists prefer the name Santa Rosa–Swift Creek. The Santa Rosa pottery types are variants of the same types found to the west in the
Marksville culture centered along the Gulf coast and in the lower Mississippi River valley. In Florida, Gordon Willey and Richard Woodbury
(1942:241–242; Willey 1949a:366–396) recognized this overlap, de-
scribing it as a merging of two ceramic styles and leading them to
define a Santa Rosa–Swift Creek culture: "In both vessel shapes and
vessel decoration the Santa Rosa–Swift Creek period was one of fusion
of two rather strikingly different sets of ideas: on the one hand, the
conoidal-based pots decorated with the stamping technique; and on
the other, globular bowls, beakers, collared jars and unusual forms
decorated with incision, punctation, rocker stamping or red zoned
painting" (Willey 1949a:544).

As Tesar (1980:87–198) states in his discussion of Santa Rosa–Swift
Creek, other archaeologists since have noted the same phenomenon.

In village middens, Santa Rosa pottery is almost never found in the
panhandle east of the Apalachicola drainage. In their surveys in Leon
County and the Lake Seminole region, respectively, Louis Tesar
(1980) and Nancy White (1981a) found no mixed Santa Rosa and
Swift Creek sites. But in the western panhandle mixed deposits exist.
At the Hawkshaw site near Pensacola, for instance, Judith Bense
found pottery of the Santa Rosa and Swift Creek series in about the
same amounts, comprising 2.7 percent and 3.1 percent of the nearly
15,000 potsherds excavated. Apparently, no archaeological village or
special-use sites in the western panhandle contain only Santa Rosa
pottery.

Santa Rosa pottery is found in mounds in the eastern panhandle,
however. In such contexts the vessels most likely represent items of
special significance or status that were brought to the sites via trade or
other means.

Comparisons of two sites in Bay County reported by Bense and
Watson (1979:110) suggest that Santa Rosa pottery is found in early
Swift Creek sites (e.g., 8By74), but not in later Swift Creek sites (e.g.,
8By73), at least along the western coast. These data also could be used
to support the contention that on the coast, the Santa Rosa–Swift
Creek period lasted longer than some archaeologists have supposed, as
late as A.D. 350 or even later (Bense 1992). As noted, the exact temporal

relationships among Deptford, Swift Creek, Santa Rosa–Swift Creek, and Weeden Island in coastal and inland northwest Florida remain ambiguous.

Recent research focusing on the Santa Rosa–Swift Creek culture (Thomas and Campbell 1990; Bense 1992) has made it clear that the Santa Rosa–Swift Creek culture is a discrete culture that can be differentiated from Swift Creek. The pottery made by the Santa Rosa–Swift Creek peoples includes both Swift Creek types and types of the Santa Rosa ceramic series originally defined by Willey (1949a:372–378; and see Bense 1985:56–66). The latter series consists of Alligator Bayou Stamped, Basin Bayou Stamped, Santa Rosa Stamped, and Santa Rosa Punctated ceramic types. In excavations at the Hawkshaw site, sherds of these four ceramic types were found by Gadus and Bense, along with Marksville Incised and Marksville Stamped potsherds. The latter two types, whose surface treatments are closely related to the Alligator Bayou types, but which are made from quite different pastes, might be "direct imports from the lower Mississippi River valley" (Bense 1985:59). This ceramic assemblage probably appears in conjunction with Swift Creek pottery at all Santa Rosa–Swift Creek sites.

The pattern of settlement of the Santa Rosa–Swift Creek culture is much like that of the late Archaic–period Elliott's Point complex. In her summary of the culture, Judith Bense (1992) notes that 87 percent of the known sites are on or near the coast, most often around the estuaries, such as St. Andrews Bay, Choctawhatchee Bay, Santa Rosa Sound, and Pensacola Bay. Annular and linear shell middens are present, along with smaller shell middens. As was true with the late Archaic Elliott's Point complex, larger sites may have functioned as centers, with other sites located nearby. Unlike the late Archaic settlement pattern, however, some Santa Rosa–Swift Creek site clusters are associated with burial mounds.

The picture that is emerging in the western panhandle is of great settlement and subsistence continuity from the late Archaic period into the Santa Rosa–Swift Creek period and probably later. The appearance of burial mounds in the Santa Rosa–Swift Creek period may reflect changes in social and political structure related to demographic increases. The precolumbian inhabitants of that region may have needed solutions to economic pressures that resulted from larger populations trying to extract a livelihood from the spatially bounded

Alligator Bayou Stamped vessel about 7½ inches high from Anderson's Bayou (Moore 1902: fig 54). The photo was probably taken by John Goggin (courtesy Smithsonian Institution).

Basin Bayou Incised vessel from Pearl Bayou (Moore 1902: 183–188), in the collections of the Smithsonian Institution (courtesy Florida Museum of Natural History).

coastal estuarine systems. Greater competition and an increase in territorialism may have resulted. Burial mounds, perhaps associated with
specific groups, may have symbolized this competition for resources.

Despite social and political accommodations, coastal resources, no
matter how productive, could not continue to support the growing
Swift Creek and Santa Rosa–Swift Creek populations. As we shall see
in the next two chapters, precolumbian populations took advantage of
inland resources, establishing more villages in the interior of northern
Florida. The number and distribution of these post–A.D. 300 Weeden
Island sites is much greater than for the Deptford, Swift Creek, and
Santa Rosa–Swift Creek cultures. During the period of regional cultures, demographic increases were a major impetus for culture
change, just as environmental and climatic changes led to culture
changes in the Archaic period.

Weeden Island Cultures
of Northern Florida

Weeden Island cultures are distributed across northwest Florida and the western two-thirds of the northern peninsula. Sites are found from Mobile Bay east to the Okefenokee Swamp and south through north and north-central Florida. Along the Gulf coast, sites are located as far south as Manatee and Sarasota counties just below Tampa Bay; to the north, sites extend into the coastal plain in southeast Alabama and southern Georgia. Like other archaeological cultures, Weeden Island has been closely linked to a ceramic complex but cannot be defined solely on the basis of ceramic typologies. Temporal and geographical variations in the distribution of the Weeden Island ceramic complex are present and, in conjunction with traits such as environmental adaptations, allow archaeologists to define and study several Weeden Island cultures.

At the turn of the century, archaeologist C. B. Moore excavated more than fifty mounds in Florida containing human interments and Weeden Island pottery. Over two decades, Moore dug in Weeden Island sites from northwest Florida to Tampa Bay (Moore 1900, 1901, 1902, 1903a, b, 1905, 1907, 1918). The reports of those mound excavations, as well as the collections, remain a major source of information on Weeden Island cultures.

The distinctiveness of Weeden Island pottery found in mounds was recognized early on by William H. Holmes (1903:104–114, 125–128), who described ceramics from archaeological sites in the panhandle and the Gulf coast. But neither Moore nor Holmes recognized the temporal placement of Weeden Island relative to earlier Deptford and Swift Creek assemblages or to later cultures. They were hindered by their data: Moore's excavations had centered on mounds, representing relatively discrete deposits made at a single or almost-single point in time. There were no stratigraphic data on ceramic assemblages that might have been obtained had excavations been carried out in village middens.

Shortly after Moore's activities ended, J. Walter Fewkes of the Smithsonian Institution undertook excavations in a large shell midden on Weeden Island (spelled *Weedon* Island on some maps) at the mouth of Old Tampa Bay in Pinellas County. During the winter of 1923–1924, Fewkes dug in the midden and in an adjacent burial mound that contained Weeden Island pottery. Fewkes's site, today located in a state park, would give its name to the Weeden Island culture.

The excavations at Weeden Island led Fewkes to conclude that the ceramic complex from the mound was precolumbian in time and was more closely related to other, more northerly southeastern ceramic complexes than to the ceramic assemblages known at that time from the Caribbean (Fewkes 1924:23–26). His investigations also pointed out a phenomenon that eventually led to a taxonomic reappraisal of Weeden Island: the Weeden Island ceramic complex in the mound was quite different from the pottery assemblage in the midden. (It is not clear from Fewkes's report that he thought the mound was actually made by the same people who deposited the nearby midden.) This dichotomy—one ceramic complex associated with mounds and another associated with village middens—was what William H. Sears (1973) would label the sacred-secular dichotomy and is true for all the Weeden Island cultures in peninsular Florida, both those in north-central Florida and those along the Gulf coast. Because Moore's early excavations focused on mounds, archaeologists failed to realize the extent of village ceramic variation within the overall Weeden Island region. It was not until a half century after Fewkes's excavations that the concept of sacred (mound) and secular (utilitarian) ceramic complexes became a part of Weeden Island studies.

In 1941, stimulated in part by the work of Moore and Fewkes and their descriptions of Weeden Island ceramics, two Columbia University graduate students surveyed a number of archaeological sites along the panhandle coast to establish a chronology for Weeden Island and other northwest Florida archaeological assemblages. Gordon Willey and Richard Woodbury (1942) published their results the following year. In that paper they formally named and began to define the Weeden Island ceramic assemblage and to order it chronologically, recognizing that Weeden Island Incised pottery was early and Wakulla Check Stamped pottery was late. The basic separation of Weeden Island into two periods, Weeden Island I and II, was established. Willey and Woodbury also began to record other Weeden Island traits in northwest Florida, including the coastal cultural adaptation, settlement systems, and artifacts.

Three years later, Willey (1945) published another important paper on Weeden Island, building on the previous survey and synthesizing data from fifty-six mounds, mainly sites excavated by Moore. This and the earlier article noted similarities between some Weeden Island ceramic decorative motifs and motifs present in the Coles Creek ceramic assemblage of the lower Mississippi River valley. These similarities, remarked on since by other archaeologists (e.g., Sears 1956a:74–83, 1992; Belmont and Williams 1981), suggest that aspects of ideology may have been shared by the peoples living across the Gulf coast from Louisiana, Mississippi, and Alabama to northwest Florida. Such ideas may have spread west from Florida.

Willey continued his research into Weeden Island and in 1948 wrote an article on the Weeden Island period cultures of the Manatee region, just south of Tampa Bay. Today this region is part of the central Gulf coast region, which encompasses greater Tampa Bay and includes the Weeden Island type site excavated by Fewkes. Willey (1948) noted that in the Manatee region Weeden Island pottery was present in burial mounds but not in village middens. He also developed a relative chronology for the region: the Weeden Island culture was followed in time by a ceramic assemblage he named Englewood, which in turn was followed by the late precolumbian–period Safety Harbor culture (Willey 1948). The check-stamped ceramics found at Weeden Island II sites in northwest Florida were not present in the Manatee area. Indeed, village pottery was mainly undecorated, causing Willey erroneously to suggest that at least some sites were affiliated with the south Florida Glades ceramic assemblage, also characterized by undecorated pottery. Like Fewkes, Willey did not fully realize that the village (utilitarian) ceramics of the peninsular Gulf coast Weeden Island cultures were quite different from the contemporary assemblage in the mounds.

The Manatee region chronology has been revisited by George Luer and Marion Almy (1979, 1982). Combining old and newly excavated data they have defined a Manasota culture for the central Gulf coast region (see chapter 6).

In 1949 Gordon Willey published his important book *Archeology of the Florida Gulf Coast*, which included a description of the Weeden Island culture based in part on the information gathered by Moore, Fewkes, and other researchers during the previous half-century. The volume remains an important archaeological reference nearly five decades later, a reflection of the quality and pioneering nature of Gordon Willey's field investigations and analysis.

Surveys and excavations carried out in the intervening years have enhanced Willey's synthetic treatment of Weeden Island, especially for inland locales that were not a focus of his book. And, as archaeological theoretical emphases have shifted, so has the problem orientation of Weeden Island studies. In the 1940s Florida archaeologists were concerned with establishing culture sequences and with isolating traits, largely ceramics, that could be used to define cultures. Using these culture histories as a basis, archaeologists now seek to reconstruct and explain the cultural processes involved in the development of the Florida Weeden Island cultures (cf. Brose and Percy 1974; Percy and Brose 1974; Milanich, Cordell et al. 1984:187–200). Numerous survey projects and excavations in north, north-central, and northwest Florida and along the peninsular Gulf coast from Sarasota County northward have yielded data on Weeden Island and helped us to recognize that, as with other time periods and cultures in Florida, temporal and spatial variations exist within it.

Temporal and Spatial Variations

Early archaeologists (Willey and Woodbury 1942; Willey 1945, 1949a) divided the period of the northwest and peninsula Weeden Island culture(s) into two periods. The earlier Weeden Island I period is characterized by the presence of Swift Creek types of complicated-stamped pottery along with undecorated pottery and Weeden Island pottery with punctated and incised decorations. These latter plain and decorated vessels, when recovered from mound contexts and, less often, from village middens, exhibit ornate and stylized designs, are shaped into animal effigy forms, and/or have animal effigy adornos (modeled clay heads, tails, and such attached to vessels before firing). Such decorative motifs are applied to a wide range of vessel shapes. Similar stylized motifs and vessel shapes occur over a wide geographical region, from northwest Florida to Sarasota County south of Tampa Bay. Punctated, incised, and some pinched surface treatments also are found on Weeden Island pottery vessels, most often on simple bowls.

The Weeden Island II period ceramic assemblage is characterized by a decrease of complicated-stamped pottery and the presence of a distinctive new type, Wakulla Check Stamped. During this period, according to Willey and Woodbury, other of the Weeden Island pottery types continued to be manufactured, but less than in the early period.

The sequence of Deptford, Swift Creek (and Santa Rosa–Swift Creek), Weeden Island I, and Weeden Island II remained relatively unquestioned in Florida for two decades following the publication of *Archeology of the Florida Gulf Coast*. The ceramic-based chronology associated with that sequence served as a template to which other culture sequences in the Southeast, especially areas adjacent to the Gulf coast in Florida, Georgia, and Alabama, were correlated, or against which they were contrasted (e.g., Sears 1956a, 1992). The Gulf tradition, defined by Goggin (1949b:34–39) to encompass the Swift Creek (and Santa Rosa–Swift Creek) and Weeden Island cultures, was seen as a major culture center from which influences were felt throughout the Southeast. Contacts were suggested with the Troyville and Coles Creek cultures of the lower Mississippi valley west of northwest Florida and with Hopewellian cultures to the north. The concept of a Gulf tradition and the culture sequence represented by that tradition became popular in published literature on Florida and the Southeast and remains in use by some archaeologists today.

As new data were collected, archaeologists realized that the original culture and ceramic sequence(s) proposed in the 1940s could be refined and defined for smaller regions, such as the central peninsular Gulf coast and the northern Florida regions. Cultural distinctions were made within the overall rubric of Weeden Island, and Weeden Island is no longer viewed as a single culture. We recognize several related but geographically separated Weeden Island cultures that probably shared aspects of social and ideological life, reflected in similar mound assemblages, while differing in specific environmental adaptations and related village assemblages.

Using the classic Weeden Island ceramic complex as a defining characteristic, we can outline a large geographical region in which those ceramic types are found in both mound and village contexts during the Weeden Island I period. That heartland region encompasses northwest and north Florida and adjacent portions of Alabama and Georgia. Differences allow us to distinguish the northwest Florida Weeden Island culture from the contemporaneous culture in north Florida, the McKeithen Weeden Island culture (Milanich, Cordell et al. 1984).

As we saw in chapter 4, the Swift Creek culture is present in the eastern panhandle in northwest Florida, but not in north Florida. Nor is the late Weeden Island–period Wakulla culture that is present in the northwest region found in north Florida. Nor, as we shall see in chapter 10, is the Fort Walton culture that develops out of the late Weeden Island Wakulla culture in the panhandle present in north Florida. These differences make it taxonomically possible to distinguish among the northwest and north heartland cultures.

Louis Tesar (1980:112) has suggested that the northwest region can be further divided, separating the coastal region culture from the culture present in the Apalachicola River valley and adjacent inland areas.

Early Weeden Island cultures.

South of the heartland region—in north-central Florida, along the northern peninsular Gulf coast, and in the central peninsular Gulf coast region—the early Weeden Island ceramic assemblage is found in mounds but not in village contexts (except for a very few punctated and incised sherds). As was true in the heartland region, we can use a variety of criteria to divide the Weeden Island period cultures of these three regions into separate cultures. Those cultures—the Weeden Island I period Cades Pond culture in north-central Florida, the middle and late Manasota–period (A.D. 300–700) culture of the central peninsular Gulf coast, and an unnamed north peninsula Gulf coast culture—are described in chapter 6.

Although differences in geographical and temporal distributions, village ceramic assemblages, environmental adaptations, and evolutionary trajectories provide the basis for the taxonomic division of Weeden Island into these various cultures, similarities in the ceramic assemblages found in mounds allow them all to be called Weeden Island. All of the cultures must have shared aspects of ideology and social and political organization. But local environments necessitated differences in economic adaptations that had been established in the late Archaic period, well before the onset of the Weeden Island period.

Chronology

Just as new data have led to a revision of the concept of Weeden Island and the designation of cultural variants, so have archaeological investigations resulted in refining the Weeden Island chronology. George Percy and David Brose (1974) were the first to present such a refined chronology for a portion of the heartland region, basing their revision on changes in utilitarian (village) ceramic assemblages from Swift Creek and Weeden Island sites in the upper Apalachicola River valley. Their period designations for approximately A.D. 200 to 1000 or 1200 are shown in the table on page 203.

This sequence has been used elsewhere in northwest Florida (for Leon County, see Tesar 1980:602) and may apply to other inland locales there as well. As yet, however, an exact frequency-based ceramic seriation has not been correlated with the Percy-Brose sequence, making its application to specific collections difficult (cf. White 1981a: 647–648).

Another Weeden Island chronology similar to that found in northwest Florida has been proposed by Timothy Kohler for the McKeithen site in Columbia County in north Florida (Kohler 1978; Milanich, Cordell et al. 1984:76–81, 185–187). Kohler's chronology covers the early Weeden Island period and the early portion of the equivalent of the late Weeden Island period, about A.D. 200–900 (Percy and Brose's periods 1–4). Because Swift Creek culture sites are not present in north Florida and because check-stamped pottery is not the majority decorated type after about A.D. 750 as in northwest Florida, Kohler's three-period McKeithen chronology differs in detail from those presented by Willey and by Percy and Brose.

Kohler's chronology is based both on actual sherd counts and on an analysis of pottery attributes. It is tied to radiocarbon dates, to other artifacts, and to the community pattern of the McKeithen site (in Milanich, Cordell et al. 1984:78–81; and see Johnson 1985). Whether Kohler's detailed analysis applies to other north Florida sites as well as to panhandle sites remains to be investigated. One facet of the chronology proposed by Kohler is the presence of both cord-marked and check-stamped pottery, the latter in small quantities (especially when compared to northwest Florida), in north Florida during the post–A.D. 700 period. Additional research by Kenneth Johnson (1991) and John Worth (in Weisman 1992) has verified this finding and further refined the ceramic inventory for north Florida for the period from the end of the early Weeden Island period (A.D. 750) into the colonial period. That ceramic assemblage and the culture with which it is associated, Suwannee Valley, are discussed in chapter 9.

Archaeologists have been successful in their efforts to refine chronologies in the Weeden Island heartland region. Deriving ceramic assemblage–based sequences for the Weeden Island period cultures of north-central Florida and the peninsular Gulf coast is much more difficult because utilitarian (village) pottery in the peninsular cultures is almost all undecorated. As we shall see in the next chapter, one solution has been to use ceramic attributes such as rim forms to find chronologically sensitive traits (Luer and Almy 1982).

In summary, Weeden Island cultures include (1) the coastal plain, inland culture of northwest Florida and adjacent portions of Georgia and Alabama; (2) a panhandle coastal Weeden Island culture; (3) the north Florida McKeithen Weeden Island culture; (4) the late Weeden Island Wakulla Weeden Island culture of northwest Florida; (5) a northern peninsular Gulf coast culture; (6) the middle and late Manasota–period culture in the central peninsular Gulf coast; and (7) the Cades Pond culture in north-central Florida.

Heartland Cultures

Much of our knowledge of the northwest Florida early Weeden Island cultures comes from the syntheses of Gordon Willey (1949a) and George Percy and David Brose (1974; Brose and Percy 1974). In the north Florida region of the McKeithen culture, we have information from the McKeithen and other sites (Kohler 1978; Milanich, Cordell et al. 1984; Johnson 1985) and from surveys and test excavations (Sigler-Lavelle 1980a, 1980b).

Differences in the sequence of regional cultures in north and northwest Florida certainly exist. In north Florida, Deptford sites are rare and Swift Creek sites almost nonexistent, unlike northwest Florida. The McKeithen Weeden Island culture develops directly out of the Deptford culture and appears to represent the first major post-Archaic occupation of north Florida. Radiocarbon dates from the McKeithen site indicate that the appearance of Weeden Island in north Florida is earlier than in northwest Florida, based on available dates from the latter region.

No Yent or Green Point complex mounds appear in north Florida because there are no major late Deptford or Swift Creek sites. Yet McKeithen Weeden Island ceremonialism is indistinguishable from early Weeden Island ceremonialism in the panhandle. And radiocarbon dates from the McKeithen site indicate the period of this ceremonialism is the same in the two regions. McKeithen ceremonialism is clearly from the same tradition as the northwest Florida Yent and Green Point ceremonial complexes. As people began to establish villages in interior locations in northwest and north Florida after about A.D. 100, peoples in the two regions must have been in constant contact.

But cultures in north and northwest Florida took different directions after the early Weeden Island period. The archaeological assemblage associated with the late Weeden Island Wakulla culture in the panhandle is quite different from that associated with the contemporaneous Suwannee Valley assemblage in the McKeithen region (see chapter 9). And the post–late Weeden Island development of the Fort Walton culture in the panhandle did not occur in north Florida, where the Suwannee Valley culture continued into the early colonial period.

Early Weeden Island–period archaeological sites in the heartland region.

In the colonial period these two regions continued to be distinct: in northwest Florida were the Apalachee Indians, and in north Florida were Timucuan speakers. This is quite remarkable, considering that the distance from Tallahassee (in northwest Florida) to Live Oak (in north Florida) is only seventy miles.

The discussion that follows of these two inland heartland cultures and the coastal panhandle Weeden Island culture emphasizes their differences (settlement patterns and economic orientation) and their similarities (ceremonialism and social organization). Unfortunately, our information on Weeden Island is not yet fine-grained enough to compare these three heartland cultures beyond the most obvious traits, such as coastal versus inland economic patterns. Although the McKeithen site (Milanich, Cordell et al. 1984) and the surrounding region are used to interpret contemporary traits in northwest Florida and to suggest cultural similarities, such an application someday may be shown to be in error. There is much to learn about Weeden Island.

The distribution of early Weeden Island sites in north and northwest Florida reflects the continuation of a change that began at the end of Deptford and Swift Creek times as people began to establish inland villages in larger numbers. In northwest Florida it is Swift Creek villages that first appear in relatively larger numbers in interior locales; in north Florida it is Weeden Island villages.

The early Weeden Island settlement pattern in northwest Florida resembles that of the preceding Swift Creek culture, although there are more Weeden Island sites. Many of the Swift Creek sites, including the annular middens, contain a Weeden Island component. The settlement continuity between Swift Creek and early Weeden Island is striking; clearly the two practiced very similar economic systems. In fact, the biggest difference noted thus far between the two cultures lies in their ceramic assemblages, which as we have seen represent a developmental continuum.

Coastal Weeden Island middens in northwest Florida are found on the barrier islands as well as on the adjacent mainland close to freshwater sources and not far from the salt marsh: "Although there are some exceptions, most sites do not front on open Gulf waters. Instead they tend to be concentrated on estuaries, lagoons, sounds, and small saltwater bays or coves which are relatively sheltered. . . . [S]ites are located near a freshwater source, . . . not more than several hundred feet from brackish or salt water, and . . . tidal marsh is usually near at hand" (Percy and Brose 1974:19). These coastal middens probably represent fishing and shellfish-gathering locales (Percy and Brose 1974:20). As was true of coastal Swift Creek sites, the shell middens contain oyster, *Rangia* clams, and other shellfish, along with fish remains.

As also was true of Swift Creek sites, some early Weeden Island coastal sites are found just back from the coast in forested locales, but still near the coastal marshes. These sites, usually annular middens, probably represent villages, and they may articulate with the special-use shell middens nearer the coast. David Phelps and his students from Florida State University located and tested a number of these sites, including Bird Hammock, Snow Beach, Hall, and Mound Field (Bense 1969; Phelps 1969; Penton 1970), each of which contained a Swift Creek component as well.

Other than ceramics, artifacts from these early coastal Weeden Island sites are poorly known, and large expanses of the panhandle coast remain to be surveyed before we can fully understand the coastal early Weeden Island settlement system.

In the interior of the panhandle, early Weeden Island villages are often present at the sites of earlier Swift Creek villages (Percy and Brose 1974:28). C. B. Moore (1903a, 1918) excavated mounds at several early Weeden Island sites in the Apalachicola River valley, including the Aspalaga site in Gadsden County, a mound-village complex of the Swift Creek and early Weeden Island periods.

In his Leon County survey, Louis Tesar (1980:604–606) noted that Weeden Island sites occurred in clusters around Lake Miccosukee and Lake Iamonia. Fewer early than later Weeden Island sites were present. These clusters, also present in the McKeithen Weeden Island region, probably each were associated with several contemporary villages. Over time villages budded off, resulting in a larger number of villages. Villages were built in the locales best for the nonagricultural economic pursuits of the early Weeden Island peoples.

This and other settlement, social organization, and ideological aspects of the early Weeden Island heartland cultures have been investigated most thoroughly in north Florida, the McKeithen region. Surveys by Brenda Sigler-Lavelle (1980a, b) and excavations by Tim Kohler (1978, 1980) and others (Milanich, Cordell et al. 1984) have produced a model of the early Weeden Island settlement and social system that can be applied to northwest Florida.

The McKeithen region is centered in Columbia, Suwannee, and Hamilton counties. Early Weeden Island–period sites occur in the largest numbers in the highland forests of the Middle Florida Hammock Belt, which extends in a north-south line through the central portion of this region, roughly between Live Oak and Lake City. Fewer sites are found in the lowlands to the east and west. Madison County remains almost terra incognita, and the extent of sites in the formerly forested zone across the northern section of that county is unknown.

In the McKeithen region, Weeden Island sites of several types were located: (1) villages; (2) village(s) with burial mounds; (3) village(s) without mounds but within three miles of a village with one or more mounds; (4) mound-village complexes, consisting of a village with two or more mounds; (5) isolated burial mounds (most likely the villages associated with these mounds were destroyed by modern development); and (6) task-specific (special-use) sites, including lithic quarries, used for hunting or resource procurement. Villages were nuclear settlements, and, as in northwest Florida, the village middens often are horseshoe shaped. The association of village clusters with at least one burial mound is very similar to the pattern described by Louis Tesar for northwest Florida. In both regions each cluster probably represents a community that shared social and ceremonial ties, including participation in mound-building and burial activities.

Weeden Island village locations in north Florida exhibit physiographic similarities. All are near permanent freshwater sources, and all are located in mesic hammocks, the dominant hardwood forests of the highlands in that part of the state. Although the large lakes found in Leon County are not present in Columbia and Suwannee counties, there are a large number of wetlands, and villages are always located within one-half mile of these aquatic habitats, including ponds, small lakes, creeks, wet prairies or marshes, and swamps. It is clear that the Weeden Island villagers sought maximimum access to such resources as well as to the hardwood forests.

Because the distribution of vegetative communities in the McKeithen region is like a patchwork quilt, villages were located where their residents had easy access to the most diverse vegetation. Sigler-Lavelle found that, although mainly placed in hardwood communities, villages always lay within a mile of the pockets of sand hills, pine scrub, and flatwoods interspersed among the deciduous forests.

How best can we explain this pattern of village clusters, each associated with one or more burial mounds? The explanation offered by Sigler-Lavelle both fits the data at hand and is predicted by anthropological theory (in Milanich, Cordell et al. 1984:41–43,187–189). Her model suggests that each village contained households that formed an interacting community of families linked by kinship and other social and ideological practices. Over time, a village population ultimately reached a size that culturally and economically was outside a normal range. One or more households then budded off, forming a new village near the parent village and in a similar environmental setting. Over many generations a cluster of villages resulted, including both contemporary villages and abandoned sites. The peoples living in the cluster continued to share a common identity, reflected in lineal kinship ties and various social and ideological symbols and behavior.

One physical way in which lineage or other kin ties were demonstrated was in mound burial. Villagers who shared kin ties were interred in kin-related burial mounds associated with each village cluster. We might expect that a charnel house was used to store the bodies of deceased relatives. From time to time the stored remains, perhaps represented by cleaned bones, were interred in a mound. A single mound could have been used several times to deposit groups of stored bodies.

Lineage or kin interment also served to centralize rituals and other activities associated with burial. One or more religious specialists coordinated and led the ceremonies associated with the mortuary rites, as well as other ceremonial activities. Their knowledge gave those individuals power and social status, reinforced through village ceremonies. Within a cluster of villages—a community—religious specialists were thus important figures who had special status that might have transcended a single village or kin group. The specialists used symbols and paraphernalia associated with group ceremonies and beliefs and provided a means by which ordinary villagers could communicate with the supernatural.

Within clusters of villages, a village or a certain kin group within a village could achieve special, higher status because of greater relative access to resources, a slight economic advantage that afforded the kin group or village an advantage in community wide activities, such as in sponsoring feasts or ceremonies. Such a village might well be the one in which burial activities took place. These higher-status mound villages were centers not only for burial and communal religious activities, but also for other types of intervillage or interlineage exchange. As might be expected, within such a center the religious specialist might have achieved higher status, becoming a village leader or "big man," whose status was derived from and reinforced by the importance of his or her village as a mound-village center.

The importance of a Weeden Island mound-village center and its leader must have risen or fallen as economic fortunes increased or decreased. Because the early Weeden Island villagers were not maize farmers, their ability to maintain the competitive economic and social edge associated with a mound-village center depended on their ability to maintain their productive advantage. That advantage was afforded by village location vis-à-vis environmental resources. As populations grew and local resources became relatively more difficult to access, and as new villages budded off, a single mound-village could not hope to retain its status. The resulting loss of status and decline in inter-village or interlineage exchange and communal activities ultimately led to the establishment of another mound-village center elsewhere. Big men came and went.

The social differentiation associated with this system could not be maintained indefinitely because the economic system of the early Weeden Island villages, unlike that of later maize farmers, could not support the food distribution requirements. A village and its big man maintained its status at most for a generation or two.

Village Life

Investigation of the McKeithen site in north Florida provided an opportunity to explore this model in more detail (Kohler 1978, 1980; Milanich, Cordell et al. 1984). The site, covering approximately 120 acres, is composed of three sand mounds arranged nearly 300 yards apart in a large triangle. A horseshoe-shaped village midden extends around the three mounds. Enclosed by the mounds and midden is a plaza. The northern limits of the site are defined by a small creek, which would have provided fresh water for villagers.

Before modern agricultural activities intervened, extensive mesic forests and other vegetative communities surrounded the site. Centrally located in the Hammock Belt zone, the McKeithen site is quite

Excavations at Mound B, the McKeithen site.

close to what is known to have been a major east-west trail in the early colonial period. This location probably was the catalyst for the site's becoming a mound-village center and, for a time, the most important Weeden Island village in north Florida.

Kohler (1980, 1991; also see Steinen 1976) has argued that this location allowed the McKeithen village to function as a gateway community through which trade goods from the north passed on their way south into peninsular Florida. This gateway status would have been a factor in the site's becoming a center for intervillage activities.

Kohler's excavations in the village were intended to produce evidence of social differences as measured by differential access to certain types of artifacts, including types of pottery and trade goods. A similar approach was used by G. Michael Johnson (1985) with lithic artifacts excavated by Kohler. Using the radiocarbon-dated chronology that he tied to ceramic types and vessel attributes, Kohler could analyze changes that took place in artifact distribution and use through the approximately 600-year period the site was occupied (A.D. 200 to 750 or 800).

Chert projectile points from the McKeithen village (courtesy Timothy A. Kohler).

Kohler's data (1978:224–229) indicate that in the village during the middle period of occupation, about A.D. 350–500, nonrandom distribution of status artifacts reached a peak. He found that the distribution of elite ceramics—Weeden Island Incised, Weeden Island Punctated, Weeden Island Red, and Weeden Island Zoned Red types—was unlike the distributions of earlier and later periods of occupation. In the middle period, these ceramic types were much more widely distributed across the site, suggesting that social factors were at work that gave higher status to the entire village, not just one group within it.

Kohler's study of status items, some of which were nonlocal to the region, showed that their distributions did not change through time, suggesting that it was not necessarily contact with non–Weeden Island peoples that increased the status of the village but interaction among Weeden Island peoples. Johnson's (1985) analysis of lithic artifacts from the village supports this contention. He found that during the middle period of site occupation there was the greatest spatial clustering of lithic debitage and the greatest spatial differentiation of lithic reduction activities, reflecting greater specialization.

Mound Ceremonialism

Excavation of the three mounds at the McKeithen site provided an additional opportunity to test Sigler-Lavelle's model of early Weeden Island settlement and social organization. It also provided another perspective on the nature of the McKeithen site during the middle occupation period, when it is believed the site functioned as a mound-village center.

Investigations showed that all three mounds were built about A.D. 350 and used until A.D. 475; the actual period of construction and use could well have been a much shorter time within this century and a quarter. All the mounds were associated with mortuary and related ceremonial activities that could have been coordinated by a religious specialist or big man, such as an individual found interred in Mound B. The mound excavations strongly support Sigler-Lavelle's model of Weeden Island societal organization. They also indicate, just as predicted from Kohler's village investigations, that during the middle occupation period the McKeithen site served as a mound-village center.

Additional analyses of the mound's contents by Ann S. Cordell and Vernon J. Knight, Jr. (Cordell 1984; in Milanich, Cordell et al. 1984), yielded information on ceremonialism and ideology that helps in interpreting other Weeden Island cultures. It may be that this model of Weeden Island settlement and social systems and their relationship to mound ceremonialism can also be applied to the earlier late Deptford and Swift Creek cultures and to the Yent and Green Point ceremonial complexes. Just as there was great cultural continuity and similarity among the late Deptford, Swift Creek, and early Weeden Island cultures, so were there similarities among the ceremonial complexes (Brose 1979). The McKeithen mounds thus may provide important information not only for understanding Weeden Island but for interpreting other northern Florida cultures of the 100 B.C.–A.D. 750 period.

Mound B was at the apex of the triangular arrangement formed by the three mounds. The mound was originally constructed as a small, rectangular platform less than two feet high. This platform mound served as base for a rectangular building made of pine posts placed in individual post holes. Perhaps thatched (no evidence of daub was found) with rounded corners, the structure apparently functioned as the residence of a religious specialist or big man.

Within the building were several hearths. Small posts along the interior walls may have supported benches. Positioning of the interior posts suggested that the structure had been refurbished at least once. Food bones, quartz pebbles, mica flecks, red ochre, Weeden Island pottery, and stone artifacts were found strewn about the floor of the structure, especially against the interior walls and outside of the doorway.

The presumed resident of the house, an individual mid- to late thirties in age, died and was buried in a very shallow grave dug into the floor of the house. This person was either a very gracile man or a woman: the "big man" may have been a "big woman." The person was lying face up with arms bent at the elbows and palms up. Red ochre, possibly used to color the hair, was found beneath the skull along with a single piece of human occipital bone from another person. Also found under the back of the head was the lower leg bone (tibiotarsus) of an anhinga or water turkey (*Anhinga anhinga*). The piece of skull and the bird bone could have been parts of a headdress worn by the individual.

After having been placed in the grave the individual was allowed to lie exposed for an unspecified length of time, perhaps several days (it is also possible that the body was not in the grave when exposed). During that period rodents chewed on the body, leaving tooth marks on those skeletal elements covered only by thin layers of flesh or skin. Chewing marks, some large enough to have been from a dog, marred the person's shoulder, one upper arm, both shin bones, and even the brow ridge above the left eye.

As an adult, the individual had been shot in the left buttock (ilium) with an arrow. The 1.25-inch arrow point, similar to those found by Kohler in the village, was still embedded in the bone. William R. Maples, forensic anthropologist at the Florida Museum of Natural History, examined the wound and concluded the person had been shot at least several months before death. A severe infection had developed around the wound, especially next to the base of the point where pitch or another substance would have been used to haft the chert point to the arrow shaft. The infection could have been the cause of death.

After the body was exposed for a period of time, a small tomb made from vertical posts set into the ground (with some sort of covering) was erected over the shallow grave and the body within it. Then a small, low mound of earth was deposited over the grave and the tomb. The building containing this tomb was then burned to the ground and the charred remnants scattered. A red-painted bird head adorno broken off of a Weeden Island ceramic vessel was placed in a small hole dug near the individual's feet. Next a mantle of earth was placed over the entire platform mound, the small tomb containing the individual, and the charred remains of the rectangular structure strewn about the periphery of the platform. The result was a circular mound five feet high.

Ceramics recovered from the floor of the structure and from outside the door included portions of six Weeden Island Zoned Red oblong plates, each decorated with a stylized bird motif; portions of a stylized "column" or carved post may also be depicted on at least some of the plates. It is easy to speculate that the raptoral bird represented on the plates and by the bird-head effigy found near the burial were symbols associated with the house's occupant, the presumed religious specialist or big man. The average of three radiocarbon dates from the charred structure indicate that it had been built in A.D. 350.

Mound A, the largest mound at the McKeithen site, began like Mound B with the construction of a rectangular platform mound, much larger in extent than at Mound B, but still less than two feet high. Its main function seems to have been for ritual activities associated with cleaning human bodies for storage and later interment in Mound C. This apparently involved interring bodies, allowing them to decompose, and then cleaning the bones. The part of the platform mound on which this occurred was a rectangular area on the back portion of the platform.

This rectangular area contained a number of empty burial pits, most of which had been redug and reused. As many as ten pits or graves, some large enough for several bodies, were placed adjacent to one another. New pits overlapped old ones. From the size of the few single graves present, we can guess that the bodies were originally interred in flexed positions.

Large pine posts or markers, some more than two feet in diameter, were erected within the charnel area in the deep ends of long, narrow, sloping trenches. In some cases individual markers had been taken out of the ground, perhaps to be reused elsewhere in the charnel area.

Numerous small fire pits dotted the floor of the charnel area. Some were filled with ash and burned material that was not charred wood. Fire pits that used wood as fuel also were present. Liberal amounts of red ochre were strewn about the floor of the platform mound where the charnel activities took place. One pit contained the ochre supply.

This rectangular burial preparation area was centered exactly over a portion of the platform mound that had been partially built out of intentionally deposited alternating layers of soil and organic material. These strata appeared as five thin layers of alternating grey humus and tan sand, the two sand layers sandwiched between the three organic layers. All five overlay the ground surface under the platform mound.

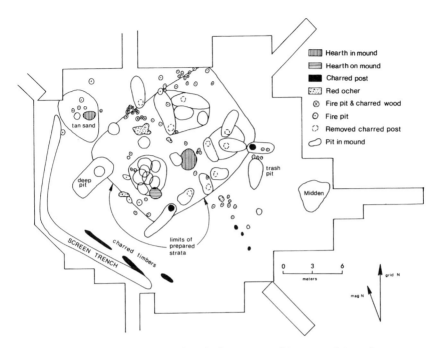

Various features on the top of the platform mound in Mound A at the McKeithen site.

They were covered by a layer of earth approximately eight inches thick, part of the same soil used to construct the rest of the platform mound. These alternating strata were thus buried in the platform mound and could not be seen from the mound's surface. Yet the charnel activities only took place on the mound's surface directly above the rectangular extent of these strata. The various pits that had contained human remains were dug down from the top of the platform mound into these banded layers.

A fire had been lit in a hearth on top of the specially prepared strata before the rest of the mound had been constructed over them. After the entire platform mound had been constructed, a curving screen of pine posts was set in an anchoring trench on the mound's surface. Its location suggests it shielded the mortuary area from the adjacent village.

When it was time to halt the activities on the platform mound, all of the human remains were removed from the pits dug into the mound.

Some of the marker posts were left in place, but the pole screen was removed and its posts placed on top of the rectangular charnel area and lit. The large fire that resulted left the soil in the mortuary area scorched. The fire also deposited a thick layer of ash. Some of the charred wood and ash from the fire was removed to the edges of the platform mound. The platform mound and the remains of the fire, including the charred debris moved to the side, were then covered with an oval-to-rectangular cap of sand 145 by 260 feet and 6 feet deep at the center. The sequence of fire, scattering burned debris, and ritually burying the platform mound and charred debris was the same as in Mound B. Five radiocarbon dates from the charred remains of the screen and post markers yielded an average date of A.D. 350, the same date as obtained from Mound B.

The ceramic assemblage recovered from Mound A was quite different from that present in Mound B. Ann Cordell's analysis of the 1,836 potsherds from the platform mound's surface indicated that at least twenty-seven separate vessels were represented. The collection closely resembles the types found in the village. The elite ceramics found in Mound B were not present, supporting the contention that the activities associated with Mounds A and B were quite different.

Some feasting, especially consuming deer, was associated with those Mound A activities. Arlene Fradkin's analysis of the bones of animals recovered from two small dumps on the platform mound (in Milanich, Cordell et al. 1984:102) identified parts, especially haunches, of at least nine deer. Other animal bones identified from the dumps came from a mallard duck, a ring-necked duck, and a fish.

In addition to the bones of animals and the ceramics, artifacts from the platform mound included mica, several stone knives or points, a quartz-sandstone grinding stone, and two small caches of freshwater mussel shells.

The cleaned bones resulting from the charnel activities on Mound A are thought to have been stored in a charnel house erected on a third platform mound, the platform within Mound C. Unlike the Mound A and B platform mounds, the Mound C platform was circular, about three feet high. The building on the mound, probably a charnel house, had wall posts that were beveled on their bases.

At some time, (radiocarbon dates suggest A.D. 480), the stored burials in the Mound C charnel house were removed, and the charnel house was burned to the ground. Unlike Mounds A and B, however, little or no effort was made to remove the burned debris. Clean soil was scattered over parts of the burned debris and bundles of human bones were placed around the edges of the platform. The bundles contained arm and leg bones, occasionally hands and feet, and skulls. Deposits of teeth and lower jaws also were placed on the platform. Sometimes a bundle contained bones or teeth from two or more individuals. Two flexed, partially articulated burials also were deposited. Both were probably partially cleaned before being placed on the mound. One was missing some skeletal parts, and the other did not have the bones arranged in proper anatomical position. The mound had been severely disturbed by modern looters prior to excavation, and the remains of the thirty-six people found in the mound are thought to be about 60 percent of the estimated fifty-seven people buried there.

As a part of the interment ritual a fire was lit on the eastern part of the platform mound atop the clean sand placed on the burned stratum. Bones of animals, perhaps the remains of a ceremonial meal, were found in and around this hearth. They included one fish, a mud turtle (*Kinosternon* sp.), and an unidentified rodent. The menu from this meal was quite different from that of the dining on Mound A.

The ritual associated with the fire on Mound B may have included the taking of sacred medicines, such as black drink, because immediately beside the hearth was a Weeden Island ceramic bowl with four animal-head effigies. The bottom of the unique vessel had been killed. The four animal heads were arranged evenly around the rim of the vessel. Two opposite one another are probably dogs; the other two may be vultures. The dog heads and one vulture head all faced inward, and the eyes of all three had been "blinded": while the clay was still wet a finger or thumb had been used to smudge the eyes of the animals, closing them. The fourth head, perhaps a bird, faced outward and was hollowed so it could function as a spout.

At least seventeen other Weeden Island vessels were placed on and beside the southeast quadrant of the platform mound in and around

Early Weeden Island Plain effigy vessel 5½ inches high at lip with animal-head adornos excavated from Mound C at the McKeithen site.

interments. The types and shapes of vessels are very like those found in early Weeden Island mounds excavated by C. B. Moore in north-west Florida and by William Sears (1956a) from the early Weeden Island mounds at the Kolomoki site in southwest Georgia. Numerous limestone and coarse sandstone rocks were also placed atop the primary mound with the pottery vessels.

Weeden Island Red derived turkey vulture effigy 8¾ inches high at lip with triangular cutouts from McKeithen Mound C.

After deposition of the human remains, the limestone rocks, the pottery vessels, and (after the ritual involving the fire and consumption of food had taken place) the entire platform mound and the deposits were covered with a mantle of earth six feet thick. The result was a Weeden Island burial mound.

In addition to the four-headed effigy bowl, the seventeen vessels placed on the Mound C platform mound at the McKeithen site included a number of ornate Weeden Island vessels. Two were pedestaled effigies, five were derived animal effigies, and three others depicted bird motifs or had bird-head adornos. The two pedestaled

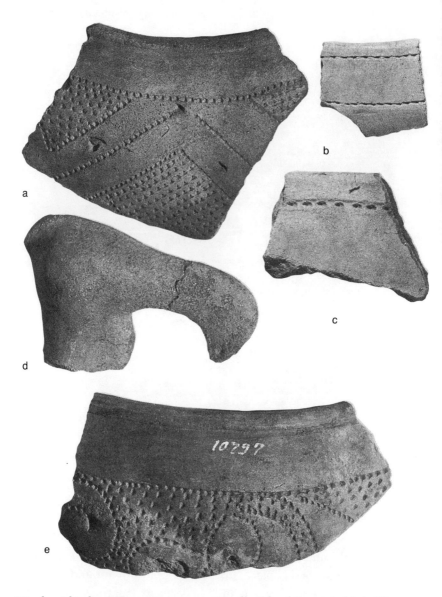

Weeden Island prestige pottery: *a–c, e,* Weeden Island Punctated (*a* is 2¾ inches high); *d,* bird-head effigy.

Weeden Island utilitarian pottery; *a–b,* St. Andrews Complicated Stamped (*a* is 2 inches high); *c,* New River Complicated Stamped; *d–f,* Carrabelle Incised; *g–i,* Carrabelle Punctated.

Weeden Island utilitarian pottery; *a–c,* Keith Incised (*a* is 2⅜ inches high); *d–g,* Weeden Island Plain rims.

effigies may represent a quail and an owl. Both have triangular cutouts as part of their decoration and both have hollow, flat bases. These effigies were never intended as vessels; with their hollow bottoms and the cutouts in their sides they could not have functioned as containers. Rather, they are sculptures made of fired clay. The battered bottoms on both suggest that the effigies had been placed on a tenoned pole or similar pedestal that protruded into their flat, hollow bases. One suggestion is that these and the other vessels originally were used at Mound A, where they perhaps were displayed on the marker posts. A single sherd from Mound A may have come from an effigy vessel, but it could not be cross-mended or fitted with certainty to any of the Mound C vessels. The effigy vessels from Mound C could also have been displayed in the charnel house on that mound.

When all of the ceramic vessels and sherds from the three McKeithen mounds and the village are taken as a whole and compared with other collections from Weeden Island sites such as Kolomoki, several informative trends are evident. One is that rather than simply a sacred-secular (mound vs. village/utilitarian) dichotomy in the distribution and presumed use of Weeden Island pottery, a tripartite division exists: mortuary pottery, prestige or elite pottery, and utilitarian (or village) pottery. Mortuary pottery includes the effigy vessels like those from Mound C at the McKeithen site and those excavated and described by Sears from Kolomoki (1956a). Such vessels depict animals and often have a hollow base. The heads and tails of the animals are hand modeled separately and attached to opposite sites of the vessels near the rims or shoulders. Frequently the vessels are red slipped and incised, or red paint is used to portray animal body contours, such as wings. The form of the animal may be further emphasized by circular or triangular cutouts made in the body of the vessel before firing. Animals portrayed on these mortuary vessels include vultures, owls, water and wading birds, dogs, panthers, deer, and, occasionally, reptiles or fish. Mortuary wares are found only in the contexts of charnel activities; the vessels or even sherds from them are never found in village middens.

Prestige or elite ware, the second class of Weeden Island pottery, is thought to have had relatively high value, limited distribution within sites, and special functions. These vessels are intricately incised, punctated, and/or painted and often depict highly stylized animals. Small, somewhat flattened animal effigy heads are applied to vessel rims or shoulders. The incised and punctated lobe, teardrop, and scroll designs on the bodies of the vessels portray stylized bird motifs. Designs may be set off or highlighted by closely spaced incised lines, cross-hatching, or small punctations. Vessel shapes include globular bowls and jars, squared jars, shallow plates, and uniquely shaped forms. Prestige vessels and sherds are most common in mounds but are found in village middens in relatively small amounts. At McKeithen 4 percent of the ceramics from the village were prestige wares. Apparently activities in which these vessels were used occurred both at mounds and in villages.

The third category of Weeden Island pottery is utilitarian ware, largely bowls and jars probably used in everyday cooking and storage activities. Most are undecorated. Decorative elements found are not as finely executed as on mortuary and prestige wares. Utilitarian Weeden Island pottery types were found in Mound A, where they may have been associated with feasting or with bone cleaning. They also were found in the McKeithen village, accounting for 96 percent of the village ceramics.

Ideology

Why are only certain animals portrayed on Weeden Island vessels, both mortuary and prestige wares? Why are animals portrayed at all? Why are Weeden Island mortuary wares or large amounts of prestige wares not found in villages? Reconstructing what may have gone on in the minds of people who lived and died hundreds of years ago is a difficult task, and we can only hope to sketch the broad outlines of aboriginal belief systems like those of the early Weeden Island societies in northern Florida.

To investigate Weeden Island ideology, Vernon J. Knight, Jr. (in Milanich, Cordell et al. 1984:163–184) has derived a model from the methods and theories of symbolic anthropology to explain both the animals portrayed and the context in which mortuary and prestige wares are found. The process of developing the model involved several assumptions and steps. The first assumption was that the animals depicted on Weeden Island vessels were important within the symbolic system of that culture. The next question was, Why these animals? Anthropologists know that all societies tend to attach symbolic importance to animals they judge to be anomalous within their classification system. These animals are anomalies because of behavior or appearance. For example, a duck or a wading bird may be anomalous

Weeden Island Incised derived duck effigy 8¾ inches high with triangular cutouts from the Hall Mound (Moore 1902: fig. 254; courtesy Smithsonian Institution).

because it moves from what is viewed as a normal habitat (the sky and trees) into an abnormal one (lakes). Other animals are seen as anomalous because they cross normal habitat boundaries into contexts that are important to humans, and they display what is interpreted as inappropriate behavior. Dogs, for example, are wolves, but they live with humans. These anomalous and boundary-crossing animals often become cultural symbols.

The next step is to look at the contexts of the animal symbols within the culture. The Weeden Island culture depicted the animals on clay vessels found in mortuary contexts; they are rare or absent in villages. Last, this knowledge is combined with information about the behavior of those animals to determine what the animals mean in the Weeden Island ideological system.

Information regarding belief systems of southeast native American Indians in the sixteenth, seventeenth, and eighteenth centuries aids in this process (Swanton 1946: Hudson 1976). Simply stated, the southeastern native Americans believed that the cosmos was organized into three worlds: the upper world, inhabited by special beings such as the sun and moon; this world, inhabited by the native peoples and including the earth, its waters, and the animal kingdom; and the underworld, inhabited by monsters and ghosts. The upper world represented order and unity, predictability and expectability. In opposition was the underworld, associated with change and disorder. The sun, an upper-world being, was represented on earth by fire, and ceremonial fires were never extinguished with water, associated with the underworld.

Native peoples lived between the upper and underworlds in this world. They sought to maintain the status quo between the two. Violating taboos disturbed the state of normalcy or homeostasis that generally prevailed, upsetting the balance of the three worlds. As a consequence, many rituals, such as the taking of black drink and other medicines, were performed to cleanse individuals of impurities, helping them to exist in a normal state and keeping balance in the world.

The southeastern peoples further believed that this world was inhabited by three types of nonspiritual beings: humans, animals, and plants. Humans and animals were seen as being in opposition to one another, while plants were viewed as the friends of humans. Animals, with which we are most concerned here, were classified into three groups: the four-legged animals (the most important of which was the deer), the birds (associated with the superior status of the upper world because of their ability to fly), and the vermin (including lizards, frogs, fish, and snakes).

Animals that did not readily fit into this tripartite classification system or that behaved abnormally by crossing boundaries were thought of as anomalous or special and were awarded ritual status. These are the animals depicted on Weeden Island vessels. Some examples are the kingfisher, a bird that normally should live in the forest eating insects, seeds, and berries and nesting in trees. As a bird, it is associated with the upper world and the sky. But kingfishers do not behave properly; they are anomalous. They dive into water to eat fish and make their nests in burrows in the muddy banks of rivers or lakes, habitats affiliated with the underworld. The crested birds depicted on some Weeden Island derived and pedestaled effigy vessels are probably kingfishers.

Dogs also are depicted on Weeden Island vessels. Unlike its relative the wolf, the dog lives with humans and eats discarded garbage and offal. And dogs are incestuous, thus guilty of further improper behavior. To the Weeden Island peoples, dogs probably were a symbol of impropriety. On the other hand, deer, a dietary mainstay, possibly symbolized proper behavior. Deer was a food that was ritually taken at feasts and other special occasions, including the feasting that took place on Mound A at the McKeithen site.

In order to maintain order in the cosmos and to keep this world at its proper position between the upper world and the underworld, it was necessary for anomalous animals, such as the kingfisher, to mediate between impropriety, symbolized by animals such as the dog, and propriety, symbolized by the deer. These mediating animal symbols were probably exhibited at many ceremonial occasions in Weeden Island life, and they undoubtedly had complex beliefs associated with them.

But why would these symbols be found in burial mounds or associated with the individual interred in Mound B at McKeithen? For an explanation it is again necessary to turn to anthropology and theories concerning ceremonial behavior, especially ceremonies that are rites of passage. Such rites include naming ceremonies, puberty rites, marriages, and funerals. Their common theme is that during the ritual, an individual changes status. In a naming ceremony an unnamed nonentity becomes a person with a true identity, a name. In a funeral, a person leaves the realm of the living and becomes an ancestor, a dead person.

Anthropologists (e.g., Turner 1969) have noted that in each rite of passage there is a period in which the initiate is between statuses. During this liminal period, which may last several hours or even days, a person may be secluded, may undergo special rites or fasting, or may be attired in a special costume. Rites of passage also may be community-wide ceremonies in which a society publicly exhibits or parades those symbols associated with shared values, such as those necessary for maintain the status quo. Ceremonies and displays of symbols, including the animals depicted on Weeden Island vessels, offer occasions to reinforce belief systems regarding the cosmos and the proper place of humans within it. Consequently, symbols associated with proper and improper behavior, life, death, vitality, and fertility are displayed and often juxtaposed.

What archaeologists excavated at Mound C at the McKeithen site was the end result of a rite of passage that involved the display of animal symbols, as well as fire building, food consumption, and probably the taking of sacred medicines. The bodies of the dead may have been involved in a long rite of passage. At death an individual entered a period of liminality: initial interment and decomposition in Mound A, followed by the cleaning of the bones. Later the cleaned remains were stored in a charnel house. If it did not end with storage in the charnel house, the period of liminality ended still later when the remains were deposited and buried in Mound C. Elaborate rituals, symbols, and behaviors would have surrounded this entire process, including the animal symbols so important to maintaining the stasis between proper and improper, between life and death, between the upper world and the underworld.

The animals depicted on the Mound B and C vessels and on other Weeden Island elite and mortuary wares are symbols—that is, ritually important animals. Some symbolize anomalous behavior, and therefore mediation; others symbolize improper behavior; and still others symbolize propriety. The spoonbills on a squared, globular Weeden Island bowl recovered from Mound C are mediating symbols. The spoonbill is a wading bird that feeds in shallow water, peculiar behavior for a bird. Adding to its anomalous nature are its spoon-shaped bill, its red color—a color associated with clay and earth—and its propensity for feeding with the ibis or wood stork, which is colored white and black (white is a color associated with the upper world). The ibis, depicted on another of the Mound C vessels, is itself anomalous, another bird that feeds in water.

Several of the derived effigies represent turkey vultures. Vultures, like dogs, probably are symbols of impropriety. These boundary-crossing birds stay close to villages, where they can dine on offal and carrion. The Mound C bowl with two dog-head and two vulture-head adornos may symbolize the height of impropriety. The hollow vulture head looking outward may also represent a tail, further emphasizing the impropriety symbolized in this vessel.

The two pedestaled effigies, an owl and a quail, also might be anomalous birds, mediators within the Weeden Island ideological system. Owls are nocturnal animals who are carnivores, while quail fly only in short bursts, live on the ground, and often are seen in coveys with their young, scurrying through the undergrowth like mammals.

Ritual animal symbols are exhibited in the bird-of-prey or vulture motifs depicted on the plate-form vessels found in Mound B and the ceramic bird head found buried next to the feet of the leader interred in Mound B. Certainly a rite of passage was associated with the burial of that person in the platform mound. The period of liminality was the time when the body was allowed to lay exposed. "Not alive," the person had yet to enter a new status, that of ancestor.

The mounds at the McKeithen site and their contents are not unique within the Weeden Island culture. Similar mounds and ceramic collections are known from a number of Weeden Island sites, though only at Kolomoki have excavations focused both on extensive village and mound contexts. Much of our data on other sites comes from the reports of C. B. Moore, which do not always provide contextual information as detailed as one would like.

One mound-village complex similar to McKeithen that Moore investigated is the Aspalaga site (Moore 1903a:481-488). Aspalaga, in Gadsden County in northwest Florida, like McKeithen, consists of three sand mounds arranged in a rough triangle around an apparent

Weeden Island Incised pedestaled owl effigy 8½ inches high from Mound Field (Moore 1902: fig. 298; courtesy Smithsonian Institution).

plaza. A horseshoe-shaped village curves around two sides of the plaza. One mound contained at least fifty-five burials, including flexed burials, bundled burials, and single-skull burials. A cache of pottery vessels present on the east side of the mound included a number of early Weeden Island vessels (Willey 1949a:390). Moore reports that the other two Aspalaga mounds were low and "domiciliary in character," suggesting that they were not burial mounds but, like McKeithen Mounds A and B, were probably platform mounds later covered with mound caps. Overall, the pattern of the mounds appears to resemble that at McKeithen.

The evidence from Mound C at McKeithen suggests that a ritual took place at the time interments were made, perhaps the taking of black drink or of other sacred teas. Similar ceremonialism is suggested

A unique polychrome funerary urn recovered from the Buck Mound in Fort Walton Beach. The extraordinary vessel, which is 15 inches high, apparently had been deliberately broken and the sherds scattered on the top of a primary mound (see Lazarus 1979; courtesy Fort Walton Temple Mound Museum).

from another early Weeden Island mound in northwest Florida, Davis Field Mound in Calhoun County (Moore 1903a:468–473). The mound was constructed in two stages. On the surface of a primary mound (perhaps a platform, as in McKeithen Mound C), a small mound or tomb had been built. Lying on top were three small bowls. Two shell drinking cups were placed on the side of the small mound, and immediately next to them was a hearth. All were then covered by the mound cap.

The models of Weeden Island society and ceremonialism derived from the McKeithen culture provide valuable insights into the lifeways of the early Weeden Island peoples. Those lifeways seem to have persisted until about A.D. 750. After that date, especially in northwest Florida, changes began to occur that ultimately resulted in a new social, political, and economic order. In northwest Florida these changes are first associated with the late Weeden Island–period Wakulla culture.

Wakulla Weeden Island Culture

Gordon Willey and Richard Woodbury's (1942) investigations on the panhandle coast recognized that in that region the Weeden Island ceramic complex changed over time. In the late Weeden Island period Wakulla Check Stamped pottery became the most common decorated type in nonmound contexts. Excavations by Joseph R. Caldwell (1978) at Fairchild's Landing on the lower Chattahoochee River and by Arthur R. Kelly (n.d.) on the Flint River clarified the geographical extent and temporal position of what has come to be called the Wakulla culture.

The Wakulla period, which dates from Weeden Island 3–5 periods according to Percy and Brose's (1974) chronology, lasts from about A.D. 750 to 950. Wakulla develops out of the early Weeden Island coastal and inland cultures of northwest Florida and reflects the adoption of maize agriculture into the Weeden Island economic system. Such an economic change had far-reaching implications for the native societies of the panhandle, leading to cultural changes that are manifested in the appearance after about A.D. 950 of the Fort Walton culture (see chapter 10).

The Wakulla region in northwest Florida.

Wakulla sites, like the early Weeden Island sites that preceded them, are distributed both along the coast and in the interior of northwest Florida, as well as in adjacent portions of southwest Georgia and southeast Alabama (e.g., Kelly n.d.; Sears 1963; Dickens 1971; Nance 1976; Percy and Jones 1976; Steinen 1976; Jeter 1977; Walthall 1980:167–171; Mikell 1993). Wakulla sites are rare east of the Aucilla River drainage in peninsular Florida. Eventually, inland and coastal variants of Wakulla culture may be defined. Although we have a relatively large amount of information about the inland culture, especially in the upper Apalachicola River valley, many questions about the coastal region remain unanswered, among them that of the relative importance of agriculture on the coast.

Archaeological surveys and investigations in interior northwest Florida suggest two Wakulla settlement trends: more sites than in the early Weeden Island period and sites in locales not previously occupied or only occupied sparsely (e.g., Percy and Jones 1976: Tesar 1980:600–604; White 1981a:702). Such data reflect larger populations and the necessity for people to locate in new areas, perhaps a result of both increased population and the need for soils suitable for maize agriculture. In his Leon County survey, Louis Tesar noted a marked preference by Wakulla peoples for soil types not preferred by earlier Weeden Island peoples.

George Percy and David Brose (1974:31–32) have described the Wakulla settlement patterning in northwest Florida:

> In late Weeden Island, there is a very significant increase in the number of sites; also, many sites are now established in the uplands bordering the east side of the upper Apalachicola [River]. These same basic trends—new site locations and many more sites—also appear to be characteristic of scattered localities throughout the Marianna Lowlands in central Jackson County and along the lower Chattahoochee and Flint rivers in southeastern Alabama and southwestern Georgia. These latter areas are not pioneered by late Weeden Island people, as is sometimes suggested; rather, Swift Creek and early Weeden Island occupations are present, but are less populous than late Weeden Island.

Percy and Brose (1974:74) offer the hypothesis that this change in settlement pattern involved "a significantly greater dependence on agriculture" undertaken by small family groups. Increased agriculture exhausted soil faster, requiring more settlement shifts; it eventually filled up the usable locales across the landscape. This in turn led to population pressure, in part an impetus for the subsequent development of the Fort Walton culture. Although this model has not been explicitly tested, it does explain the data collected thus far in the panhandle.

Another aspect of Wakulla settlements is the absence of the large nucleated villages and mound centers present in earlier Weeden Island times. The settlement stability and economic cooperation present in earlier periods probably eroded under the competition among smaller independent groups for agricultural lands. This time of relative social instability (Percy and Brose 1974:32) gave way to the new social and political order associated with the Fort Walton culture. With new economic systems came new social and political systems.

Mounds (or strata added to earlier mounds) associated with the Wakulla peoples for the burial of their dead also reflect the societal and settlement changes that occurred after A.D. 750. Although some of the ornate Weeden Island prestige vessels still are found in mounds, they are much fewer in number; the mortuary, pedestaled effigy vessels no longer were made. Cooperative ceremonial activities, like those suggested for the McKeithen site, disappeared along with cooperative economic efforts. No longer did one social group or village gain economic advantage and, hence, higher social status. Wakulla mounds were for the interment of family members and give little indication of the ceremonial and social elaboration present in early times. Often earlier mounds were reused, rather than new ones built, perhaps a decline in communal activities.

Our knowledge of how the Wakulla peoples lived is skewed, with most of the information coming from inland locales (but see Mikell 1993). In addition to the information from the surveys carried out by Louis Tesar (1980) in Leon County and Nancy White (1981a) in the Lake Seminole area near the confluence of the Flint and Chattachoochee rivers, most of the data come from the Torreya Ravines, on the eastern side of the Apalachicola River between the towns of Chattahoochee and Bristol. George Percy and his students carried out intensive archaeological surveys of sites in that region and excavated portions of a large Wakulla village site located in Torreya State Park (Percy 1971a, b; Percy and Jones 1976). Under the auspices of the Division of Archives, History, and Records Management (now Historical Resources), other investigations were carried out in the Torreya Ravines at the Sycamore site, a Wakulla household dating to about A.D. 860, and at a camp several miles away (Milanich 1974). The data gleaned from those projects are probably applicable to other Wakulla sites in the inland portions of the eastern panhandle, but it is doubtful if they can be said to describe the way of life of the coastal Wakulla peoples.

Within the Torreya Ravines two types of Wakulla settlements are found: short-term, special-use camps and villages. The camps are located along freshwater streams in the foothills of the ravines back from the Apalachicola River. At least some of these sites probably were deposited by deer hunters. Their size and the artifacts present differ from those of village sites.

The two village sites excavated are quite similar to each other. Both are characterized by "hot spots" of artifacts—concentrations of midden thought to be from individual households. At the Torreya State Park site, thirteen such house middens were strung out in a crescent-shaped line around the spring heads of a small creek (Percy 1971b). At least two distinct periods of occupation were noted, comparable to periods 3 and 5 in the Percy and Brose chronology. Although the community pattern was the same for both periods, the two villages were placed in spatially distinct areas. The best estimate of houses occupied at any one time is five to seven. Small burial mounds were constructed near the villages.

The community pattern at the Wakulla-period Sycamore site located farther north in the Torreya Ravines is much the same (Milanich 1974). Midden concentrations are thinly distributed over a roughly circular area about 900 yards in diameter. The early Weeden Island Aspalaga mound and village complex is located within the central portion of the Wakulla settlement area. The large, dense midden of the early Weeden Island nucleated village contrasts with the Wakulla pattern of small, widely spaced middens.

The Sycamore excavations focused on a single household area including a cold-weather house, a small midden off to one side that probably was associated with a second building (perhaps a warm-weather house), a second small midden (perhaps a second warm-weather house), and a freshwater shell midden (Milanich 1974; this interpretation differs from that published in the original report). These household features extend over an area about 100 by 150 feet.

Subsistence information gathered from the presumed winter house and the nature of the house itself—a wigwam or hothouse like those built in the Southeast in later times—suggests that the house was occupied during the fall and winter months. Evidence for the two

Nancy White in the early 1980s testing the Mercer site, a late Weeden Island village in Jackson County on the east side of Lake Seminole (courtesy University of South Florida).

nearby warm-weather houses is much less definitive because of erosion. However, presence of summer and winter structures within a single household would certainly be consistent with archaeological and ethnohistorical information from elsewhere in the Southeast (Swanton 1946:386–420; Faulkner 1977).

Food remains in the cold-weather structure and the shellfish midden show a tremendous reliance on deer and acorns, as might be

Late Weeden Island–period Wakulla sites.

expected from a fall occupation. In projected weight (ignoring shell-fish), venison accounted for 88.2 percent of the meat diet. Other mammals eaten include black bear, raccoon, rodent, wood rat, squirrel, and opossum. Turtles comprise the second-largest meat source. In addition, some freshwater fish, freshwater mussels and clams, and turkeys were eaten.

Plant remains from the winter house include acorns, walnuts, hickory nuts, and wild plums. Some maize kernels were recovered, indicating that maize horticulture was practiced by Wakulla peoples. The Sycamore site occupants gained much of their livelihood by hunting and gathering foodstuffs from the nearby river valley hard-wood forests and the small streams draining into the Apalachicola River. They also grew maize.

The Sycamore house structure, radiocarbon dated to the latter portion of the ninth century, was an oval wigwam about 18 by 27 feet. A description by John Lawson of an eighteenth-century Siouian wigwam from Virginia aptly describes the Sycamore house:

These [people] live in wigwams, or cabins built of bark which are made round, like an oven, to prevent any damage by hard gales of wind. They make the fire in the middle of the house and have a hole at the top of the roof right above the fire, to let out the smoke. These dwellings are as hot as stoves, where the Indians sleep and sweat all night. The floors thereof are never paved or swept, so that they have always a loose earth on them. The bark they make their cabins withal, is generally cypress or red or white cedar; and sometimes, when they are a great way from any of these woods, they make use of pine bark, which is the worser sort. In building these fabrics, they get very long poles of pine, cedar, hickory, or any other wood that will bend; these are the thickness of the small of a man's leg, at the thickest end, which they generally strip of the bark, and warm them well in the fire, which makes them touch and fit to bend, Afterwards, they stick the thickest end of them in the ground about two yards asunder, in a circular form, the distance they design the cabin to be (which is not always round, but sometimes oval) then they bend the tops and bring them together, and bind their ends with bark of trees, that is proper for that use, as elm is, or sometimes the moss that grows on the trees, and is a yard or two long, and never rots; then they brace them with other poles to make them strong, afterwards they cover them all over with bark so that they are very warm and tight; and will keep firm against all the weathers that blow. (quoted in Swanton 1946: 410–411)

The Sycamore house had a large shallow hearth in its center. Several circular fire pits or earth ovens with straight sides and basin-shaped bottoms also had been used for cooking. Later they were filled with discarded refuse. One such pit was inside the house, and two were outside near the door. In addition to cooking, the outside fire pits might also have been used to smoke meat. One was centered among several post molds, indicating, perhaps, a rack.

Several large, deep, circular storage pits (or wells) with straight sides and flat bottoms were spaced around the outside of the house. One inside contained large amounts of oxidized acorn meats and shells as well as hickory shells, maize kernels, and a wild plum seed. The depth of these pits, thirty to thirty-six inches, varied according to the depth of an almost impermeable clay zone that underlay the house; the deeper the clay stratum, the deeper the pit. It is possible that the pits were dug to gain access to the groundwater found above the clay.

The size of the house, its structural features, and the associated pits and artifacts all suggest that the structure was used during a portion of the year by a single family. The quantity of debris further suggests that the house was reoccupied over at least several years, perhaps as many as ten or more.

South of the house was the shellfish dump, which also contained other refuse, including animal bones, potsherds, ash, and charcoal. The dump probably accumulated over a similar period and likely represents garbage discarded by the occupants of the house. The charcoal and ash could have been cleaned out of the house hearth or the cooking pits and dumped with other garbage.

A large assortment of pottery, tools, and other artifacts was recovered from the winter house, the area immediately around it, and the two smaller house sites. The lithic assemblage is probably typical of inland Wakulla peoples in northwest Florida. Pottery types also are typical of the Wakulla Weeden Island culture, although the exact frequencies of pottery types probably vary through time across the region. At the Sycamore site, dating about A.D. 860, the ceramics included Wakulla Check Stamped (48 percent), undecorated (41 percent), and Northwest Florida Cob Marked (5 percent), with the remainder 6 percent.

Nearly all of the lithic tools were made of local chert. About 10 percent showed evidence of thermal alteration. One chert blade appears to have been manufactured out of material quarried in the Georgia Piedmont, as do several pieces of stone gorgets and a steatite sherd. None of the tools displayed a high degree of artisanship; all were

The Percy-Brose Weeden Island Chronology

Swift Creek	Swift Creek pottery, A.D. 200–1000
Weeden Island 1	Swift Creek pottery and the appearance of Weeden Island pottery.
Weeden Island 2	Increase in Weeden Island pottery, decrease in Swift Creek ceramics, and appearance of new Weeden Island types.
Weeden Island 3	Appearance of Wakulla Check Stamped pottery and further decrease in complicated stamping.
Weeden Island 4	Decline in previous Weeden Island types, increase in Wakulla Check Stamped pottery, and disappearance of complicated-stamped pottery.
Weeden Island 5	Wakulla Check Stamped most frequent (about 55 percent of all pottery), appearance of corncob marked pottery as a minority ware, limited occurrence of Weeden Island incised and punctated pottery.

worked only enough to make them functional. Only the Hernando projectile points showed any pressure retouch. The points (Bullen 1975:24) probably were used to tip the arrows.

Other tools included bifacial and unifacial end and side scrapers made from linear flakes and crude blades; turtle-backed scrapers made from expended cores; hafted, stemmed scrapers fashioned out of reworked projectile points or knives; and small flake scrapers. All of these scrapers were probably used to clean and process hides and to work wood and prepare split cane for making baskets. Small triangular knives, flake knives, and stemmed knives (the latter similar in appearance to stemmed Archaic projectile points) were common tools used for cutting. They might well have been salvaged from earlier sites. River cobbles were fashioned into crude choppers and hammers. Foods such as nuts and seeds could have been processed on flat grinding stones, some made of nonlocal granite, where they were ground with river cobbles. Fist-size quartz river rocks were used as cooking stones.

Other artifacts and ornaments used by the Wakulla Weeden Island peoples are hematite paint stones, from which red pigment was taken to decorate pottery and probably to paint other items; flat, slate gorgets used as bow-string wrist guards or ornaments; shell pendants, both circular and shoehorn-shaped; and fired clay pipes. The pipe stems, measuring a little more than an inch in diameter, had a small hole cast in them to draw the smoke through. The hole was made by placing a twig in the unfired clay stem. During firing the twig burned out, leaving the hole. Pottery earspools more than two inches in diameter were worn by some individuals.

The Sycamore excavations provide a detailed look at a single Wakulla household at a single point in time. Such family-based households were probably widely distributed across the interior of northwest Florida, as well as on the coast. As we shall see in chapter 10, these people were the immediate ancestors of the Fort Walton culture. The distributions of the Wakulla and Fort Walton cultures are much the same.

In the chapter that follows, the Weeden Island cultures of peninsular Florida are described. As we shall see, aspects of ceremonialism were like those of the more northernly Weeden Island cultures that inhabited different environments and had different histories. Certain beliefs and practices must have been shared by many of the people of precolumbian Florida.

Weeden Island Cultures of Peninsular Florida

6

During the period that Weeden Island cultures flourished in north and northwest Florida, other Weeden Island cultures occupied north-central Florida and the peninsular Gulf coast from Charlotte Harbor north. Those cultures shared aspects of Weeden Island ideology, as evidenced by the Weeden Island ceramics found in burial mounds. But their styles of village life differed from one another and from the Weeden Island heartland cultures. Each of the peninsular Weeden Island cultures adapted to its local environment.

In each peninsular region where Weeden Island mounds are found, cultural developments differed over time, and the sequences of cultures present after 500 B.C. were distinct from each another and from the sequences of the heartland region. For instance, as noted in chapter 4, Deptford sites are found on the north peninsular Gulf coast but are much less common south of Levy County and are absent on the central peninsular Gulf coast. Swift Creek sites are absent on the peninsular Gulf coast and in north-central Florida. Deptford sites are found in north-central Florida, but in that region Deptford developed into Cades Pond, a cultural adaptation to the extensive wetland resources of that area.

The situation is even more complicated. In the central portion of the Gulf coast, from Charlotte Harbor to the Withlacoochee River, the late Weeden Island–period cultures developed into the Safety Harbor

Weeden Island cultures in peninsular Florida.

culture. But that culture was not present in north-central Florida, where the Cades Pond culture was replaced by the Alachua culture, whose origins probably lie in the Georgia coastal plain.

This bewildering list of cultures results from several factors. First, Florida's varied environments led to the evolution of a variety of pre-columbian cultures, often in relatively close proximity to one another. Second, utilitarian pottery of Weeden Island–period cultures of the central and north peninsular coasts is largely undecorated or decorated with motifs not temporally sensitive, thwarting archaeologists' attempts to use ceramic types to order those cultures in time. Recognizing and differentiating an A.D. 300 site from an A.D. 900 site in Dixie or Pasco counties can be embarrassingly difficult without data from excavations that produce radiocarbon dates or without extremely large samples of pottery. It is nearly impossible to assign cultural provenience to a small sample of potsherds that may contain all undecorated specimens with a variety of paste types. Third, following Willey's initial research on the Gulf coast in the 1940s, for several decades relatively little research built on his work.

Adding to this uncertainty and confusion was the failure of early archaeologists to recognize the sacred-secular dichotomy in ceramic assemblages. Although ceramics from mounds on the Gulf coast could be compared to ceramic sequences from northwest Florida, the peninsular coast utilitarian assemblages—largely undecorated pottery—could not be tied to the better-known ceramic sequences. It was not recognized that the people who made undecorated pottery could be associated with a mound that contained Weeden Island ceramics.

Still another factor was what in chapter 4 was termed the "ceramic transition problem." The geographical distribution of utilitarian ceramic assemblages along the Gulf coast from the panhandle in the northwest, with its well-defined ceramic sequence, to Charlotte Harbor represents a continuum. Village sites on the Gulf coast from Sarasota County to Taylor County are characterized by distributions of undecorated pottery containing limestone, quartz sand, or Fuller's earth as temper, paste inclusions, or both. Because the geographical and temporal distributions of these ceramic paste categories overlap— ceramic transitions—it has been almost impossible to do much more than focus on specific sites. Before the 1990s no synthesis was undertaken, except in the central Gulf coast region where a relatively large amount of data from a number of sites exists. The result of all of these factors has been a great deal of uncertainty by archaeologists when dealing with the cultures of the peninsular coast north of Charlotte Harbor.

But the confusion concerning coastal cultures is being cleared up. New data are being collected from excavations and surveys, older data are being reexamined, and a more complete picture of the coastal cultures is emerging. In the sections that follow we will examine some of these new interpretations for three regions: the north peninsular coast, the central peninsular coast, and north-central Florida.

North Peninsular Coast

The north peninsular Gulf coast, from Pasco County northward to Taylor County, is not a homogenous region, for a great deal of ceramic variation exists. Fortunately, we have recent overviews by Timothy Kohler (1991) and Nina Borremans (1991) to help clarify the Weeden Island–period cultures. Kohler's study resulted in part from survey work he and G. Michael Johnson undertook in Dixie County for Washington State University (Kohler and Johnson 1986; Johnson and Kohler 1987). That project built on earlier excavations by Kohler (1975) at the Garden Patch site in Dixie County. Borremans's research was stimulated by the University of Florida's ongoing Seahorse Key Maritime Adaptations Program in Levy County, directed by Michael Moseley (Borremans and Moseley 1990; Jones and Borremans 1991).

Pertinent archaeological surveys and excavations carried out in the Cove of the Withlacoochee in Citrus County (Weisman 1986; Mitchem 1989) have further helped to unravel the story of the precolumbian cultures. These new data can be used to interpret better the work carried out by Adelaide and Ripley Bullen and other excavators at sites along the coast, including the Crystal River site with its Yent complex burial mound and surrounding platform (e.g., Moore 1903b: 379–413, 1907:406–425, 1918:571–573; Bullen and Bullen 1950, 1953, 1954, 1961b, 1963; Bullen 1951a, 1953b, 1965, 1966; Weisman 1987).

One theme emerging from these studies is that defining a north peninsula Gulf coast region is not necessarily a useful concept when trying to understand the aboriginal cultures of its six coastal counties, although it may be a useful taxonomic device for writing a book. Even though the distance along southern Pasco County to northern Taylor County is only about 155 miles, the length of indented coastline is more than ten times that figure, offering ample space for geographical variations in cultures.

The region also is much more environmentally diverse than it first appears. The coastal marshes, extensive in places, are fed by freshwater rivers (e.g., the Aucilla, Suwannee, Waccasassa, Withlacoochee, and Crystal rivers) and creeks, which in turn are fed by wetlands. Some of the latter are huge, such as Gulf Hammock in Levy County, Chassahowitzka Swamp in Hernando County, and the Cove of the Withlacoochee in Citrus County. Near the coast and in adjacent inland

Weeden Island–period archaeological sites in the Gulf coastal regions.

1   Battery Point
2   Bayshore Homes
3   Burtine Island
4   Crystal River
5   Garden Patch
6   Gator Mound
7   Hope Mound
8   Horseshoe Point
9   Manatee Springs
10 Myakkahatchee
11 Safford Mound
12 Sarasota County Mound
13 Seahorse Key
14 Shired Island
15 Thomas Mound
16 Wash Island
17 Weeden Island

areas, stands of pine and scrub lowlands are common, although hardwood hammocks also occur. In several places, such as in Taylor County and the region around Crystal River, extensive hardwood hammocks once extended to the coast. In interior Hernando County, forested rolling hills predominate, topography quite different from the rest of the coastal region.

Nina Borremans (1991) has offered this cogent description of the region:

The north peninsular Gulf coast lies within the Gulf Coastal Lowlands province.... Inland from the Gulf a series of old dune lines runs parallel to the coast and interrupts the gentle westward slope.... The interior coastal mainland is a patchwork of upland hammocks and ridges and

lowland wetlands, including sawgrass marshes, vast cypress and hardwood swamps, and bayheads. . . . Unlike the rest of Florida, much of the
north peninsular coastline has not been ditched, diked, graded, filled or
otherwise altered by modern development, giving us a glimpse of what a
soggy place the Gulf coast of Florida used to be.

To document thoroughly the various ceramic assemblages found in
the region would require sampling each ecological zone, including
each drainage-estuary system. However, progress has been made in
geographically documenting ceramic assemblages, although a lack of
radiocarbon dates still makes it difficult to order the assemblages in
time.

Numerous islands dot the shoreline of the north peninsular Gulf
coast. Rather than being true barrier islands, these offshore keys were
formed either as the Gulf inundated the coastline, making islands of
tracts of land of various sizes, or they are relic Pleistocene sand dunes.
The latter, most common from Levy County north, are high enough
(up to forty-five feet above sea level) to escape being inundated by the
Gulf.

As during earlier periods, the shallow waters of the Gulf of Mexico
and the salt marsh and tidal stream systems provided the coastal
dwellers with a variety of fish, shellfish—especially oysters—and
water birds. The inland wetlands, such as the Cove of the Withlacoochee, also provided mollusks—mostly freshwater snails—fish, and
other animals.

Ceramic Variations and Settlements

Deptford sites extend down the peninsula coast at least as far as the
Cedar Key region, although Deptford pottery and an occasional site
are found even farther south. Below Cedar Key in Citrus, Hernando,
and Pasco counties the most prevalent ceramic assemblage during
Deptford times is a mixture of undecorated wares whose paste contains either sand (quartz) or crushed limestone. The limestone type,
called Pasco Plain, seems to be related to Perico Plain, an earlier limestone-tempered type found in the central Gulf coast region (Willey
1949a:364–365; what are sometimes described as limestone inclusions
can be Fuller's earth, see Mitchem 1986).

Throughout the northern peninsular coast region after the end of the Deptford period, about A.D. 100, these same two wares (Pasco Plain and sand-tempered plain) continue to predominate at Weeden Island–period village sites on the coast and at some inland locations. Depending on relative north-south location on the coast, the exact percentages of these two undecorated wares differ, as do the relative percentages of decorated sherds, which are nearly always minority types on the coast. For instance, Kohler and Johnson (1986:14) have noted that in southern Taylor County at what is probably a post–A.D. 100 village site, Swift Creek pottery constituted as much as 10 percent of an otherwise largely undecorated ceramic assemblage. Just to the south in Dixie County, excavations at Shired Island (Goldburt 1966) and the Garden Patch site (Kohler 1975) yielded utilitarian assemblages that were almost all undecorated (about 90 percent). At those two sites sand-tempered sherds were 80 percent of the total and limestone-tempered pottery 20 percent. Decorated sherds were of a variety of minority types, including Swift Creek, Weeden Island, and cord-marked types. St. Johns paste sherds, as at most sites in the region, also are a minority type. The Shired Island and Garden Patch sites are thought to span at least the Weeden Island period.

Farther south in Levy County, Jones and Borremans (1991) located thirty-seven sites in Gulf Hammock thought to span approximately the same period, A.D. 300–1200. They report that at some sites Pasco Plain pottery predominated, although undecorated pottery with quartz inclusions was the most frequently occurring ware overall. The most common surface decoration was check stamping, usually never more than 8 percent at any one site. Other decorated pottery types were present, such as Weeden Island, but in very small amounts.

Still farther south in coastal Citrus County—such as in the middens associated with the Crystal River site, the nearby Wash Island site, and several sites on Burtine Island—and in coastal Hernando County at the Battery Point site, the Weeden Island–period assemblages (and those extending probably to several hundred years B.C.) contain a higher percentage of limestone-tempered ware. At Crystal River, 84 percent of the pottery was limestone tempered (Bullen 1953b); at Wash Island, 57 percent limestone tempered, 13 percent decorated (Bullen and Bullen 1963); and at Battery Point, 71 percent limestone tempered, 14 percent decorated (Bullen and Bullen 1953b). Two sites on Burtine Island had 43 percent limestone-tempered and 3 percent decorated ware, and 51 percent and 9 percent, respectively (Bullen 1966a). As yet, there is no reliable seriation to order these collections in time.

A third site on Burtine Island is a complete anomaly. Only 6 percent of the pottery was limestone tempered, and 48 percent was the type Ruskin Dentate Stamped (Bullen 1966a). Other decorated ceramics from the two tests in this site include cob-marked sherds.

Almost all of the coastal Weeden Island–period sites are shell middens in which oysters are most common. Some middens are strung out along the edge of the salt marsh, often with open water close by. Others are adjacent to estuaries, such as on the Crystal River. Many of the shell middens are linear, several hundred yards long, while others are amorphous in shape. Rarely are they more than five or six feet high. But there are exceptions, such as in the Cedar Key area where much higher shell middens are located (Bullen and Dolan 1960). Rich humic middens with only small amounts of shell are found at a few sites, often occurring with shell middens.

Weeden Island (and earlier) burial mounds are present at coastal village sites, though at times they are found away from habitation areas (e.g., Gator Mound in Levy County, Jones and Borremans 1991:63–64). C. B. Moore excavated in a number of Weeden Island burial mounds along the coast from Taylor County to Pasco County, including at the Horseshoe Point mound complex and the Crystal River site (for summaries of Moore's mound excavations and those by other early archaeologists, see Willey 1949a:301–330). Those two sites, and perhaps others in the region, such as the Garden Patch site just south of the Horseshoe Point site, could at various times have been intervillage centers like the McKeithen site described in the previous chapter. Indeed, there is no reason to suppose that the social and political system of these coastal Weeden Island–period villagers differed greatly from those present in the Weeden Island heartland region to the north.

Cultures with a coastal settlement and economic system were not the only ones present in the north peninsular Gulf coast region during the Weeden Island period. Inland in Taylor, Dixie, and Levy counties, in some cases only a few miles inland, Kohler and Johnson (1986) found sites whose ceramic assemblages are related to the post–A.D. 600

Alachua culture of north-central Florida (see chapter 9). That culture is associated with a way of life quite different from that of the coastal villagers. At some of these Alachua-related sites the two distinct ceramic assemblages, Alachua and coastal Weeden Island, are both present. Similar Alachua-related ceramics have also been noted at Manatee Springs (Bullen 1953a) and at sites in Levy County (Milanich 1971:3).

Could two such different cultures occupy the same general region at the same time? Kohler (1991:98, 101) suggests that indeed this could be the case. Alachua farmers expanded into regions near the coast suitable for agriculture, while Weeden Island–period peoples continued to live on the coast proper, each occupying and exploiting a different environmental niche. The Alachua-related sites surveyed by Kohler and Johnson tend to be closer to soils better suited for agriculture than do the Weeden Island–period sites. One such Alachua-related village near Chiefland recorded by archaeologists in the early 1970s was in a similar setting, and a burial mound was present. No evidence has yet been found to support the suggestion that agriculture was present at these inland Alachua-related sites. Perhaps other reasons for the expansion of Alachua-related populations into the northern peninsular Gulf region should also be explored.

Surveys and excavations in the Cove of the Withlacoochee, inland in Citrus County and south of the distribution of Alachua-related sites documented by Kohler and Johnson, have turned up sites characterized by the same Pasco ware present immediately west on the coast proper. Weisman's (1986) tests at the Board Island site, which produced a radiocarbon date of A.D. 520, and collections from a number of other sites on both sites of the Withlacoochee River, some in westernmost Marion and Sumter counties (Johnson 1987), all are dominated by undecorated, limestone-tempered pottery. In villages in that region, Pasco limestone-tempered ware continued to be used throughout the later Safety Harbor period as well (Mitchem 1989), just as it was on the coast.

Weisman's surveys indicate that within the extensive wetlands of the cove, early Weeden Island–period peoples lived adjacent to the Withlacoochee River and its back swamps, locales where they could fish and collect freshwater snails and mussels. After about A.D. 600, Weisman's data suggest "a general shift away from a riverine-based subsistence," possibly correlated with "the need for better-drained agricultural soils" (1986:20). Thus, as in the area immediately to the north where Alachua-related sites are found, populations developing or moving into suitable locations for cultivation at a relatively early date are suggested. Evidence for what crops may have been grown or the nature of the agricultural practices is lacking, however. As in other parts of northern Florida, it is uncertain that maize agriculture actually was present before about A.D. 1000.

Subsistence Activities

During the Weeden Island period the peoples living in the north peninsular Gulf coast region can be matched with several different subsistence systems, each correlated with different environmental niches. The people on the coastal salt marshes and near the mouths of freshwater rivers lived like their coastal ancestors. They collected shellfish (mainly oysters); fished (catfish, sharks, mullet, jack, sheepshead, drum); hunted deer, raccoon, bear, opossum, and other animals; and collected small mammals, wild plants, and a variety of marine, land, and freshwater turtles. But marine resources were their mainstay. Kohler (1975) calculates that 75 percent of the meat in the diet of the people at the Garden Patch site in Dixie County came from the salt marsh and from the shallow inshore waters of the Gulf.

The ceramic assemblage associated with these people is largely undecorated, and sherds are tempered with limestone or contain quartz inclusions; at least during the Weeden Island period both wares are present at the same sites. Many of their tools probably were wood and have not been found by archaeologists. What we do have are a very few flint chips and a large number of tools made from conch and whelk and clam shells, including hafted hammers, pounders, picks, adzes, anvils, cups, celts, and perforators (Borremans 1991). Stone and bone tools (points and basketry-making fids) also are present. It is highly likely that all of the gear—nets and the like—present in earlier cultures such as the Deptford culture also were in use.

A second subsistence system was that practiced by the early Weeden Island–period peoples living in the Cove of the Withlacoochee and probably in other riverine and freshwater wetland locales as well. Their subsistence pattern was like that described by Weisman (1986) for the cove, with heavy reliance on riverine resources. Most of their pottery was undecorated and tempered with limestone.

Still another economic system possibly included horticulture and, if Kohler, Johnson, and Weisman are correct, first appeared in the north peninsular Gulf coast region after about A.D. 600. If this is true, then inland Alachua and possibly Suwannee Valley culture farmers might have expanded west into Taylor, Dixie, and Levy counties, establishing homesteads in locales suitable for cultivating crops. Horticultural practices were possibly adopted by the peoples in the Cove of the Withlacoochee and similar inland wetland locales. But although food production, and perhaps gardening, may have been added to their economic system, the cove dwellers did not relinquish the riverine and other wetland resources so important to them.

As Kohler has suggested (1991:98), the coastal hunter-gatherers and inland farmer-gatherers in the north peninsular Gulf coastal region would have interacted, developing mechanisms for mutually beneficial exchanges of food and other resources. If these exchanges are reflected in what appear to be nonlocally made potsherds at the various post–A.D. 600 sites in the region, such mechanisms were indeed present.

The question of whether agriculture was present during the Weeden Island period in this region remains unresolved. To date, definitive evidence—charred cobs or kernels—have not been found at any precolumbian sites in the north peninsular Gulf coast region. Nor have any other cultigens been identified.

Mounds and Ceremonialism

Our knowledge of the ideology and ceremonialism of the Weeden Island–period peoples and their immediate ancestors in the north peninsular Gulf coast region is based heavily on the work of C. B. Moore and other early archaeologists. No archaeologist since the 1930s has excavated a Weeden Island–period mound in that region, leaving us to rely on the sketchy descriptions in Moore's reports (1902, 1903b, 1907, 1918) and the more complete records of the 1896 Pepper-Hearst Expedition (see Bullen, Partridge, and Harris 1970; Smith 1971b). Unlike the village middens of the region, ceramic inventories from some mounds do contain significant amounts of decorated Weeden Island pottery. Earlier mounds related to the Yent complex also are present. Green Point complex mounds, however, apparently are not present in peninsular Florida.

The earliest north peninsular coast mounds are contemporary with the Deptford mounds of the northwest Florida coast, and at least one of them, Crystal River, was used by William Sears (1962) in his original definition of the Yent complex. Today a state park, the Crystal River site—a complex of shell middens, shell mounds and platforms, and two burial mounds, one with a surrounding platform enclosed by a circular embankment—is located on the bank of the Crystal River several miles from the Gulf. The village areas at the site probably span the millennium and a half after A.D. 1. It is possible that some or all of the platform and shell mounds and the smaller burial mound date from the Safety Harbor period, but this is uncertain. A large piece of limestone with a crude figure incised on it found at the site has been described as a stela, a stone marker set upright in the ground (Bullen 1966b), but its true function is unknown.

The larger burial mound with its platform and surrounding enclosure was excavated by Moore during three visits to the site. Ripley Bullen (1953b, 1965) later excavated in these earthen structures as well. Bullen's analysis of Moore's reports and his own excavations led him to suggest that the mound, platform, and enclosure actually were constructed and used over several hundred years, a conclusion with which Sears concurs (1962:5). Earliest construction was the lower portion of the mound itself, which contained the Yent artifacts; next, the surrounding platform and earthen enclosure were built; lastly, additional strata were added to the mound. At least some of the later features were constructed in the early Weeden Island period. Bullen's suggestion that the upper portion of the mound with its bundled burials dates from the late Weeden Island period appears to be in error.

Within the Yent portion of the mound, a number of shell, metal, and bone artifacts like those from the Pierce and Yent mounds in northwest Florida clearly show the relatedness of the complex to Hopewellian-affiliated complexes elsewhere in the Southeast and the Midwest. The artifacts include copper pan pipes; copper earspools, some with natural silver plating and one with pearl insets; elongate plummets (of copper, shell, and stone); a cut panther jaw and the worked teeth of other carnivores, including bear, believed to be parts

The largest shell mound at the Crystal River site in 1964, when a significant portion was being removed. Few visitors to the site, today a state historic site, realize that the present mound is only about half of its original size. When the mound was built is uncertain (photograph by Ripley Bullen; courtesy Florida Museum of Natural History).

Adelaide Bullen standing beside the famed Crystal River stele in 1966. The limestone rock has a crudely drawn face and upper torso etched on it (see Bullen 1966b). Whether the rock was actually used as a stele is uncertain (courtesy Florida Museum of Natural History).

of masks; two-hole, stone bar gorgets; cut shell ornaments (oblong and circular gorgets, a flower-shaped ornament with central perforation and six petals, and "scoop-shaped" ornaments); and platform pipes (Moore 1903b:397–413; Sears 1962). Although a few of these types of shell artifacts—though not the copper ones—have been reported in collections taken from other mounds in the north peninsular Gulf coast, none of those sites is known to have the rich assortment of materials recovered from Crystal River. Crystal River appears to have been a center associated with trade routes that reached from Florida northward into the contemporaneous cultures of the midwestern United States.

The ceramics from the Crystal River mound include Yent complex types, many with functional podal supports (Willey 1949a:319–322; Sears 1962; Bullen 1965). As in the Yent mounds in northwest Florida, miniature vessels are found at Crystal River, as are uniquely shaped vessels (e.g., a four-lobed tetrapodal vessel and a doughnut-shaped vessel with three spouts). Some vessels have flanged or T-shaped rims or scalloped and notched rims, and at least one has a hand motif incised on it. Specific pottery types from the Yent mound include Crystal River Incised, Crystal River Negative Painted, Crystal River Zoned Red, Pierce Zoned Red, Swift Creek Complicated Stamped, and Deptford Check Stamped. In addition a few examples of Weeden Island Plain, St. Johns Plain, and Oklawaha Incised vessels came from the mound.

In contrast to this assemblage are the ceramics excavated by Moore from the surrounding platform and enclosure, which contain early Weeden Island–period pottery like that found in mounds in north and northwest Florida, including various Weeden Island Plain, Incised, and Punctated mortuary wares. Also present are the types St. Johns Plain, St. Johns Incised, and Crystal River Incised and various Swift Creek series ceramics.

By Moore's calculations this ceremonial complex, measuring 270 feet across, contained 411 human burials. Gordon Willey suggests the complex probably contained 500–600 people (1949a:317), about 60 percent primary burials (bodies placed directly in the earth) and the remainder secondary burials, either bundled burials or single skull, which had been cleaned or stored prior to burial. Relative to other Gulf sites, Crystal River must have functioned as an important center for a number of years just prior to and into the early Weeden Island period.

Other mounds along the coast must be contemporary with the pre–Weeden Island deposits at Crystal River, but no single component mounds of that period have yet been reported. Some, like the Aucilla River mound reported by Moore (1902:325–330, 1918:564–567), may date from both the Yent complex and the early Weeden Island periods.

Early Weeden Island–period mounds, many with Swift Creek ceramics in them, are much more common in the region than are Yent complex–related mounds, suggesting that during or just prior to the Weeden Island period burial mound ceremonialism became widespread on the coast. The ceramics from the coastal mounds are much the same as the early Weeden Island assemblage found in mounds in northern Florida, including derived effigies. But it has not been established that the ornate, pedestaled effigy vessels—Weeden Island mortuary ware—are present in Gulf coast mounds.

Many of the Gulf coast mounds appear to be of the continuous-use type, with strata and burials—both primary and secondary—added over time. Some contain early and late Weeden Island pottery, also indicating use over considerable periods of time. Other burial mounds might have been built in a single episode, and some of these contain a mass interment of secondary burials.

Two early Weeden Island–period mounds located at the southern end of the northern peninsular Gulf coast region were excavated by members of the Pepper-Hearst Expedition in 1896. Hope Mound, in western Pasco County, was excavated by Wells M. Sawyer, the artist and photographer for the now-famous expedition. The expedition was led by Frank Hamilton Cushing (Smith 1971b). Later that year Cushing and the expedition's members would excavate the Key Marco site in Collier County (see chapter 8).

Sawyer's field notes, interpreted by Samuel Smith (1971b), suggest that the mound was built in at least two stages. The early stage may have been a circular-to-oval platform mound, similar to the platform in Mound C at the McKeithen site; a central burial was placed under the platform mound (Smith 1971b:126). Most of the ceramics and other artifacts recovered were apparently deposited on the surface of the primary mound, although burials and some artifacts came from within the platform as well. Ceramics included St. Johns Plain, Dunns Creek Red, and Pasco Plain vessels, some of which were quite small, four to five inches in diameter and approaching the size of Yent miniature vessels. A Dunns Creek Red effigy vessel depicting a gourd dipper was found, along with at least several *Busycon* shells. Overall, 27 percent of the ceramics were undecorated with quartz paste inclusions, 23 percent were limestone tempered, 27 percent St. Johns Plain, and 22 percent Dunns Creek Red. Less than 1 percent, literally a handful of sherds, were Swift Creek, Weeden Island, Oklawaha Plain, and Oklawaha Incised.

On the surface of the primary mound at least one individual was buried near a cache of flat copper ornaments and a mass of shell and pearl beads. Copper items are found in many west and north Florida mounds of the period A.D. 100–300, roughly the period of the late Yent and Green Point complexes. An upper sand stratum covered the primary mound. A number of individuals were buried in the upper portion of this stratum; many were secondary interments, suggesting use of a charnel house. The construction sequence of the mound is similar to that of the McKeithen mounds.

Another similarity with the McKeithen and other Weeden Island mounds is evidence for a black drink ceremony. Shell cups and ceramic vessels were found with a hearth on the surface of the primary mound. A large ceramic vessel was found on the hearth, around which were placed a pan-shaped vessel (possibly for parching leaves), a miniature pot with a killed bottom, three gourd-shaped water jars (one killed), one large killed bowl, and a second bowl. These were accompanied by six *Busycon* drinking cups, all suggestive that medicines were brewed and drunk as a part of the burial ceremony.

The same pattern of mound use is found at another early Weeden Island mound just south of the north peninsular Gulf region in northern Pinellas County. Excavation of the Safford Mound also was carried out by the Pepper-Hearst Expedition in 1896, directed by Cushing himself. Ripley Bullen, William Partridge, and Donald Harris (1970; and see Smith 1971b) analyzed the materials from the mound, guided by Cushing's field notes. The mound contained a very large number of Weeden Island vessels along with Swift Creek, Crystal River Incised, Oklawaha Incised, and Deptford vessels. The full range of Weeden Island Incised, Punctated, and red-painted mortuary pottery was present, including at least two lobed vessels and a compartmental vessel. Small amounts of Safety Harbor pottery were also recovered.

The mound seems primarily to have been used during the early Weeden Island period, although it may have been reused later. It is impossible to document mound construction from the limited information on hand, but Cushing's notes do refer to charred posts, which may be the remains of an intentionally burned charnel house. The ceramic vessels were found in small caches at a number of locations within the mound.

Other artifacts include greenstone celts, a variety of large lithic blades and other lithic tools, *Busycon* cups, pieces of copper, and many plummets made from bone, shell, quartz crystal, and stone. Pieces of galena (a shiny grey mineral) and mica also were found.

The lack of data from good archaeological contexts makes it difficult to assess the exact relationships between the Weeden Island period cultures of the north peninsular Gulf coast and the contemporary Weeden Island heartland cultures. At this time, however, the evidence we do have suggests a great deal of similarity between the mounds of the two regions. Presently, no data suggest that the two regions did not share many aspects of social and political organization as well. As we shall see in the next section, Weeden Island mounds, and perhaps other cultural similarities, also extended southward into the central peninsular Gulf coast region.

Manasota and the Central Peninsular Coast

The central peninsular Gulf coast region extends from Pasco County south to Sarasota County through Pinellas, Hillsborough, and Manatee counties. Inland the region reaches nearly to the Peace River drainage in Polk, Hardee, and DeSoto counties.

During the Deptford and early Weeden Island periods (and encompassing what has been called the Perico Island period), this was the territory of the Manasota culture. For a time (A.D. 300–700) the Manasota culture, which derives its name from Manatee and Sarasota counties, practiced early Weeden Island burial ceremonialism. Indeed within this region lies the Weeden Island mound that gave its name to the culture, excavated in the 1920s by Jesse Fewkes.

As was true for the coastal region to the north, C. B. Moore's various excavations provide data on mound sites along the central coast (Moore 1900, 1902, 1903b). In addition, excavations by Fewkes at the Weeden Island site (Fewkes 1924; also see Willey 1949a:105–113) and various state and federally sponsored projects in the 1930s (Willey 1949a:30–34) provide data, as does the work of Ripley Bullen, William Sears, and others (e.g., Bullen 1950, 1951b, 1971; Sears, 1960, 1971b; Bullen and Bullen 1976; Bullen, Askew et al. 1978). Their information has been synthesized by George Luer and Marion Almy (1979, 1982), who have reordered Willey's original cultural sequences for the region and defined the Manasota culture as beginning about 500 B.C. and extending to the late Weeden Island period, about A.D. 700. Their taxonomy emphasizes the continuity in the coastal lifeway from the end of the late Archaic period until the Safety Harbor culture. During the early Weeden Island period, influences from northern Florida reached down the coast, resulting in the Weeden Island burial mounds in the central Gulf coast region.

Since the 1970s a relatively large number of surveys and testing projects have been undertaken in the greater Tampa Bay region, including locales away from the coast (Hemmings 1975; Luer 1977a, b; Luer and Almy 1980; Welch 1983; Austin and Russo 1989; see Welch 1983:20–21, for a more complete listing). These projects have provided perspectives on the Manasota culture, including a number of radiocarbon dates.

Cultural resource management projects continue to be a major source of information for the central peninsular Gulf coast, where development since the turn of the century, especially from the 1940s to the present, has destroyed much of the archaeological record. Such destruction makes the reports from these management projects and the reports and museum collections obtained by early archaeologists all the more important.

Luer and Almy (1979:40–41) have described the Manasota culture as

characterized by ... sites which yield evidence of an economy based on fishing, hunting, and shellfish-gathering. The sites yield evidence of burial practices involving primary, flexed burials.... Ceramic manufac-

Excavations in 1965 or 1966 at the Sarasota County Mound, a Manasota shell midden (see Bullen 1971; courtesy Florida Museum of Natural History).

turing was limited to sand-tempered, undecorated . . . pottery such as . . . flattened-globular bowls and pots with a converged orifice. Many shell tools were used . . . including fighting conch shell hammers, left-handed whelk shell "spokeshaves," . . . columellae, and hammers. . . . There was little use of stone tools. . . . Bone tools include barbs and simple points made from long bones.

Ceramics and Chronology

Almost all Manasota utilitarian ceramics are undecorated, as is true for Weeden Island–period and earlier pottery in the north peninsular coast region. Attribute analysis of temporally sensitive vessel and rim shapes, however, has helped construct a ceramic-based sequence for the culture (Luer and Almy 1980, 1982:41, 44–45). Flattened globular bowls with in-curving rims and beveled lips are characteristic of the early Manasota period (500 B.C.–A.D. 400). After that time deeper vessels with straight rims and rounded lips are most common. Another shape—a pot-shaped vessel with slightly in-curved rim and rounded lip and a slightly converging orifice—is found from about 200 B.C. to A.D. 700. Late in the Manasota period simple bowls with out-curving rims and flat lips appear; the earlier varieties are thicker than the later ones, often in excess of 0.2 inch thick. All Manasota vessels after A.D. 400 tend to be thinner than this.

At post-Manasota sites (after A.D. 700, the late Weeden Island period) both Wakulla Check Stamped and St. Johns Check Stamped sherds occur in sites (e.g., the Clearwater and Boca Ciega sites in Pinellas County; Willey 1949a:332–333). Check-stamped ceramics also are found in burial mounds from this time.

Subsistence and Settlements

During precolumbian times, the central peninsular Gulf coast was probably wetter than it is today but still less soggy than the Gulf coast further north. An extensive system of small rivers (e.g., Anclote, Hillsborough, Alafia, Little Manatee, Manatee, Myakka) and creeks drain the interior pine forests. Locales along some of the drainages are swampy, often with bayheads; further inland the topography is higher. In the past, pine flatwoods and scrub forests predominated.

Tampa Bay is a large inlet that offers numerous estuaries and, in the past, extensive marsh and mangrove stands. The amount of shoreline within the bay, including Hillsborough and Old Tampa bays, is almost equal to the entire Gulf shoreline of the region. The waters and estuaries of Tampa Bay were a giant food basket of fish and shellfish that could support relatively large precolumbian populations. Along the adjacent Gulf coast were more mangroves and salt marshes as well as narrow barrier islands.

Most Manasota sites are shell middens found on or near the shore, where the aboriginal villagers had easiest access to fish and shellfish. Both large and small middens are known, and most often sites are multicomponent; some were occupied during the Safety Harbor period. This is not surprising, because people continued to use the same locations and resources for hundreds, even thousands of years. Sand burial mounds are present at some of the coastal sites.

The coastal shell middens, usually linear deposits parallel to shore-lines, sometimes form undulating ridges, and several have shell ramps constructed to provide access to the tops of the middens. These middens, with shell mounds and ramps, are like those found on the southwest Florida coast (see chapter 8).

As was true elsewhere in Florida, the wetlands provided the Manasota peoples with most of their meat diet. At their coastal settings, the Manasota villagers could take advantage not only of marine resources but of the resources of the wooded locales and the inland rivers and wetlands. As yet, evidence for any type of agriculture is lacking, and it is doubtful if extensive farming ever took place in the region from Tampa Bay south.

Zooarchaeological studies of coastal Manasota sites (Brooks 1974; Luer 1977a, b; Fraser 1980; Austin and Russo 1989) have identified fifteen species of fish, ten of sharks and rays and fifteen of shellfish, the most common of which is oyster. A few sites with mainly clams are known. Other creatures documented as having been used by the Manasota people are deer, wolf, dog, opossum, raccoon, rabbit, rat, various reptiles and amphibians, red-breasted merganser, and bald eagle.

Not all Manasota sites are on the coast. What are presumed to be short-term villages (without extensive middens) and special-use camps are found in the interior pine flatwoods on higher ground near water sources and wetland habitats (Austin and Russo 1989). Scatters of shell midden are present at some, and in at least one instance an interior site was deliberately built up to increase its elevation (Almy n.d.). Some of the special-use sites contain scatters of lithics and ceramics; others are probably lithic workshops (Hemmings 1975; Padgett 1976). More intensively occupied interior villages (with dirt middens) have been found in wetland locales (e.g., the Myakkahatchee site, Luer et al. 1987).

An inventory of some of the shell and bone artifacts from Manasota sites (Luer and Almy 1982:41–42, 44, 45) shows shell tools were common. Marine shell was durable and available. Shell tools include *Strombus* two-holed hammers; *Busycon* spoons or small dippers, pounders, celts, columellae, columella barbs, cutting-edge tools, and hammers; *Pleuroploca* columella adzes; *Noetia* net weights (made from the valves); and *Mercenaria* anvils, choppers, hammers, scrapers, and digging tools. *Busycon* shell was made into gorgets, and *Oliva* shells were fashioned into beads.

The Manasota bone tool assemblage is less extensive. Shark teeth scrapers and knives have been recovered from sites, along with points made from stingray spines. Shark vertebrae were drilled and used as beads, and bone was used for projectile points, barbs, and awls. Stone tools, most often chert and agatized coral, also are fewer relative to shell tools. Scrapers, knives, drills, and projectile points have been identified. The latter are Sarasota, Hernando, and Westo types (see Bullen 1975). A few tools were made from fossilized bones that can be recovered from Gulf beaches and inland rivers (including shark teeth and dugong ribs).

Analysis by Bullen (1971) of collections from the Sarasota County Mound suggests an increase in tools in the Weeden Island portion of the Manasota period relative to earlier times. More plummets, bone and shell tools, stone points and knives, and various types of shell beads were found in the late Manasota (early Weeden Island period) component at the site. This distribution also may reflect a denser occupation. The same types of artifacts were found throughout the midden deposits, attesting to the conservative nature of the maritime economic system.

William Sears's (1960, 1971b) excavations at Bayshore Homes and at the Weeden Island site demonstrate that a cultural continuum existed between the late Weeden Island period and the succeeding central coast Safety Harbor culture. There is not enough information to quantify the relative size and numbers of late versus early Manasota sites. The data that exist, however, suggest that many new villages were established during the late Manasota period and that most were occupied into the Safety Harbor period.

Ceremonialism

Luer and Almy (1982:42, 46–47) have suggested a chronology for Manasota burial ceremonialism. That scheme is used here, with some alterations. During early Manasota times, 500 B.C.–A.D. 100, human burials were flexed, primary interments in shell middens or in cemeteries. Burial in intentionally constructed burial mounds evidently was not practiced until after A.D. 100. These early mounds, until about A.D. 300, also contain primary, flexed interments and, occasionally, extended or semiflexed burials. The mounds are located adjacent to villages and often contain sherds of locally made pottery.

During the next period, A.D. 300–700, which was the early Weeden Island period, Manasota mounds contain secondary burials accompanied by almost the full range of Weeden Island ceramics and, often, complicated-stamped sherds. Post–A.D. 700, late Weeden Island period burial mounds also are present. They often contain Wakulla Check Stamped and St. Johns Check Stamped sherds, in addition to fragments of broken Weeden Island vessels. Some of these mounds contain pieces of Safety Harbor vessels, indicating they were used over many generations. The reuse or continued use of mounds was apparently a common practice in the central Gulf coast region during Manasota and later times. One example of such a mound is the Thomas Mound on the Little Manatee River.

The Manasota peoples and their coastal neighbors immediately to the north practiced an economic system well-suited to making a living in the coastal realm. With their Weeden Island relatives in north and northwest Florida they shared beliefs and practices that helped them to explain the world around them. Another Weeden Island–period culture, Cades Pond, similarly used techniques well suited to its environment and shared ideology with the Weeden Island societies to the north.

Cades Pond in North-Central Florida

The Cades Pond culture was originally defined by John Goggin (1948a: 58, 60, 1949b:25), who named it after a site mound near Lake Santa Fe excavated in the 1870s. Goggin assigned the name to mounds in north-central Florida that contained ceramics bearing resemblances to the St. Johns culture in east Florida and the Weeden Island period cultures. Because of the types of St. Johns ceramics present in the mounds, Goggin correctly dated the culture to the late St. Johns I (post-Deptford) period, that is, after A.D. 100.

In 1951 Goggin excavated an important village site in Alachua County, the Melton site, located on the north side of Paynes Prairie. Because the dominant ceramic type at the site—more than 90 percent of the 12,000 total sherds—was an undecorated, quartz sand-tempered ware rather than a St. Johns or Weeden Island pottery type, Goggin concluded that the site was not contemporary with nearby Cades Pond mounds. The concept of secular and sacred ceramic series had not yet been introduced, and Goggin did not realize that a culture's utilitarian ceramics could be so different from their mound ceramics. Notes at the Florida Museum of Natural History indicate that Goggin assigned the Melton village site to the time before the Cades Pond period, a period he named pre–Cades Pond.

Subsequent research revised and corrected Goggin's chronology. The pre–Cades Pond period is not a viable concept because it is known that Cades Pond mounds were associated with the village sites previously placed in the pre–Cades Pond period (e.g., the Melton village).

At Cades Pond villages undecorated ceramics are 85–95 percent of the utilitarian pottery, while many of the mounds contain Weeden Island ceramics dating from the early Weeden Island period, probably A.D. 300–600. Slightly earlier Cades Pond mounds, A.D. 100–300, contain Deptford ceramics, along with St. Johns Plain and Dunns Creek Red pottery.

Before the establishment of year-round villages in north-central Florida by late Deptford–early Cades Pond peoples, the region seems to have been occupied only part-time by Deptford people. After approximately A.D. 100 or slightly before, late Deptford populations began to establish sedentary settlements in the region, where they could take advantage of the wetlands, which were year-round sources of food. Perhaps population pressures to the west on the Gulf coast influenced this shift in settlement. Such pressures may have been caused in part by rising sea levels, which for a time inundated estuaries. Whatever the reason, late Deptford populations moved into the area and soon developed into the distinctive Cades Pond culture.

Most of our knowledge of Cades Pond village life comes from the 1971 reinvestigation of the Melton village site by Charles Fairbanks and his students. Stephen Cumbaa used the data to prepare a detailed analysis of Cades Pond subsistence for his master's thesis, "An Intensive Harvest Economy in North-central Florida" (1972). In the summer of 1974, another Cades Pond village site, 8Al46, was excavated just west of Newnan's Lake, and a third, the Hawthorne site, was excavated in 1976 (Milanich 1978). Radiocarbon dates from the Melton and Hawthorne sites are A.D. 220 and A.D. 210, 275, and 490, respectively.

Cumbaa's research was preceded by the research of Samuel Smith, who studied the mounds associated with the Cades Pond culture. Smith's thesis, "A Reinterpretation of the Cades Pond Archaeological Period" (1971a), draws on data from a Cades Pond mound excavated by William Sears (1956b), as well as on information gathered by University of Florida excavations carried out in 1957, 1964, and 1970 at the Cross Creek and Melton mounds (see also Hemmings 1978; Milanich 1978).

The Cades Pond culture occupied a restricted geographical and physiographic region in north-central Florida. All of the known sites are in the area bounded on the north by the Santa Fe River and on the south by Orange Lake. None is found in western Alachua County, and most are located in the better-watered regions of eastern Alachua and western Clay and Putnam counties, where there are numerous wetlands. All of the village sites are adjacent to extensive wetlands, large lakes, or both. Once again, the availability of wetlands and the resources they presented were a determining factor in site selection.

Many locales of Cades Pond village and mound complexes maximized access to wetlands. Rather than lying on the south end of Orange Lake, sites lie near the north end or the east side where there is easy access to additional wetlands and lakes. The same is true for other locales: sites are located between Paynes Prairie and Newnans Lake, between Orange Lake and Lake Lochloosa, between Paynes Prairie and Levy Lake, and between Orange Lake and the wetlands in the River Styx drainage. From such sites Cades Pond people also could have had ready access to the resources available in the nearby hardwood oak and hickory forests.

Although the forests provided deer, nuts, and other animals and

1 8Al46
2 Cross Creek sites
3 Melton mounds 1-2
4 Melton Mound 3
5 Melton village
6 River Styx

Cades Pond archaeological sites in north-central Florida.

plants, the wetlands provided most of the meat diet. Of the more than 1,500 separate individuals identified in faunal collections from the Melton village, almost 90 percent were taken from either lake or marsh habitats (Cumbaa 1972).

Melton village provides an informative look at Cades Pond subsistence strategies. Hickory, pine, and oak nuts were gathered, stored, and eaten. The most popular nut was the mockernut hickory (*Carya tomentosa*), which contains about twice as much meat as the next most frequently used nut, the pignut hickory. Acorns and pine nuts, the latter from both slash and long-leaf pines, also were eaten. Other wild plant foods were the Chickasaw plum, wild cherry, and persimmon. These could be collected, dried, and stored for future eating.

Other than a few large animals—deer, black bear, and panther—most of the mammals used by the Cades Pond villagers could have been taken with small snares or traps. Bones of muskrat, opossum, mole, rabbit (two species), squirrel (two species), skunk, rat (two species), grey fox, red wolf, and pocket gopher have been identified.

The large sample of deer bone present allowed Cumbaa to reconstruct some butchering techniques. Deer were apparently butchered at the kill site. Metacarpal and metatarsal bones showed evidence of cut marks made during skinning. Hides could be used as pouches to carry the meat and choice parts of the carcass—the haunches—back to the village, where their remains were found.

Birds also were eaten. Cumbaa (1972) reports finding significant amounts of young bird bones together, indicating that the animals were collected in quantities from rookeries. Several of the birds—white ibis, sandhill crane, coot, egret, and heron (two species)—normally establish nests in wetlands. Other bird remains came from bald eagle and turkey, which, like the other birds, provided feathers as well as meat.

Reptiles and amphibians, mostly snakes, frogs, and toads, could have been taken in the hammocks, although they are more plentiful and more easily collected near the lakes and marshes. A second group of snakes and turtles of several species inhabit only wetlands. They, too, provided meat. The entire list of amphibians and reptiles from the Melton sites includes Southern toad, frog (*Rana* sp.), Southern leopard frog, amphiuma, greater siren, mud turtle (at least two species), musk turtle (several species), pond turtle, chicken turtle, box turtle, gopher tortoise, soft-shelled turtle, black snake, indigo snake, rat snake, mud snake, king snake, coach whip, water snake, brown water snake, cottonmouth moccasin, eastern diamondback rattlesnake, and alligator. The water snakes, cottonmouths, and mud snakes were the most numerous. Pond snails and clams, also collected from wetlands, were often found in large deposits, indicating mass collection and processing.

The single most important food taken from the lakes was fish. Eleven freshwater species were identified at Melton village: gar, mudfish, gizzard shad, chain pickerel, lake chubsucker, catfish, sunfish, warmouth, largemouth bass, and speckled perch. Their sizes ranged from four-inch catfish to eight- to twelve-pound largemouth bass. Gar scales were found from fish as much as three feet long. Although some fish, such as the large gar, were probably speared with bone-tipped gigs or spears, the most common fishing technique seems to have been netting with seines. The species and size of the fish remains analyzed by Cumbaa suggest that the Cades Pond fishers practiced total catch— that is, fish netted were the same range of sizes and species occurring naturally in lakes. Hook-and-line fishing or spearing would not reflect such normal distributions.

A variety of stone and bone tools were used to help hunt or process these animals, including chert projectile points classified as Columbia, Jackson, and Bradford types (Bullen 1975:19, 21, 14). Battering on the edges of some of the specimens indicates use as hafted knives. Small triangular points probably used to tip arrows have been recovered from Cades Pond sites (Milanich 1978:165). If indeed these are arrow points, they are as early as similar points from the McKeithen site.

Lithic tools other than projectile points include nutting and seed-grinding stones, medium-sized triangular knives, stemmed and hafted drills, and triangular perforators. The last, named Cross Creek perforators by Samuel Smith (1971a), seem to be diagnostic of the Cades Pond culture.

Bone tools include perforators, flakers, scrapers or fleshers, punches, and awls made from deer ulnae and from bone splinters. Bone items exhibiting wear patterns that suggest their use as tools for basket weaving also were found, as were a number of double-pointed bone points showing marks and discoloration from pine pitch used to attach them to a shaft. Fossil and nonfossil shark teeth used as cutting tools were hafted by drilling or by using notches cut into their bases. Bone was also carved and decorated for use as gorgets.

No complete house patterns were excavated at the Melton site, nor have any been found at other Cades Pond villages. At the Melton site, however, a large number of storage pits were excavated. Often overlapping, most were basin-shaped, about three feet deep. Smaller pits possibly anchored support posts for structures.

Cades Pond people did not live in isolation. They acquired a variety of artifacts and even some foods from elsewhere. Most were obtained from the Gulf coast and northern Florida, but the Cades Pond people also took advantage of trade routes reaching into the Appalachian

Cades Pond points and knives: *a* is 2⅝ inches long; *i–j*, similar to Pinellas points; the others are varieties of Columbia, Jackson, and Bradford types that appear to be resharpened and reworked.

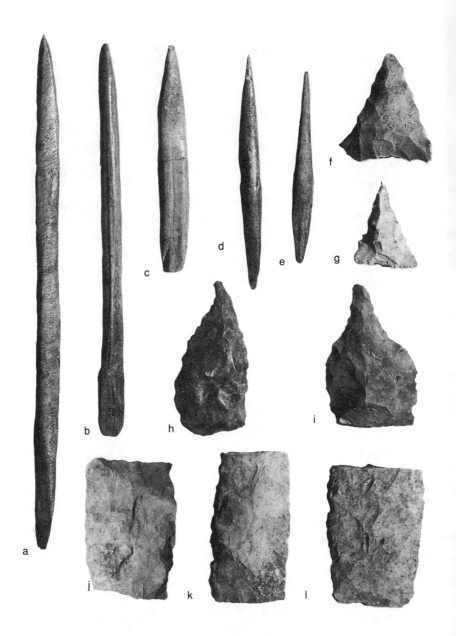

Cades Pond artifacts: *a–b*, bone "points" or leisters (*a* is 6⅝ inches long);
c, bone fid or shuttle for weaving; *d–e*, double-pointed bone points; *f–g*, Cross
Creek perforators; *h–i*, perforators; *j–l*, broken bases of bifacial knives.

piedmont and beyond, probably the same ones that had brought Yent complex stone and copper to Florida.

The St. Johns Plain and Dunns Creek Red pottery found in the Cades Pond mounds could have come from east or central Florida or even from peninsular Gulf coast Weeden Island–period sites, where similar ceramics are found in mounds. Items that came from the Atlantic or Gulf coasts include marine food remains—white, mako, requiem, tiger, and hammerhead sharks—and large sea turtles. In addition, mullet and several species of marine mollusks were brought inland to the Cades Pond region. One adze or scraper was fashioned out of marine conch shell.

Exotic objects that originated outside Florida, most likely in the southeastern piedmont, included gorgets and plummets manufactured of slate and greenstone. Rolled copper beads and a copper boatstone-shaped object came from the Melton village.

Mounds and Villages

Five Cades Pond mounds, each associated with or near a village, have been excavated and a number of others surveyed. Arranged from the earliest to the most recent, these five mounds are River Styx, Melton Mound 1, Melton Mound 3, Cross Creek Burial Mound, and Cross Creek Platform Mound. In addition, a number of Cades Pond village sites are known.

These Cades Pond mounds and villages can be separated into at least six separate clusters, groupings of villages and one or more mounds. Each cluster is located near wetlands. Although several of the clusters with the earliest type of mounds may have been "founded" first, at some later time all six clusters had villages that were contemporaneous with one another. In this model of Cades Pond settlement, each site cluster probably represents a separate community (Milanich 1978:166–171).

The earliest two site clusters are probably the Cross Creek–River Styx sites and the north Levy Lake–southwest Paynes Prairie sites. In each there is at least one small mound surrounded by a horseshoe-shaped embankment adjacent to a village site. Similar to the Yent complex burial mound and embankment at Crystal River, these are the earliest mound type in the Cades Pond region.

When these early villages and their associated mound and embankment complexes were abandoned, new villages with mounds were established nearby. As villages grew, additional villages budded off to locate close by. This process resulted in the clusters of mounds and villages we can observe today. When the total population within a cluster placed pressure on local resources, a new cluster must have been founded in a geographically removed locale. From the two earliest clusters, the Cades Pond population apparently grew to six spatially distinct communities, each with old and new villages and mounds.

Why did Deptford coastal populations who previously had occupied camps in north-central Florida become year-round Cades Pond villagers? One explanation mentioned earlier is population pressure along the coast: at some point it was easier for some of the Deptford population to remain inland, taking advantage of the extensive wetlands there, than to stay on the coast. These late Deptford–period peoples began to remain in north-central Florida year-round, establishing villages and constructing mounds with embankments around them like that at the contemporary Crystal River site to the west. As these early Cades Pond peoples were able to become sedentary through their intensive use of wetland and forest resources, their burial practices, as evidenced by changes in mound construction, diverged from those of the Gulf coast cultures.

We can trace the history of specific site clusters following the initial sedentary occupation of the region. For instance, around A.D. 200 at least some of the River Styx villagers evidently moved several miles south and established the Cross Creek site as a new mound and village center. The mound at that village still had an earthen embankment surrounding the mound (one much larger than at the River Styx site), but that mound contained no Deptford pottery. Through time more burial mounds were built at Cross Creek, but these did not have embankments. Let us look at the archaeological evidence.

The River Styx Mound, unfortunately, was partially bulldozed before investigations were undertaken by Ripley Bullen in 1971. It is the earliest dated mound in north-central Florida, radiocarbon dated to A.D. 180. A detailed map of the ceremonial earthworks made by Thomas Hemmings allows interpretation of the site along with Bullen's data. The complex consists of a burial mound constructed over cremated burials. Whether or not cremations or other types of burials were present in the constructed mound itself is not certain. The earthwork surrounding the mound was horseshoe-shaped; a nearby borrow pit, which contains water much of the year, was the source of earth for construction. The embankment and the area enclosed within it around the mound also contained cremated interments. A village is present on the opposite side of the borrow pond from the mound. The embankment and mound complex measured roughly 140 by 190 feet.

The ceramics from the River Styx Mound, studied by Ann Cordell, include Deptford Check Stamped, Bold Check Stamped, and Linear Check Stamped pot-shaped vessels and several St. Johns vessels—including two compartmental forms, a unique boat-shaped oval bowl with lug handles, and a rectangular plate or dish with rounded corners. Some of the vessels are reminiscent of Yent complex vessels. Two bowls, one with a roulette-stamped design and one incised, are unique to Florida and most closely resemble Hopewellian period pottery from the western Great Lakes.

Found with some of the vessels were rolled copper beads like those recovered from other Cades Pond mounds and villages. University of Georgia scientists analyzed a sample of the beads and found their ultimate source was the copper deposits of the Lake Superior area copper formations.

The layout of the River Styx mound complex—a mound enclosed by a horseshoe-shaped embankment with a borrow adjoining—is similar to that of the Crystal River site and the Cross Creek site and to the mound–charnel pond and embankment at the contemporary Fort Center site in the Lake Okeechobee Basin (described in chapter 8). All of these complexes date within the period from about A.D. 100 to 300.

Related in form to the River Styx complex and part of the same cluster is the Cross Creek village and mound complex, consisting of two mounds placed roughly 590 feet apart on a northeast-southwest axis. A village area is located between the two mounds, closest to the southernmost mound. The more northerly mound, Cross Creek Mound 1, is a conical, sand burial mound. A curving trench 6–7 feet wide and 4 feet deep with an earth embankment thrown up on its south (interior) side had been dug around the burial mound at a distance of approximately 160 feet, forming a semicircular enclosure. The enclosure looks like the one at River Styx, except the Cross Creek earthwork and mound are much larger. Two borrow pits between the mound and the village most likely provided the earth to construct the mound.

The southern mound, Cross Creek Mound 2, is a low, flat-topped platform measuring 150 by 125 feet at the base. The larger axis runs north and south. A midden stratum extends under the mound, indicating that the village was occupied before the mound was constructed. South of the platform mound is a pond, probably the borrow pit from which mound fill was taken. This second mound contained no intentionally deposited artifacts or interments and appears to have been a platform for a structure.

The human burials excavated by the University of Florida team in its 1964 investigation of the burial mound, Cross Creek Mound 1, were in an extremely bad state of preservation due to the acidic soil present at the site, and no analysis was done. More than 500 potsherds from a number of different vessels had been deposited in the mound. The potsherds, now curated at the Florida Museum of Natural History, included undecorated sherds with quartz sand temper or inclusions (49 percent), Weeden Island series types (40 percent), and St. Johns Plain (11 percent). The relative frequencies of pottery types from the mound contrast sharply with those in the village, where 94 percent of the sherds were undecorated, an amount similar to that from other Cades Pond villages. The ceramic data suggest that the Cross Creek mounds, contemporary with the early Weeden Island period, were built after the River Styx Mound, which dates from the late Deptford period. The associated villages most likely are similarly sequential in time.

Three other mounds found near the Cross Creek site (Smith 1971a) lie roughly in a line extending south from the flat-topped mound at distances of 380, 485, and 940 yards. All have been heavily disturbed by looters. Several small habitation areas have been found close to these three southern mounds, but none have been excavated. Surface collections indicate that they are Cades Pond occupations. These outlying mounds and villages probably were established after the main Cross Creek complex to the north.

Most likely, then, River Styx and Cross Creek were sequentially occupied by the same group of Cades Pond peoples. Cross Creek is more elaborate and larger than River Styx. Mounds and villages south of the Cross Creek site probably postdate it, perhaps an example of population growth and the founding of new settlements within the general locale of an established community. Together, all of these sites and mounds form a single cluster spanning the temporal range of the Cades Pond culture.

In contrast to this cluster is the Melton cluster, which contained at least five ceremonial mounds and ten villages and special-use camps. Three Melton mounds were located west of their presumed associated villages. The distance from the westernmost mound, Melton Mound 1, to the easternmost village site (8Al46) is about three miles. The mounds and villages are strung out in an east-west line parallel to the north edge of Paynes Prairie, up to one mile from the prairie's edge. There is no early mound with an embankment in the Melton cluster, suggesting it was founded later than the Cross Creek cluster.

Melton Mound 1 is a burial mound constructed of sand taken from a borrow pit to the west. Another low sand burial mound lies 225 feet north, Melton Mound 2, believed to have been excavated in the 1880s by James Bell (Bell 1883:635–637; Bell apparently also dug into the other two Melton mounds). Mound 2 contained many human interments and early Weeden Island–period mortuary ceramics, including animal effigies. No Cades Pond village area is evident in the immediate vicinity of these two mounds. The nearest villages are the Melton village site and site 8Al46, with which the mounds probably were associated.

Melton Mound 1 contained seventeen human interments, most represented only by a few fragments of tooth enamel (Smith 1971a). The acidity of the soil destroyed most of the bone tissue. Two better preserved burials seem to have been secondary bundled burials, suggesting the use of a charnel house. The mound appears to have been reused after its initial construction, and two primary burials, one a female in a flexed position, were interred in graves in the center of the mound. Broken pottery vessels were placed in the mound fill during construction. Of the nearly 1,600 sherds recovered, half were St. Johns Plain, and a third were undecorated with quartz sand inclusions. Some Dunns Creek Red sherds (6 percent of the total) also were present.

Melton Mound 3, excavated by William Sears (1956b), is smaller than the other Melton mounds, measuring forty-eight feet in diameter

Two pottery vessels excavated in the early 1880s by James Bell from a mound in Alachua County, probably Melton Mound 2. *Left,* Swift Creek Complicated Stamped; *right,* apparently a portion of an animal effigy vessel. Both are in the collections of the Smithsonian Institution (courtesy Florida Museum of Natural History).

and four feet in height. The distance between the two Cades Pond villages to the east, Melton village and site 8Al46, is roughly the same as between Melton Mounds 1 and 2 and Melton Mound 3. If mound-to-village distances were relatively constant, this would suggest that the former two mounds were associated with the Melton village site, while Mound 3 was associated with village 8Al46.

Although direct evidence was lacking because of soil leaching, the patterning of artifacts and human interments in Mound 3 led Sears to conclude it was constructed in two stages. The primary mound, about two feet high and twenty-eight feet in diameter, contained a deposit of pottery sherds and several central burials. Later, before the second mound was added, a deposit of seven or eight bundled burials was placed on the primary mound's surface near its center, perhaps burials stored in a charnel house. At the same time more bundled burials, perhaps as many as twenty people, were placed elsewhere across the primary mound's surface. At least two groups of cremated burials also were deposited. Just west of the central mass interment, an adult female was arranged on the primary mound in a flexed position. The woman had fragments of an infant skeleton in her abdominal area indicating, as Sears notes, that she died during pregnancy. Two undecorated vessels, one globular in shape with nonfunctional podal supports, were placed next to this burial.

Between the flexed burial and the western edge of the mound, Sears uncovered a deposit of more than 1,000 potsherds deliberately deposited on the primary mound surface. Other sherds were scattered throughout the fill of both mound strata. St. Johns Plain sherds accounted for nearly 70 percent of the total, a number significantly greater than in the other Cades Pond mounds. Weeden Island sherds also were present in the mound.

In the Cross Creek, River Styx, and Melton mounds St. Johns Plain, Dunns Creek Red, and undecorated sand-tempered ceramics are most common. Deptford ceramics, found in the earliest mound, and undecorated sand-tempered wares decrease over time, while Weeden Island and St. Johns wares increase. In all but the earliest mound, most burials were stored as bundles in a charnel house before interment in the mounds. Skeletal remains of a number of individuals were buried at the same time, usually by placing them on the surface of a primary mound and then covering them with a layer of sand. A few cremations and flexed burials also occasionally were placed in the later mounds; cremations were most common in the early mound.

Cades Pond was a unique cultural adaptation to the extensive wetlands and forests of north-central Florida. Although the peoples' basic economic orientation differed from those of the contemporary precolumbian societies of the central and north peninsular Gulf coast, they shared many aspects of ceremonialism with them and with the Weeden Island cultures to the north. North-central Florida would see an influx of new peoples after about A.D. 600. Those Alachua culture peoples, possibly expanding out of south-central Georgia, are described in chapter 9.

Cultures of Eastern and Central Florida

Like the Gulf coastal regions of peninsular and northwest Florida, the riverine, lacustrine (lake), and coastal zones of east and central Florida contain extensive shellfish middens, evidence of large precolumbian human populations. Indeed, the most extensive freshwater shellfish middens in Florida are found within the St. Johns River drainage. And in a number of locales within the coastal lagoon in east Florida, the marine shell middens once rivaled those of the Gulf coast in size.

East and central Florida is a region composed of the lower (northern) and central portions of the St. Johns River, its tributaries, adjacent portions of the coastal barrier island–salt marsh–lagoon system, and the central Florida lake district. Its middens, and numerous other sites in the region, were home to the post-Archaic St. Johns cultures. The St. Johns I and II cultures developed out of the fiber-tempered Orange culture found in the same region during the late Archaic period. There was great continuity in east Florida from the time of the Orange-period peoples to the time of the various eastern Timucuan-speaking Indian groups who lived there in the colonial period.

The shell middens within the St. Johns drainage and those along the Atlantic coastal lagoon of northeastern Florida were visited by two early archaeologists, Jeffries Wyman and Andrew Douglass, who wrote about their observations:

St. Johns region and variant cultures in east and central Florida.

The shell deposits on the [St. Johns] river are entirely different as to their characteristics from the mounds of the sea coast. The last extend around the shores . . . and . . . are of gigantic proportions. They are composed exclusively of marine species. . . . The mounds on the river, on the contrary, consist exclusively of freshwater species. Anyone who for the first time views the larger ones [shell mounds], sometimes covering several acres . . . rising to the height of fifteen, twenty, or twenty-five feet, might well be excused for doubting that such immense quantities of small shells could have been brought together by human labor. (Wyman 1875:9, 11)

Throughout the extent of this lagoon, on the one side or the other, appear the shell mounds or ridges left by the Aborigines in consuming shell fish during a vast number of years. Equal in frequency, but vastly

Green Mound, a large shell midden in Volusia County on the Halifax River. In 1948 John Griffin described it as "one of the last of the once numerous large shell heaps of the region" (Griffin 1948a:1). By 1933 one-third of the site had been mined for shell (courtesy Florida Museum of Natural History).

inferior in dimensions, the sand mounds keep pace with the shell mounds. . . . It can hardly admit to question that the same people constructed both kinds. (Douglass 1885b:74–75)

Wyman and Douglass were among the first of the late nineteenth-century visitors to the St. Johns region who recognized that the "immense quantities of small shells" were piles of refuse left by the precolumbian people and not natural formations (see also Wyman 1867, 1868; Douglass 1884, 1885b; Moore 1892–1894).

Wyman, in addition to noting both the differences in composition of coastal versus freshwater middens and the presence of numerous sand burial mounds in the region, astutely recognized another type of site that he referred to as "shell fields" (Wyman 1875:9, 11). We think today that such "fields" were actually village sites typified by sheet middens of variable thickness. The shell was refuse discarded within and around houses and other structures.

Unfortunately, many of the St. Johns shell middens and mounds observed by early archaeologists have been destroyed, mined for their shell to be used as paving material or obliterated by land clearing and development. At one time the freshwater and marine wetlands of east Florida were blanketed with archaeological sites, mute testimony to the St. Johns culture people who had lived there.

Chronology

Wyman and other early archaeologists soon established that the St. Johns region shell heaps were deposited in discrete layers or strata, suggesting a considerable period of time for their deposition. In addition, it was determined that some of the middens contained no aboriginal pottery in their lowest levels. These astute scientific observations came at a time when other archaeologists were arguing over whether or not a lost race of Mound Builders had been responsible for mounds in the eastern United States.

By 1918 the observations of Nels C. Nelson (1918; and see Mitchem 1990) combined with those of archaeologists like Wyman, who actually quantified ceramic differences from arbitrarily excavated levels, produced the following sequence of aboriginal pottery in the St. Johns region shell middens (from earliest to latest): (1) no pottery; (2) pottery tempered with vegetable fiber; (3) disappearance of fiber tempering and the appearance of chalky ware pottery; and (4) the appearance of chalky ware pottery that was check stamped on the surface (Goggin 1952c:38–39).

Essentially this is the same sequence in use today: (1) Mount Taylor middle and late Archaic period (no pottery); (2) Orange late Archaic period (fiber-tempered pottery); (3) St. Johns I period (chalky ware, often decorated with incisions); and (4) St. Johns II period (chalky ware with check stamping). Since the 1940s archaeological investigations have confirmed this sequence many times over, and with the advent of radiocarbon dating in the early 1950s, absolute dates have been tied to the rise and fall in popularity of the various ceramic types, providing a well-dated chronology for the St. Johns region.

The appearance of chalky ware ceramics—pottery chalky to the touch because of the presence of microscopic spicules of freshwater sponges in the clay used to make the pottery—corresponds to the beginning of the St. Johns culture at about 500 B.C. The same ware continued to be made for 2,000 years, into the colonial period. As noted, changes in surface decoration on this ware provide archaeolo-

St. Johns Region Chronology

Period	Dates	Distinguishing ceramics, other traits, and cultural influences
St. Johns IIc	A.D. 1513–1565	St. Johns Check Stamped pottery; European artifacts in some middens and mounds. Burial mounds still present early. The St. Johns IIc people are the various Timucuan-speaking groups described in European documents of the early sixteenth century.
St. Johns IIb	A.D. 1050–1513	St. Johns Check Stamped pottery; some Fort Walton and Safety Harbor pottery and Southeastern Ceremonial Complex objects in mounds. Mississippian influences.
St. Johns IIa	A.D. 750–1050	Appearance of St. Johns Check Stamped pottery in villages and mounds; large number of mounds and villages, reflecting larger populations; late Weeden Island pottery and copies in some mounds.
St. Johns Ib	A.D. 500–750	Weeden Island, Dunns Creek Red (early), and St. Johns pottery in mounds; village ceramics almost all plain St. Johns ware; Weeden Island influences; some pottery caches in mounds.
St. Johns Ia	A.D. 100–500	Village pottery nearly all plain St. Johns ware; Hopewellian-Yent complex objects in early mounds (pre–A.D. 300); some possible log tombs. Late Deptford and Swift Creek pottery traded and copies locally manufactured; Dunns Creek Red common. Weeden Island influences appear late.
St. Johns I	500 B.C.–A.D. 100	Village pottery all St. Johns ware, both plain and incised; some Deptford pottery or copies present. Burial mounds appear for first time. All pottery coiled; some pottery punctated or pinched; side lugs rare; at times mixed quartz sand and fiber temper.

gists with a basis for establishing relative chronologies within the St. Johns culture. One of the most temporally significant changes in surface decoration was the practice of impressing check-stamped motifs on vessel surfaces by using a carved wooden paddle. This practice appeared at about A.D. 750, as it did in northwest Florida, and marks the beginning of the St. Johns II period.

A chronology for the St. Johns culture is shown in the table. It is no coincidence that the dates for the various periods correspond to other chronologies in northern Florida. First, ceramic changes on which archaeologists base definitions of temporal periods spread across northern Florida at approximately the same time. Second, the same precolumbian developments that influenced other cultures in the Southeast and in Florida—for instance, the appearance of Hopewellian-related burial ceremonialism—also affected the St. Johns cultures. Third, some ceramics found in St. Johns sites, especially mounds, are copies of vessels being made at that time elsewhere in Florida, or they are items brought from those other cultures (e.g., Weeden Island ceramics). The St. Johns region, home to a way of life that persisted for hundreds of years, was not isolated from events elsewhere in Florida. Those events, reflected in the archaeological record, help establish the St. Johns chronology. The table also includes a brief summary of external influences useful in dating St. Johns archaeological assemblages. The presence of ceramics and other traits similar to those found elsewhere in northern Florida reinforces the contention that, although regional lifeways developed in precolumbian Florida, many aspects of the native cultures were shared by different groups because of a common heritage and continual communication.

Regional Variations—St. Marys and Indian River

The St. Johns region is not a single, homogenous culture area. Regions of ceramic transitions have been documented on its northern and southern fringes: the St. Mary's variant to the north and the Indian River Zone to the south.

In their survey of Amelia Island, Ripley Bullen and John Griffin (1952) located a number of archaeological sites characterized by Savannah pottery types documented for the Georgia coast after A.D. 1200. Subsequent research at the mouth of the St. Johns River and the area just north of the river's mouth has confirmed the presence of a ceramic complex related to that of the Savannah culture in that salt marsh–barrier island–estuary region (Sears 1957; Lee et al. 1984; Saunders 1987; Russo 1992a). One explanation is that during the

Savannah period, coastal Georgia peoples expanded southward, filling an environment niche similar to the Georgia coast itself. Another is that St. Johns peoples living in northeastern Florida adopted Savannah pottery along with other practices, perhaps including maize agriculture.

Many sites in the region contain mixed St. Johns and Savannah or other typical Georgia ceramics. Such mixed sites also are documented for southeast Georgia immediately north of the St. Marys River (Larson 1958; Smith et al. 1981; Saunders, DesJean, and Walker 1985). One implication may be that, rather than representing a zone where first one and then another culture held sway with peoples moving in and out, this transitional zone, like others in Florida, was the home of a permanent population who made the same types of pottery as did their neighbors to the north and south. Michael Russo has named this transitional area in northeast Florida and southeast Georgia the St. Marys region (Russo 1992a), noting its correspondence to the northern St. Johns region defined by Lewis Larson (1958).

During the St. Johns I and II periods the people of the St. Marys region probably used their coastal habitats in the same fashion as the contemporaneous population of coastal Georgia, including cultivating maize after about A.D. 1200 or earlier (Lee et al. 1984). Excavations at the Dorian site on Amelia Island (Saunders 1987) indicate that at the time of first European contact, the Timucuan-speaking people of that locality continued to make Savannah pottery, rather than the St. Johns pottery made by the other Timucuan speakers to the south. Clearly, in transition zones, established correlations between language, ethnicity, and archaeological assemblages do not always hold true.

The second transition zone, in the Indian River area at the southern end of the St. Johns region in Brevard, Indian River, and St. Lucie counties, encompasses the Indian River, a coastal lagoon, from near Merritt Island south to St. Lucie Inlet. It includes the wet marshlands, braided stream system, and lakes that comprise the St. Johns River basin ten to twenty miles inland from the coast (the St. Johns River flows north; its headwaters lie in southern Florida).

Irving Rouse was the first to describe the precolumbian cultures of the area, defining a chronology that paralleled that of the St. Johns region (Rouse 1951:70). His Malabar I period is coeval to the St. Johns

I period, and Malabar II, characterized by the appearance of St. Johns Check Stamped pottery, is the temporal equivalent of St. Johns II. But although St. Johns ceramics are present in the Indian River region, there also are significant amounts of undecorated pottery tempered with quartz sand. Rouse (1951:222) and other early researchers (e.g., Ferguson 1951) originally called this undecorated pottery Glades Plain or Belle Glade Plain, depending on temporal provenience, attempting to demonstrate affinities to south Florida assemblages and cultures. Other researchers have taken another tack, noting that some of the quartz-tempered pottery is "resistant to more detailed typological assignment" and simply calling it "sand-tempered ware" (Jordan in Jordan, Wing, and Bullen 1963:10). More recent analysis of Indian River–region ceramic samples has shown that both the St. Johns and quartz-tempered pottery are made from local clay sources (Espenshade 1983), suggesting that one group made both wares.

Ann Cordell's analysis of pottery samples from several Indian River region sites in southern Brevard County has demonstrated continuity in ceramic manufacturing from the Orange period into the Malabar II period (Cordell in Sigler-Eisenberg et al. 1985:118–134). Her study showed that sand-tempered pottery reached its greatest popularity, 41 percent, during the middle portion of the Malabar I period. This seriation holds for other Indian River locales, suggesting that, as in the St. Marys region, ceramic studies provide one line of evidence for treating the Indian River region as a discrete culture area.

Site surveys and zooarchaeological analyses of Malabar sites also provide data that distinguish the Indian River region from the St. Johns region (Knoderer 1972; Sigler-Eisenberg et al. 1985; Russo 1986, 1988; Bense and Phillips 1990). Such investigations underscore the importance of correlations between local environmental conditions and the nature of precolumbian occupations.

Michael Russo's (1986:37–53; 1988) studies of Malabar subsistence in the interior marshes provides the following overview. During the late Archaic period, because of lower than present groundwater and sea levels, the marsh region was drier than at present and freshwater wetlands were not as extensive or as deep. Mussels, well adapted to these conditions, and small, shallow-water-dwelling fish were important meat sources. With prairies, pine flatwoods, and cabbage palm hammocks predominating across the landscape, terrestrial habitats were not as productive as they are under modern drainage regimes. The Orange-period population probably was much smaller than at more productive locations to the north in the St. Johns region.

Gradually, through the Malabar I period, wetter conditions began to prevail as local water levels rose. Wetlands became more numerous. In Malabar middens larger fish and more species are apparent, as are more mussels. More food resources led to larger human populations living year-round in the upper St. Johns Basin.

The expansion of wetlands continued into the Malabar II period. But Russo found that the situation was more complex than just a simple increase in wetlands leading to more wetland resources. Deeper and more expansive waters indeed provided increased habitat for more and larger fish, such as bass and pickerel, which found their way to Malabar peoples' hearths along with the smaller species. But drying of wetlands in winter and spring, periods of lesser rainfall, reduced the amount of deepwater fish at those seasons. The density of species such as bowfin and gar, that could survive in muddy-bottomed, shallow ponds increased, and Malabar villagers were quick to take advantage of that boon. They also availed themselves of the turtles that were forced to find new homes as water levels dropped in the dry season. Migratory ducks who wintered there, taking advantage of the expanded marshlands, made up another food source that flourished in Malabar II times.

Terrestrial resources—deer, raccoons, rabbits, and the like—also were used for food. But when minimum edible meat weight is calculated, land mammals only accounted for 15 and 14 percent of total edible meat for the Malabar I and II periods, respectively; the bulk of the meat diet was provided by fish and reptiles (80 percent for both periods; Russo 1986:23, 29).

A survey of aboriginal sites within the interior marshlands provides a picture of the types of camps and villages of the Malabar peoples (Sigler-Eisenberg et al. 1985:195–198; Russo 1988). Small artifact scatters or sites with only small amounts of animal remains probably are camps used a single time to gather some specific resource. Other sites were clearly used intermittently for short periods of time. The latter sites are multicomponent, usually under a quarter-acre in extent, with small and discontinuous individual midden strata. Like the camps, such sites are located apart from permanent settlements, although some are located near larger settlements. They probably were special-use sites, used either on a seasonal basis or for gathering a specific resource.

Both camps and intermittently occupied sites are distinct from the large, multicomponent sites that exhibit extensive middens and a wider range of tools and resources than are found at smaller sites. Such household sites, some several yards thick (e.g., the Duda Ranch Mound south of Lake Winder, Bense and Phillips 1990), are always near wetlands and are surrounded by the smaller special-use sites. The picture is one of small villages occupied at any one time by several families who expertly collected a variety of foods and other resources from the marshes of the uppermost St. Johns River drainage.

Similar, smaller artifact scatters and larger shell and dirt middens were noted by Irving Rouse (1951:115–151) in the St. Johns drainage within the Indian River region, especially around the lakes. He also found sand mounds containing human burials near the middens. Pottery from the mounds suggests that they are from both the Malabar I and II periods.

Within the Indian River region, Malabar sites are not restricted to inland locations. Marine resources were used extensively, and a number of sites formerly dotted the shores of the coastal lagoon, the adjacent portions of the mainland, and the narrow barrier islands to the east (Rouse 1951:151–220; Jordan, Wing, and Bullen 1963; Russo 1985, 1992b; Sigler-Eisenberg and Russo 1986). Unfortunately, twentieth-century development has destroyed many of these coastal Malabar sites, a number of which contained Orange-period components.

Archaeologists have developed a model of Malabar coastal settlement, based on data from the Zaremba site (a Malabar II coastal oyster shell midden north of Vero Beach; see Sigler-Eisenberg and Russo 1986), and the Futch Cove site (a Malabar I coastal site in southern Brevard County; see Russo 1992b). Zaremba, a special-use camp, is thought to have been occupied intermittently in the spring and summer by small groups. The season of occupation was deduced from an analysis of lengths of coquina shells. The site seems to have been used for collecting shellfish, mainly oysters, and fishing, primarily for marine catfish. The varieties of small sites in the Indian River region "reflect the diversity and frequency of economic activities that occur away from the primary household sites" (Sigler-Eisenberg and Russo

Over the years archaeologists in Florida have had field crews of students, Girl Scouts, Boy Scouts, and hired workers. Construction of U.S. Highway l in southern Brevard County (the Indian River region) in 1958 led to the emergency excavation of a shell midden with still another labor source: a road crew of convicts complete with armed guard. Archaeologist William Sears took this photograph of the Grant site excavations (courtesy Florida Museum of Natural History).

1986:29). Such an economic pattern in the context of coastal and inland environments of the Indian River region suggests that the Malabar people, like their colonial-period descendants the Ais, were foragers rather than agriculturists and practiced a way of life quite removed from that of their late precolumbian agricultural neighbors in the lower (northern) St. Johns region.

Data from the Futch Cove site support this model of settlement. Russo (1992b:25–29) found that Futch Cove was likely occupied infrequently by a limited number of persons, rather than by entire families. Presumably more permanent settlements occupied by full family households existed apart from the camps, which served as temporary, logistical sites for collecting certain foods (Russo 1992b). At Futch Cove, in addition to fish, cold-weather taking of birds and collection of coquina were also indicated. At the site, the range and intensity of use of shell tools was smaller than at permanently occupied sites, and the range of shellfish taken for food also was less. Fishing at the site was probably done by individual fishers using hook and line or gigs rather than by groups using nets.

What is uncertain is the articulation between inland and coastal Malabar sites. Did the same population move between these areas, or were there two groups, one primarily coastal and the other living only a few miles away in the upper St. Johns drainage? The latter seems unlikely. Perhaps the more permanent settlements were the large middens found inland in the marshes of the St. Johns River drainage. Such central settlements could have articulated with both the coastal and inland logistic camps, with individuals traveling to those locales to gather specific resources as they were needed.

Much remains to be learned about the regional precolumbian cultures of Florida, especially those that lie at the fringes of regions that have received the most archaeological scrutiny in the past. In the study of the St. Johns region it is easy to overlook the unique ways of life of the native peoples of the St. Marys and Indian River regions.

St. Johns I Culture

The basic lifeway of the St. Johns I period peoples—hunting, fishing, and collecting wild resources and occupying villages and camps adjacent to the numerous freshwater and coastal resources in the region—seems to have been little changed from that of their late Archaic, Orange-period predecessors. Villagers continued to live along the St. Johns River and its tributaries, such as the Oklawaha River, down to western Brevard County, and they lived around the numerous lakes that make up the central portion of the St. Johns and those in central Florida, especially in Orange, Lake, and northern Osceola counties. People also lived adjacent to the coastal lagoons and on some of the barrier islands from the area around the mouth of the St. Johns River south into Brevard County. At some locales in that coastal area are salt or freshwater marshes (e.g., the Guana Tract or the Tomoka River localities) that provided important habitats for St. Johns people.

Archaeological surveys and excavations have demonstrated that, throughout the St. Johns region, Orange-period and St. Johns I–period components are found in the same locales, often at the same

St. Johns archaeological sites.

site (e.g., Bullen and Griffin 1952; Goggin 1952c; Jahn and Bullen 1978; Newman and Weisman 1992; Russo, Cordell, and Ruhl 1992; Wayne and Dickinson 1993; Weisman 1993). This continuity is illustrated in a study by James Miller (1991:155, 172), who plotted locations of all known Orange and St. Johns I sites on the St. Johns River from Lake George north. Miller's study demonstrated similar settlement continuity between the St. Johns I and St. Johns II cultures (1991:172, 176). Such continuity is to be expected in a region where wetlands were so important.

A second trend observable in the St. Johns region is an increase in population over time from the Orange period into the St. Johns II period. Such an increase is strongly suggested from indices calculated by Miller that chart numbers of sites per century per period (Miller

1991:152, 180). For the Orange period there are 4.5 sites/century, while the numbers for the St. Johns I and II periods are 9.3 and 21.1, respectively. These indices offer strong credence to a picture of growing populations, especially during the St. Johns IIb period when agriculture is thought to have been important to local economies.

Village Life

Although the basic lifeway of the St. Johns culture was established by the end of the late Archaic period, the culture was not unchanging. Cultural changes after 500 B.C. grew out of inventions and new ideas—the latter reflected in the appearance of new and nonlocal ceramic styles—along with larger populations and increased use of domesticated plants. After about A.D. 1050, although that date has not been verified with radiocarbon dates, at least some of the St. Johns IIb period groups living along the middle and lower portions of the river developed complex social and political structures similar to those of the Fort Walton, Pensacola, and Safety Harbor cultures in contemporary northwest Florida and the Tampa Bay region. These societies, typified by large mound centers and, apparently, by a chiefly level of social organization, are discussed in the section on St. Johns II cultures. Because maize agriculture never became as important to the economic system of the St. Johns people as it did to the Fort Walton culture or other late precolumbian societies of the interior Southeast, the complex social and political systems associated with these St. Johns IIb societies may not have been sustained over time, and their geographical distribution within east Florida is limited.

Few occupational sites of the St. Johns I period have been extensively studied. One excavation, however, provides important data on the nature of St. Johns I occupation of the coastal zone, confirming the presence of shellfish-gathering stations occupied irregularly by small numbers of people at various times throughout the year (Russo et al. 1989). Excavations at two coastal middens at Edgewater Landing in Volusia County also provided radiocarbon dates confirming the temporal placement of the St. Johns I ceramic assemblage. The recognition of Orange-period permanent village sites along the coast (Russo in Russo, Cordell, and Ruhl 1992) and the data from the Edgewater Landing sites strongly suggest that year-round St. Johns I settlements also were present in the coastal zone and that such sites articulated with the special-use camps.

Evidence suggests that most tools and other St. Johns I–period artifacts were the same as those found associated with Orange-period sites. In fact, from the end of the Orange period on, the same types of shell tools, bone pins, bone awls, and bone points appear to have been used. Occasionally, stone points, hollow bone sockets, plummets, or net weights are found, but these are less common.

St. Johns pottery, the distinctive chalky ware, is ubiquitous at sites. In middens, the majority type in the St. Johns I period is always St. Johns Plain. Pinching and incised designs, some of which are the same as the designs on fiber-tempered pottery, appear on some early St. Johns I vessels. Over time the trend is for fewer decorated sherds. Sherds tempered with quartz sand also are found in some locales, and the variation in paste types is greater than is apparent to the naked eye (see Cordell in Russo et al. 1989 for a study of St. Johns I pottery).

Some archaeologists have suggested that changing sea-level conditions and water salinity during the St. Johns I period led to the first appearance of significant oyster populations in the coastal lagoons, drawing St. Johns people. This view may be incorrect, and the observation that during the St. Johns I period large numbers of sites first are found near the coast must be tempered by the fact that many earlier sites, such as those of the Orange period, have been inundated. As more surveys are completed, more and more Orange-period sites continue to be found in coastal regions (see chapter 3).

The coastal shell middens, composed mainly of oysters (60 percent to more than 90 percent of the shell), are among the largest shell middens in the United States. Perhaps the most extensive is Turtle Mound near New Smyrna. Before its partial destruction during the late nineteenth and twentieth centuries, various observers estimated its height at as much as seventy-five feet. In the sixteenth century it served as a landmark for sailors and was known to the colonial-period native peoples as the mound of Surruque.

Archaeological investigations in coastal shell heaps indicate that by far the most extensive occupations occurred during the St. Johns II period, the time of the largest populations. Excavation of sites such as Castle Windy (Bullen and Sleight 1959) and Green Mound (Bullen

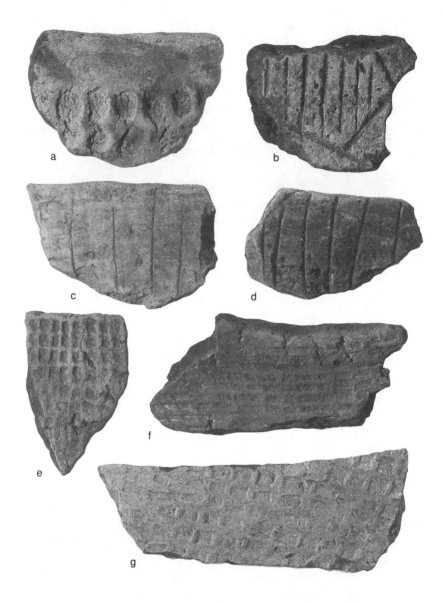

St. Johns pottery: *a*, St. Johns Pinched, 1¾ inches high; *b–d*, St. Johns Incised; *e–g*, St. Johns Check Stamped.

The bottom of a St. Johns Plain pottery vessel found at Tick Island (*right*) was impressed with a plaited fabric, shown in the plasticene impression on the left (courtesy Florida Museum of Natural History).

and Sleight 1960) have determined the nature of these shell heaps and provided information on the coastal subsistence pattern during the St. Johns I and II periods. Animals eaten for food at the coastal sites included deer, turkey, raccoon, opossum, rabbit, wildcat, and a variety of fish, especially snook, mullet, shark, and redfish. As elsewhere, fish were probably the most economically important vertebrate meat source. An occasional porpoise was also caught. Birds taken include loon, gannet, double-crested cormorant, duck, black brant, turkey vulture, razor-billed auk, herring gull, black-backed gull, glaucous gull, laughing gull, wood ibis, brown pelican, great blue heron, bald eagle, and great auk—the last extinct today. The array of animals at the large coastal sites, which must represent the refuse from year-round settlements, contrasts with the more meager species list from the special-use camps, like those excavated by Russo at Edgewater Landing (Russo et al. 1989).

Ceremonial Life

St. Johns I ceremonialism appears to combine indigenous elements with aspects of practices present elsewhere in Florida, such as those of the Yent, Green Point, and Weeden Island complexes. Exactly what the presence of copies of Weeden Island vessels in St. Johns I mounds signifies is uncertain. At the least, finding the same stylized bird motifs on St. Johns vessels and on early Weeden Island vessels suggests that some aspects of ideology were shared, as they may have been across northern Florida.

Much of our knowledge of St. Johns ceremonialism comes from burial mounds excavated in the late nineteenth century by Clarence B. Moore (1894a, 1896a, b, c). In his synthesis of the St. Johns–region cultures, *Space and Time Perspective in Northern St. Johns Archaeology, Florida,* John Goggin (1952c) provided an interpretive framework for much of Moore's work. The discussion that follows is based in part on that synthesis.

Constructed sand burial mounds are present in east Florida during the St. Johns I period, prior to A.D. 100, just as they are on the Gulf coast and in northwest Florida. Goggin (1952c) describes the mounds as low rises or truncated cones usually less than four feet high, although a few are as high as ten feet. Deposits of red ochre or a similar mineral were often placed in mounds. Use of a charnel house for burial preparation is suggested by the presence of secondary bundled burials. Primary flexed or extended interments and cremations also were placed in mounds. The number of individuals in any one mound ranges from two to a hundred, although most mounds contain less than twenty-five individuals. As with the early Weeden Island burial mounds described in chapter 5 and 6, the people interred in some St. Johns I mounds may all have been members of the same lineage or kin group.

The most common St. Johns I burial ritual resembled that found elsewhere in north Florida at the time. The deceased first were prepared and stored in a charnel house. Later, the bundled skeletal remains were placed on a specially prepared surface and ritually covered with earth, resulting in a mound. The same mound might have been used more than once for interments, resulting in several mound strata and multiple layers of human burials.

After A.D. 100 during the St. Johns Ia period, new ideas must have entered east Florida along with items exotic to the region. The same trade networks that brought materials from outside of Florida to northern Florida and the Gulf coast also brought them to the early St. Johns people. Such objects, placed in caches in mounds or with individual burials, include mica and galena, copper-covered animal jaws and wooden effigies, greenstone celts, quartz plummets, copper discs, copper cymbal-shaped earspools, and bird-effigy elbow pipes. Locally made Dunns Creek Red and St. Johns Plain vessels, some with podal supports like those on Deptford pottery, were placed in the mounds. At times Deptford-like check- and simple-stamped surface decorative motifs were copied on vessels made from St. Johns paste. Deptford vessels also are found in St. Johns Ia mounds, as are shell columella beads, drinking cups, tools, and pendants.

The mounds of the St. Johns Ia period tend to be larger than those dating from earlier in the St. Johns I period, and all are constructed in the shape of truncated cones. In later mounds of this period Swift Creek Complicated Stamped vessels and vessels with Swift Creek motifs and St. Johns chalky paste replace the Deptford vessels.

Two late St. Johns Ia or early Ib period mounds were excavated by Ripley Bullen, Adelaide Bullen, and William Bryant (1967). Located at the Ross Hammock site on the coastal lagoon in Volusia County, the mounds were constructed of earth scooped from moatlike borrow pits beside each mound. Neither mound contained exotic items related to the Yent or Green Point complexes. The mounds did contain relatively large amounts of Dunns Creek Red pottery, a type that may be typical of the St. Johns Ib period and that is also found in Cades Pond mounds of the same period in north-central Florida and in mounds of the peninsular Gulf coast.

One of the Ross Hammock mounds contained a small log tomb. Such tombs are known from Hopewellian mounds elsewhere in the Southeast. Human burials in the mound were both mass and single interments, all in flexed position. Charnel house preparation and storage of bodies may not have been practiced.

A log tomb also has been identified in a St. Johns Ia mound, the Queen Mound located east of Jacksonville just south of the St. Johns River (LaFond 1983). In addition to the log tomb, the mound, 5.5 feet high and 65 feet in diameter, contained items that clearly are related to the Hopewellian Yent complex, including cut carnivore jaws, galena, miniature vessels, and St. Johns Plain and Deptford pottery. Cremated burials, bundled burials, and flexed burials all were present. A small effigy bird head, possibly made from galena, also was recovered (LaFond 1972). The overall artifact assemblage of this St. Johns Ia mound is similar to contemporary assemblages from the northern peninsular Gulf coast.

During the St. Johns Ib period, the growth and spread of Weeden Island ritual and beliefs are reflected in the types of nonlocal pottery found in the mounds. Late varieties of Swift Creek Complicated Stamped, Tucker Ridge-pinched, and Weeden Island Incised and Punctated vessels occur with St. Johns Plain and Dunns Creek Red vessels. Greenstone celts are present, but some nonlocal objects, especially copper ornaments, were evidently no longer obtained through trade.

Some St. Johns Ib mounds contain vessels made with St. Johns chalky paste but in Weeden Island shapes and decorated with Weeden Island motifs. These copies of Weeden Island vessels sometimes depict animals, such as a duck effigy and other ceramics from a mound on Tick Island (Goggin 1952c:100, pl. 3; Moore 1894a:58–63). That mound also contained shell cups, galena, and mica.

By the end of the St. Johns Ib period at A.D. 750, native groups were living in villages throughout the St. Johns River drainage as well as on portions of the coast and around the many lakes in the central lake district. As was true of other contemporary native societies in Florida, they lived near wetlands and made their living by hunting, fishing, gathering, and collecting wild resources. Some gardening may have taken place. At the least, the St. Johns I people certainly encouraged the growth of wild plants, which they used for food, containers, and other purposes. The manipulation of plants so they would grow close to settlements probably was practiced throughout Florida at this time.

St. Johns II Culture

The appearance of check-stamped pottery in the St. Johns region at about A.D. 750, the same time it appeared in regions of the Weeden Island cultures, provides archaeologists with an important temporal marker that allows St. Johns II archaeological deposits to be distinguished from St. Johns I deposits (see table, this chapter). Less easy is an explanation of why check-stamped pottery suddenly became so popular. Archaeologists have speculated that, as in northwest Florida, the spread of check-stamped pottery correlates with the spread of maize agriculture. Whether this is true or not, the reasons for any relationship between ceramic style and maize remain to be proven. Indeed, the evidence for precolumbian maize agriculture in the St. Johns region is almost nonexistent.

More certain is the theme of continuity between St. Johns I– and St. Johns II–period populations. Types of artifacts found in sites show little change, sites are found in the same locations (not surprisingly, given the reliance on wetlands), and ceramic seriations from stratigraphic tests show a development from the St. Johns I to the St. Johns II period.

But several changes are apparent. One, alluded to earlier in this chapter, is the increase in numbers of sites or components within sites. There is little doubt that in the St. Johns II period there were larger human populations. And with larger populations at least some locales within the St. Johns drainage apparently developed a more complex political organization, a system more like that of the Fort Walton– and Mississippian–period societies than like the big-man, lineage-group level of social integration present earlier in the St. Johns region.

Whether or not the economic system of the St. Johns region could sustain chiefdoms like those in northwest Florida (see chapter 10) is not at all certain. However, there is evidence that at least one of the St. Johns IIb period mound sites interpreted as center of a chiefdom was still occupied when European influences first reached Florida.

Gourds and Squashes

Another phenomenon in the St. Johns II period is the use of bottle gourd (*Lagenaria siceria*) and a gourdlike form of squash (*Cucurbita pepo*). Identified from St. Johns II–period deposits at Hontoon Island, both plants probably were used as containers rather than as food (Newsom 1986:88, 1987:71, 74). More than 2,000 cucurbit seeds were recovered along with rind fragments. Bottle gourd remains were much fewer. Both plants are most likely examples of encouraged plants rather than crops that were cultivated. Well documented from the

St. Johns II– and colonial-period aboriginal midden deposits at Hontoon Island and apparently found in earlier strata at that site as well, both plants certainly were in use in the St. Johns I period. As we have seen, one or the other of these plants has been found in early Archaic deposits at the Windover Pond site, and they now have been documented for the Orange period in east Florida as well (Russo et al. 1992).

Indeed, new evidence indicates that wild *Cucurbita pepo* gourds were present in Florida at least by the time of Paleoindians and that *Lagenaria* gourds have nearly as long a history here. Wild ancestors of these plants are most likely native to Florida (Newsom, Webb, and Dunbar 1992). Their origin was not Mesoamerican, an explanation once proposed for their presence in the eastern United States.

As samples of plant remains collected from the freshwater-saturated midden deposits at Hontoon Island are processed, the presence of both types of gourd, as well as other plants, is certain to be demonstrated for the St. Johns I period. With new methods of recovering plant remains and the recognition that wet sites preserve these remains well, these and other plants yet to be identified probably will be shown to have been used by nearly all precolumbian native Floridians.

Subsistence, Village Life, and Hontoon Island

A tantalizing glimpse of inland St. Johns IIb period subsistence is provided by pottery effigies excavated from a ceremonial cache at the Thursby Mound site (Moore 1894a:69–81). These fired-clay, toylike effigies are modeled in the forms of corncobs, squashes, gourds, and acorns, as well as several animal species. Corncob-marked pottery from the St. Johns area also verifies the presence of maize in that region during the St. Johns IIb period, although the exact importance of maize within the diet remains uncertain.

All four of the plants depicted in clay effigies at the Thursby Mound site have been identified from the wet deposits at the Hontoon Island site, excavated in the 1980s by Barbara Purdy (Purdy 1987a, b, 1991). Hontoon Island, more than two miles long, is bordered by the St. Johns River and several of its braided streams. The site investigated by Purdy is on the north end of the island, directly across the St. Johns River from the Thursby site. Her excavations revealed an extensive precolumbian snail midden, dating to the St. Johns I and II periods.

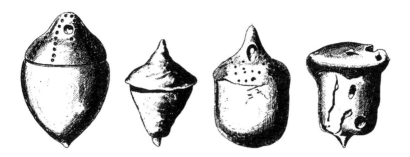

These four clay acorn effigies were recovered by Moore from the Thursby Mound (from Moore 1894a: figs. 84–87). Specimen at left is 2 inches high. Other objects of similar size resemble an ear of corn, gourds, and a variety of animals, dippers, vessels, and other implements.

Radiocarbon dates and ceramic collections indicate that the portion of the snail midden deposited in the water is from the St. Johns II period (Purdy 1987a:36, 1987b:11). In portions of the site, including the area of the wet deposits, the snail midden is overlaid by a mussel shell midden dating to the postcontact period, that is, after contact with Europeans. Elsewhere on the island are additional middens, some of which predate the St. Johns culture.

Purdy's initial tests in the wet midden strata produced a remarkable assortment of St. Johns II–period artifacts, along with extraordinarily well-preserved plant and animal remains. The artifact assemblage included more than 82,000 potsherds (largely St. Johns Plain and St. Johns Check Stamped), 177 bone artifacts, 147 stone artifacts, 80 wooden artifacts, and thousands of wood chips and other debris from woodworking, probably including dugout canoe making (Purdy 1991: 117, 120).

Pinellas projectile points, used to tip arrows, were common, as were sandstone abraders used to work wood (Purdy 1991:125). The array of bone and shell artifacts is similar to that found at other St. Johns sites: deer ulna awls; bone pins, pendants, beads, a dagger, and fishhook; shark teeth; *Busycon* shell hammers and receptacles or cups; and a fish-hook made from mussel shell.

It would not be surprising to find this entire assemblage, except for the Pinellas points, at St. Johns I–period sites. Many of the same wetland-oriented subsistence practices and other activities of the St.

Johns II people at Hontoon Island were practiced by their pre–
A.D. 750 ancestors.

This continuity is true as well for the faunal remains identified from
samples taken from the wet deposits (Wing and McKean 1987). The
same animals were used for food in the St. Johns I and II period. The
Hontoon assemblage was dominated by freshwater species such as catfish, gar, bass, mullet, aquatic turtle, and alligator. A number of other
fish and reptiles were eaten, along with ducks (some migratory),
Canada geese, and terrestrial species, such as gopher tortoise, rabbit,
deer, and turkey. Most popular in the meat diet were snail, catfish,
pond turtle, and gopher tortoise. All of these last species could be
taken with simple but efficient technologies: gathering snails and
gopher tortoises by hand, using hook and line and nets for catfish (clay
plummets which may be net weights were found), and catching turtles
with traps or by hand.

One remarkable aspect of the Hontoon Island collections is the
range and quantity of plant remains, materials normally not found by
archaeologists because they are not preserved in land sites. Analysis of
the archaeobotanical samples by Lee Newsom (1986, 1987; and see
Purdy 1991) provides a look at the species of plants used for artifacts,
types of wooden artifacts in use at the site, and the plants that were
used for food. Thirty separate wood species were identified along with
eighty-two species of seeds or other plant parts. Woods included
cypress, pine, willow, ash, bay, staggerbush (*Lyonia* sp.), oak, elm, but-
tonbush, cedar, and persimmon. Several tropical woods not native to
Florida were identified. Cypress chips were common, quite likely
debris produced in adzing dugout canoes out of logs. One broken
canoe paddle was recovered, along with a red cedar bird effigy ornament, perhaps a hair pin. Posts, fire-starters (parts of bow drills),
shafts, plugs, a wedge, tool handles, small points, and a bowl were present, along with numerous notched sticks, some of which could be
throwing-stick shafts, while others resemble the pegs used today to
anchor tent supports (Purdy 1991:120).

Just as the native peoples made use of the wide range of animals
that could be taken from their immediate surroundings, so did they
use the plants that grew around them. Hickory nuts, acorns, and cabbage palm remains were especially prominent, along with may pop,
grape, and saw palmetto. Other plants with edible parts were huckle-

Barbara Purdy at her excavation on Hontoon Island, which produced one of the largest assemblages of plant remains recovered from a Florida site. Pumps and hoses were used to wash the soggy deposits through screens (courtesy Barbara A. Purdy).

berry, blueberry, elderberry, blackberry, peppervine, black gum (the fruit is eaten), groundcherry, amaranth, bristlegrass, pokeweed, broomweed, smartweed or knotweed, bulrush, nut sedge, button-bush, water shield, and spatterdock.

Maize cobs and kernels were found at Hontoon Island, but as yet only in samples taken from the colonial-period mussel shell midden. Based on the clay effigies from the nearby Thursby mound, we would expect maize to have been cultivated by the St. Johns IIb peoples living at Hontoon Island. As Purdy (1988) has noted, Hontoon Island, like other Florida wet sites, is a true storehouse of knowledge about the precolumbian peoples who lived in Florida.

Political and Ceremonial Life

As for many other parts of Florida, our knowledge of St. Johns II ceremonialism and associated ideology comes almost entirely from mounds excavated by C. B. Moore (1884a, b, 1886a, b, c). His reports suggest that St. Johns IIa–period mounds tend to be somewhat larger

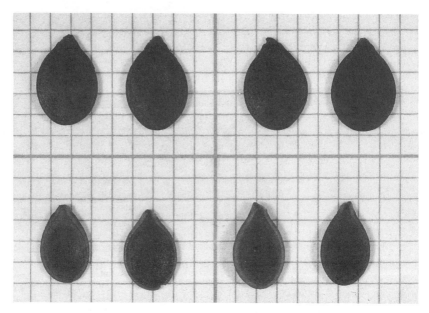

Cucurbita (squash) seeds recovered from Hontoon Island (courtesy Lee Ann Newsom).

than those of the earlier St. Johns I period and that they continued to be used for kin-based, perhaps lineage, interments. St. Johns Check Stamped pottery, a horizon marker, provides a convenient chronological tool for dating the mounds.

During the St. Johns IIb period, a time contemporaneous with the Mississippian Fort Walton culture in northwest Florida, at least some mounds were apparently used as tombs for elite individuals. This finding suggests that in some portions of the St. Johns region, perhaps those with the largest populations and most efficient economies, chiefdoms replaced big-man societies. Although the archaeological evidence is sketchy, it is likely that agriculture never was as important in the St. Johns region as it was for Mississippian societies with their complex forms of social and political organization. Agriculture-based economic systems could support higher levels of population density and more complex levels of social integration; St. Johns IIb economies based largely on fishing, hunting, and gathering and supplemented by agriculture might, in some instances, support higher populations and more complex political integration for a time. But sooner or later local resources would not be enough to sustain such intensification, and the complex political constructs would dissolve. Although this may have been true, at least some large St. Johns mound and village complexes—for instance, Thursby Mound—probably continued to be occupied into the St. Johns IIc period, the early colonial period.

Archaeological evidence suggests Mississippian cultures did have some influence on St. Johns IIb societies, and some artifacts like those found in Mississippian mounds have come from sites in the St. Johns region during that period.

One St. Johns IIa mound investigated in modern times is the Walker Point Mound on Amelia Island (Hemmings and Deagan 1973). Like many of the mounds reported by C. B. Moore, Walker Point was a conical mound composed of a lower submound stratum containing interments and a covering upper cap of red ochre–impregnated sand. Burials were extended, flexed, and bundled. Fragments of skeletal material, such as teeth, cranial fragments, and phalanges, also were found in the red ochre–colored stratum. These may have been left over from burial preparation activities in a charnel house, put in the mound when the other skeletal remains were interred. In many ways, the burial ceremonialism is similar to that of St. Johns I mounds.

But the St. Johns IIb period, A.D. 1050–1513, as noted earlier, is characterized by the adoption of some Mississippian traits. Several large pyramidal mounds like those at Mississippian sites were excavated by C. B. Moore. Such large mounds are not known for earlier times in the St. Johns region. Decorative motifs and types of objects found by Moore in the Mt. Royal Mound on the St. Johns River in Putnam County are identical to those found elsewhere in the southeastern United States dating to A.D. 1050–1150. These artifacts and symbols are associated with the Southeastern Ceremonial Complex, an assemblage of artifacts and art styles widespread in time and space and associated with various Mississippian beliefs and practices (Brown 1985; and see chapter 10).

The three best-known St. Johns IIb mounds, all excavated by Moore (1894a, b), are Shields (also called "mound near Mill Cove") in Duval County, Mt. Royal in Putnam County, and Thursby Mound in Volusia County. All three are located on the St. Johns River, and their respective natural settings, perhaps in combination with agriculture, could have supported large populations, at least for a time.

Shields Mound is a typical Mississippian truncated pyramidal mound with a ramp leading up one side. The square base measured roughly 190 feet on a side (Moore 1894b:204–205). Evidently built in several stages, the mound probably served as the base for a building. Moore's excavations uncovered about 150 sets of badly decomposed skeletal remains, suggesting that the mound may have been used both as a burial mound and, perhaps later, as a structure base.

The famous Mt. Royal site contained a copper plate displaying Southeastern Ceremonial Complex forked-eye motifs like those found at other Mississippian sites. Copper beads and copper ornaments also were found, evidence of contact between the St. Johns region and societies to the north and northwest.

At the time it was excavated by Moore, the Mt. Royal mound was 15 feet high and 160 feet across. One of the most intriguing features of the site is a causeway leading 820 yards from the mound to a small lake. The causeway, which varies from 12 to 25 feet across, was built by scraping soil from the ground surface and piling it on both sides of the causeway. These parallel piles or, more correctly, ridges, were nearly 3 feet high and as much as 12 feet wide.

Earthworks have been identified from another St. Johns II–period site in east Florida, Murphy Island near Palatka (Goggin 1952:55). That site may be the aboriginal town of Edelano, said by French explorers in the 1560s (the St. Johns IIc period) to have been located on a large island in the St. Johns River (Laudonnière 1975:115, 131). The French account says in the town was a walkway 300 paces long and 50 paces wide, with huge trees growing on both sides with their branches intertwined overhead. A similar walkway also is mentioned as having been present at the main town of Chief Utina located to the north in the St. Johns drainage (Laudonnière 1975:115, 137).

The naturalist William Bartram visited Mt. Royal in 1765 and 1774, publishing the description quoted in chapter 1 ("a noble Indian highway, which led from the great mount, on a straight line, three quarters of a mile . . . about fifty yards wide, sunk a little . . . , and the earth thrown up on each side, making a bank of about two feet high"; Bartram 1928:101–102).

As with other St. Johns IIb mounds, the Mt. Royal Mound appears to have been capped with a red ochre–impregnated sand stratum. Artifacts excavated by Moore from the mound had been deposited both in

Drawing of a copper breast plate, about 10½ inches high, recovered by
C.B. Moore from the Mount Royal site (Moore 1894a:4). The copper depicts
forked eyes, a Southeastern Ceremonial Complex motif. Moore (1894a:32)
noted, "Beneath the upper plate [shown here] was a layer of reeds . . . bound
together by closely woven vegetable fibre. On one side . . . , the reeds were
replaced by twisted vegetable fibre of equal length and diameter. Behind this
layer was a backing of bark about .25 of an inch in thickness. Next came
another copper plate bent over on itself. . . . Behind [this plate] were fragments of wood one inch in thickness."

separate caches and with interments. The distributions of these objects
suggest the mound was constructed during at least several different
building phases before receiving the final cap. Artifacts included
Busycon shells (none of which were made into drinking cups, although
many seem to have been "killed"), greenstone celts, spatulate greenstone celts, ceramic biconical tubes, and numerous fired-clay vessels.
The last were constructed into a variety of unique shapes and must

A limestone earspool covered with copper sheeting,
1¼ inches in diameter, from the Mount Royal site
(from Moore 18942:33). "In every portion of the
mound . . . were various objects wrought from or
coated with sheet copper" (Moore 18942:30).

have had special ceremonial use, such as for the brewing and drinking
of black drink or other ceremonial teas.

The Thursby Mound, located near the Hontoon Island site excavated
by Purdy, is a truncated cone thirteen feet high and about ninety feet
in diameter. A constructed shell causeway led from the mound to the
nearby St. Johns River. The causeway may have been the equivalent
of the broad walkways at Mt. Royal and the St. Johns villages documented in the colonial period. The presence in the Thursby Mound of
gold and silver ornaments is evidence that it continued to be used into
the colonial period. Purdy's excavations at Hontoon Island indicated
that it similarly was occupied into the St. Johns IIc period and, perhaps, later (Newsom 1986:128–129).

The Thursby ceremonial mound contained numerous flexed burials,
many in deteriorated condition. The exact construction sequence of
the mound is not known, although Moore's description of strata indicates that at least a large portion of the mound was originally built in
a single phase. Later, additional strata were added, and interments and
artifacts were placed in the mound.

In addition to a large variety of unusually shaped vessels, some quite
similar to those from Mt. Royal, Moore recovered the cache of plant
and animal effigies mentioned earlier. In all, forty-eight separate animals were recovered, including eight fish and ten turtles. Other animals were felines (probably panthers), bears, squirrels, turkeys, dogs
(?), and beavers (?), many depicting the same animal species identified
among the Hontoon Island fauna collections. Some of the figurines are

A wooden owl carving recovered from the St. Johns River near Hontoon
Island in 1955. The rotted bottom portion was later cut off and radiocarbon
dated (see Bullen 1955b; courtesy Florida Museum of Natural History).

easy to identify, while others are crude. Several of the effigy vessels
from the mound resemble *Busycon* shells, while others may represent
sea urchins.

Another piece of information about St. Johns IIb–period ideology
surfaced in 1955 when a dragline operator pulled a large carved
wooden "totem" out of the muck of the St. Johns River near the
Thursby site (Bullen 1955b:61). Carved from a single log by burning
the wood and then scraping with a shark tooth tool and, possibly, a
stone knife, the "totem" is an owl with distinctive feather "ear" tufts,
representing either a great horned owl or a screech owl. The carved
owl, which measures about six feet from head to talons, is portrayed
perched on a roost. Evidently originally stuck in the ground, the
bottom end of the roost is rotted away. A radiocarbon date of A.D. 1300
was obtained from a wood sample taken from the carving.

It is doubtful if the carved figurine represents a true totem, like the
clan totem poles found on the northwest coast of North America. The
sound of owls was viewed by the Timucuan-speaking native peoples
of the St. Johns region as a symbol of evil or bad luck (Milanich and

Sturtevant 1972:24, 26, 44). They were anomalously behaving animals—symbols like the animals depicted on effigy vessels of the Weeden Island culture; like them, they may have been displayed near a charnel house or burial area. Similar large wooden carvings have been recovered from the Fort Center site in the Lake Okeechobee Basin, where they were associated with mortuary activities (see chapter 8).

The owl carving is not an isolated find. In 1978 smaller wooden carvings of an otter and a pelican were found in the St. Johns River quite near the place where the owl was found (Purdy 1991:110, 119–120). Like the owl, both the otter (a mammal that swims in water and is a carnivore) and the pelican (a water bird with a peculiar way of feeding) may have been viewed as anomalously behaving animals and served as symbols in the St. Johns ideological system.

The social and political systems of the St. Johns IIb–period societies, and the related ideological system, must have been similar to those found elsewhere in northern Florida at the same time. After A.D. 1050 many of the southeastern native societies, including the St. Johns peoples, apparently shared new aspects of ceremonial and political lives while retaining their individual economic adaptations. Those adaptations, while differing in specifics, all involved hunting, gathering, fishing, and cultivating crops. The level or intensity of agricultural production differed, however, across the entire region.

The native cultures of south Florida were among the groups in Florida who did not practice maize agriculture in the late precolumbian per d. But they, too, shared aspects of ideology and other traits with the native groups of northern Florida with whom they shared a common heritage, as we will see in chapter 8.

The South Florida Cultures

8

At one time archaeologists viewed south Florida as a single, large culture region that stood in contrast to the regions of northern Florida (e.g., Goggin 1947, 1949b:14, 28–32). There were several reasons for this belief. First, excavations at south Florida sites had revealed ceramic assemblages that included large amounts of undecorated pottery tempered with sand. The small amount of decorated pottery present helped to construct a chronology for the post–A.D. 500 period. The vast majority of the ceramics, however, appeared to be undecorated, sand-tempered, simple bowl-shaped vessels. As a whole, this south Florida assemblage differed markedly from the contemporary assemblages found in northern Florida, where decorated pottery in a variety of pastes was common.

A second factor was the small range of excavated data from south Florida relative to that from regions in the north. All of the geographical locales had not been sampled adequately, and the variability in archaeological assemblages that did exist was not emphasized. Indeed, from the time the Florida Park Service's archaeology program was halted in the early 1950s until the death of John Goggin in 1963, few other archaeologists ventured into south Florida. By tacit agreement Goggin had monopolized research in the area for more than a decade. Even into the 1970s fewer large archaeological projects were begun in south Florida than elsewhere in the state, and complete data from them did not appear until the 1980s. These projects include John

Griffin's excavations in Everglades National Park (Griffin 1988); the Fort Center project, directed by William Sears in the Lake Okeechobee Basin in the mid-1960s (Sears 1982); and the Granada project in Miami undertaken by the Florida Division of Historical Resources in the late 1970s (Griffin et al. 1985). The lack of information about the variety of south Florida cultural assemblages also contributed to the erroneous view that, except for the Lake Okeechobee Basin, archaeological sites tended to be distributed in largest numbers around the coast. The potential of the interior freshwater wetlands, such as the Everglades, as habitats for precolumbian peoples was not given sufficient credence by some investigators (Milanich and Fairbanks 1980:181).

A third reason that archaeologists treated south Florida as a separate culture region unique from northern areas was the lack of evidence of maize agriculture in the south. Documents written in the sixteenth century by Spanish sailors, priests, and survivors of shipwrecks led to the conclusion, accepted by a century of naturalists, historians, and archaeologists, that the native societies of northern Florida practiced agriculture; the native peoples of south Florida did not. One could draw a line across the state from the north side of Charlotte Harbor in the west to Fort Pierce in the east to separate northern, agricultural Florida from the nonagricultural south. A widespread belief was that the precolumbian societies of south Florida continued to have an Archaic-like way of life into the colonial period, practicing the same pattern of hunting, gathering, and fishing that had been present in northern Florida thousands of years earlier, but which in the north had evolved into new economic systems with the adoption of agriculture. South Florida, extending as it does into the Caribbean, was seen as a special case, the home of unique precolumbian cultures who subsisted by using a broad spectrum of animals and plants, as Archaic peoples had done earlier. The presence of large numbers of vertebrate species—especially fish and reptiles—in south Florida middens seemed to substantiate this view.

But this view would begin to change in the 1960s and 1970s. As data gathered from the late 1930s to the early 1950s by John Goggin (1949a, n.d., 1950a, b, 1951, 1952a, b; Goggin and Sommer 1949) was added to new information coming out of Fort Center in the Lake Okeechobee Basin (Sears 1971a, 1974) and other sites, it was becoming obvious that south Florida was not a single-culture region. A revised taxonomy was needed that expanded Goggin's concept of a single Glades culture for south Florida (cf., Sears 1967a; Griffin 1974). Variations in archaeological assemblages existed among geographical areas as well as through time, suggesting that cultural regions could be defined within south Florida.

The first revised taxonomy defined three regions: Okeechobee (the Okeechobee Basin and adjacent areas to the east and west), Calusa (the southwest coast and adjacent inland area), and Teksta (the remainder of south Florida, including the Florida Keys) (Griffin 1974:343; these names had been used earlier by John Goggin but were never published; Goggin n.d.:69). This initial reorganization and nomenclature were not entirely satisfactory, because it was not a certainty that either the Calusa or the Teksta (Tequesta) Indians of the colonial period correlated with the archaeological assemblages found in the regions that bore their names. Also, new information concerning ceramic distributions and other archaeological data showed that this taxonomy could be refined further. Consequently, a second, revised taxonomy has been offered, although it is still being altered as more information is gathered (Carr and Beriault 1984; Griffin 1988).

The most recent scheme divides south Florida into three culture regions: Okeechobee, Caloosahatchee, and Glades or Everglades (Glades is used here to distinguish the region from the Everglades habitat and to preserve at least some of Goggin's original nomenclature). The Ten Thousand Islands on the lower Gulf coast may be a separate region or subregion related to the Glades. Likewise, the Florida Keys is a subregion related to the Glades region. East Okeechobee, the interior portions of Palm Beach and Martin counties, may be a subregion related to the Okeechobee Basin.

Throughout their histories, the people living within all of these regions must have been in contact with one another as well as with cultures to the north, and they probably shared many aspects of their cultures. Indeed, the lifeways of the precolumbian native American Indians who lived in these southern regions after 500 B.C. were probably not too different from those practiced by many northern Florida societies. Wetlands, either coastal or freshwater, were major producers of fish and other animals taken for food in both north and south. Dugout canoes were a major means of travel for precolumbian

Culture regions of south Florida.

peoples, whether they lived in the marshes of the upper St. Johns River drainage, the wet prairies surrounding Lake Okeechobee, or the saw grass of the Everglades. Rather than envisioning a marked contrast between northern Florida agriculturists and south Florida Archaic-like peoples, a more correct view might be that the importance of agriculture lessens as one moves southward through Florida from the interior of the eastern panhandle—the region of the Fort Walton culture (see chapter 10)—down the peninsula. As we saw in previous chapters, the regional cultures of the peninsular Gulf coast and the upper St. Johns River basin probably placed little economic reliance on maize agriculture, and other coastal peoples in north Florida probably were not agriculturists at all.

South Florida cultures were not unique as previously thought. The large range of fish and reptile species in south Florida middens, both inland and on the coast, have now been duplicated at almost every wetland-related site in Florida where modern methods of recovering faunal remains have been employed. Although some species may vary by site and local catchment area, nearly all precolumbian cultures in Florida relied heavily on vertebrates that could be taken from rivers, lakes, wet prairies, coastal estuaries, and other wetlands.

Okeechobee Region

Today sport anglers troll and cast the shallow waters of Lake Okeechobee. The same resource that draws them to fish camps in the towns of Okeechobee, Moorehaven, Clewiston, and Belle Glade on the lake shore drew precolumbian fishers with nets and dugout canoes. From at least as early as 500 B.C., Lake Okeechobee and the surrounding area—pine and palmetto flatlands, creeks, wet prairies, and cypress swamps—were home to people of the Belle Glade culture, named for an archaeological site excavated in the 1930s (Willey 1949b; Sears 1967a:101).

Although ditched, diked, and drained, the Okeechobee Basin still retains some of the appearance it had when Belle Glade peoples occupied a series of large and small sites within the region. Huge by Florida standards, the lake averages 645 square miles in surface area. Lands near it are flat with little relief, hindering water runoff and drainage. Forested hammocks are home to cabbage palms, oaks, palmettos and scrub vegetation, but they have relatively low soil fertility.

Fisheating Creek and other creeks drain the surrounding flatlands into the lake. On the north side, the Kissimmee River, now channelized, also empties into the lake. To the west is the Caloosahatchee River, channelized and connected to the lake. The carefully controlled flow of that river, however, actually drains water from the lake.

At many of the sites in the Okeechobee region the precolumbian peoples constructed earthworks, including mounds, ponds, borrows, ditches, canals, and linear and annular embankments, some in peculiar geometric shapes. As a whole, the assemblage of earthworks is unique to the Okeechobee region, which encompasses the area

1 Bear Lake
2 Belle Glade
3 Big Mound City
4 Fort Center
5 Granada
6 Honey Hill
7 Horr's Island
8 Key Marco
9 Margate-Blount Mound
10 Mound Key
11 Onion Key
12 Ortona
13 Tony's Mound
14 Turner River

South Florida archaeological sites. Individual sites in the San Carlos Bay (e.g., Pineland, Useppa, Josslyn, Buck Key, Wightman) and Charlotte Harbor (e.g., Gasparilla, Solana, Big Mound Key) locales are not shown.

around the lake, including Glades, Hendry, Palm Beach, and Martin counties on the west, south, and east. The region also takes in much of the Kissimmee River drainage in Okeechobee, Highlands, and probably Osceola and Polk counties to the north. This northern end of the region has more relief than the basin itself because a southern finger of the central highlands topographic feature reaches down from northern Florida into eastern Polk and Highlands counties.

The exact cultural relationships between the Kissimmee River drainage and Belle Glade sites in the basin were a subject of contention for decades. Recent investigations have shown that earthworks like those found in the basin proper are found at least as far north as Lake

Kissimmee (Hale 1984), while Belle Glade pottery is found even farther north, having been documented as the majority ware at components in a site near Lake Hatchineha in eastern Polk County (Austin and Hansen 1988). Other data also support the inclusion of the Kissimmee River drainage in the Okeechobee region (see Allerton, Luer, and Carr 1984; Austin 1987b; Hale 1989; Luer 1989; W. Johnson 1991; and see Austin 1992, for an overview of archaeological research in the Kissimmee River area).

Also debated is the cultural relation of sites east of the basin in the flatwoods of eastern Palm Beach and Martin counties, the East Okeechobee area (e.g., Jaffee 1976). Belle Glade pottery, a type associated with the Belle Glade culture of the Okeechobee region, is found in relatively large quantities in coastal sites in Palm Beach County (Fury 1972:39). Better defined is the southern periphery of the Okeechobee region at the northern extent of the Everglades, the river of grass that is part of the Glades region.

Much of our information on the Belle Glade culture comes from surveys and test excavations, including the recording of earthwork complex sites, which can be discerned on aerial photographs (Carr 1975, 1985; Hale 1984, 1989; W. Johnson 1991). Although test excavations have been carried out at three earthwork sites—Tony's Mound (Hale 1989) and Big Mound City and the Belle Glade site (Willey 1949b)—the only site thoroughly excavated is Fort Center on the west side of Lake Okeechobee. Over a six-year period in the 1960s, William Sears directed excavations, and the information he gathered provides a mainstay for understanding the Belle Glade culture (Sears 1971a, 1974, 1982; Sears and Sears 1976).

Although Sears was the first to mount a long-term project in the Belle Glade region, the unique nature of the earthwork complexes had not escaped the notice of earlier archaeologists and observers. In the 1930s and 1940s, Federal Emergency Relief Agency archaeologists and others recorded and, in some cases, tested several of the sites. In addition to Big Mound City (described by the botanist John Small in the 1920s) and the Belle Glade site, both in Palm Beach County, other sites noted early on include Tony's Mound in Hendry County (visited and mapped by Allen [1948]), and the Ortona site in Glades County.

Big Mound City, Tony's Mound, and similar sites are collectively known as "Big Circle" sites, a name given to them by Allen (1948:17)

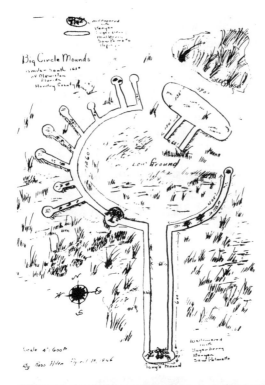

Ross Allen's original sketch of Tony's Mound (1946). In his original report (Allen 1948) and in this drawing, he noted an associated mound a quarter mile northeast of the main complex (from the files of the Florida Museum of Natural History).

Subsequent to Allen's visit, the site was plowed, ditched, drained, and put into improved pasture. Many of the mounds and earthworks were plowed flat, as shown in this 1960s aerial photograph. The white dots on the right are cows (courtesy William Sears and Florida Museum of Natural History).

because of the narrow, semicircular or horseshoe-shaped sand embankments present at each. These embankments average about 500 feet across at the opening. Extending outward from each semicircular embankment are five to ten linear embankments, each terminating in a small round or oval mound. Usually other mounds and embankments, or other types of earthworks, are present at the sites, including large middens sometimes deposited across the openings to the horseshoe–shaped mounds. William Johnson (1991:153–179, 182) has provided a typology for the earthworks and attempted to order them chronologically, using information gleaned by Sears from Fort Center and a chronology developed for the Belle Glade site by Gordon Willey (1949b:125–126).

Another feature of the Belle Glade region is the canals found at sites like Ortona. Similar canals, some several miles long and presumably used to facilitate canoe travel between villages and rivers or as shortcuts across coastal islands, are known from other locations in south Florida (Kenworthy 1883; Douglass 1885a; Luer 1989). The earthworks and canals of the Okeechobee Basin are extraordinary.

Fort Center

As noted, the Fort Center site provides much of our information on the Belle Glade culture (Sears 1982). Sears selected the Fort Center site for excavation because it contained middens and earthworks of the same types found at other sites in the Okeechobee Basin: mounds, linear embankments, a burial mound adjacent to what appeared to be an artificial pond (and borrow), extensive middens (along Fisheating Creek, which runs through the site), and several overlapping circular ditches. This large complex of earthworks and middens is located in a hammock that extends along Fisheating Creek for a mile. Outlying middens are found along the creek, such as the one tested by Goggin (1952a).

The name of the site, Fort Center, is derived from a Second Seminole War–period fort established near the creek in the late 1830s. In 1926 a hunter observed a wooden carving of an eagle sticking up out of the muck in a small pond near a large mound at the site. The carving eventually found its way to Bartow and then to the Florida State Museum in Gainesville (Anonymous 1933). The eagle would

Aerial view of the Fort Center site (see Sears 1982). North is to the right (courtesy William Sears and Florida Museum of Natural History).

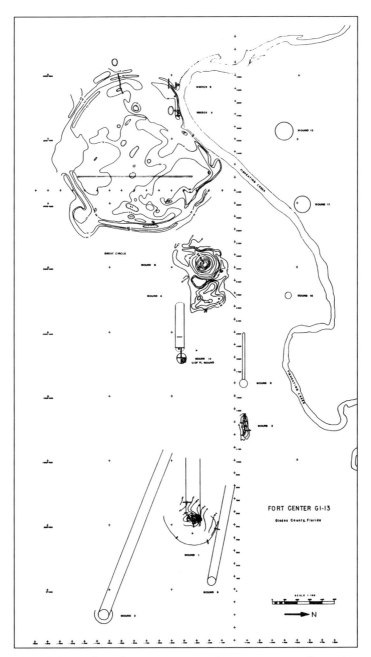

Plan of the earthworks at Fort Center (from Sears 1982: fig. 1.1).
Compare this drawing with the aerial photograph opposite.

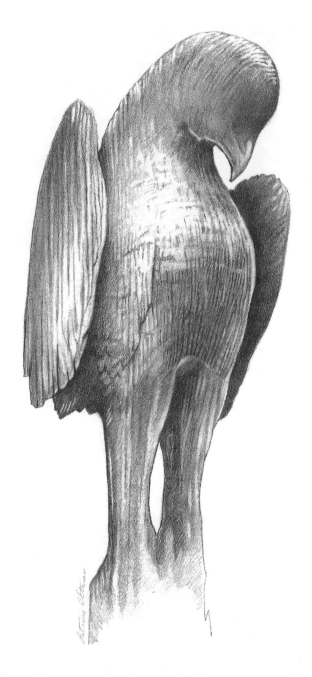

The wooden eagle carving taken from the Fort Center pond in 1926. The portion shown here is 27 inches high; the entire carving is 63 inches high (drawing by Patricia Altman; courtesy Florida Museum of Natural History).

prove to be a clue that led Sears to excavate an extraordinary collection of similar wooden carvings from the Fort Center charnel pond.

As Sears suspected, the various Fort Center earthworks date from different temporal periods and have different functions. The site was first occupied in the late Archaic period, sometime between 1000 and 500 B.C. The subsequent early Belle Glade peoples lived by hunting, fishing, and gathering, and they mostly made undecorated pottery of the type many archaeologists refer to as Glades Plain. Some potsherds contained fiber as temper along with sand. A radiocarbon date of 450 B.C. is consistent with the fiber-tempered pottery.

Early Maize Agriculture?

That people were living in the Okeechobee Basin by 500 B.C. was not as surprising as both the radiocarbon sample and the pottery coming from the fill of a circular ditch. More intriguing was the identification of maize pollen grains from soil removed from that same fill (Sears 1982:177–178). Maize pollen grains were identified from other contexts at the site, including (1) a lime-based paint found on a wooden carving excavated from the pond that had produced the eagle carving; (2) paleofeces excavated from a midden deposit beside the pond; and (3) other soil samples (Sears and Sears 1976).

Maize cultivation at 450 B.C. in the Lake Okeechobee Basin is astounding and, as might be expected, controversial. As much as some archaeologists would like to explain it away by pleading sample contamination or suggesting that the pollen was not from maize but from another plant, they cannot.

The artifact collections from Fort Center, including the pollen samples, are now curated at the Florida Museum of Natural History. There archaeologists meticulously reviewed the contexts of the soil, paint, and paleofecal samples from which maize was identified. Some maize pollen may have turned up where it did as a result of sample contamination, but other samples appeared to be good contexts. The pollen slides also were reidentified by a palynologist in the museum's paleoecology laboratory. All involved in the reanalysis came to the same conclusion Sears had reached: well before the time maize is known to have been cultivated in northern Florida, the Belle Glade people were growing the crop at Fort Center.

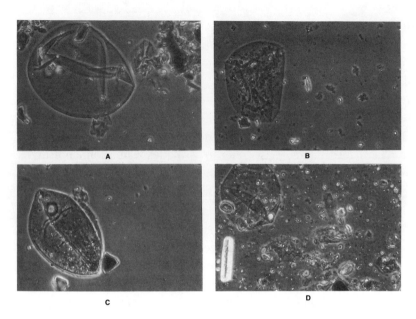

Microscopically enlarged maize (*Zea*) pollen grains from Fort Center: *a*, from white pigment on one of the wooden carvings from the charnel pond; *b*, from a coprolite; *c*, from the Great Circle ditch; *d*, from a single linear mound (from Sears 1982: fig. 8 .1; courtesy Elsie O'R. Sears, William Sears, and Florida Museum of Natural History).

How could agriculture be present at such an early date at Fort Center, especially if, as noted earlier, the colonial-period native American Indians in south Florida did not practice maize agriculture? Does any explanation fit other archaeological data from Fort Center?

At least one such explanation is possible, following Sears (1982:145, 147, 178, 186, 192–194). Maize was cultivated in a garden plot adjacent to the Fort Center middens along Fisheating Creek. Because maize will not grow in conditions that keep the plant's roots wet, the Belle Glade people needed a means to keep the field where maize was planted drained and dry. This was accomplished by digging a circular ditch about 375 yards in diameter, averaging 28 feet wide at its top, with walls that sloped to a flat bottom 6 feet below the ground surface.

Sears suggests that the ditch cut through the underlying hardpan, a humite stratum (a spodic horizon in which humic materials percolating down through the soil collect) that underlies the site and kept water from percolating into the ground. Excavations on the western side of the ditch showed that it did extend below the level of the hardpan stratum. By cutting through the hardpan, water within and outside of the circle could drain downward, flow along the top of the hardpan, and then drain where the hardpan had been excavated away. The result would be a roughly circular drained field, slightly larger than the ditch itself.

Excavations indicated that the ditch contained standing water and that a mucky layer accumulated in its bottom. Sears (1982:189) suggests that one by-product of cleaning muck out of the ditch and distributing it across the drained field was the natural fertilizer provided by the "quantities of fish and amphibian small-fry and eggs" found in the muck. This "protoplasmic" muck would have contained phosphorus and been high in nitrogen (Sears 1982:182). At least two "causeways," unditched walkways across the ditch, allowed access to the interior of the field.

Aerial photographs and excavation revealed that this circular ditch was not the only one constructed at the site. Two smaller, earlier ditches had been built, first one and then the other, in the same location. The largest and most recent ditch overlapped these older ditches, both constructed before 450 B.C., the radiocarbon date obtained from the fill of the larger, more recent ditch. Sears believes that the ditch method of field drainage continued to be used to about A.D. 600 or 800, with the land's usefulness maintained by fertilization.

Sears makes the point that the Lake Okeechobee Basin greatly resembles the lowlands of the Gulf coast of Mexico in terms of vegetation, rainfall, growing season, and day length. Maize is a crop that requires adaptation to local conditions. If maize were introduced to south Florida from Mesoamerica it could have been grown in the basin. South Florida is accessible from Mexico by boat, either around the Gulf coast or, more likely, via Yucatan and the Caribbean islands

(Sears 1977b). Because ditched and drained agricultural fields are found elsewhere in the tropical savanna in the western hemisphere (Denevan 1970), Sears implies that the entire complex of maize cultivation and ditched fields could have been introduced into south Florida.

The three Fort Center circular ditches are neither the only ones recorded in the basin nor in south Florida. Other circular ditches have been located using aerial photographs and by site surveys (Carr 1975). One such ditch, about 420 yards in diameter, is several miles south of Fort Center (Milanich 1968). Another is west of Lake Okeechobee on the Caloosahatchee River. It appears to have been round but later was extended so it would intersect the river. Still another is on Pine Island in Lee County.

Were these circular ditches indeed drained fields? Some authors have argued for a ceremonial function (Goggin and Sturtevant 1964; Carr 1985), an explanation offered for other Okeechobee earthworks as well, such as the linear embankments at Fort Center and other sites. Another explanation for these embankments has been suggested by Stephen Hale (1989), who noted that the orientation of the sites seems to be related to the direction of flow of surface water. The linear constructions could have helped steer water away from village sites to keep them dry.

Soil coring at the Fort Center sites has shown that at least one place along the circumference of one of the earlier ditches was not dug deeply enough to penetrate the spodic horizon (W. Johnson 1991:72). And analysis of soils from the ditched area showed that the underlying soils that characterize the site have low fertility and high aluminum and are acidic, all indicators that the soils would have been very poor for growing maize. Particle size analysis of the cores suggests that the bottom of the ditch was not periodically cleaned, with the fill distributed across the field enclosed by the ditch (W. Johnson 1991:60–72). These results conflict with the model that views the ditches as a way to drain agricultural fields, leaving the question of how maize was grown at Fort Center unresolved. Perhaps, as has been suggested (Milanich and Ruhl 1986:2), maize was grown at the site not as a dietary staple, but as a high-status food or for some other special purpose. Through time, with increasingly wetter conditions, maize gardening simply became too difficult and was abandoned. By the colonial period maize was not present in the Okeechobee region.

The question of Okeechobee-region maize agriculture is one of the most intriguing in Florida archaeology. Additional research at Fort Center and other sites is needed to clarify the issue. The presence after A.D 1200 or 1400 of linear embankments at Fort Center further clouds the debate, because these have been interpreted as raised agricultural plots (Sears 1982:200).

Fort Center through Time

Sears (1982:111–117, 184–201) divided the Fort Center Belle Glade culture sequence into four temporal periods based on ceramic inventories. He correlated the periods with mound and midden patterning and, in some instances, with radiocarbon dates. The site was first occupied during the earliest of these periods, from 1000 or 800 B.C. to A.D. 200. Population of the site during Period I was probably less than 100 persons, who lived on the higher places along Fisheating Creek or on small house mounds in the creek meander belt. During this period the three ditches were constructed and used.

During this and later periods a variety of animals was collected and hunted; in fact, almost every edible species was utilized. The only exceptions are birds, sparingly eaten perhaps due to cultural taboos. No single species constituted more than 10 percent of the meat diet, although together, several turtle species accounted for a significant portion of it, and fish and turtles together were the most important component (Hale 1984). Some of the turtle shells from Fort Center are perforated, suggesting turtles were tethered, a way to store meat for future use. Creatures eaten for food include opossum, mole, fox squirrel, muskrat, cotton rat, raccoon, gray fox, blue goose, green water snake, brown water snake, black vulture, bobcat, deer, turkey, frog, siren, nine species of turtle, mud snake, king snake, cottonmouth, alligator, gar, mudfish, and a variety of other species of fish. This basic way of life—the collecting of plants and a variety of local animal species, especially animals from the lake and other wetlands—probably continued to the colonial period.

Excavations in the middens along the creek and in other middens, ceremonial mounds, and house mounds at the site produced a large sample of artifacts—tools and the like that apparently were used throughout the occupation of site. Many of the items resemble those in the smaller samples excavated in the 1930s from the Belle Glade site located on the southeastern edge of the lake (Willey 1949b), suggesting that the Fort Center collections are typical of the Okeechobee region.

Analysis of the Fort Center nonceramic artifacts by Karl Steinen (1971; and in Sears 1982:68–110) revealed a large variety of tools. Shark teeth, hafted either singly or in groups by perforating, notching, or thinning the bases, were used for cutting, carving, and sawing wood. Striations on some of the wooden figures recovered from the Period II charnel pond (described later) suggest that hafted shark teeth were used for detailed wood carving. Bone leisters (probably used for spearing fish and animals), fids (used for weaving or basketry), awls, and points were also common implements. Collections at the Florida Museum of Natural History also contain a number of bone drills or bits from bow drills; all display extreme circular use on their well–worn tips.

Lithic tools, including items made from chert, are relatively common, although the nearest chert outcrops are in the Peace River valley 40–60 miles to the northwest. Trade is indicated by a few steatite sherds and by tools made from igneous rocks not found in Florida.

Stone points are of three main types: small to medium triangular projectile points; Hernando-like, basally notched projectile points; and a variety of triangular-blade, stemmed, Archaic-like specimens, most of which appear to have been hafted knives, although a few were used as saws. Limestone abraders, hones or sharpening stones, and food grinders also were used.

Tools made from marine shells brought inland from the coasts are the same types found throughout south Florida and include celts, adzes, gouges, picks, and hammers. The last two, manufactured from *Busycon* shells, were often hafted by cutting one to three holes in the outer shell.

Throughout Period I, sand- and fiber-tempered pottery continued to be manufactured at the Fort Center site; in later periods it declined rapidly in popularity, giving way to pottery containing only quartz sand or sand and freshwater sponge spicules in the paste. Most of the

Fort Center ceramics closely resemble the varieties manufactured elsewhere in south Florida at the same period, although some of the Period I pottery was crudely made of a laminated, crumbly paste.

Period II at Fort Center, A.D. 200 to A.D. 600 or 800, is delineated by changes in the ceramic assemblage, notably the absence of fiber tempering and the appearance and subsequent increase in the ceramic type Belle Glade Plain. This type, manufactured in the same bowl forms as the earlier sand-tempered ware, is distinguished by a smoothed or tooled surface achieved by scraping or cutting the almost dry clay surface with a wooden tool, leaving characteristic drag marks caused by grains of sand being pulled across the surface. The lips of the bowls are often flattened by similar cutting. Belle Glade Plain pottery continued to increase in popularity until it was the majority utilitarian ware in Period III.

Subsistence during Period II seems to have been little changed from that of the preceding period. Sears suggests that maize was still grown in the circular ditched field, and most of the inhabitants of the site lived on the various middens adjacent to or near the creek. Maize pollen was identified from seven samples dating from this period, about the same number as from the earlier period.

A major change in site orientation took place in Period II with the construction of several structures used in charnel activities. The structures formed a small complex consisting of a low platform mound, an adjacent artificial aboriginally dug pond, a dense midden across the pond from the mound, and a surrounding earthwork (Sears 1982: 145–175). The low, flat-topped platform mound was constructed as the base for a charnel-house structure. The deceased were prepared in the charnel house, perhaps in conjunction with a bathtub-shaped pit dug into the platform mound surface. Bodies were cleaned of flesh, tightly wrapped in bundles, and then stored.

On the floor of the charnel house, refuse was mixed with small human bones and teeth, the latter apparently lost during preparation of the bodies. The special nature of the charnel structure is emphasized by a deposit or offering placed on the edge of the platform nearest the pond, consisting of an infant skullcap, an adult skull, a worked carnivore mandible, two bird-bone tubes, three *Mercenaria* clam shells, seven *Busycon* cups, and a nested set of four scallop and four clam shells (Sears 1982:157).

Immediately adjacent to the charnel platform was the pond, measuring about 120 feet across and 5 feet deep. Dark brown earth dug out of the pond was used as fill to build the platform mound. A wooden platform supported by tree trunks and unshaped timbers was built in the pond. The bundles of skeletal remains from the charnel house were stored on this platform.

Vertical corner and side posts supporting the wooden platform were anchored in the muck at the bottom of the pond. Above-water portions of many of these wooden supports were carved into an incredible array of large animals: life-size cats, a bear, foxes, and larger-than-life birds, including an eagle. The eagle recovered in 1926 also came from this pond.

Other smaller carvings, many with tenon bases, were placed along the edges of the platform on the tops of mortised posts. The largest number of the carvings are of birds, both raptors and water birds. One of the smaller carvings depicts an otter with a fish in its mouth. Wooden tools and a set of wooden deer antlers also were found in the pond. Perhaps the animals depicted in the carvings or by the antlers

The Fort Center charnel pond before excavation in the mid-1960s. Sears and his students are standing on the slope of Mound B (courtesy William Sears and Florida Museum of Natural History).

Wooden carvings with pole bases excavated by Sears from the Fort Center charnal pond: *top*, possibly dogs; *bottom*, panthers (*a–d,* respectively, are 24, 39, 56¾, and 50¼ inches high; from Sears 1982: fig. 4.5).

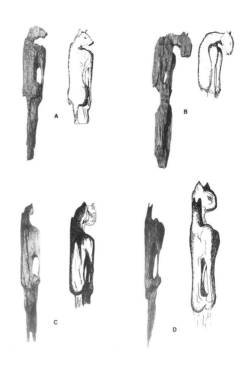

Small wooden carvings from Fort Center; *top and middle*, otters, 15¾ and 15 inches long; *bottom*, a running panther 15½ inches long (from Sears 1982: fig. 4.10) .

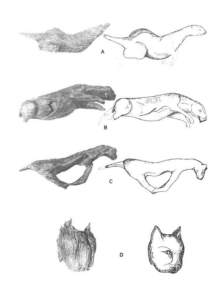

were symbols, like those represented by Weeden Island ceramic effigy vessels.

Eventually the platform, loaded with 150 or so individuals, collapsed into the pond. Many of the burials were salvaged and redeposited on the platform mound after removal of the charnel house and the deposition of a layer of clean sand. Groups of bundles probably were placed on the mound and covered with sand. This process was repeated several times. Numerous *Busycon* and *Pleuroploca gigantea* shells were deposited also. When this process was completed, the entire deposit was buried beneath a deep cap of sand. The result was a large mound fourteen feet high.

The wooden carvings and platform supports that had fallen into the pond were preserved by the water and muck for 1,500 years. Sears pumped the pond dry and excavated the remnants of the platform and those burial bundles that had not been salvaged and put in the mound. The remarkable assemblage of wooden carvings, although eroded somewhat by time and especially by the hooves of cattle that congregated in the pond in modern times, provides us with another example of the importance of wet sites.

Across the pond from the platform mound and its charnel house was a dense midden deposit, which Sears suggests was a place of residence for the individuals who participated in the charnel activities. After the collapse of the platform and the capping of the platform mound, this midden area continued to be occupied.

A large quantity of refuse was deposited in the midden, forming a low rise. The refuse included quantities of potsherds (some four-inch-thick excavation levels in five-by-five-foot excavation units produced more than 3,000 sherds), even larger quantities of bones of animals used for food, and stone and shell tools. Lime, obtained from burning freshwater mussel shells, was found on and around the area. Sears suggests that the lime was used to process maize, a technique common in Mesoamerica. It might also have been used to make the white pigment that was found on some of the carvings in the pond and that contained maize pollen. Around the edges of the lime deposit were a number of human paleofeces preserved by the lime. Several of these also contained maize pollen.

Included in the collections from this midden are a number of fired clay platform pipes and a cache of chert nodules. Shell, shark teeth, and stone tools probably used to make the wooden carvings also were found. Overall the assemblage of artifacts and the density of the midden is quite unlike that found anywhere else on the site.

A circular earthen embankment constructed from fill dug from the pond (like the platform mound) connected the two ends of the dense midden and surrounded the pond and charnel mound. This Period II ceremonial center has features similar to those found at contemporary sites elsewhere in Florida, such as the Crystal River site and River Styx sites (see chapter 6). Items such as a galena hemisphere, flint (as opposed to chert) tools, and plummets of quartz crystal suggest that the Belle Glade people were part of the trade networks functioning in Florida and the southeastern United States at this time. Included among the artifacts is a grapefruit-size piece of freshwater sponge with spicules like those found in some south Florida pottery (the object is mistakenly identified in the site catalogue as petrified wood; Steinen in Sears 1982:76, fig.6.2, *h*).

By Period III at Fort Center, A.D. 600 or 800 to A.D. 1200 or 1400, the importance of the site as a ceremonial center seems to have ended with the collapse of the charnel platform. Ceremonial activities may have been transferred to another center in the Okeechobee Basin, perhaps in part for reasons similar to those that caused Weeden Island–period centers in north and northwest Florida to rise and fall in importance. The ceramic inventory during this period remained unchanged with Belle Glade Plain being the majority ware. People continued to live along the creek middens, and some individuals continued to live adjacent to the charnel pond.

During Period IV, A.D. 1200 or 1400 to A.D. 1700, changes again took place at the site, and earthwork construction increased and included well-made house mounds. Circular ditch construction and use had long since ceased, and a new type of earthwork was constructed: linear, raised earthen embankments. The linear earthworks measure 180 to more than 580 feet long, and some have circular house mounds built on one end. This type of raised embankment is present at many of the other mound complex sites in the Okeechobee region, such as Big Mound City and Tony's Mound.

Sears (1982:200) recovered maize pollen from samples taken from buried surfaces in two of the linear embankments. He suggests that maize continued to be cultivated at the site on the raised plots, noting that raised fields are found elsewhere in the circum–Caribbean region and other areas of North and South America. Those fields, however, are quite different from the Okeechobee embankments and typically contain evidence of features intended to intensify agricultural potential, such as walls to contain the raised fields to prevent erosion or the deposition of organic matter on the fields to increase fertility (Parsons and Denevan 1967; Denevan 1970; Siemans and Puleston 1972; Farrington 1985). The Fort Center embankments do not contain such evidence.

The maize pollen samples collected from the linear embankments were among those whose contexts were questionable. It is not certain that the pollen grains could not be explained by contamination, especially the washing down of pollen grains through the sandy, porous spodosols used to construct the embankments. Maize agriculture at Fort Center in Period IV is not a certainty. Whether or not maize was grown at Fort Center can only be clarified through long-term archaeological investigations that produce plant remains.

Glades Region and Related Cultures

The largest of the south Florida regions in geographical extent is the Glades region, comprising all of south Florida east and south of the Okeechobee and Caloosahatchee regions. Environmentally diverse with a variety of wetlands that were important to the precolumbian inhabitants, the region includes the Everglades itself—a largely sawgrass marsh in Hendry, Palm Beach, Broward, Dade, and Monroe counties; the Big Cypress Swamp west of the Everglades in Collier County; and extensive saltwater marshes and mangrove forests once found along both coasts, now almost totally destroyed on the Gold Coast in Broward and Dade counties.

Within the flat, wet Everglades, Big Cypress Swamp, and other wetlands of interior south Florida are small, palm tree–studded elevations that resemble islands in a sea of grass. Such raised islands of dry ground provided space for settlements, and numerous archaeological sites are found on them (Laxson 1970; Ehrenhard, Carr, and Taylor 1978, 1979; Ehrenhard and Taylor 1980; Ehrenhard, Taylor, and Komara 1980; Carr 1981, 1990; Ehrenhard, Komara, and Taylor 1982; Taylor and Komara 1983; Taylor 1984, 1985; Griffin 1988; Lee and

This everglades hammock (the tree island in the distance) is a small Glades midden in western Broward County (courtesy Florida Museum of Natural History).

Beriault 1993). Drier pine and scrub flatwoods along the north–south Atlantic coastal ridge that parallels the east coast also drew pre-columbian people.

Overall, however, the densest site distribution is along the coasts; at one time nearly every bit of higher land adjacent to the coastal salt marshes and estuaries probably had archaeological sites on it. Sites are largest where rivers, even small ones, drain interior wetlands.

Unfortunately most of the precolumbian sites on the lower Atlantic coast have been destroyed by twentieth-century development. Others, such as those on the lower west coast around the Ten Thousand Islands, may have been inundated by the rising waters of the Gulf of Mexico. As development has moved westward in Broward and Dade counties, even sites on the edges of the saw grass have been destroyed. Ditching and draining portions of the Everglades has disturbed and destroyed sites as well.

Relationships between the diverse Glades habitats and different pre-columbian archaeological assemblages of the late and post-Archaic period will no doubt receive more research focus in the future. Already investigations have led to recognition of the Ten Thousand Island region as a subregion, encompassing the coastal keys and the adjacent mainland wetlands in portions of Collier and Monroe counties (Carr and Beriault 1984; Griffin 1988). And, as noted earlier, the Florida Keys, stretching southwesterly from Biscayne Bay to the Marquesas Keys west of Key West, probably also should be designated a separate culture area (see Goggin 1950a; Goggin and Sommer 1949).

Chronology and Material Culture

Very early in his archaeological career John Goggin began to develop a typology and relative chronology for south Florida (Goggin 1939, 1940, 1944b, n.d.) based largely on ceramic decorative motifs. That ceramic chronology, now recognized as applying to the Glades region, has been refined based on John Griffin's excavations at the Bear Lake and Onion Key sites in Monroe County, and it has been correlated with radiocarbon dates from Bear Lake and the Granada site (Griffin 1988:181–226; and see Widmer 1988:80–82). A version of that chronology incorporating data from excavations in Collier County (Russo et al. 1991:578) is summarized in the table opposite.

Analysis of the pastes used to manufacture precolumbian Glades pottery also has been undertaken (Russo et al. 1991:556–591). A study of samples from Horr's Island has shown some of the same varieties of paste present there as in the Caloosahatchee region, suggesting that paste categories may prove successful as interregional chronological indicators (Russo et al. 1991:556–591). Paste studies also have called into question previous taxonomies using poorly defined undecorated pottery types like Glades Plain and Goodland Plain.

Pottery vessels in the Glades region are typically bowls with incurving walls and rim. Nearly all of the pottery was shaped by the coiling method, although what appears to be modeled pottery has been found at some sites. The modeled pottery appears laminated in cross section and does not exhibit coil fractures. Glades decorative motifs include linear and curvilinear incision and rim ticking. The type Glades Tooled, which appears late in the precolumbian period, exhibits elaborated lip treatments, either pinched (to produce a piecrust edge), folded, or dowel impressed. The bodies of the Glades Tools vessels are undecorated carinated bowls, often extremely shallow.

As is true of the Okeechobee and Caloosahatchee regions, the Glades region does not contain deposits of chert, and such stone artifacts are rare. Those chert tools present appear to be items brought to

Glades Region Ceramic Chronology

Period	Dates	Distinguishing ceramics
Glades IIIb	A.D. 1400–1513	Almost no decorated ceramics; Glades Tooled rims.[a]
Glades IIIa	A.D. 1200–1400	Appearance of Surfside Incised (parallel incised lines below lip); some lip-grooving; St. Johns Check Stamped and Safety Harbor sherds found in this and subsequent periods.
Glades IIc	A.D. 1100–1200	Almost no decorated ceramics; some grooved lips; Plantation Pinched (lines of finger-pinched indentations below lip on rim).
Glades IIb	A.D. 900–1100	Key Largo Incised still majority decorated type; some incision on rims and some lip grooving; Matecumbe Incised appears (cross-hatched incisions below lip on rim); more incurving bowls.
Glades IIa	A.D. 750–900	Appearance of Key Largo Incised (loops or arches incised below lip); Opa Locka Incised (half–circles or arches incised below lip in vertical rows with open sides down); Miami Incised (diagonal parallel incised rims below lip on rim).
Glades I late	A.D. 500–750	Appearance of decorated pottery (less than 10 percent of ceramics at sites); Sanibel Incised (ticking to form running lines of inverted V's below lip); Cane Patch Incised (incised looping line with stab-and-drag punctations, below lip); Fort Drum Incised (vertical or diagonal ticking on lip or rim); Fort Drum Punctated (punctations around vessel below lip).
Glades 1 early	500 B.C.–A.D. 500	First appearance of sand-tempered pottery (Glades Plain or undecorated Glades Gritty Ware—both types subsumed under plain, sand-tempered, not separated as to type); no decoration.

a. Glades Tooled may appear slightly earlier in time, in period IIIA, or the A.D. 1400 date for the beginning of period IIIB may be earlier.

the area from elsewhere and reused. Tools of sandstone, limestone, and similar sedimentary rocks, mined from local sources, were used as hones, abraders, and pounders or hammers. Limestone plummets and grooved pebbles could have been weights for fishing line or for nets, but more likely plummets were items of adornment (Reiger 1990).

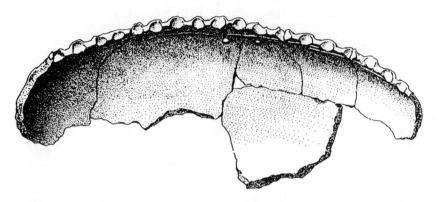

Glades Tooled pottery; the carinated bowl is approximately 2 inches high (drawing by Merald Clark; courtesy University of Florida Institute of Archaeology and Paleoenvironmental Studies).

Perforated bivalve shells, especially *Noetia* shells, probably served as net weights as well.

Instead of stone, shell and bone were used as raw materials for tools, many the same types as those found elsewhere in southern Florida. Shell picks, hammers, adzes, celts, gouges, chisels, awls, knives, scrapers, cups, and dippers are made from *Busycon, Pleuroploca,* and *Strombus* shells; clam shell anvils are common (Goggin n.d.; Luer 1986; Griffin 1988:82–88).

One excellent study of bone tools is the analysis of the large collection from the Granada site carried out by Sue Richardson and Mary Pohl (in Griffin et al. 1985:83–111; also see Griffin 1988:91–98). As with shell tools, the same bone tools are found throughout the south Florida regions. Although an archaeological test may produce only one or two bone pins or other tools, the large variety of bone artifacts from Granada is duplicated across the entire Glades region.

Bone tools include pins, awls, fids, and points often made from deer bone or antler; fish spines and stingray tail spines used as perforators; and shark teeth cutting and engraving tools (see Kozuch 1993 for information on south Florida sharks and shark products). Pins and points, some hollow, come in a variety of shapes. Other tools have been made from animal jaws and barracuda teeth. Rectangles of turtle bone and shell are almost surely gauges used in making nets (Walker 1989).

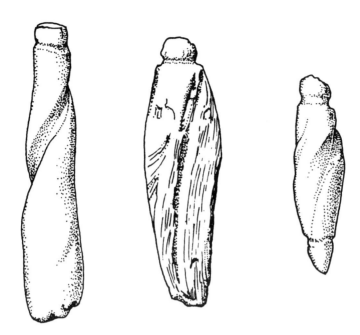

Plummets made from shell columella, the longest 3⅛ inches long (drawing by Merald Clark; courtesy University of Florida Institute of Archaeology and Paleoenvironmental Studies).

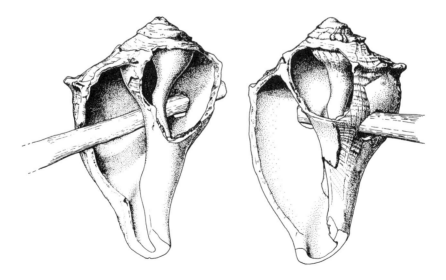

Busycon shell tools showing hafting method. The cutting edges are down; specimen at left is 5½ inches long (drawing by Merald Clark; courtesy University of Florida Institute of Archaeology and Paleoenvironmental Studies).

Shell beads, fish vertebrae ornaments, and worked carnivore teeth are present, as are small animal figurines (especially birds) made from limestone, shell, and bone. In style some of the latter resemble bird heads on early Weeden Island pottery, while others are more like the Fort Center carvings.

Wooden artifacts have been recovered from several wet sites in the Glades, often discovered as a result of construction activities, such as digging boat slips or dredging canals. Canoe paddles, dumbbell-shaped wooden pounders, anthropomorphic figurines, bowls, and other wooden implements have been found. The shell, bone, and wooden tool and weapon assemblages of the Glades culture are as varied as the artifact assemblages of northern Florida.

Key Marco

This discussion of artifacts associated with the Glades region people would end here were it not for the extraordinary objects excavated by Frank Hamilton Cushing in 1896 from the Key Marco site (Cushing 1897; and see Gilliland 1975, 1989). The Key Marco collection contains a host of wooden and fiber items that were preserved in muck. Some are identical to items from other south Florida wet sites.

Wooden items in the remarkable Key Marco collection include bowls, mortars and pestles, pounding tools that look like dumbbells, boxes, trays, and hafts or handles for a variety of adzes, knives, and other cutting tools. Some tools were recovered with the shell, bone, or shark teeth bits or working edges still affixed. Long bone pins and bone tools are common, as are stone plummets. Most of these wooden and bone items are expertly carved, some with intricate designs or animal adornos. A toy catamaran canoe, a canoe paddle, throwing stick handles and darts, and other tools, all of wood, came from the muck. Most of the wood used to make the tools is cypress, button-wood, and gumbo-limbo.

Pieces of fish nets, some with floats and shell or stone weights still attached, attest to the importance of fishing to the Glades people. Gourd (*Lagenaria siceria*) and squash (*Cucurbita pepo*) were present (Cutler in Gilliland 1975:255–256). The same weedy varieties found at Hontoon Island in the St. Johns River drainage, they probably were used as containers, net floats, or both. Rectangular and square net gauges provide further evidence of the importance of net fishing to Glades subsistence.

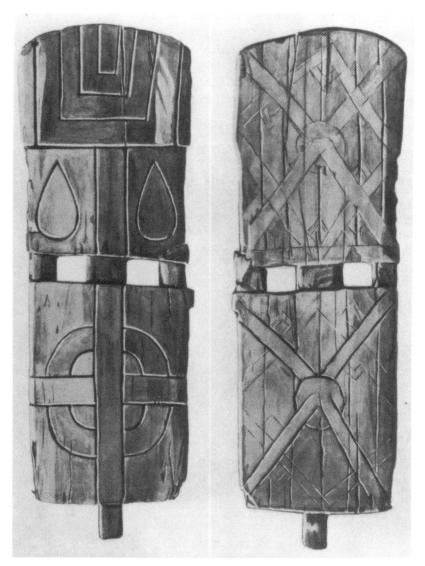

Front and back of a wooden spider tablet found near Fort Myers (from
Fewkes 1928: plate 2). Its exact size is unknown.

Among the Cushing collection are a number of expertly carved
(some painted) wooden specimens that illustrate the artistic skills of
the Glades peoples. Exquisite carved wooden masks, some with shell-
inset eyes and others painted, may have been used in ceremonies.
Wooden animal masks were worn; two of those found were composite
masks depicting a wolf's head and an alligator.

Wooden tray 15 inches long made of gumbo-limbo from Key Marco (inventory photograph courtesy Florida Museum of Natural History).

A wooden pounder 5½ inches long from Key Marco (inventory photograph courtesy Florida Museum of Natural History).

The original of this wooden tablet with a woodpecker painted on it was excavated from Key Marco
by Frank Hamilton Cushing. This painting was done
by Wells Sawyer, a member of the expedition.
Cushing found it "perhaps the most significant
object of a sacred or ceremonial nature . . . a thin
board of a yellowish wood, a little more than sixteen inches in length . . . which I found standing
slantingly upward. . . . On slowly removing the
muck from its surface, I discovered that an elaborate
figure of a crested bird was painted upon one side of
it, in black, white, and blue pigments" (Cushing
1897:56; courtesy Smithsonian Institution).

A variety of wooden plaques or "standards," some more than twenty inches long, deserve special mention. The plaques include both flat planks and carved specimens. Perhaps the most famous of the former is a rectangular flat plank with a woodpecker painted on it. Another type of carved plaque is two sectioned with a tenon on one end. Some specimens had a stylized motif, possibly representing a spider, carved on them. Similar wooden and colonial-period metal examples have been found in south Florida (Fewkes 1928; McGoun 1981; Allerton, Luer, and Carr 1984). Plain, carved two-part standards and one standard with a carved dolphin also came from Key Marco. Exactly what purpose the standards served is unknown.

Two truly magnificent wooden objects are a painted deer head and a kneeling feline figurine. The deer head is beautifully painted, and the ears were made with pegs to fit them on the head. Four inches high, the feline may be a person with a feline mask or costume. Both are exquisite works of art, as is a two-inch-square turtle plastron plaque incised with two realistic dolphins placed tail to nose.

The remarkable Key Marco assemblage is another illustration of the importance of wet sites for providing information that cannot be obtained from terrestrial sites.

Site Types

The variety of archaeological sites in the Glades region rivals that found in any region in northern Florida. Along the coasts marine shell and earth middens predominate, especially where freshwater rivers meet the coast. Some of the shell middens are extensive, such as those on the Turner River site in Collier County or the middens that once fronted the Miami River. Many of these middens were probably used over many generations, such as those at the Granada site on the Miami River (Griffin et al. 1985). Such middens may represent villages. Shell constructions—embankments, ramps, and the like—are present at some of these sites.

Other middens probably represent camps that were occupied for short periods of time to gather certain resources. Examples include the oyster-gathering station on Horr's Island in Collier County (Russo et al. 1991), the small sites on Pine Island in Dade County (Carr 1990), and a probable deer-hunting camp in inland Collier County (Lee and Beriault 1993).

Earth middens, characterized by a dark color resulting from high organic content, are more common than shell middens in some locales. In the Everglades National Park about two-thirds of the middens were earth middens, while the remainder were shell (Griffin 1988). Earth middens, some containing freshwater shell, are found on hammocks throughout the saw grass and seem to date from all Glades periods (and some date from the late Archaic period as well). The overall picture is of coastal and inland populations who maintained central settlements and used a variety of nearby special-use sites (see Athens 1983).

Sand and stone burial mounds are present, and interments also were made in and beside middens (Goggin n.d.; Jaffee 1976; Isçan 1983; Williams 1983; Felmley 1990; Newman 1993). Evidence from the Margate-Blount Mound in interior Broward County suggests that a charnel house had been present and that the mound was in use in the Glades II period (Williams 1983:145, 152). Two circular ditches like those present in the Okeechobee Basin have been located in Dade County by Robert Carr (1985).

Whether changes in settlement patterning occurred in the Glades region after 500 B.C. is not clear. Evidence suggests that the Florida Keys subregion may not have been occupied until the first millennium A.D. Based on the information gathered by William Marquardt and his research team in the Caloosahatchee region (Marquardt 1992), we would expect the history of precolumbian settlement in the Glades region to have been as complex as it was on the southwest coast. Sea-level fluctuations and fluctuations in ground- and surface water had far-reaching consequences for all the precolumbian people of south Florida.

Evidence for an increase in population over time has been gathered from the Glades region by Laura Kozuch (1991:121). She used site file data to report 170 sites (or components) in the Glades I period, 270 in Glades II, and 280 in Glades III.

Subsistence

The dependence of Glades people on wetland resources is reflected in the faunal and floral data collected from sites like Granada on the southeast coast (Griffin et al. 1985); site 8Cr201 and the Key Marco site, both on the southwest coast (Russo et al. 1991; Wing 1965); and freshwater wetland sites in the Big Cypress area (Wing 1984). At all of these, various combinations of shellfish, vertebrate and cartilaginous fish (marine or freshwater), and reptiles provided the bulk of the meat biomass (edible meat). At Granada, sharks were 30 percent of the biomass, sea turtles 9 percent, vertebrate fish 42 percent, and other reptiles 10 percent (Griffin et al. 1985:325–326). Deer and other mammals were only 7.5 percent of the total biomass. These percentages remained relatively unchanged over the history of the site, signifying that the pattern of subsistence and the environment remained stable throughout Glades I–III. Although marine mammals have been found in south Florida middens (Cumbaa 1973), including at Granada, they must have been only infrequently used for food.

The most important edible plants at the Granada site—all with edible fleshy fruits—were mastic, cocoplum, cabbage palm, saw palmetto, sea grape, and hog plum, seeds of which were found in almost all samples analyzed by Margaret Scarry (in Griffin et al. 1985:222, 230–232). Acorns and red mangrove sprouts were eaten also. All of these plants could be collected from adjacent pinelands and hammocks. Indeed, the primary wood in use at the site (identified from charcoal samples) was pine. The same array of fleshy fruits were identified from the Honey Hill site, a black-earth midden on the eastern edge of the Everglades (Masson and Scarry n.d.).

An interesting piece of data from the Granada site archaeobotanical analysis is evidence that the site was probably only occupied during the fall and possibly the winter months throughout its history (Griffin et al. 1985:232, 386). If true, this suggests a model of subsistence and settlement different from that in the Caloosahatchee region with its rich natural coastal resources. It may be that in the Glades region, coastal resources in specific locales could not support year-round village populations. Instead people could have used a number of different locales, gathering fall resources and marine foods at one, oysters at another, and freshwater fish and reptiles at still another.

Did the same Glades people move among coastal and inland locales, taking full advantage of seasonally available resources? Did the same people occupy sites like those in the Ten Thousand Island locale and inland sites to the east in the Big Cypress Swamp? These interesting questions for future research are pertinent to our understanding of the Glades region. Comparisons of subsistence strategies among the south

Florida regions and subregions promises to provide new insights on the ways people who depended on hunting, gathering, and fishing lived in precolumbian Florida.

Caloosahatchee Region

During the post–500 B.C. period the southwest Florida coast from Charlotte Harbor to just south of Estero Bay south of Fort Myers was perhaps the most productive marine region in the state. Fed by nutrients brought to the coast by the Peace, Myakka, and Caloosahatchee rivers, the shallow, grassy subtropical waters of the region afforded its precolumbian inhabitants a rich larder of shellfish and fish. The estuary and bay systems of Charlotte Harbor, Pine Island Sound, and San Carlos and Estero bays with their numerous barrier and inshore islands, many rimmed with mangrove forests, supported a vast marine food chain that could be systematically harvested by the Caloosahatchee people.

Although early archaeologists such as Frank Hamilton Cushing (1897; and see Simons 1884; Goggin and Sturtevant 1964) could marvel at the many huge shell middens there, it was not until the 1970s that indepth investigations began to focus on the region (e.g., Fradkin 1976). It is significant that local residents, members of the Sanibel-Captiva Conservation Foundation who wished to be better informed about the archaeological sites around them, were responsible for attracting archaeologists to the region in the mid-1970s (e.g., Wilson 1982). Archaeological research in the region has since boomed, and public participation and education remain important aspects of investigations (Marquardt 1992). Perhaps more than for any other region in Florida, our knowledge of the archaeology of the Caloosahatchee culture is a product of the post-1980 era (Luer 1986; Widmer 1988; Marquardt 1992a; Walker 1992b).

The Caloosahatchee region is immediately west of the Okeechobee Basin and the Belle Glade culture. During the precolumbian period the Caloosahatchee River could have functioned as a canoe highway connecting the cultures of the basin with those of the coast. Throughout their histories, the cultures of these two adjacent regions must have been in continual, close contact with one another. That they were is suggested by the concurrence of ceramic types over time, such as the appearance of the type Belle Glade Plain (for a study of Caloosa-hatchee pottery, see Cordell 1992).

It is likely that cultural and, perhaps, political relationships between the two regions were closer than suggested by our present taxonomy, which divides them into separate areas. As yet this aspect of south Florida cultural dynamics has not been adequately explored. Indeed, our present taxonomy focusing on the uniqueness of each of these regions may be hindering archaeological studies to articulate relationships between them.

Coastal and Inland Sites

A single visit to one of the large shell mound and midden sites in the Caloosahatchee region leaves the observer with at least two questions. First, how could such large shell heaps have escaped the attention of archaeologists for so long? Second, were the food habits of the pre-columbian inhabitants truly responsible for the millions of whelks and oysters that comprise the bulk of the shell?

The size of the shell heaps and the numbers of individual mollusks within them are staggering, as is the number of sites along the coast (see Kennedy 1978; Widmer 1988; Marquardt 1992). In the Caloosa-hatchee region surveys have noted shell mounds, middens, or both on almost every island. Some islands, such as Cayo Costa, North Captiva, Captiva, Sanibel, and Pine Island, have extensive, multiple sites. Other, smaller keys seem to be one large site, such as Cabbage Key, Josslyn Island, Demere Key, and Mound Key (Cushing 1897; Marquardt 1984). Still more sites are distributed around Charlotte Harbor (e.g., Big Mound Key) and along the shorelines of Charlotte and Lee counties.

These coastal shell sites are most often adjacent to bay-estuary waters. Today some are in or immediately adjacent to mangrove forests, although it is likely that the growth of the mangroves occurred after the sites were abandoned. At many of the sites, long, linear shell middens snake through the mangroves for several hundred yards. Others seem to be circular middens. And many others are complex structures combining shell middens with what appear to be mounds and causeways constructed of shell. In some instances shell mounds as much as 375 feet long and 15 feet high have other, smaller mounds built on the top. Often the mounds have very steep sides.

Artificial canals lead into some of these large shell mound complexes. Today mangroves often choke these silted-in canals, which once provided canoe access into the sites. Mound Key in Estero Bay near Fort Myers Beach and Pineland on Pine Island are two such sites cross-cut by aboriginally built canals. Mound Key contains large artificial mounds built of earth and shell that probably served as platforms for the civic and ceremonial structures of the Caloosahatchee people. Middens, some more than twenty feet thick, cover portions of the island. A canal on Pine Island apparently cut across the entire island, providing a canoe shortcut and passing by a major site. Another canal is known from Cape Coral (Luer 1989). These canals are reminiscent of the canals in the Lake Okeechobee Basin.

While a visitor's initial impression of these sites is one of immensity and large quantities of shells, more informed observation reveals details. The species of shells often differ among sites, and even within a single shell mound. Some are almost entirely *Busycon* shells, others are almost all oyster, and still others contain strata of mixed species. Some of the shell mounds appear to be intentionally constructed with distinct strata, while others are middens that accumulated more casually or combinations of the two.

Other differences are apparent. Test excavations have shown that some shell strata contain dense amounts of animal bone, mainly fish, while some are almost entirely shell, with little bone. Within some sites, sea urchin spines occur in large numbers.

In some locales, such as Buck Key where mosquito control ditches have cut through shell sites, the bottom of shell strata can be seen to extend as much as 3 feet below the present water level, clear evidence of a postoccupation sea-level rise.

In several coastal locales, such as on Useppa and Captiva islands and Buck Key, human interments have been found in sand mounds or shell middens (Collins 1928, 1929; Marquardt 1992a). Some burial sites around Charlotte Harbor contain Weeden Island or Safety Harbor pottery, in addition to locally made undecorated wares. Safety Harbor pottery, common in mounds in the central peninsular Gulf coast region (see chapter 11), occurs in late Caloosahatchee sites south of Charlotte Harbor.

Not all Caloosahatchee sites are found in coastal settings. Sites are distributed along the shore of the Caloosahatchee River and in other inland locales (Austin 1987a), although many have been destroyed by modern development. Sand burial mounds and shell and earth middens are most common on the river, while smaller dirt middens are found on interior hammocks near freshwater marshes. Small shell scatters, perhaps special-use camps, have been recorded in the interior of the Caloosahatchee region. The distribution of sites inland along the Caloosahatchee River makes it difficult to draw a sharp line separating the Caloosahatchee region from the Okeechobee region to the east.

Chronology, Site Use, and Subsistence

The archaeological remains of the precolumbian Caloosahatchee people—a complex array of sites in different settings and exhibiting different processes of formation—challenge archaeologists. Were the sites occupied at the same time? Do sites represent long occupations? When did the construction of shellworks begin? Does the construction of large platform mounds reflect a complex form of social and/or political organization? Do different sites containing different patterns of faunal remains reflect different patterns of subsistence at a single point of time, or at different times, or both? What effects have sea-level fluctuations had on the patterning of sites and subsistence?

These are difficult questions to answer, requiring excavations in a number of sites and the analysis of large amounts of faunal remains. Also required is a detailed understanding of the history and functioning of the natural environment of the Caloosahatchee region.

Excavations at the Wightman site on Sanibel Island (Fradkin 1976) and tests on Useppa Island (Milanich, Chapman, et al. 1984) emphasized the complex nature of settlement and subsistence patterns. Shell heaps that looked like intentionally constructed mounds contained midden strata as well as layers of shell deposited as fill. Frequencies of fish and shell species differed between sites, as well as within a single site. The history of human occupation and the relationships between precolumbian people and their environment were clearly complex. Although it seemed certain that marine resources provided the economic base for Caloosahatchee cultural developments, it was just as clear that subsistence and settlement strategies varied among sites and at the same site over time. Also, the shellworks were nearly as complex as the earthworks found in the Okeechobee region.

Caloosahatchee Region Ceramic Chronology

Period	Dates	Distinguishing ceramics
Caloosahatchee IV	A.D. 1350–1500	Safety Harbor, Glades Tooled, Pinellas Plain; Belle Glade Plain diminishes.
Caloosahatchee III	A.D. 1200–1350	St. Johns Check Stamped, Englewood ceramics, Belle Glade Plain.
Caloosahatchee IIb	A.D. 800(?)–1200	Belle Glade Plain, Belle Glade Red.
Caloosahatchee IIa	A.D. 500 or 650–800(?)	Belle Glade Plain appears, undecorated plain, Glades Red; thinner ceramics.
Caloosahatchee I	500 B.C.–A.D. 500 or 650	Thick, sand-tempered, plain pottery, with round and chamfered lips.

Source: Based on Cordell 1992.

A model to explain the development of the Caloosahatchee culture and its relationships to the natural environment was conceived and later revised by Randolph Widmer (1978, 1984, 1988). Widmer's model, simply stated, emphasizes the propitious nature of the marine resources (Widmer 1988). Precolumbian people of the Caloosahatchee region harvested the shallow coastal waters for the shellfish and fish that provided the economic base for their society. The appearance of such a coastal economic pattern is believed by Widmer to have occurred after about 700 B.C., when modern optimum coastal conditions were reached as a result of sea-level changes. The resulting marine-oriented subsistence system allowed population expansion and growth.

All of the zooarchaeological studies carried out in the region (Fradkin 1976; Marquardt 1992; Walker 1992b) have emphasized the importance of marine foods in a diet supplemented by animals and plants gathered from terrestrial and mangrove forests. The species from these habitats are as varied as those from the Glades region listed earlier in this chapter. Analysis by Karen Walker (1992b) has shown that sizes and species of fish available in local site catchment areas depend on water salinity and the relative position of the site within the coastal estuarine system. For some species larger individuals are found closer to open, deeper water, while smaller, juvenile individuals are found in shallower, more sheltered locations.

Randolph Widmer (in dark glasses) excavating at the Solana site on Charlotte Harbor in 1977. His environmental reconstructions for the site postulated higher sea levels at A.D. 400 (Widmer 1986), an observation that has stimulated additional studies of sea levels in the Caloosahatchee region (courtesy Rebecca Storey).

Busycon snails, once so numerous on the sandy bottom of the bays of the region, were especially important as a food source. A single large adult specimen can produce nearly two pounds of meat, and some sites contain millions of individual shells, many with a hole knocked in the end, presumably to cut the muscle that attached to the shell, thus allowing the meat to be extracted.

Analysis of archaeobotanical samples from six Caloosahatchee sites (Scarry and Newsom 1992) identified twenty-three different woods collected from the adjacent terrestrial and mangrove forests. The samples were dominated by pine (51 percent), black mangrove (33 percent), and red mangrove and buttonwood (together, 11 percent). Like the Glades people, the Caloosahatchee villagers collected the fleshy fruits of several species for food—cocoplum, sea grape, mastic, prickly pear, cabbage palm, saw palmetto, and hog plum. Acorns also were collected. Seeds of weedy plants, such as chenopods, have been found, along with gourdlike squashes (*Cucurbita pepo*), which may have grown wild in the region (Scarry and Newsom 1992).

Widmer's model further suggests that by about A.D. 300, the need "for continuity in the maintenance and regulation of efficient coastal resource exploitation" led to the development of a more complex form of political organization, one in which hereditary chiefs provided leadership. Chiefs could control access to and distribution of resources, assuring the continued ability of the population not only to survive, but to prosper and grow. As elsewhere in precolumbian Florida, social and political systems were tools that allowed societies to use their environments more effectively and to reproduce themselves.

Such managerial oversight was especially necessary in southwest Florida because agriculture was not an economic option (Widmer 1988:279). Soils in the Caloosahatchee region are not productive. The precolumbian inhabitants found it necessary to make the most of their abilities to harvest marine resources, even using social and political means to do so.

But the Caloosahatchee population could not expand forever. By about A.D. 700–800 the population had reached the maximum level that the natural environment could support. Competition among groups resulted, along with military efforts by chiefs to control other chiefs and their people and resources. Widmer (1988) suggests that such conditions would encourage alliances with other south Florida groups or annexation of those groups, both enforced by military means. The Caloosahatchee extended their political sway over much of southern Florida, giving them access to more resources and allowing people to move outside the coastal zone proper.

The power of chiefs is reflected in mound building and the construction of the other shellworks present at numerous sites in the region. What we see today are the remains of the villages ruled by those precolumbian chiefs. Their power and the range of their hegemony might also be reflected in their ability to obtain goods from other groups and to provide symbols of their importance to the leaders of those groups. Safety Harbor Incised pottery from the Tampa Bay region found at late precolumbian sites in the Caloosahatchee region may be an example of the former, if it can be shown that the pottery was not manufactured locally.

One item reflecting the geographical extent of alliances or the political influence of the Caloosahatchee chiefs may be the postcontact distribution of small metal plaques displaying the same possible spider motif found on wooden standards at Key Marco and elsewhere (Cushing 1897; Fewkes 1928; Griffin 1946; and see McGoun 1981; Allerton, Luer, and Carr 1984; Luer 1985). The latter are from the precolumbian period, while the metal plaques, fashioned of gold and silver salvaged from the cargos of Spanish shipwrecks, are clearly postcontact.

A factor in the Widmer model recognized as absolutely essential for any model of the Caloosahatchee region is sea-level fluctuations (Widmer 1988:279; and see Widmer 1986, reporting work at the Solana site that initiated archaeological studies of sea-level fluctuations in the region). For the post–500 B.C. era, geological evidence suggests periods of higher and lower sea levels. Such fluctuations, as Widmer notes, would have a tremendous effect on settlement patterns and other aspects of Caloosahatchee cultural developments.

Since the publication of Widmer's model, additional field research has been undertaken in the Caloosahatchee region by a number of archaeologists, including William Marquardt and his associates and students (Marquardt 1992; Walker 1992b). Those interdisciplinary field studies provide data that further articulate the complex relationships that existed among the precolumbian cultures and their dynamic environment, including details on post–500 B.C. sea-level fluctuations, subsistence, and variations in water salinity affecting shellfish and fish species. Marquardt and his team also have refined previous (Widmer 1988:83–87) ceramic-based chronologies for the region, providing a radiocarbon-based ceramic sequence (see table on page 315) that has been correlated with sea-level data and settlement information.

The beginning of the Caloosahatchee I period, 500 B.C., correlates with a sea-level stand that at its height was two to three feet lower than the present level of the Gulf of Mexico (Marquardt 1992a:425, 428–431; and see Walker 1992b). Thus it is not surprising that some middens extend below the present water level or that other middens have suffered mangrove encroachment. Consequently, as elsewhere along the Florida coasts, attempts to determine population increase by counting sites must be tempered by the realization that what we see today is only a part of the overall distribution of sites.

This low sea-level stand reversed by 150–50 B.C. and was followed by a period of rising seas that persisted to about A.D. 450 (see Widmer 1986). During that time the Gulf was higher than it is at present. Walker (1992b) has shown that at some sites this period correlates with higher salinity that affected the relative availability of crested oysters, crown conchs, and ribbed mussels.

After about A.D. 400 the southwest Florida environment was affected by the Scandic climatic episode, a drier period of cooler temperatures that lasted until about A.D. 900 and correlates with a second period of lower sea level. Marquardt and his team noted that during that 500-year period, when sea level fell about two feet, the number and size of shell middens increased, pottery types changed, shell tools became more diverse (conch- and whelk-hafted hammers and cutting tools), and Columbia projectile points or knives appeared. Belle Glade Plain pottery, the same type found in the Okeechobee region at this time, first appears in middens, as does Weeden Island pottery, presumably originating from more northerly Florida regions. Shell mounds and embankments appear at some sites. These changes, noted at Big Mound Key, Galt Island, Josslyn Island, Pineland, Useppa Island, Wightman, and other sites mark the beginning of the Caloosahatchee II period, A.D. 650 to A.D. 1200.

During this period sand burial mounds were being used for interring the dead, as were natural sand ridges. Interments included both bundled secondary deposits and primary flexed burials.

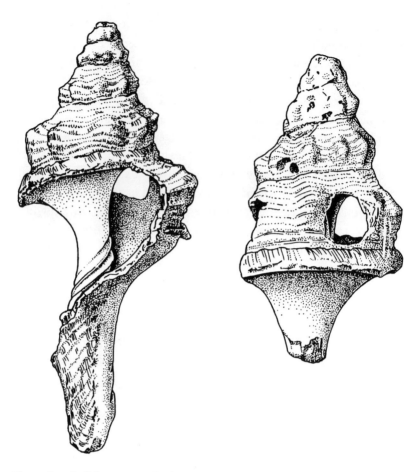

Pleuroploca shell hammers; the longer is 5½ inches long (drawing by Merald Clark; courtesy University of Florida Institute of Archaeology and Paleoenvironmental Studies).

The shellwork constructions and new burial patterns of this period might well correlate with the period of political intensification suggested by Widmer's model. The presence of Weeden Island and Safety Harbor pottery in Caloosahatchee II village sites and some mounds may reflect increased contact between the Caloosahatchee region and the cultures along the Gulf coast to the north.

During the later part of this period, after A.D. 950, the climate was stormier and warmer than at present and the level of the sea may have risen one foot, perhaps leading to settlement shifts. Minor perturbations in sea levels continued after this time, possibly affecting some specific site locations.

The Caloosahatchee III period, A.D. 1200 to 1350 or 1400, is marked by the appearance of St. Johns Check Stamped pottery in middens. Although we cannot be certain that such pottery came from the upper St. Johns region in eastern Florida, its appearance may signal expansion of Caloosahatchee political influence in that direction. With higher-than-present water levels from A.D. 950 to 1450, such political expansion might have been a response to reductions in local catchment areas, although this is by no means certain.

Sand burial mounds continued to be used in the Caloosahatchee III period, and Safety Harbor pottery is found in a number of them. During this time it is difficult to use pottery in mounds to mark a point geographically dividing the Safety Harbor culture of the central peninsular Gulf coast from the Caloosahatchee culture. Increasingly, archaeologists are questioning whether the presence of Safety Harbor pottery in mounds in southern Sarasota and northern Charlotte counties—localities around Charlotte Harbor—means the region was occupied by Safety Harbor villagers (Luer 1980; Marquardt 1992a:431). The problem is in large part a taxonomic one that will be sorted out as more archaeological data are gathered.

The final Caloosahatchee precolumbian period, Period IV, dates from A.D. 1350 or 1400 to European contact and is marked by a decline in the popularity of Belle Glade Plain pottery. In many ways the ceramic inventories of the Glades region and the Caloosahatchee region are most similar at this late time. Most pottery is undecorated, and Glades Tooled pottery is present in both regions. Again, such ceramic evidence may reflect the geographic area encompassed by the political might of Caloosahatchee chiefs.

When the first Europeans entered the realm of the Caloosahatchee peoples in the sixteenth century, they would find the Calusa Indians, a people whose chiefly political system was remarkably like that modeled by archaeologists for the precolumbian period. The Caloosahatchee region, with its rich archaeological evidence and its equally rich documentary record (Zubillaga 1946; Hann 1991), offers archaeologists an extraordinary laboratory for the study of precolumbian Florida.

Coastal Technology

The shell and bone tools of the Caloosahatchee region are much like those found in the Glades region and described earlier (Marquardt 1992b; Walker 1992a). Karen Walker (1989, 1992a) has argued that given the marine-oriented subsistence strategies of the precolumbian people in southwest Florida, archaeologists need to examine artifact collections and determine what part each tool might play in fishing technology. Although it is easy to discern the purpose of some artifacts, such as the palm fiber netting recovered from muck deposits at the Key Marco site at the north end of the Ten Thousand Islands, it is not as easy to prove the purpose of others. However, it is logical that artifacts found in shell middens containing fish remains might well have been used in fishing.

To examine this possibility Walker examined artifacts from several Caloosahatchee and Glades sites, including Key Marco, and compared them with similar items from other maritime societies, tools documented as fishing gear. One such item is the bone point. Small, bipointed points could have functioned as fish gorges, according to Walker. Others could have been attached to wooden shanks to form composite fishhooks for use in deep water. Such composite specimens were found by Cushing (1897:39) at the Key Marco site. Still other single-pointed bone tools could have been attached to hafts and used as fish spears. Bipointed shell specimens also are found at some south Florida coastal sites.

Walker has suggested that another artifact possibly used in fishing technology, a shell or pottery disk with a central hole, was part of a spindle whorl used to spin fiber cordage for netting and fishing line. The use of spindle whorls is common in many societies, and it would be surprising if such tools were not used in Florida. As yet, no one has examined any of the spun cordage from the Key Marco site to determine the method of manufacture.

One last artifact type is polished shell or bone rectangular tablets. Walker suggests that these objects are not gaming pieces or something similar but net gauges, also called mesh sticks, used in net weaving to assure uniform mesh size. One made of fossilized bone has been recovered from Charlotte Harbor, and other examples made of wood came from the Key Marco site. Examples studied thus far tend to group the net gauges into five width sizes: 50, 35, 25, 18, and 14 mm (two to just

Artist's reconstruction of a fish net with gourd floats and shell weights attached to hold it horizontal in the water (drawing by Merald Clark; courtesy University of Florida Institute of Archaeology and Paleoenvironmental Studies).

over 1/2 inch). One section of Key Marco netting has a mesh size of 35 mm, the same as a gauge from the site.

Because of the importance of fishing to precolumbian people in Florida, it would not be surprising to find similar artifacts throughout the state. Indeed, other examples of fishing gear and of other tools probably have already been excavated at aboriginal sites, but not yet identified as to use. The tool assemblages of the precolumbian Floridians probably were as specialized as those found in a modern Floridian's home tool drawer.

Other Cultures of the Late Precolumbian Period

 **PART III**

In part 2 we saw that distinctive lifeways had developed by at least 500 B.C. in east and central Florida, as well as in the southern portion of the state. When the first Europeans arrived on Florida's shores some of those same regional cultures—St. Johns, Belle Glade, Glades, Caloosahatchee, and others—were flourishing.

Agriculture, apparently present though not extensive in the northern St. Johns River valley after A.D.1000 or so, may have been associated with changes in that area, notably increased political complexity. Elsewhere, such as in the upper St. Johns drainage as well as in southern Florida and a large part of coastal north Florida, maize agriculture did not become a local subsistence pattern. Soils in these areas are not well suited to aboriginal agricultural practices, at least the extensive cultivation of maize. Even without an agricultural base, in the Caloosahatchee region marine resources from shallow waters near shore supported larger populations and a more complex political system than could be sustained in other regions where extensive agriculture was not present.

In a few regions of the state, maize agriculture did become a part of local economies, although the exact date this occurred is a matter of controversy, a point examined in chapter 9. What is certain is that the agricultural cultures present in the late precolumbian period differed considerably from those that preceded them and from the nonagricultural societies. For instance, in north-central and north Florida, respectively, the Alachua and Suwannee Valley farming societies differed from those of the Weeden Island–period peoples who had occupied those regions before A.D.750.

Another agricultural region, the most developed in the state, was northwest Florida, especially the eastern panhandle, where the Fort Walton culture developed out of the late Weeden Island Wakulla culture after A.D. 900. Taking advantage of the relatively fertile soils of the Tallahassee Red Hills and the Apalachicola River valley, Fort Walton populations extensively cultivated maize and other crops. That subsistence base led to denser populations and a more complex level of political organization than were found anywhere else in Florida during the precolumbian period.

Fort Walton societies were undoubtedly organized in similar fashion to contemporaneous cultures occupying the river valleys of interior Georgia and Alabama. Archaeologists call these Mississippian cultures, naming them for the Mississippi River valley where they once were thought to have originated. The type of political system shared by Mississippian societies, found from the region of the Fort Walton culture northward throughout the agricultural zone of the interior eastern United States, is a chiefdom. Villages, groups of villages, and even confederations of village groups were ruled by hereditary chiefs who held life and death power over their subjects. Lesser chiefs and their subjects paid tribute to the higher chiefs. Chiefly respect and power were maintained by ideology and especially by military force or its threat. Chiefdoms arose in response to the need to coordinate larger populations, defend territory needed for agricultural pursuits, and assure agricultural success. Anthropologists have noted that, in general, subsistence systems of precolumbian native societies who practiced agriculture were more specialized than the generalized economies of hunting-gathering-fishing societies. With less room for error— as, for instance a bad harvest—agriculturists had to institute both social and supernatural controls to try to prevent the unexpected. This is why agricultural populations generally have complex, intricate, and intertwined ideological, social, and political institutions. As we shall see in the discussion of the Fort Walton culture, the greater a society's reliance on agriculture, the more complex its social institutions.

The presence of the Fort Walton culture with its chiefly organization must have affected the nature of the late precolumbian cultures in

Florida's wetlands (*shaded*) are extensive, especially in coastal regions and in the central and southern portions of the state. They are less extensive in the northern peninsula and in interior northwest Florida, the regions where agriculture was present. (Illustration based on the map *Wetland Resources of the United States,* compiled by Thomas E. Dahl, National Wetlands Inventory, U.S. Fish and Wildlife Service, St. Petersburg.)

adjacent regions and localities, such as the Pensacola culture of the western panhandle, where such influences are apparent. But Fort Walton seems to have had little influence on the Suwannee Valley culture of north Florida or the Alachua culture in north-central Florida. Its absence is difficult to fathom, because both cultures were agricultural and near the Fort Walton region. However, no evidence suggests that they relied as heavily on agricultural products as did the northwest Florida cultures.

Another late precolumbian culture flourishing at the time of European contact was Safety Harbor, which developed out of Manasota and late Weeden Island–period cultures in the central peninsular Gulf coast region, especially around Tampa Bay. Like the Pensacola culture in the panhandle, the Safety Harbor culture also was influenced by Fort Walton, although the processes by which that influence reached the Safety Harbor region are poorly understood. As we shall see in chapter 11, the region of the Safety Harbor culture extended north at least to the mouth of the Withlacoochee River in northernmost Citrus County. The Tampa Bay area Safety Harbor people seem not to have been maize agriculturists. Ample coastal resources in tandem with relatively unfertile soils must have been factors influencing the nonagricultural subsistence pattern of the Tampa Bay populations. Other Safety Harbor peoples farther north may have grown maize, though not as extensively as in the Fort Walton region.

Although all the evidence certainly is not in, it seems likely that the coastal Pensacola culture likewise was not based on extensive farming. The same may have been true of the coastal Fort Walton populations south of the Tallahassee Red Hills. Increasingly, archaeologists are understanding that where marine and wetland resources were available, the precolumbian peoples of Florida did not need extensive agriculture to sustain themselves. This was especially true in regions where local soils are relatively infertile compared with those found in the river valleys of the interior southeastern United States, localities where Mississippian agriculturists lived and where annual floods replenished soil fertility. Where wetlands are present—the bulk of the state of Florida—extensive agriculture was absent; where there are no extensive wetlands, such as in the Tallahassee Hills in the panhandle and the highlands of north and north-central Florida, agriculture was adopted.

In the next three chapters five late precolumbian-period cultures are described: Alachua, Suwannee Valley, Fort Walton, Pensacola, and Safety Harbor. Together they provide a laboratory in which archaeologists can study the reasons some cultures became agriculturists and others not, the reasons chiefdoms of political complexity were sustained by some societies and not by others, and the influences that a Mississippian culture like Fort Walton had on neighboring cultures. Pensacola and Safety Harbor are examples of largely nonagricultural coastal economies that, as a result of contact with a Mississippian society (Fort Walton), developed some aspects of chiefdom political systems. On the other hand, Suwannee Valley and Alachua are agricultural cultures whose archaeological records show little or no evidence of chiefly developments. It is to them we turn first.

Alachua and Suwannee Valley Cultures

9   Driving north from Miami modern-day visitors to Florida receive a firsthand introduction to some of the state's
physiographic zones that directly influenced the nature
of late precolumbian cultures. On U.S. Highway 27 out
of Miami one first drives across the Everglades and then
through the Okeechobee Basin, both of which can be
succinctly described as flat and wet. Northwest of Lake Placid, the
same highway reaches the southern extension of the central highlands
at the western edge of the Kissimmee River drainage. Farther north,
west of Orlando, U.S. 27 enters the central lake district with its extensive wetlands.

Farther north, at Belleview in southern Marion County, the scenery
changes. Stands of live oaks and magnolias appear among the gently
rolling hills, interspersed with horse farms of the thoroughbred racing
industry. This vegetative transition marks the southern limits of north-
central Florida, the region of the Alachua culture. The oaks and magnolias are part of the hardwood forests that once characterized the
vegetative zone known as the Middle Florida Hammock Belt. The
Hammock Belt, which extends north-south through the region, contains loamy, fertile soils excellent for agriculture.

North of Gainesville, U.S. 27 intersects Interstate 75, which runs
northward into the region of north Florida, following the Middle
Florida Hammock Belt through Columbia and Hamilton counties to

Alachua and Suwannee Valley regions in north-central and north Florida.

the Florida-Georgia border. The Hammock Belt extends north a short way farther, ending at the wire grass region of southern Georgia.

The vegetation of the Hammock Belt in north and north-central Florida contrasts sharply with that of the more tropical and subtropical central and southern portions of the state, as well as with the vegetation of the east and west peninsular regions. The forests, soils, and freshwater sources provided the late precolumbian inhabitants of north Marion, Alachua, Suwannee, Columbia, and Hamilton counties with the environmental necessities for combining farming with hunting and gathering. In this, both regions resemble the Tallahassee Red Hills zone of the upper eastern panhandle. In the eighteenth century settlers from Georgia and the Carolinas came to these same areas to establish farms. They sought the same constellation of environmental conditions that native American Indians had utilized earlier.

Although north and north-central Florida shared similar natural environments (one major difference is more large lakes in north-central Florida), different late precolumbian–period cultures lived in each region and can be differentiated on the basis of their respective archaeological assemblages. Although differences exist, so do similarities. This is predictable: the populations of the two regions lived in similar environments and maintained contact with one another for nearly a millennium.

Alachua Culture

In north-central Florida the late precolumbian Alachua culture originally was defined by John Goggin based on archaeological surveys and excavations he and his students conducted in Alachua County (Goggin 1947, 1948b, 1949b, 1953). Goggin (1949b:39) defined the culture as

> basically a sedentary agricultural complex with extensive villages situated
> in regions of good soil.... [C]ord-marking and cob-marking are important
> as decorative techniques for pottery.... Burial mounds were apparently
> constructed, but are not common and do not appear typical.... [N]o
> temple mounds have been found. In many respects this complex appears
> more like cultures from elsewhere in the Southeast than like the sur-
> rounding Floridian [cultures]. The use of cord-marking and cob-marking
> does not reach the popularity [elsewhere in] Florida that it does here.

Following Goggin's initial work in the late 1940s and early 1950s, two generations of archaeologists have continued to study the Alachua culture, building on Goggin's observations (Milanich 1971, 1972; Milanich et al. 1976; K. Johnson 1991).

Alachua site locations and the archaeological assemblage found at those sites contrast sharply with both the Cades Pond Weeden Island period culture that preceded the Alachua culture in north-central Florida and with other cultures to the south, east, and west. Most Alachua sites are large middens with little or no freshwater shell; pottery, bone tools, and lithic artifacts occur in relatively large amounts.

1 Carter mounds
2 Chiefland Golf Course
3 Henderson Mound
4 Ichetucknee River
5 Law School Mound
6 Leslie Mound
7 Manatee Springs
8 Woodward Mound

Alachua and Suwannee Valley archaeological sites.

Chert used for the stone tools was easily mined from local limestone outcroppings common in the karstic geologic strata of the region. The amount of lithic artifacts is much greater than it is at St. Johns sites or at the sites of coastal northern Florida.

While Cades Pond sites are located to provide access to extensive wetlands, Alachua villages are in locales where good agricultural soils are found, mainly in the Hammock Belt. Some such locations are near larger wetlands, such as on the north side of Paynes Prairie, the north side of Levy Lake, and the west side of Orange Lake. Others are near small lakes or spring-fed sinkholes.

Differences in site selection criteria between the Cades Pond hunter-gathers and the later Alachua agriculturists become most apparent when individual site locations are mapped and it is seen that they are mutually exclusive. For instance, although Cades Pond sites are found on Orange Lake and Paynes Prairie, and Alachua sites are found adjacent to those same extensive wetlands, specific locations differ. Sites of the two cultures are almost never contiguous. Alachua sites lie at higher elevations where drainage is better and where deciduous hammocks and loamy soils are found. Cades Pond sites are in lower, less well-drained locales where soil type was not a factor. Within Alachua and northern Marion counties, Alachua sites are found in many localities where extensive wetlands are not present, miles away from the nearest Cades Pond site clusters.

The different subsistence emphases of these two cultures also is reflected in their zooarchaeological records. The number of individual animal species used for food by the Alachua peoples is much less than for the Cades Pond culture. This finding suggests that with agriculture providing a portion of the diet, the Alachua villagers used fewer animal resources. As they placed less emphasis on hunting and gathering, they became more selective of the animals they did hunt and collect.

Origins and Distribution

The differences between the Cades Pond and the Alachua cultures strongly suggest that one did not develop out of the other. If this is true, where did the Alachua culture, which appears after A.D. 600, originate? In his original definition Goggin (1949b:39) noted similarities between Alachua pottery and ceramics found to the north in Georgia. Subsequent research (Milanich 1971) confirmed similarities in projectile-point types and cord-marked and fabric-marked pottery between the Alachua culture and the Wilmington and Savannah cultures of the Georgia coast. It violates intuition however, to suggest that coastal populations who probably relied not on maize agriculture but on marine resources migrated to or colonized inland north-central Florida.

A better explanation—a more likely Georgia source for the Alachua culture—emerged from tests and surveys carried out in southern Georgia well inland from the coast (Milanich et al. 1976; Snow 1978). Those studies located previously unstudied Ocmulgee culture sites with a ceramic complex like both the Wilmington and early Alachua assemblages. Ocmulgee sites are numerous in the river valleys of southern Georgia, especially in the physiographic region known as the Dougherty Uplift, a highlands zone that cuts diagonally across Georgia from Augusta to northwest Florida.

The presence of such sites and an archaeological assemblage like that of the early Alachua culture suggests another explanation for the origins of the latter, subject to revision as more information is collected. That is, at about A.D. 600 Ocmulgee populations expanded beyond the boundaries of their Georgia region, moving south around the McKeithen Weeden Island villages in north Florida and into north-central Florida. There, especially in the western part of that region away from the Cades Pond sites that are located among the more easterly wetlands, the Ocmulgee culture–derived population found a suitable area to settle.

This explanation, unfortunately, is little more than a Just-So story at present. Precolumbian migrations, easy to hypothesize, are much harder to prove. We also lack an explanation of why Ocmulgee culture people moved southward at about A.D. 600. One explanation—expansion of agricultural populations seeking additional lands—seems unlikely. There is no evidence that the Ocmulgee villagers practiced agriculture, and we would not expect it to be present at that early date. We can only suggest that this is a problem worthy of research.

However the Alachua culture came to be in north-central Florida after A.D. 600, its village sites soon occupied locales throughout the area. Sites are found from just south of the Santa Fe River southward to Belleview in Marion County, about the southern extent of the magnolia and live oak forest of the Middle Florida Hammock Belt. The eastern boundary is marked by the eastern extent of those forests, a north-south line through easternmost Alachua and eastern Marion counties. As we saw in chapter 6, Alachua sites extend westward into Levy and Dixie counties. The latter are well west of the main distribution of Alachua villages in Marion and Alachua counties. Where relatively large ceramic inventories (fifty or more potsherds) have been collected from such sites, such as Manatee Springs and the Chiefland Golf Course site, it is apparent that the utilitarian pottery assemblage differs from that present at the more eastern sites. More fabric-impressed pottery and less corncob-marked pottery is present in Levy and Dixie counties. These western sites have not been radiocarbon dated, but the ceramic assemblages associated with them appear to be early within the time frame of the Alachua culture. Could they be sites occupied by the Ocmulgee peoples who entered Florida by following the Alapaha-Suwannee River system to Levy and Dixie counties, later expanding eastward into north-central Florida?

Within Alachua County, Alachua culture sites are most often found in clusters, perhaps representing the budding-off of new villages from older ones, the establishment of new villages as nearby soils lost fertility, or both (for recent survey results, see K. Johnson 1987, 1991; Johnson, Nelson, and Terry 1988). Such clusters are known from west Orange Lake, north Levy Lake, the north-central side of Paynes Prairie, the northwest side of Paynes Prairie (extending to the Idylwild locality), near the town of Rochelle, the Moon Lake locality, the Devil's Millhopper locality, near the town of Alachua, and in the Robinson Sinks locality in northwest Alachua County. Some of these clusters contain sand mounds.

Using maps from the eighteenth and nineteenth century in combination with on-the-ground surveys, Kenneth Johnson (1991) reconstructed many of the major colonial- and postcolonial-period trails in north-central Florida. Most of the Alachua site clusters lie on or quite near this road system. The implication is that the roads follow earlier, precolumbian trails that connected aboriginal towns. It would be surprising if this were not true. Similar trails must have been present throughout precolumbian Florida.

All of these site clusters, except those immediately south of Paynes Prairie, contain at least one site where sixteenth- or seventeenth-century Spanish artifacts have been found, indicating the Alachua culture continued to occupy north-central Florida into the colonial period. Fewer surveys have been carried out in Marion County, but the absence of similar site clusters there would be surprising.

Ceramic Chronology

During the millennium that the Alachua peoples occupied north-central Florida, the relative frequencies of various pottery-decorating techniques rose and fell as culturally defined styles changed. Because many sites from different time periods have been excavated, a seriation table charting these changes through time can be constructed. Such tables are useful tools in helping archaeologists to date components in sites. Unfortunately, Alachua ceramic seriation is not yet firmly tied to radiocarbon dates and can only be used to relatively order sites and provide "guess dates."

Based on the ceramic changes evident in the seriation chart, the precolumbian portion of the culture can be divided into two main periods: Hickory Pond, A.D. 600 to about 1250; and Alachua, A.D. 1250 to 1539. The date of A.D. 1250 is little more than a guess, while 1539 marks the entry of the Hernando de Soto expedition into the Alachua region. Postcontact periods also have been defined.

During the earlier Hickory Pond period, 45–70 percent of the pottery was cord marked; vessel surfaces were roughened by malleating the unfired clay with a wooden paddle wrapped with twisted fiber cord. Through time, this technique rose and then fell in popularity. Some Hickory Pond–period pottery was similarly roughened or impressed with fabric-wrapped paddles.

The start of the Alachua period marks the point when a new technique—malleating or scratching the pot surface with a dried corncob—became more popular than cord marking. Fabric-impressed pottery is not present in the Alachua period.

Subsistence and Settlements

Although Alachua ceramic inventories changed over time, other culture traits seem to have remained the same. As yet, we cannot see changes in settlement patterns or subsistence strategies during the precolumbian history of the culture. Alachua culture villages are found on higher ground close to lakes, ponds, or other freshwater sources. These freshwater habitats provided both drinking water and access to fish, turtles, and wading birds. Catfish, gar, bowfin, blue gill, sunfish, and bream bones have all been identified from Alachua villages. Some of the panfish remains are headless and articulated, suggesting the fish were filleted and then, perhaps, smoked. No fishhooks or bone gorges of any kind have been recovered from Alachua sites; it seems likely that the fish were taken in nets. The lack of extremely large bass, gar, and catfish—such as those found at earlier Cades Pond sites—and the lack of bone points used as gigs suggest that fish spearing or bow-and-arrow fishing was not important.

A number of species of turtles were collected from wetland and terrestrial habitats. Box, snapping, cooter, softshell, mud, slider, and musk turtles and gopher tortoises all were eaten. Occasionally box turtle shells (without the carapace) were used as small cooking vessels. Freshwater habitats also provided mud eels and alligators.

Using snares, traps, and, perhaps, bows and arrows tipped with small triangular projectile points made of whitish local chert, the Alachua peoples caught and hunted a variety of animals from the forests of north-central Florida. The white-tailed deer was probably the single most important meat source. Deer were butchered at the kill site, and the haunches, hide, lower jaw (probably with tongue attached), and antlers were taken to the village. At least some of the haunches were roasted over open fires inside of houses. Other mammals in the diet include opossum, rabbit, raccoon, brown bear, skunk, round-tailed muskrat, and squirrel.

Hunting seems to have been for specific species, as opposed to casual collecting. For example, hunters may have gone after squirrels one time and deer another. In a single refuse pit bones of five individual squirrels representing more than one species have been found. Presumably the squirrels were collected en masse, butchered and eaten, and their remains discarded, all at one time.

Freshwater mussels were occasionally collected and eaten, as were wading birds. But, unlike the Cades Pond culture, birds were not an important part of the Alachua diet.

As yet, evidence for Alachua plant use is scarce. Palm berries, acorns, and hickory nuts have been found at sites. No doubt many additional wild plants were used. Maize agriculture is indicated by the impressions of corncobs—some with kernels—on vessel surfaces. Thus far, charred kernels and cobs have been recovered from only one late precolumbian–early colonial period site (Milanich 1972; and see Kohler 1979). Members of the Hernando de Soto expedition described maize fields in north-central Florida at villages that certainly must have been Alachua sites (Ranjel in Bourne 1904:69).

As yet we have no direct evidence that maize agriculture was present in the early history of the culture, during the early Hickory Pond period. Could the appearance of cob-marked pottery correlate with the appearance of maize agriculture? Is it possible that the early Alachua villages grew crops, but that only after A.D. 1000 or so did agricultural practices include growing corn?

Excavations at the Richardson site on the west shore of Orange Lake (Milanich 1972) indicate that the village covered an area 200 yards on a side. Within the village, houses were circular, about 25 feet in diameter, and placed about 70 feet apart. Drying racks and storage cribs were interspersed among the houses. Houses were constructed by anchoring wall poles 2 to 3 feet apart in the ground. The tops of the poles were probably bent over and tied together to form a domelike roof. Palmetto or palm fronds could have been used as thatch to cover the pole frame.

Within the houses were shallow pits in which cooking fires were lit; other, deeper pits were possibly lined with hides or grass and used for food storage. Along the inside walls of the houses sleeping and sitting platforms were constructed by setting small posts vertically in the ground and then attaching horizontal poles. As anyone who has ever camped near a lake or sinkhole in north-central Florida can attest, the aboriginal villages must have been invaded by mosquitoes during much of the year. To avoid the insects, the aborigines lit small smudge fires under the beds and slept in the smoke.

Technology

Small, triangular Pinellas arrow points are typical throughout the temporal range of the Alachua culture (Bullen 1975:8). At village sites these points often are the most numerous lithic tool recovered. Other stone tools include expanded-base drills, linear drills that are round to lenticular in cross section, gravers, spokeshaves, and sandstone hones. Flakes and small blades struck from irregular polyhedral cores were used as knives and scrapers. Some large blades were worked into end scrapers and bifacial knives. Bifacial, ovate knives are also common.

A variety of grinding equipment, both mortars and manos, most likely was used to process maize, nuts, and seeds. Ovate hand axe–shaped implements were used as choppers, perhaps for working or cutting wood. Some exhibit silica polishing, which suggests they were hoes.

Many fewer types of bone tools have been recognized. Only a few awls and pins, the latter perhaps used as clothing or hair fasteners, have been recovered. Potsherds with grooves worn in them were used as hones to sharpen these tools.

Items of personal adornment—shell ear pins made from the columella of *Busycon* shells—have been recovered from one village site and one mound, as have fragments of *Busycon* shell drinking cups. Red

Alachua culture lithic tools: *a–b,* ovate bifacial knives (*a* is 2¾ inches long); *c–e,* linear bifacial knives; *f–k,* Pinellas points; *l,* Tampa point; *m–n,* Ichetucknee points.

Alachua culture lithic tools: *a*, spokeshave, 3 inches long; *b–d*, perforators; *e–f*, blade knives; *g*, hoe.

ochre—hematite or a similar iron oxide pigment—was probably used as body paint.

The pottery of the Alachua culture peoples is distinctive from that of the earlier Cades Pond culture. Alachua vessel shapes include both cylindrical pots, smaller than those of the Cades Pond people, and simple, small bowls ten inches or less in diameter at the mouth. Some of the pots made during the Hickory Pond period had clay lumps and quartz sand present in the paste as temper. In later ceramics only quartz sand inclusions are present. In the manufacturing process, nearly all of the clay vessels had their surfaces malleated and roughened before firing. Perhaps this helped to compact the clay coils, adding more strength to the vessels. About half of the individual vessels were then smoothed over on the outer surfaces, appearing undecorated, although occasionally some of the roughening still shows.

Roughened-surface Alachua pottery types include Prairie Cord Marked, Alachua Cob Marked, Lochloosa Punctated, Prairie Punctated-over-Cord Marked (rare), Prairie Fabric Impressed (plain twined openwork and plain plaited fabric were used, both rarely), and Alachua Net Impressed (rare). A few potsherds were ground down into discs one to two inches in diameter, possibly for use as game counters or some other use.

Alachua Mounds

Two Alachua burial mounds have been excavated, Woodward Mound (Bullen 1949) and Henderson Mound (Loucks 1976); a third one, the Law School Mound, has been tested (Fradkin and Milanich 1977). The Woodward Mound is immediately adjacent to a village site that was investigated in the late 1960s and shown to have been occupied during the Hickory Pond period (Milanich 1971). Presumably the mound was used at the same time. Neither the Henderson nor the Law School mound is associated with any nearby village. This raises the possibility that other isolated, small sand burial mounds in north-central Florida were built by Alachua peoples. A number of such sites have been recorded, but most have since been destroyed, and their cultural affiliations remain uncertain.

The Woodward Mound is described by Bullen (1949) as an annular sand mound fifty feet in diameter and measuring about three feet in height when excavated. Initial construction of the mound was

Alachua culture pottery: *a–b, e,* Prairie Cord Marked (*a* is 1 ½ inches high; *e* exhibits a mending hole); *c–d,* Prairie Fabric Marked; *f–h,* Lochloosa Punctated.

Alachua culture pottery and sherd disks: *a–e*, Alachua Cob Marked (*a* is 2 inches high); *g–h*, sherd disks made from Prairie Cord Marked pottery.

Excavations at the Law School Mound in 1976. The mechanical sifter, engineered by Charles Fairbanks, is powered by a lawn mower engine.

preceded by digging a circular depression about eighteen inches deep and thirty-two feet in diameter. A mixture of dark gray sand and charcoal was used to fill in the depression, forming a base on which the mound would later be built. Two or three people were buried in separate graves dug into this prepared stratum. All were adults, and red ochre was placed under and beside portions of two of the bodies. After their interment, a mound was erected over the prepared stratum, covering the interments.

Over time, twenty-six additional individuals were interred. They were laid on the eastern side of the mound, most in extended positions. Each was oriented with head toward the northwestern edge of the mound and feet toward the mound's edge. After each interment, the body was covered with sand, a process that added height and diameter to the mound. Three of these burials were bundles, with only the skull and long bones buried. Two children were accompanied by shell beads. Analysis of the burial population by Adelaide Bullen suggests a normally distributed population in terms of gender and adult-child ratios (although the sample was small). Most likely, all villagers or all the members of a certain village lineage who died over an unspecified period of time were buried in the mound.

The Henderson Mound (Loucks 1976) was similar in size and content to the Woodward Mound. It was slightly oblong, thirty-two feet long and three feet high. Initially, a platform or primary mound two feet thick was built on the ground surface. Several crania, one flexed interment, and five extended burials were placed in or on this stratum. Sand was scraped up from around the mound and used to cover this first mound and the burials. Over time, other interments were made on the surface of this primary mound and covered with sand. Most of these individuals were placed on the mound's east side. This practice eventually gave the mound a slightly oval shape.

The mound contained 41 individuals: 24 were interred in an extended position, 10 were represented only by crania; and 5 were flexed (2 were too fragmented to ascertain burial form). As with the Woodward Mound, age distribution ratios seemed normal. However, of the 16 individuals whose gender was determined, 15 were female, perhaps evidence that the mound was used for a single matrilineage.

Many of the burials were interred with red ochre deposits around the head, shoulders, and chest. Thirteen individuals had wood charcoal, in some instances identified as portions of charred planks, placed on, beside, or under the body. Apparently the wood was used to line and cover individual shallow graves. Fires were lit on top of the graves, igniting the wood, and then sand was used to cover the still smoldering wood and the grave.

Three radiocarbon dates were obtained from charred wood associated with human interments in the Woodward Mound. Those dates—A.D. 590, 740, and 1110—suggest that the mound, like Woodward Mound, was constructed during the Hickory Pond period, although the range of dates seems to be in error, extending over too long a time. The Law School Mound (Fradkin and Milanich 1977) also is thought to date to the Hickory Pond period.

That all three mounds date from the Hickory Pond period raises the question of whether or not burial mounds were constructed during the post–A.D. 1250 Alachua period, when cob-marked pottery provides good evidence for maize agriculture. Could a seeming lack of Alachua-period mounds signal a change in burial practices or social organization, one tied to an increased reliance on maize agriculture? This is a question future investigations should address.

Suwannee Valley Culture

By A.D.750 sufficient changes had occurred in the ceramic inventory of the early Weeden Island–period McKeithen culture in north Florida for archaeologists to recognize a new culture, Suwannee Valley. It seems clear that this new archaeological assemblage developed out of Weeden Island and overlaps temporally with both the late Weeden Island–period Wakulla culture in northwest Florida and the Alachua culture in north-central Florida. The year A.D. 750 seems to have been key in the history of precolumbian Florida, a date when changes in archaeological assemblages, especially ceramic inventories, occurred across northern Florida, from the panhandle into the St. Johns region. Archaeologists have long assumed that such changes were related to the addition of maize agriculture to subsistence systems or, perhaps, to an increase in the economic importance of agriculture in those systems. But once again, direct evidence for maize in early Suwannee Valley sites is lacking (corncob impressions are present on pottery from the late Suwannee Valley culture, after about A.D. 1200).

It was only in the late 1970s that the regional cultures of north Florida began to be the focus of archaeological investigations. Surveys and test excavations at a number of locales and sites and extensive village excavations at the McKeithen site in western Columbia County indicated that following A.D. 750 a previously unrecognized ceramic assemblage was found throughout the region (Kohler 1978; Loucks 1978; Milanich, Cordell et al. 1984). The assemblage consists of both undecorated and decorated pottery, the latter displaying a variety of surface-roughening techniques, including check stamping, cord marking, cob marking, punctating, and brushing. Some of these types are the same as individual pottery types present in the contemporaneous Wakulla assemblage (e.g., check stamping) and the contemporaneous Alachua assemblage (e.g., cord marking, cob marking, and punctating, the latter similar to the type Lochloosa Punctated). But when the total Suwannee Valley assemblage is examined, it is distinct from either Wakulla or Alachua ceramics.

More recent surveys and excavations have produced evidence that the Suwannee Valley ceramic assemblage was still present in north Florida into the early sixteenth century (K. Johnson 1986, 1987, 1991; Johnson, Nelson, and Terry 1988; Johnson and Nelson 1990; 1992; Worth in Weisman 1992). As with the Alachua culture, variations in frequencies of pottery types over time are present and have resulted in the recognition of a late precolumbian–early colonial Suwannee Valley phase called Indian Pond. An earlier manifestation is present at a site adjacent to the Ichetucknee River from which radiocarbon dates of A.D. 950 and 1250 have been obtained. Certainly other phases and periods will be defined in the future.

Apparently there also are regional variations in the assemblage. Because much of our present information about the nature of the Suwannee Valley ceramics comes from surface collections, it is difficult to define these variations with certainty. What is known is that the Suwannee Valley culture occupied north Florida after A.D. 750, developing out of the early Weeden Island McKeithen culture. It continued to occupy that region at least to the time of European contact. Late precolumbian sites are contemporary with the Fort Walton culture of the panhandle, but as yet no contact of any sort between the two cultures has been recognized.

Sites

As noted in chapter 6, the north Florida region of the Suwannee Valley culture contains two vegetative zones. Extending northward through the central portions of Columbia and Suwannee counties is the Middle Florida Hammock Belt. Similar mesic forests once also extended westward across north Florida, through Hamilton and northern Madison counties. This L-shaped distribution of hardwood forest provided important natural resources for the aboriginal populations of north Florida, including loamy soils good for agriculture. Lower, less well drained lands, a second vegetative and topographic zone of lowland forests, are present on the eastern side of the hardwood hammock (e.g., in the Osceola National Forest and portions of Baker, Union, and Bradford counties), as well as on the southwestern side (e.g., San Pedro Bay in Lafayette and Taylor counties).

When compared to sites of the early Weeden Island period, Suwannee Valley village sites seem less densely distributed, more numerous, and smaller. Many appear to be small hamlets, and they are found both in the Middle Florida Hammock Belt as well as in lowland locales. Surveys by Kenneth Johnson, Bruce Nelson, and their research teams (Johnson 1986, 1987; Johnson, Nelson, and Terry 1988; Johnson and Nelson 1992) have located several hundred of these hamlet sites as well as smaller sites that may be special-use camps. This settlement pattern is similar to that noted in the Wakulla Weeden Island region in northwest Florida during the late Weeden Island period: less nucleation of villages, the presence of smaller and more numerous settlements (probably hamlets), the presence of special-use camps, and occupation of locales that were little utilized previously. As was suggested for the Wakulla culture in northwest Florida, this settlement system may correlate with increased reliance on agriculture. But hard evidence for early Suwannee Valley–period agriculture has not yet been found.

By the period of the Indian Pond phase, however, nucleation of villages may once again have occurred. Kenneth Johnson (1991; Johnson and Nelson 1990) has located several late precolumbian– early colonial period clusters of village sites and special-use camps. These clusters, similar to those in the Alachua region, may date from the time when intensive maize agriculture was practiced. Several clusters are known to have been associated with one or more mounds containing human interments.

What appear to be early Suwannee Valley mounds—for example, Leslie Mound and the three Carter Mounds (Milanich, Cordell et al. 1984:202–206)—are found in both highland and lowland locales. In each case a village site is associated with the mound. Leslie Mound and its village are located on a small creek in a region of well-drained soils. Construction of the circular mound began when the ground surface where the mound was to be built was cleaned of humus. Then a four-inch-thick layer of clean, clayey sand was laid down. On top of that a low platform mound one foot high and at least thirty feet long on one side was built. A humic zone formed on top of this platform, which may have been the base for a charnel structure. Bundles of skeletal remains—long bones and crania—were placed on the mound surface on the humic stratum; these individuals may have been stored previously in the charnel house. Sand was brought in and used to cover the platform mound and the burials, forming a second platform mound

Excavations at the Leslie Mound, Columbia County (1979).

three and a half feet thick. This flat-topped mound probably also was used as the base for a charnel house, and a second humic zone accumulated on its surface. Bundled burials were similarly placed on the surface of that mound and another mound cap laid down on them, burying both platforms mounds and the human interments and forming a rounded mound.

Most of the potsherds in the Leslie Mound appear to have been accidental inclusions scraped up with the fill used to build the various mound strata. Three sherds from the same well-worn Weeden Island Incised vessel with a red-slipped interior appear to have been deliberately placed on the surface of the first platform mound, however; perhaps these were relics from earlier times.

Carter Mound I also was constructed by first cleaning the ground surface and building a two-foot-thick sand platform. Bundles of human bones were placed on the platform and covered with sand. Subsequently, other burials were laid down and covered with more sand. The mound contained two stone celts, a Carrabelle Punctated bowl, and a collared Carrabelle Punctated bowl with pinching encircling the collar. None of the Suwannee Valley mounds contained examples of the well-made Weeden Island pottery vessels typical of early Weeden Island–period mounds in north and northwest Florida.

Suwannee Valley pottery: *a–c,* St. Johns Check Stamped; *d–f,* Lochloosa Punctated; *g–i,* Ichetucknee Roughened.

Material Culture

The pottery types that define the precolumbian Suwannee Valley culture include Alachua Cob Marked, Prairie Cord Marked, Lochloosa Punctated, Prairie Fabric Impressed, Ichetucknee Roughened, and Alachua Plain (Worth in Weisman 1992:191–195; also see Milanich, Cordell et al. 1984: 201–202, 204; Johnson and Nelson 1990; Weisman 1992;127–130). St Johns Plain and St. Johns Check Stamped potsherds and other check-stamped sherds are also a part of the ceramic assemblage.

Small arrow points—Pinellas, Ichetucknee, and Tampa types (Bullen 1975:8–10)—and other small bifacial tools have been recovered from Suwannee Valley sites along with flake tools. Definition of the full assemblage of lithic and other tools associated with the culture, however, awaits more excavations.

This brief description of the Suwannee Valley culture has not done justice to the precolumbian Floridians who lived in north Florida after A.D. 750 and whose descendants occupied that region when the first Europeans invaded their land in the early sixteenth century. Archaeological investigations are ongoing in north Florida, and we have much to learn. At present, we can do little more than sketch the barest of outlines of the Suwannee Valley culture. Our knowledge of the Fort Watlon culture is much greater, as we shall see in the next chapter.

Fort Walton and Pensacola Cultures

10 The most politically complex culture in Florida and the regional culture with the densest population was Fort Walton in the northwest region of the state. During the late precolumbian period, the Fort Walton culture, which developed out of the late Weeden Island Wakulla culture (see chapter 5), practiced patterns of mound building, intensive agriculture, and hierarchial settlement arrangements like those of the Mississippian societies flourishing during the same period in the interior of the Southeast.

Excavations at the Lake Jackson site in Leon County, directed by B. Calvin Jones of the Florida Bureau of Archaeological Research, recovered many examples of highly ornate and beautifully crafted copper and shell Mississippian artifacts similar to those found at Mississippian sites like Etowah in northern Georgia or Spiro in Oklahoma. Such artifacts are paraphernalia associated with high-ranking Mississippian chiefs and priests and with the power and ideology that surrounded them.

Such archaeological evidence leaves no doubt that Fort Walton was a Mississippian culture with social and political systems much more developed than had existed previously anywhere in Florida. The presence of Fort Walton, especially the grandeur and the military might manifested in the various Fort Walton societies that rose and fell through time, must have been well known to contemporary precolumbian peoples across northern Florida. To be able to interact with the Fort Walton chiefs, adjacent groups must have developed social systems that mirrored, albeit perhaps only partially, the Fort Walton political system. Although it is not always possible to see such influences in the archaeological record, it seems clear that Fort Walton developments did affect the nature of late precolumbian societies around Tampa Bay (Safety Harbor culture) and in the western panhandle (Pensacola culture). Historical documents from the colonial period suggest similar influences on the Suwannee Valley culture of north Florida, although archaeological evidence from that region thus far has eluded researchers. One key to understanding these late precolumbian developments is to understand Fort Walton, and it is to that culture we turn next.

Fort Walton Culture

Fort Walton, like most other northwest Florida regional cultures, was first recognized by Gordon Willey and Richard Woodbury (1942; also see Willey 1949a:452–470, 512–513). Based on the distribution of Fort Walton pottery in both mound and midden sites, the region of the culture was defined as northwest Florida. Sites were recorded along the coast as well as at inland locales, such as around Tallahassee and in the Apalachicola River valley. Some coastal villages featured large flat-topped mounds, but such mounds were said to be more common in interior, noncoastal locales (Willey 1949a:453–454).

The pottery associated with these sites was so different from that of the earlier Weeden Island–period peoples that archaeologists believed the Fort Walton culture represented a late (ca. A.D. 1500) intrusion of Mississippian peoples into northwest Florida from Alabama and western Georgia. In the 1940s, the appearance of Mississippian cultures across the Southeast, including northwest Florida, was thought by archaeologists to have been the result of migrations of intensive agriculturists, rather than in situ developments. But by the late 1940s sufficient ceramic similarities between Weeden Island and early Fort Walton were recognized for John Griffin to postulate development of Fort Walton out of earlier Weeden Island cultures in northwest Florida, rejecting "migration and replacement of peoples" as an explanation (Griffin 1949a:46; 1950).

Fort Walton region in northwest Florida.

Beginning in the 1970s and continuing to the present the Fort Walton culture has been the focus of a number of important archaeological investigations (Fryman 1971b; Brose and Percy 1978; Scarry 1980, 1981a, b, 1984, 1990a, Tesar 1980, 1981; Payne 1981, 1991a, 1993; White 1981a, b, 1982, 1986; Jones 1982; Brose 1984; Scarry and Payne 1986; there also have been numerous archaeological surveys; see Scarry 1990a:230–231 for an overview of Fort Walton research). Investigators have now examined the culture's origins, development, and spatial variations; the nature of the social and political structures reflected in settlement and community patterns and in artifact assemblages; subsistence; and the relationship of the culture to other Mississippian cultures and to the colonial-period native peoples of northwest

Florida, such as the Apalachee. These investigations have refined our knowledge of Fort Walton and its place in the history of Florida. They also have provided a detailed picture of a remarkable native culture, different from all others in precolumbian Florida.

Spatial and Temporal Variations

Fort Walton sites are distributed across northwest Florida from the Aucilla River west through the Apalachicola River drainage, perhaps as far west as Mobile Bay. Fort Walton also extends north into the Chattahoochee River drainage in southeastern Alabama and southwestern Georgia and the adjacent coastal plain. Much of this geographical distribution is almost the same as that of the earlier Wakulla culture, and it is certain that Fort Walton developed out of that late Weeden Island–period culture during the period A.D. 900–1000.

Within the Fort Walton region both spatial and temporal variations have been defined (Scarry 1990a; Payne 1991a). These variations, which allow archaeologists to begin to chart both the emergence of the culture out of its Weeden Island roots and its expansion within northwest Florida, continue to be refined as more information is collected.

In addition to the Chattahoochee River valley and adjacent portions of Alabama and Georgia, Fort Walton variants are recognized in the Apalachicola River valley, the Tallahassee Hills, the Marianna Lowlands, and the Gulf coastal region from the mouth of the Aucilla River west to St. Andrew Bay near Panama City. The distribution of Fort Walton sites extends even farther west, past Choctawhatchee Bay to Fort Walton Beach and beyond. But in that far western portion of the coastal region, archaeologists have had trouble differentiating Fort Walton sites from sites of the Pensacola culture by means of ceramic inventories. Ceramic assemblages in that area are often mixed, and determining what is and what is not Fort Walton is not always an easy task. This results from two factors. First, the western panhandle area is a ceramic transition zone; the distribution of Fort Walton ceramics there overlaps with that of Pensacola ceramics, the latter characterized by shell tempering. Second, in the western panhandle the Pensacola culture, which dates after A.D. 1200, follows (overlies) early Fort Walton, meaning that at some sites components of both cultures may indeed be present. As yet, largely because of a dearth of radiocarbon-dated assemblages from the western panhandle, the exact spatial and

Fort Walton regional variants.

temporal relationships between Fort Walton and Pensacola in that area remain to be determined.

The Fort Walton variant cultures in the eastern panhandle have been investigated much more fully, and the taxonomy is clearer in that area. In the Apalachicola River valley, sites are found along both the upper and lower reaches of the river. From Bristol northward the river valley is typified by low rolling hills or the steep ravines of the Torreya physiographic zone. Soils that would have been excellent for aboriginal agriculture are present; in some aspects the upper valley resembles the Appalachian piedmont. From Bristol to the river's mouth the valley is flatter as the river gradient drops, eventually reaching the coastal estuaries and marshes. Along the river's lower portion below Bristol lie numerous expanses of freshwater wetlands.

Fort Walton sites, including large mound complexes, are found all along the river valley from the Georgia-Alabama state line to Apalachicola Bay. More large sites, however, appear to be found away from the coast in or near the upper Apalachicola valley.

John Scarry (1984, 1990a) has used archaeological assemblages and radiocarbon dates to divide the Apalachicola sites into early, middle, and late Fort Walton phases, naming the phases Cayson (A.D. 1000–1200), Sneads (A.D. 1200–1400), and Yon (A.D. 1400–colonial period). Phases are archaeological cultures that are tightly defined in space and time; a single culture period may be composed of several phases or sequences of phases. The societies associated with the early Fort Walton Cayson phase have been described as "simple chiefdoms, with clear social distinctions between high and low status individuals—distinctions revealed in residential segregation and the extraction and allocation of community surplus labor. The people relied on cleared-field agriculture for a significant portion of their diet" (Scarry 1990a:232).

At least several chiefdoms are thought to be represented in the Cayson phase, probably each controlling a mound center and nearby outlying homesteads. During the following Sneads phase, Fort Walton people continued to live within the valley, probably increasing in population. Late Fort Walton times, the Yon phase, saw changes in the valley archaeological assemblages. Scarry (1990a:232–233) has suggested attributing these changes to "disruption of interregional trade networks . . . , the collapse (or restructuring) of individual Fort Walton [chiefdoms] . . . , and the establishment of new systems of alliance and exchange with other Mississippian [societies]." Although dated to the post–A.D. 1400 period, future research and tighter radiocarbon dating may show that these changes were a result of the impact the European presence made on native American Indian societies following Christopher Columbus's 1492 voyage. Such impact may have preceded the actual entrance of Europeans into northwest Florida in the late 1520s and 1530s.

The density of sites immediately to the east of the Apalachicola drainage in Gadsden and Liberty counties is much lower than in the river valley itself, suggesting that area was a buffer zone between the Apalachicola valley sites and those of the Tallahassee Hills. This

Fort Walton archaeological sites.

evidence supports the contention that the Fort Walton culture in northwest Florida was never a single political unit but comprised several regional chiefdoms.

A second area of dense Fort Walton sites is in the Tallahassee Hills region, an inland, upland region between the Aucilla and Ochlockonee rivers above the coastal flatlands in Leon and Jefferson counties. The area of this Fort Walton variant culture is characterized by mixed hardwood and pine forests and by loamy, clayey soils that are excellent for farming.

Scarry has defined two Fort Walton phases for this region: Lake Jackson (A.D. 1100–1400, early and middle Fort Walton) and Velda (A.D. 1400–colonial period, late Fort Walton). In the colonial period, the Tallahassee Hills region was the home of the Apalachee Indians, whose precolumbian ancestors are known to be the people of the Lake Jackson and Velda phases.

Fort Walton sites blanket the locality around Tallahassee, decreasing as one moves eastward toward the Aucilla River. Writing about the Tallahassee Hills, Charles Fairbanks (1971:39) noted that "almost any- where where there is either red clay soil ... or where there are sandy well-drained clay loams, we will find Fort Walton sites. . . . The largest of them is considerably less than an acre and a good many of them would be only the size of [a large] room."

That Fort Walton populations within the Tallahassee Hills greatly outnumbered those of earlier precolumbian cultures is verified by Louis Tesar's survey of six selected Leon County locales (Tesar 1980). Of 174 site components (150 sites) recorded (encompassing all periods from Paleoindian times into the colonial period), 97 (56 percent) were Fort Walton. An additional 18 percent were from the colonial (mis- sion) period, while the remaining 26 percent were from periods earlier than Fort Walton. A similar increase in sites during the Fort Walton period was noted by Nancy White (1981a:702) in her Lake Seminole survey at the Chattahoochee-Flint River confluence at the north end of the Apalachicola River. These data suggest an expanding population after about A.D. 1000 throughout the Fort Walton region, the result of farming.

One settlement change associated with the Lake Jackson phase from that of the late Weeden Island Wakulla culture in the Tallahassee Hills is the hierarchial ordering of sites, thought to reflect social and polit- ical hierarchies as well. Payne (1982; and see Scarry 1990a:238) notes four Lake Jackson phase site types: (1) small farmsteads like those described earlier by Fairbanks, each consisting of one or two houses; (2) larger hamlet settlements with five to ten houses and a larger building that probably served the community for certain specialized religious or governmental activities; (3) small mound centers, each with a single pyramidal mound; (4) and a major mound-village center with multiple mounds (the largest one is the Lake Jackson site). Mound centers are found around Lake Jackson, Lake Iamonia, Lake Miccosukee, and the now-dry Lake Lafayette. It is likely that the higher-status elite members of society—chiefs and their families and other officials—lived at these mound centers, while most of the population was found at the farmsteads and hamlets scattered across the landscape in localities of good agricultural soils.

A third Fort Walton variant culture is present in the Marianna Lowlands in Jackson and Calhoun counties west of the upper Apalachicola River valley. The Chipola River, a tributary of the Apalachicola, flows through this region, which also contains good agricultural soils. Archaeological research in those lowlands is much more limited than in the Apalachicola River valley or the Tallahassee Hills. Surveys along the Chipola River (White and Trauner 1987) and excavations at the Waddells Mill Pond site (Gardner 1966) suggest that farmsteads are present, but village-mound complex sites are rare or absent. Only one small platform mound has been reported for the Marianna Lowlands.

William Gardner's excavations at the Waddells Mill Pond site showed the site was palisaded, perhaps as protection against other Fort Walton peoples to the north and east. Palisades have not been found in other Fort Walton regions. Cave occupation sites present in the Marianna Lowlands have not been found elsewhere in the Fort Walton region either.

The fourth Fort Walton variant is along the Gulf coast, west of the mouth of the Aucilla River. As yet, separate phases have not been defined for the coast; future research probably will divide this culture into several variants.

Within this region there are coastal shell middens, dirt middens back from the coast in the pine flatlands, and platform mounds and mounds containing burials. Mounds and middens are most frequent on or near estuaries and bays where inland rivers flow into the Gulf of Mexico. Evidence for coastal agriculture has been found (Mikell 1990), although it is likely that farming was not as important on the coast as it was in inland areas. As noted earlier, in the western portion of the coastal area there is some confusion over what is and what is not Fort Walton, as well as over the relationships between the Fort Walton and Pensacola cultures.

Village Life, Subsistence, and Material Culture

Fort Walton represents a new cultural system, a Mississippian way of life "far different" from those present elsewhere in Florida or even in the southeast United States in earlier times, a way of life with "new technology, subsistence, settlement patterns, sociopolitical integrations, and ideology" (Smith 1986:53). The hierarchial system of different site types, agricultural practices, and the presence of ceramic vessels and other artifacts with the same complex iconography found in other Mississippian cultures across the Southeast are some of the most obvious new developments manifested in the Fort Walton archaeological assemblage. To be a Fort Walton villager was to be a very different person than a Wakulla Weeden Island person.

The inland Fort Walton peoples, like other inland Mississippian peoples, were intensive maize agriculturists who supplemented their diet with other cultigens (beans and cucurbits) and with wild foods that were hunted, fished, and collected. The difference in farming techniques between the Fort Walton populations and the earlier Weeden Island peoples might have been one of cleared-field, row agriculture versus hillock and slash-and-burn cultivation.

Evidence for agriculture comes from a number of Fort Walton sites, nearly all in noncoastal locales. Charred maize kernels or cobs have been found at sites in the Apalachicola and Chattahoochee river drainages, in Leon County, and in the Marianna Lowlands (Bullen 1958; Neuman 1961; Gardner 1966; Jones and Penman 1973:72, 88; Tesar 1980; Dunn 1981; Jones 1982:9; White 1982; Alexander 1984). Relative to earlier Wakulla Weeden Island sites in those same areas, the number of Fort Walton sites from which maize has been recovered is extremely large, reflecting the increased importance of the plant to the diet.

Beans (*Phaseolus vulgaris*) are another cultigen identified from several sites in Leon County, as is sunflower (*Helianthus annuus*) (Alexander 1984). Corn, beans, and squashes, the last not yet found at Fort Walton sites, were major crops grown by Mississippian peoples throughout the Southeast.

Michelle Alexander's (1984) analysis of botanical remains from Fort Walton sites provides some idea of the range of wild plants eaten by these Mississippian peoples. They include hickory nut, acorn, persimmon, maypop, and wild cherry. Saw palmetto and cabbage palm seeds and chinquapin, identified from Fort Walton sites, might also have been eaten.

Limited excavations in Fort Walton middens indicate that villagers drew upon the same animals as their northwest Florida predecessors. The bones of deer, turkey, squirrel, various birds, and a variety of fish and turtles have been identified, with shellfish common at coastal sites (Percy 1974:83; White 1982; Mikell 1990, 1993). These animals and the wild plants that were collected supplemented the crops obtained from agriculture, providing the nutritional base for the large Fort Walton populations.

Exactly what the farmstead and hamlet settlements of the Fort Walton villagers looked like is uncertain. There is evidence from one site in Leon County for a circular structure forty-five feet in diameter (Tesar 1976), perhaps a communal building. A similar large circular building was excavated at the Borrow Pit site. Ordinary people probably lived in smaller circular dwellings. Examples have been found at the Bear Grass, Borrow Pit, and Velda sites. Excavations by Frank Fryman (1971b) at the Lake Jackson site uncovered a portion of a wall trench believed associated with a house structure. Wall trenches are a common building technique of Mississippian peoples.

Possibly several structures, both summer and winter houses and storage structures, constituted a single household. Some of the village house structures, perhaps the winter houses, may have been made of wood and thatch. Whether wattle and daub were used in the construction of ordinary Fort Walton dwellings of the precolumbian period is uncertain. Daub has been found associated with colonial-period Apalachee Indian houses, and Payne has found daub with wattle impressions at the Lake Jackson site. The latter, however, was associated with a special structure, one probably occupied by elites, not ordinary villagers. Evidence for fire pits and cooking or smoking racks within living areas is provided by the Winewood site, but more evidence on specific household activities is lacking.

Information available from village middens suggests that the Fort Walton shell, bone, and stone artifact assemblages are not significantly different from those found during the earlier Weeden Island times. One new item is a small triangular flint or chert arrow point like those found at other Mississippian period sites throughout the Southeast.

Evidence for village ceramic and tool industries is provided by the excavations at sites 8Ja5 (Bullen 1958), Winewood (Jones and Penman 1973), Lake Jackson (Griffin 1950), and Curlee (White 1982). Like the earlier Weeden Island ceramic inventory, Fort Walton utilitarian pottery is largely plain, undecorated ware (for descriptions of Fort Walton ceramics, see Willey 1949a:458–463; Lazarus and

Fort Walton pottery: *a–b, e*, Lake Jackson Plain (*a* is 1¾ inches high; *b* has a handle); *c–d, f–h*, Fort Walton Incised.

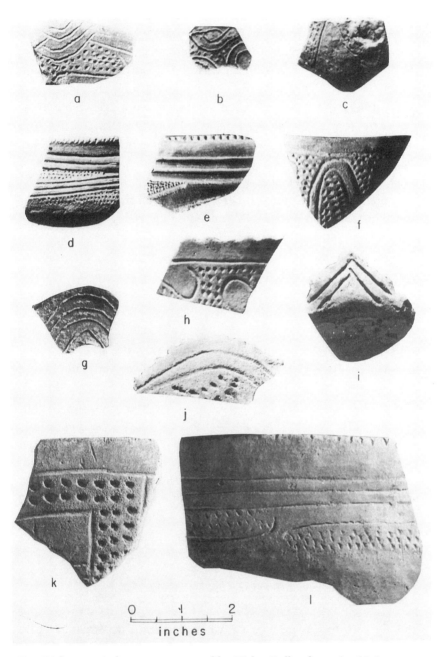

Fort Walton–period pottery excavated by Ripley Bullen from site 8Ja5: *a–c*,
Safety Harbor Incised; *d–l*, Fort Walton Incised. This illustration was
published in his report (Bullen 1958: plate 72; courtesy Florida Museum of
Natural History).

Hawkins 1976; Brose 1984:176–194; Scarry 1984:417–469; 1985). Generally 85–90 percent of the total sherds recovered from sites are plain, while only 6–10 percent are incised (e.g., the types Fort Walton Incised, Marsh Island Incised, and Point Washington Incised; see Willey 1949a:460–466). Often the incisions are not executed with as great care as the same designs made on vessels for special use. The most popular utilitarian vessel shapes, unlike those of the earlier Weeden Island period, are open bowls and collared, globular bowls. A small percentage of the plain pottery (2–6 percent of the total sherds) has notched lips, and some other vessels have small lugs or loop or strap handles (placed vertically) added as appendages. Quartz sand and crushed potsherds are the most common tempering materials; crushed shell is found in pottery of the western panhandle, some of which may be Fort Walton.

Other than the typical small, triangular arrow points, the stone tool assemblage of the Fort Walton culture seems to resemble that of the earlier Weeden Island peoples. Spokeshaves, side scrapers, polishing stones, and grinding stones have all been found, as have large, stemmed points, which probably are hafted knives. Limestone hones were used to sharpen bone and wooden tools. Shell pins and beads were found at the Curlee site. Other village artifacts include pottery and limestone discs, perhaps gaming stones; drilled discs; greenstone celts, probably used to cut wood; and equal-arm clay pipes. Charred pieces of basketry or matting have been identified from Lake Jackson.

Trade between inland and coastal Fort Walton villagers must have occurred, because marine object—shell tools and ornaments, and shark teeth—are found inland. And, as we shall see in the next section, even more exotic items were obtained by the Fort Walton elites from other Mississippian societies outside of Florida.

Site Hierarchies, Mound Complexes, and Political Structure

The hierarchy of site types recognized for the Tallahassee Hills and hinted at for the Apalachicola River valley and the Marianna Lowlands reflects the social and political reality of Fort Walton life, that is, a sociopolitical system of elites and commoners. This same hierarchial site pattern was present among other Mississippian cultures as well.

At the top of the site hierarchy in the Lake Jackson phase was the Lake Jackson site, a large multiple-mound and village complex. That

Leon County site features seven mounds (which served as the bases for structures), a plaza, and an extensive village midden (Payne 1993). It functioned for a period of time as the major Lake Jackson Fort Walton center, a true capital city, the locus of governmental and religious activities for the people it served. It also was the residence of the elite individuals—the chief and his family and associates—who ruled the capital and the surrounding villages, hamlets, and farmsteads.

By precolumbian Florida standards the Lake Jackson site was an imposing capital. Six of the seven mounds are arranged in pairs in two east-to-west rows separated by a small stream; the seventh mound is farther north. A plaza was present between two of the mounds (Mounds 2 and 4). The largest mound, Mound 2, measures nearly 90 by 100 yards along its rectangular base and is 36 feet high. It is built in typical truncated pyramid shape and had a ramp constructed up the east side, providing access to the temple or building that must have been erected on the top. Members of the ruling family or kin group lived at this capital, including the major chief.

As noted earlier Fort Walton society was stratified with some individuals and probably lineages ranking above or below others. As was true among other Mississippian peoples, the chief, who had both civil and religious duties, commanded absolute obedience from his subjects, who included residents of the capital city, residents and village chiefs of the outlying local capitals (characterized archaeologically by village sites with single mounds), and the families of common people who lived in the outlying hamlets and farmsteads. The occupants of these outlying hamlets and farmsteads made up the bulk of the population and were at the bottom of the political hierarchy.

We know from analysis of Mississippian chiefdoms like that of the Lake Jackson phase that control and redistribution of goods and resources was an important function of the chief. Tribute—probably cultigens, rabbits and other foods, feather cloaks, and other items—was paid to the chief of the capital by the chiefs of outlying villages, who collected goods from villagers. In return for this tribute and show of respect these vassal chiefs were accorded high status by the head chief. Local village chiefs and their people also received protection and other benefits from the head chief. The support and allegiance of the Fort Walton people to their leaders—maintained and reflected in ideology and practices—provided the basis for the complex political and social hierarchy that existed, a system economically sustained by farming, which allowed populations denser than any existing elsewhere in precolumbian Florida.

Villagers and the people from the farmsteads probably served as agricultural labor for fields controlled by the chiefs as well as labor to erect and maintain the mounds and associated buildings at the capital towns. Chiefs also controlled warfare. Warfare may have provided a means by which people who served as warriors could achieve higher status within the Lake Jackson chiefdom.

The status of elite individuals in life was reflected in the treatment afforded them after death. Highly ranked people were afforded special burial in the floors of the buildings erected on the pyramidal mounds. The remains of other high-ranking individuals may have been stored in temples maintained for that purpose and built atop mounds. Such practices continually validated the high status of the elites to the villagers, as did the extraordinary objects found by archaeologists with elite burials. Special paraphernalia, such as the Southeastern Ceremonial Complex objects described in the next section, were worn by the elites both in life and in death as symbols of their power.

Ordinary Fort Walton people were interred in cemeteries (Willey 1949a:456). Two such cemeteries have been excavated, and both contained about 100 persons buried either individually in flexed or extended position or buried in mass graves. Secondary burials, perhaps skeletons that had first been cleaned and retained in a charnel house, also were interred. In late precolumbian Florida such cemeteries are unique to the Mississippian Fort Walton and Pensacola cultures (earlier cemeteries are present in the Glades regions, see Carr 1990).

At the Winewood site in Tallahassee (Jones and Penman 1973), burials also were found in abandoned trash or fire pits. These were placed next to a possible cemetery area containing extended burials in separate graves. There is also evidence from site 8Ja5 (Bullen 1958) that some Fort Walton people were interred in village areas, perhaps within their houses.

Burial mounds (as opposed to platform mounds containing elite burials) are known for the Fort Walton culture but are not common. Interments in such mounds are both flexed and secondary. It is not certain if such burial practices occur early in the Fort Walton period, before social and political stratification began to develop to their fullest.

Evidence gathered thus far from analyses of the Lake Jackson phase and other Fort Walton phase settlement systems and burial patterns supports the contention that these societies were Mississippian cultures. Another line of evidence corroborates the presence of the Mississippian system of social stratification among Fort Walton peoples. Spectacular discoveries—artifacts from one of the mounds of the Lake Jackson site—provide an extraordinary glimpse into the realm of Fort Walton chiefs and other societal elites. These finds, made by B. Calvin Jones of the Florida Bureau of Archaeological Research in 1975, tie the Lake Jackson phase culture to other Mississippian societies.

Ideology, Status, and the Southeastern Ceremonial Complex

In 1975 a friend called B. Calvin Jones to ask his advice about "an odd piece of green metal" found in the yard of his new home (Jones 1982:6). Could it be an aboriginal artifact? Jones identified the object as a Mississippian-style copper celt, an object very rare in Florida. His subsequent detective work revealed the celt had been in fill dirt deposited in the friend's yard, and the fill had come from Mound 3 at the Lake Jackson site. Examination of the mound showed that, indeed, the owner of that mound was leveling it for a planned construction project and that truckloads of dirt—mound fill—were being removed. Jones immediately began a salvage excavation on the portion of the mound that remained, a project that yielded an assortment of Mississippian artifacts not duplicated elsewhere in Florida and similar to collections made only at a few large Mississippian mound complex sites—each a precolumbian capital—elsewhere in the Southeast.

Such artifacts described below reflect the importance and power of Mississippian chiefs, their ties to the supernatural, and their abilities to provide a link between villagers and their gods and the powers that controlled nature. A chief's power was displayed and symbolized in various behavioral patterns and in dress and costume and other paraphernalia. Elite individuals could immediately be recognized by their dress and ceremonial accoutrements. Chiefs, members of their families, and perhaps other individuals responsible for conducting specific rituals or ceremonies or who had other important duties dressed in "costumes" and displayed objects symbolic of their office. Those same costumes and objects accompanied elite individuals into the grave. Just as they were honored and singled out in life, so were they in death.

Some items of chiefly paraphernalia interred with the individuals have survived the ravages of time—ceramic vessels, copper and shell artifacts, rare minerals, unique lithic objects, and other similar non-perishable or less-perishable artifacts. These artifacts and the various distinctive motifs decorating some of them have been grouped by archaeologists into what is called the Southeastern Ceremonial Complex.

James Brown (1985) and other archaeologists have shown that the Southeastern Ceremonial Complex varies through time and space among Mississippian societies. There, are however, many similarities among the symbols and items. It has also been shown that the symbols and the items themselves reflect the complex beliefs that surrounded Mississippian chiefs, their military and religious power, and their relationships to nature and to supernatural powers and beings. Some symbols appear to be related to agricultural fertility, while others are associated with validating the right of elites to rule, emphasizing their hereditary ties to past elites, and providing them with arcane knowledge deemed necessary for the well-being and perpetuation of society and the Mississippian way of life. Just as the organization of Fort Walton society was manifest in the hierarchial settlement patterns and burial practices, so was it reflected in symbols and objects.

Jones's excavations at Lake Jackson revealed that Mound 3, which was fifteen feet high, had been enlarged twelve different times (Jones 1982). Each construction phase was built atop the last, and each mound had a building—a temple or similar special structure—erected on its summit. Each of the structures was represented by a floor and by rectangular arrangements of postholes.

The initial building or temple was built on the surface of the ground. It was covered with fill during the first construction phase, resulting in a low pyramidal mound on which a new building was erected. Each building was burned before the next platform mound was built over it. Over time, as each new mound was constructed over the last, Mound 3 grew in height and extent. Radiocarbon dates suggest construction and use of Mound 3 was between A.D. 1240 and 1476 (Jones 1982:

B. Calvin Jones (in striped hat) excavating Mound 3 at the Lake Jackson site. Note the complex mound strata representing multiple layers of mound fill and structure floors (courtesy Florida Division of Historical Resources).

20–21). Other of the Lake Jackson mounds might have been built in earlier times.

Some of the Southeastern Ceremonial Complex and other artifacts recovered by Jones came from the building floors themselves, but most were associated with human burials. The interments—elite individuals—were made in tombs dug through the floors of the buildings. Some floors had more than one individual associated with them. Twenty-four individuals were found, each buried separately. That children were buried as well as adults reflects the hereditary status of Mississippian elites: children not yet old enough to achieve status as chiefly officials already had such status ascribed to them by virtue of their family ties. A dog also had been buried in one floor, perhaps a beloved pet.

Bodies were placed in oval to rectangular pits three to six feet deep. Split logs were used to cover the tops of graves, forming tombs that later collapsed under the weight of other mound strata. Within these tombs Jones found fragments of woven cane mats, cloth woven from plant fibers, and leather clothing and wrappings. These normally perishable fragments were preserved by metallic salts from nearby copper artifacts. Small wooden poles with one individual suggest that the body had been laid out on a litter. The elaborate coverings encasing each entombed individual provide some measure of the high status of these elite Fort Walton leaders: "The outermost layer was usually the wooden tomb covering. The next layer included leather wrappings or coverings over cane matting (covering?), followed by woven cloth coverings, wrappings, or clothing over the body. The body usually lay on leather. When copper plates were present over the body, cloth—usually several layers in thickness—was found between the plates and the body, probably indicating that the plates were wrapped" (Jones 1982:11–12).

The number and opulence of the artifacts that accompanied the elite burials are staggering, and many of the materials from which the items were manufactured—copper, lead, mica, anthracite, graphite, steatite, greenstone—are not native to Florida. These objects and others—shark teeth, pearls, objects of marine shell and bone, pottery—reflect the power and wealth of the Lake Jackson elites. They must have benefited from complex trade networks that spread across the entire Southeast United States and perhaps beyond.

The most common artifacts were shell and pearl beads. Often these were found in positions that indicated they were worn by individuals as necklaces or were decorations on cloaks. Some of the shell beads were large columella beads like those worn by the costumed figures portrayed on two repoussé copper plates. Individuals also wore shell gorgets, shell pendants, and bone hairpins inlaid with copper. Shark teeth spangles decorated clothing, and one individual had what appeared to be a belt fastener made of galena. Copper plates were worn on breasts, and copper celts were either found lying crossed on a person's breast or by the hands, one on each side. Stone celts also accompanied individuals. Engraved shell gorgets were found under heads; perhaps they were hair decorations or parts of headdresses. Additionally, Jones reports finding copper headdress spangles, hair ornaments, copper pendants, and fragments of copper plates wrapped together in cloth or in cloth sacks next to individuals.

All of this suggests that individuals were placed in the tombs wearing full regalia and accompanied by other objects and symbols reflecting their elite positions in society. Differences in paraphernalia indicate that among the elites there were differences in status (Jones 1982:14–15), perhaps reflective of specific titles held by the leaders, for example, a paramount chief versus a member of his family (see Scarry 1990b).

The array of items placed in individual tombs is as extraordinary as the objects worn by the individuals: T-shaped steatite pipes, fired clay elbow pipes, a clay lizard-effigy pipe, *Busycon* cups, a limestone bowl, a paint palette with red ochre on it, a shark jaw knife, stone discoidals, pottery vessels, stone axes, a galena-backed mica mirror, lumps of graphite, anthracite hones, mica, small stone cups, yellow ochre pigment, and chert tools, the last including small, triangular arrow points. Deer, bird, and fish bones were found on lower building floors in the mound.

Three engraved shell gorgets and the copper artifacts, especially the repoussé plates, deserve special mention because they are Southeastern Ceremonial Complex paraphernalia that tie the Lake Jackson elites to other Mississippian chiefdoms in the Southeast. Their presence indicates that aspects of ideology associated with those chiefdoms spanned the precolumbian Southeast.

Two of the gorgets depict birdlike figures, perhaps individuals dressed as eagles. Both have birdlike faces, and one has a human body. The third gorget is engraved with two birdlike figures facing opposite directions.

Four copper plates were recovered by Jones, two associated with a single person, while two other people wore one each. The four plates were placed on their chests. Each was made from copper nuggets that had been cold-hammered into thin sheets, riveted together, and then embossed. Repairs were evident, and the thin plates were reinforced with split-cane and thin wooden laths that formed supporting frameworks. One plate measuring ten by twenty inches depicts a raptoral bird-human figure—usually described as a hawkman or a person costumed as a peregrine falcon—holding a mace or baton in one hand and a human head or mask in the other. The figure wears a necklace of shell columella beads from which a *Busycon* columella pendant is suspended. A variety of Southeastern Ceremonial Complex symbols are present on the figure, including a forked mouth, beaded forelock, and bilobed arrow headdress. The figure also is wearing an earspool, and on his head is a circular sun shield decorated with an ogee symbol. Other details include a long-nosed god mask (?), a feather cloak including a tail-like train, a waist pouch suspended from a beaded sash or belt, bracelets, anklets, and shoulder tattoos or decorations. The figure on this and the other plates may represent a deity symbolized by the chiefs themselves.

The figure on the second plate, eleven by seventeen inches, differs slightly from the first. Differences include a different headdress, painted or tattooed legs, and diamond-shaped eyes. The same columella bead necklace with shell pendant and pointed patch are present, as are an earspool, beaded wrist and upper arm bands, and a feather cloak.

Plates three and four were found with a single individual, one plate lying atop the other. The top, larger plate, six by twenty-one inches, shows a bird-person figure from the front, in contrast to the first two plates, which depicted the figure in profile. Jones (1982:17) suggests that the figure depicted on Plate 3 is dead, possibly in a state of decomposition. The individual is wearing a feathered headdress, but part of the face appears to be a skull without flesh. The cloak seems to be closed or wrapped around the figure, who also is wearing a pouch. Under that plate was a smaller one, five by twelve inches, depicting a falcon figure.

Near the head of another elite individual entombed in Mound 3 was a stack of five cut-out copper plates also depicting falcon figures. Charles Hudson (1976:129–130) suggests that these are peregrine falcons. Each of the six has a forked eye, which is derived from the natural eye markings of falcons. The array of feathers resembles the cloaks on the other plates.

Scraps and pieces of several other copper plates were found, along with pendants, arrow-shaped headdress spangles or badges, hair ornaments or plumes, and small oval plates. It seems likely that copper was

Drawing of a copper plate 20 inches high excavated from Mound 3 at Lake Jackson. The drawing
is of the back side of the plate; note the riveted
sheet-copper repairs (from Jones 1982:31; courtesy
Florida Division of Historical Resources).

a rare and highly valued metal used to depict of symbols important to the Fort Walton elites. Use of the falcon and other symbols were restricted to only a few upper-echelon individuals within this tightly stratified social system.

Ceramics and Ideology

Other symbols were used by ordinary people as well as by the elites. These appear both on pottery vessels found in special contexts, such as in mounds or cemeteries, and with interments in houses of ordinary villagers. In some instances, a single bowl might be inverted over the skull of an individual. Urn interments also are known. The implication is that the use of such vessels and the decorative symbols on them were not restricted to elites or to mortuary-related ceremonies. About 10 percent of the pottery from Mound 3 at Lake Jackson also was decorated in this fashion (Jones 1982:19–20).

Frequently the decorated vessels are in the shape of cazuela bowls or bottles. Most often they are incised with curvilinear motifs, although some rectilinear motifs are found. Curvilinear designs include volutes, scrolls, loops, and circles (many multiple lined), and they generally are interlocking and repeated around the entire vessel. Designs on cazuela bowls often are restricted to a band around the upper portions of the bowls. Punctations may occur in zones defined by the incised designs.

Other vessel shapes include shallow bowls with lateral extensions (generally forming four or six extensions), gourd effigies (dipper-shaped), collared globular bowls, and flattened globular bowls (Willey 1949a:460–462). Incised specimens may have red or white pigment rubbed into the incisions, and red-slipped vessels occasionally have been found.

Some vessels, especially bowls, have animal head adornos. Animals portrayed include eagle, woodpecker, duck, goose, quail, heron, owl, turkey, buzzard, snake, lizard, alligator, frog, fox, otter, opossum, squirrel or dog, bear, and cat (Lazarus 1971:46; Jones and Penman 1973; McCane-O'Conner 1979). This is a greater variety than the animals shown on earlier Weeden Island effigy vessels, though many of the same animals are portrayed. In addition, Southeastern Ceremonial Complex symbols or motifs are occasionally incised on special vessels, especially on the bottle forms.

Fort Walton Incised casuela bowl 6 inches high excavated in 1888 from a mound near Apalachicola (photograph by John Griffin; courtesy Florida Museum of Natural History).

Fort Walton Incised bowl 3¾ inches high excavated about 1888 from the same mound near Apalachicola as the bowl in the preceding illustration (courtesy Florida Museum of Natural History).

Fort Walton Incised bird effigy bowl 4 inches high from the Point Washington cemetery site (Moore 1901: fig. 97; courtesy Smithsonian Institution).

The bottle-shaped vessels found at Fort Walton sites are ubiquitous among Mississippian cultures. Many of the Fort Walton design motifs are similar, if not identical, to those of other Mississippian cultures. Vessel shapes and design elements, like the objects associated with the Southeastern Ceremonial Complex itself, cut across Mississippian cultures.

These objects and motifs are symbols closely associated with the social, political, economic, and settlement patterns integral to the Fort Walton culture as well as to other Mississippian chiefdoms. Beliefs concerning themselves, their origins, their leaders, and the world around them rationalized this system for Fort Walton people. A symbol as simple as a scroll incised on a pottery vessel is a reflection of the profound importance of those beliefs in helping to maintain the Fort Walton people's Mississippian way of life.

Pensacola Culture

The Pensacola culture, characterized by shell-tempered pottery but with some sand-tempered pottery also, is found in the western panhandle, from Choctawhatchee Bay west to Mobile Bay in Alabama and beyond into Louisiana (Knight 1984:199–201; Payne 1991b). Our best available evidence suggests that in Florida the culture dates from

A.D. 1200 into the colonial period. In the western panhandle the Pensacola culture follows the early Fort Walton–period culture and is contemporary with the later Fort Walton phases of the eastern panhandle. The Florida manifestation of the Pensacola culture represents only a small portion of the culture's overall distribution.

Pensacola, at least in Florida, is poorly known archaeologically. To date most of the work on Pensacola has been in the Mobile Bay area of coastal Alabama. In that locality Richard Fuller (1985) and Noel Stowe (1985) have defined two Pensacola phases: Bottle Creek (A.D. 1200–1450) and Bear Point (A.D. 1450–1700). It is not known if these same phases apply to Florida.

Vernon Knight (1984:200–202) has suggested that Pensacola contains a number of regional variants. In the Choctawhatchee Bay locale, at the easternmost edge of the overall Pensacola distribution, is the Hogtown Bayou–Point Washington variant; farther west in the Pensacola and Perdido Bay locale the variant is La Casa.

Surveys in the Florida panhandle seem to indicate that few large Pensacola sites exist in the uplands in the northern panhandle. Most of the sites noted to date have been on the coast or near it. That the Pensacola peoples continued to occupy the western panhandle in the middle and late sixteenth century is indicated by European artifacts found at sites around Choctawhatchee Bay (e.g., Point Washington, Bunker Cut-off, Hogtown Bayou, and Alaqua Bayou) (Scarry 1989).

As noted in the beginning of this chapter, confusion exists between the Pensacola and Fort Walton assemblages in the western panhandle region. Indeed, the name Fort Walton originally was derived from the Fort Walton site on Choctawhatchee Bay in Fort Walton Beach. That site, however, is associated mainly with the Pensacola culture, as it is defined today.

Increasingly, evidence suggests that aspects of the Fort Walton culture are not present in the Pensacola culture—multiple-mound village complexes with platform mounds, cleared-field agriculture, the presence of elites and social ranking, a well-developed hierarchical settlement pattern, and complex political organization. More recently, archaeologists (Sears 1977a; Scarry 1981a; Knight 1984; Fuller 1985; Stowe 1985) have tended to emphasize the differences between Fort Walton and Pensacola, noting that the latter were not the extensive agriculturists that the Fort Walton people were, nor did the Pensacola

Pensacola region in the western panhandle with site locales.

people primarily inhabit noncoastal, inland locales. The Pensacola economic pattern seems to have been centered on coastal resources rather
than inland agriculture, although the exact role of agriculture within
the economic pattern of the culture is still debated (Knight
1984:209–211). Because of this, the Pensacola culture was not a true
Mississippian culture, as was Fort Walton.

Archaeologists, including William Lazarus (1971:44) and John
Scarry (1989:7–8), have argued that the reason why cleared-field agriculture was not important to the subsistence of the Florida Pensacola
peoples is that the coastal soils, in marked contrast to those of the
inland, eastern panhandle (e.g., the Tallahassee Hills), are poorly
suited for extensive agriculture. This contention is supported by bioanthropological data from the Fort Walton Mound and other sites in the

1 Alaqua Bayou
2 Bunker Cut-off
3 Chambliss
4 Fort Walton
5 Hickory Ridge
6 Hogtown Bayou
7 McBee Mound
8 Point Washington

Pensacola archaeological sites.

Choctawhatchee Bay area (e.g., Chambliss). Human interments from those sites exhibit few of the dental caries associated with maize-consuming populations. The individuals' teeth instead show the considerable wear more commonly associated with fishing-hunting-gathering populations (Adams and Lazarus 1960). The question of Pensacola agriculture remains open, however, and it is possible that gardening of corn and beans did occur on the coast. Cultigens are reported from a coastal Fort Walton site east of the Pensacola region on St. Andrews Bay (Mikell 1990).

Material Culture

The shell-tempered Pensacola pottery series, originally defined by Gordon Willey (1949a:464–466), provides our best evidence for the geographical extent of the Pensacola culture. Sand-tempered pottery may also have been made by Pensacola people. As noted, the situation is muddied by the presence of Fort Walton ceramics (which precede Pensacola) at coastal panhandle sites west of St. Andrews Bay. A geographical ceramic transition also appears to be occurring in the Pensacola culture. William Lazarus (1971:42) has charted the relative percentages of shell-tempered and sand-tempered pottery in sites from Apalachicola Bay to Perdido Bay, finding that the percentage of shell-tempered pottery increased east to west. Sites near the Apalachicola River and on St. Andrews Bay contained 10 to 20 percent shell-tempered pottery. This number increased to 50 percent in the Choctawhatchee Bay locale and to 80 percent in locales around the city of Pensacola and Perdido Bay.

Generally at Pensacola village sites, undecorated pottery constitutes 70–80 percent of the total, while decorated pottery is 15–20 percent. At later sites, some Pensacola pottery has a brushed surface. At one site reported by Lazarus (1961:58), more than half the nonincised pottery had been brushed.

Little is known about the Pensacola lithic assemblage or other tools. A stemmed Archaic point found with a burial in the Fort Walton Mound (Fairbanks 1965:248) may indicate that, as in the Fort Walton area, Archaic-type points or knives were picked up and reused. Clarence B. Moore (1918:538) notes twenty-four "lancepoints and arrowheads or knives" from the Hogtown Bayou Cemetery in Walton County but provides no additional information. Greenstone celts are reported from the Hickory Ridge Cemetery in Escambia County (Phillips 1989) and Hogtown Bayou (Moore 1918:538). Other artifacts from Pensacola sites include mica, yellow ochre, shell beads and pins, *Busycon* columellae, bone awls, and copper (Moore 1918:538–540; Fairbanks 1965:248; Phillips 1989).

Settlements, Subsistence, and Political Organization

Pensacola sites are found predominantly in coastal lowlands and along the coast proper. Few have been found in the uplands, especially north of Interstate 10, whose east-west path roughly separates the more southerly lowlands from the northerly uplands. In this regard, the Mississippian-period Pensacola culture is similar to the Circum–

Tampa Bay variant of the Safety Harbor culture. For both cultures the coast was a crucial economic zone, and extensive maize agriculture probably was not present, or at least it was not as intensive as the agricultural practices of the Fort Walton people.

For the Pensacola people perhaps the most important coastal feature was the shallow bay–estuary systems, as it was for the cultures who inhabited the western panhandle from the late Archaic period on. The largest numbers of Pensacola sites are clustered around these bays, including Choctawhatchee, Pensacola, and Perdido bays. The first two are quite large systems. For instance, Choctawhatchee Bay is thirty-five miles long and six miles north-south. The Choctawhatchee River empties into the bay, as do Black, Alaqua, and Rocky creeks, which drain lands to the north, bringing nutrients and enriching the estuaries.

Pensacola Bay, roughly the same size as Choctawhatchee Bay, contains two separate parts, Escambia and East bays. The former is fed by the Escambia River, while the Yellow and Blackwater rivers flow into the latter. Perdido Bay, smaller than the other two, lies at the mouth of the Perdido River, which marks the geographical boundary between Florida and Alabama. These bays were rich in coastal resources, fish and shellfish, and drew Pensacola villagers just as they had earlier pre-columbian Floridians.

The economic dependence of the Pensacola culture on coastal resources is illustrated by a comprehensive survey of sites on Eglin Air Force Base on the north side of Choctawhatchee Bay, which showed that 87 percent of the late precolumbian sites lay along the coast (Thomas and Campbell 1985:36). The marine economic orientation of Pensacola is also evident at sites such as Gilligan's Island and Moccasin Mound in Santa Rosa County and Thompson's Landing in the Escambia River estuary (Claassen 1985:124–127).

Four types of Pensacola sites have been recognized in Florida (Payne 1991b): truncated pyramidal platform mounds, burial mounds, cemeteries, and coastal shell middens. Some inland sites do exist, but little is known about their distribution or nature. The only pyramidal platform mound studied to date is the Fort Walton Mound in the Choctawhatchee Bay locale (Willey 1949a:213–214; Fairbanks 1965; Lazarus and Fornaro 1975). The Jolly Bay Mound, located on the

opposite end of the bay from the Fort Walton Mound, may be a platform mound (Willey 1949a:224). A third mound, the McBee Mound
near Alaqua Bayou, also may be a platform (Scarry 1989:7).

The Fort Walton Mound, located in downtown Fort Walton Beach,
is associated with an adjacent village midden. This mound-village
complex may have been the center of a single political unit located
around the western end of the bay. A number of nearby shell midden sites may represent outlying homesteads and small villages. The
mound probably had a temple or residence for a high-ranking leader
on its summit, possibly a series of such structures as the mound was
enlarged. Human interments in the eastern side of the mound may be
elite individuals associated with the leader. Thus, although Pensacola
political and settlement systems were not as complex as those of the
Fort Walton chiefdoms, the two probably shared some similarities.
Contact with the Fort Walton chiefdoms and with Mississippian societies to the north in Alabama certainly would have influenced the
structure of Pensacola society, even if their economic orientation was
toward coastal resources and not farming.

Burial mounds seem to have been present in the Pensacola culture,
although the only certain example is the Bunker Cut-off Mound
(Moore 1918:519–520; Willey 1949a:227). More research will likely
locate additional mounds. Cemeteries are found in the western panhandle, especially around Choctawhatchee Bay, where the most survey work has been carried out (e.g., the cemeteries at Chambliss, Hogtown Bayou, Point Washington, and Alaqua Bayou). Several other
cemeteries have been recorded elsewhere in the Pensacola region
(Lazarus, Lazarus, and Sharon 1967; Phillips 1989).

The most numerous sites are coastal shell middens, but few have
been excavated. Most are located directly on the bay-estuary shores
and are characterized by oysters and clams (Willey 1949a; Lazarus
1961, 1971; Claassen 1985).

As we shall see in the next chapter, the Pensacola culture—with its
regional variants, mound-village complexes and shell middens distributed around the shores of bay-estuary systems, elites associated with
mounds, and Mississippian-related ceramic inventory—is very much
like the Safety Harbor culture, especially the variant of that culture
centered on Tampa Bay, itself a large bay-estuary system. As Claudine
Payne (1991b) has noted, the evidence gathered thus far from the

Pensacola culture in the western panhandle is more evocative of a bigman society than of a true Mississippian chiefdom (and see Scarry 1989:7). The same is true for the Safety Harbor culture, which, like Pensacola, apparently was influenced by Fort Walton developments in the eastern panhandle but was not a true Mississippian culture. What is and what is not a Mississippian chiefdom is a taxonomic problem that archaeologists continue to wrestle with. The late precolumbian cultures of northern Florida, including the Safety Harbor culture described in chapter 11, provide an excellent arena in which to examine these concepts as they are reflected in the archaeological record.

Safety Harbor Culture

11

The Safety Harbor culture, named for a site on Tampa Bay, developed out of late Weeden Island–period cultures in the central Gulf coast region after A.D. 900. Safety Harbor sites extend from the mouth of the Withlacoochee River in the north southward to Charlotte Harbor. Most of the sites—shell middens and shell and/or earth mounds—are found along the coast, especially around Tampa Bay. Other, inland Safety Harbor villages, camps, and mounds are present in the region as well.

Sixteenth- and seventeenth-century Spanish artifacts have been found at a number of Safety Harbor sites, providing ample evidence that the culture continued to occupy its traditional region into the colonial period (see Milanich and Hudson 1993:61–70, 98–110, for a summary of this evidence; also see Mitchem 1989). The presence of datable European artifacts (largely Spanish) in sites, along with radiocarbon dates from early Safety Harbor contexts associated with Englewood ceramics (e.g., Englewood Incised, Sarasota Incised, and Lemon Bay Incised), provides the basis for dividing the Safety Harbor period into two precolumbian phases: Englewood, A.D. 900–1100, and Pinellas, A.D. 1100–1500; and two colonial-period phases: Tatham, A.D. 1500–1567, and Bayview, A.D. 1567–1725 (Mitchem 1989:557–567). Additional research will no doubt provide more data for refining these phases, especially the precolumbian Englewood and Pinellas phases.

At least 95 percent of Safety Harbor utilitarian ceramics found at village sites are undecorated, making it difficult to distinguish many

Safety Harbor region on the Gulf coast of Florida.

of these wares from pottery of earlier cultures in the same region. Ceramic vessels found in mounds are often incised and display decorative motifs and symbols that are easily recognizable (some of these are similar to motifs found on Fort Walton ceramics). As a result it is the presence of mounds with Safety Harbor pottery in them that allows archaeologists to define the geographical extent of the Safety Harbor region.

Occasionally, Safety Harbor decorated vessels or sherds are found in sites well beyond the central Gulf coast, such as in the Caloosahatchee region in southwest Florida (Widmer 1988:86). But these most likely are items of trade that appear as nonlocal artifacts in other cultural contexts. The presence of Safety Harbor pottery in Caloosahatchee mortuary contexts does present a taxonomic dilemma: If the presence

of Safety Harbor pottery in mounds is the basis for defining that culture in the central peninsular Gulf coast region, why is this also not
true on the southwest Florida coast? For now, it is most convenient
simply to ignore this anomaly, as was done in chapter 8, and to keep
Caloosahatchee and Safety Harbor separate, leaving future archaeologists with more data on hand to sort out the situation.

The Safety Harbor archaeological complex was originally defined by
Gordon Willey (1949a:475–488), in part using information gathered
by C. B. Moore from various excavations on the Gulf coast (Moore
1900, 1905), as well as data from Federal Emergency Relief Agency
excavations carried out in the 1930s. Following Willey's synthesis,
John Griffin and Ripley Bullen (1950) excavated at the Safety Harbor
site itself, and Bullen reported excavations at other Safety Harbor sites
and examined the distribution of the Safety Harbor archaeological
assemblage (Bullen 1951b, 1952, 1955a).

Since the pioneering work of Willey, Griffin, and Bullen, other
archaeologists have written about coastal and inland Safety Harbor
sites (e.g., Sears 1958, 1967b; Wharton and Williams 1980; Luer and
Almy 1981, 1987; see Mitchem 1989:8–305, for a complete summary
of previous work). Jeffrey Mitchem (1988, 1989) has synthesized
Safety Harbor data, reinterpretated previous theories regarding mound
use over time, and provided a taxonomic system for ordering the culture in time and space. Most recently George Luer (1992a, b) has
investigated aspects of Safety Harbor culture.

Mitchem's information, especially his 1989 dissertation, *Redefining
Safety Harbor: Late Prehistoric/Protohistoric Archaeology in West Peninsular
Florida,* and a summary of the same (Mitchem 1991) provide much of
the background for this chapter.

Regional Variations

Although centered on Tampa Bay and adjoining river drainages, the
Safety Harbor culture defined by mound distribution extends well to
the north into Pasco, Hernando, and Citrus counties and to the south
and west into Sarasota, Polk, Hardee, and DeSoto counties. As noted,
Safety Harbor pottery also is found in mounds south of Charlotte
Harbor in the Caloosahatchee region.

Prior to the Safety Harbor period (in late Weeden Island times), the large central peninsular Gulf coast region, some 150 miles north to south, was characterized by differences in utilitarian ceramic assemblages. As we saw in chapter 6, a limestone-tempered ware was most common in the northern portion, while pottery with quartz sand was more common around Tampa Bay and south. These ceramic traditions persisted into the Safety Harbor period. Coupled with differences in settlement patterns and subsistence strategies related to geographical particulars, these data have allowed Mitchem (1989:567–579) to define several subregions for Safety Harbor (Mitchem's South Florida variant—south of Charlotte Harbor—is not used here, and the relationship between Safety Harbor and Caloosahatchee is left unreconciled). Similar to the regional variants of the early Weeden Island period, the Safety Harbor people in the four subregions shared similar patterns of burial mound ceremonialism, including the special ceramic vessels found in these mounds, while differing in village lifeways. They shared aspects of ideology and, perhaps, social and political organization, but different natural environments allowed differences in economic patterns.

Northern Safety Harbor

The Northern Safety Harbor variant encompasses Pasco, Hernando, and Citrus counties. Pasco Plain limestone-tempered pottery is most common in nonmound village and camp sites, along with undecorated pottery containing quartz sand, St. Johns Plain, St. Johns Check Stamped, and cord-marked pottery. Most settlements—residential sites and isolated mounds—are dispersed. Within the Cove of the Withlacoochee, located inland at the northern end of this subregion, several shell middens have been identified (Mitchem and Weisman 1987). More extensive oyster middens are found on the coast, such as at the Crystal River site. Relationships between coastal and inland sites are unknown.

If the large shell mounds at the Crystal River site date from the Pinellas phase, as some archaeologists have suggested, then that nucleated mound-village complex is an exception to the dispersed pattern thought to be typical of this northern subregion. Nucleated mound-village complexes are much more common in the Circum-Tampa Bay area. One large shell platform mound similar to those at

Safety Harbor culture variants.

Crystal River has been recorded on the Withlacoochee River, but it is not at all certain that it dates from the Safety Harbor period. Nor is there sufficient archaeological evidence on hand to demonstrate a major Safety Harbor occupation at the Crystal River site (Mitchem 1989:15–16, 22–23).

Within this subregion the basic subsistence patterns during the Safety Harbor period in both coastal and inland locales probably continued to reflect the marine- and freshwater-based economic strategies of the Weeden Island period, although some agriculture was apparently present within the cove itself (Mitchem [1989:588] recovered one squash seed from a mound within the cove).

At Bayonet Field, a village site within the cove, Mitchem's excavations produced an array of terrestrial freshwater animals, including

mollusks. Cherry Fitzgerald's analysis of the faunal collections identified largemouth bass, gar, deer, and freshwater snails as the most
common meat sources. Other animals probably used for food were
rabbit, squirrel, river otter, American coot, six species of freshwater
turtle, thirteen species of freshwater fish, and three additional species
of freshwater snail and two of mussel (Fitzgerald 1987). The importance of the Withlacoochee River and the adjacent wetlands to the diet
of the Northern Safety Harbor people living in the cove is abundantly
clear.

One artifact found at Northern Safety Harbor sites as well as sites in
all other subregions is the Pinellas Point (Bullen 1975:8). These small
triangular points were used to tip arrows, and their presence within
the central Gulf coast provides strong evidence for use of bows and
arrows by the Safety Harbor people.

As we saw in chapter 6, the coastal zone northward from the mouth
of the Withlacoochee River to the Aucilla River—coastal Dixie, Levy
and Taylor counties, a distance of about 110 miles—is not well-known
archaeologically, especially during late precolumbian times. It seems
odd that the Fort Walton and Safety Harbor ceramic assemblages
should exhibit such similarity when no geographically connecting cultural assemblages have as yet been identified.

Circum–Tampa Bay

The best known of the Safety Harbor regional variants, and what
might be considered the heartland of that culture, Circum–Tampa Bay
includes southern Pasco, Pinellas, Hillsborough, and northern Manatee counties, the area encompassing Tampa Bay. Most of the research
in this region has focused on mound excavations and community settlement patterns. But even though detailed data on subsistence are
scarce, especially information regarding whether maize agriculture
was present, we can project that the basic economic pattern of the
Safety Harbor villagers emphasized hunting and fishing, with a focus
on bay-estuary resources.

There are ample shell midden sites to suggest that subsistence strategies resembled those of the precolumbian peoples who preceded the
Safety Harbor culture in the Circum–Tampa Bay area and that both
saltwater and freshwater habitats provided fish and other food. Laura
Kozuch's analysis of faunal samples from five previously excavated

Safety Harbor archaeological sites.

Safety Harbor sites in this subregion supports this contention. Even though the samples were not collected using the rigorous methods employed by modern zooarchaeologists (using fine screens to collect small fish remains), her conclusions emphasize the aquatic nature of the Safety Harbor economic pursuits (Kozuch 1986). A variety of marine mollusks, several species of terrestrial animals (e.g., deer), freshwater and marine turtles, crabs, sea birds, freshwater wading birds, turkeys, alligators, rays, sharks, and a wide variety of marine fish were all represented in the collections she identified.

Safety Harbor utilitarian pottery within the Circum–Tampa Bay subregion is predominantly Pinellas Plain. Most prevalent were wide-mouthed bowls, often decorated with serrated rims (Sears 1967b, Luer and Almy 1980). The predominance of Pinellas Plain around Tampa Bay is in marked contrast to the limestone-tempered Pasco ware of the Northern area. The pattern of settlements within this subregion also contrasts with the dispersed pattern found to the north.

In the Circum–Tampa Bay area archaeologists have recorded fifteen large sites, each characterized by a platform mound and shell midden deposits thought to reflect associated village areas (e.g., Bullen 1955a:51; Luer and Almy 1981). The sites occur on the Gulf shoreline and around Tampa Bay, especially at the mouths of rivers and streams that drain into the bay or along those rivers within a short distance of the coast.

The community plan of each is much the same: a platform mound, probably the base for a temple or other important building, is placed adjacent to a plaza with surrounding village middens. One or more burial mounds are also present at the sites. None of these platform mound-village complex sites has been found very far inland in the Circum–Tampa Bay area, although a number of burial mounds, some with associated villages, are recorded back from the coast and bay.

Villages with burial mounds may once have been present within the Alafia, Manatee, and Little Manatee river drainages in interior Manatee and Hillsborough counties, but they would never have been as numerous or densely distributed as the coastal and Tampa Bay settlements. Many of these inland mounds, as well as coastal ones, have been destroyed by development and by vandals digging in them. Fortunately, several have been excavated by archaeologists and the results reported (Willey 1949a; Bullen 1952; Sears 1960).

From the locations of the sites it is probable that any villagers living nearby would have relied on freshwater habitats for a large portion of their sustenance. Some of the burial mounds recorded for the inland portion of the Circum–Tampa Bay subregion also might have been isolated, although it is often uncertain if a village midden was present when a mound was recorded. Smaller sites, perhaps short-term hunting and foraging camps, also are located in inland locales in the river drainages (Hemmings 1975; Padgett 1976).

The Circum–Tampa Bay platform mounds typically are 20 feet or less in height with the base 130 feet or less on a side. Excavations have indicated that at least some mounds were periodically rebuilt, increasing in size as new strata were added. As with Fort Walton plat-

The Madira Bickel Mound at the Terra Ceia site was entirely covered with palm trees and other vegetation when this photograph was taken in 1949. The photograph was later used by John Griffin (1951) in a popular article on the site. The truncated pyramidal mound, outlined here, is 100 by 170 feet at the base and 20 feet high. It is constructed of shell midden and dirt; there is a ramp on the left side (courtesy Florida Museum of Natural History).

form mounds, this was probably done when the structure on a mound was rebuilt.

Each mound had a ramp extending down the side toward the plaza. The mound platform served as a base for a building, perhaps the dwelling of a chiefly resident. No such building yet has been excavated, nor have any extensive excavations been carried out in a Safety Harbor village. However, a member of the Hernando de Soto expedition in 1539 described one Safety Harbor town and platform mound, the town of Uzita believed located at the Thomas Mound site on the Little Manatee River not far from Tampa Bay (Milanich and Hudson 1993:61, 70). "The town was of seven or eight houses, built of timber, and covered with palm-leaves. The Chief's house stood near the beach, upon a very high mount made by hand for defence [sic]; at the other end of the town was a temple, on the top of which perched a wooden fowl with gilded eyes" (Bourne 1866:22-23).

At the Safety Harbor site located on an arm of northwestern Tampa Bay (Griffin and Bullen 1950), the platform mound was placed on a point of land extending out into the bay with the ramp pointing inland toward the plaza. Shell middens extended down both sides of the point, enclosing most of the plaza. A burial mound was located some distance away. The temple mentioned in the de Soto expedition member's description may well have been a charnel house. At other platform mound–village complex sites where burial mounds are known to be present, they likewise are well away from the platform mound.

Each platform mound-village complex probably functioned as the center of a separate political unit. Such centers may have moved over time, accounting for the fifteen or so that are recorded. But even if only three or four were contemporaneous with one another, the total area within each polity must have been quite small, each encompassing a section of Tampa Bay shoreline and the adjacent inland and riverine area or a small locale along the Gulf coast with the adjacent mainland. Within a single polity, outlying shell middens of various sizes may reflect clusters of houses occupied by people who did not reside at the main village. At one time such middens were almost ubiquitous around Tampa Bay and the adjacent Gulf shoreline, although which ones dated to the Safety Harbor period and what percentage of those were occupied at the same time is unknown.

Whether this settlement system—platform mound–village centers with outlying habitation areas—reflects a chiefdom or some other type of political system is uncertain. Certainly the overall settlement pattern—including density—is much more like the coastal Pensacola culture than like the Fort Walton culture in the Tallahassee Hills. We can guess that the number and the density of the Safety Harbor population around Tampa Bay, probably the greatest within the total Safety Harbor region, were much less than in the Fort Walton region. Similarly the level of political integration that was present was not as complex as that reflected in the Lake Jackson or other Fort Walton settlement hierarchies. The Safety Harbor culture appears not to have been organized into Mississippian chiefdoms. This reinforces the idea that extensive agriculture—for which no evidence exists within the Safety Harbor culture—was necessary for the development and maintenance of a Mississippian political system.

One piece of evidence that the Safety Harbor peoples—even those in the Northern subregion—were not extensive agriculturists comes from bioanthropological analysis of skeletal populations from several sites. These sites include the Tatham Mound in the Cove of the Withlacoochee and the Weeki Wachee site on the coast of Hernando County (both in the Northern subregion), the Safety Harbor and Tierra Verde sites in Pinellas County, and the Aqui Esta Mound on Charlotte Harbor. Studies by Dale Hutchinson demonstrated that the populations were more typical of hunter-gatherer-foragers than farmers (Hutchinson 1991:82–94, 124, 127, 136). Additional evidence that maize was not a major constituent of the Safety Harbor diet is suggested by stable nitrogen and carbon isotopic analysis of human bone from two individuals from the Tatham Mound (Hutchinson and Norr 1991). That analysis, which measures C_4 plant foods—maize—in the diet, indicated that the cove population placed little or no reliance on maize.

Detailed studies of a number of the tool assemblages from Safety Harbor sites around Tampa Bay are lacking, but available information confirms that Pinellas points were in use throughout the region. They and the less frequent, but similar, Ichetucknee and Tampa points (Bullen 1975:8–9) have been found both in middens and in mounds. Other tools are stemmed, chert projectile points or knives that appear to be reused Archaic-period specimens, chert scrapers and flakes that show use chipping (Willey 1949a:139–140), and sandstone grinding stones (Griffin and Bullen 1950:13). Outcroppings of agatized coral are found to the north of Tampa Bay, and Safety Harbor peoples made tools from the stone, which can be worked like chert (Estabrook and Williams 1992).

Shell tools are more common than lithic artifacts at Safety Harbor coastal sites, a trend we have seen in most if not all precolumbian coastal cultures in Florida. Shell tools identified from village settings include celts, picklike artifacts, and hafted whelk shells, often called hammers. We still have much to learn about the village life of Safety Harbor people around Tampa Bay and elsewhere in the central coastal region (Luer 1992b).

Except for the arrow points, the types of stone and shell artifacts recovered are much the same as those from the earlier Weeden Island period. Although changes in social and political organization may have occurred between the late Weeden Island period and the Safety Harbor period, most likely in response to larger populations, the basic pattern of subsistence and the associated technology seem to have remained much the same.

South-Central

South from Tampa Bay in southern Manatee and Sarasota counties and extending to Charlotte Harbor is the South-central Safety Harbor subregion (Mitchem called this variant Manasota Safety Harbor; that term is not used here, to avoid confusion with the Manasota culture [see chapter 6]). Dispersed coastal and inland settlements are present, but these have as yet been little studied. As Mitchem (1989:575–576) has noted, utilitarian pottery in this area is predominately an undecorated quartz sand–tempered ware.

Marion Almy (1978:87–88) has found that the primary determinants for site location in Sarasota County are the distance to water and soil type (the two are probably interrelated). A similar pattern was found by Joan Deming (1980:22–31) in Hillsborough County. In both instances, these data likely reflect the need for proximity to potable water, the preference for camping on well- or better-drained soils, and the reliance of the precolumbian cultures—Safety Harbor included— on wetlands, both coastal and freshwater.

Inland

The fourth Safety Harbor regional variant is well inland from the coast, encompassing Polk and Hardee counties and the eastern portion of DeSoto County (Mitchem 1989:576–577). Although the density of settlements is nowhere near as great as it is in or near coastal locales, numerous surveys in the phosphate district in Hardee County and adjoining portions of the Inland subregion indicate that some dispersed settlements and isolated burial mounds are present (e.g., Wharton and Williams 1980).

Most of the sites located have not been tested, and their cultural affiliations are uncertain. One site, however, Philip Mound (Benson 1967), contained a large number of Spanish artifacts along with Safety Harbor pottery vessels and potsherds, indicating occupation of the Inland subregion during the colonial period. Most likely the area continued to be occupied by small populations (relative to the coast) throughout the Weeden Island and Safety Harbor periods.

St. Johns Plain and Belle Glade Plain utilitarian ceramics are most common, perhaps a reflection of ceramic transitions to the pottery assemblages of the Okeechobee Basin–Kissimmee River region and the lake district of central Florida. But although utilitarian pottery differs from the assemblages of the other subregions, the decorated ceramics found in inland burial mounds are the same types found elsewhere in the Safety Harbor region. Let us now examine some of those mounds and the charnel activities associated with them.

Charnel Houses, Mounds, and Their Contents

The temple described in the 1539 Spanish account quoted earlier was most likely a mortuary or charnel house, a building in which human bodies and bones partially or completely cleaned of flesh were stored before mass burial within a mound. Based on archaeological evidence, charnel houses in combination with mound burial were probably in use among many of the precolumbian cultures in Florida, including Weeden Island and Weeden Island–related cultures. There are many similarities between Weeden Island and Safety Harbor charnel-house mounds.

Some of the best documentary and archaeological evidence for charnel structures comes from the Safety Harbor culture. The documentary references, in addition to the brief mention of the temple in the town of Uzita, include a second early sixteenth-century reference to a charnel structure. When soldiers from the Hernando de Soto expedition were reconnoitering the locale around Uzita after the town was secured for use as a base camp, they found a Spaniard, Juan Ortiz, who had been held captive by native groups since 1528. Shortly after Ortiz's capture the chief of Uzita ordered the Spaniard burned to death, but a daughter of the chief interceded and Ortiz was spared. Instead of dying, Ortiz was assigned to guard a charnel house, possibly the same "temple" described in the 1539 description of the town of Uzita. "When Ortiz got well, he was put to watching a temple, that the wolves, in the night-time, might not carry off the dead there. . . . One night they snatched away from him the body of a little child, son of a principal man; and, going after them, he threw a dart at the wolf that was escaping, which, feeling itself wounded, let go its hold, and went off to die" (Bourne 1866:30).

This same incident is recounted in a secondhand account written by Garcilaso de la Vega, who interviewed some of the participants in the de Soto expedition. Although Garcilaso often embellishes anecdotes and confuses events, his description of Ortiz and the mortuary facility adds information that, if true, confirms that bodies were stored before burial, mostly likely in a charnel house.

> The Cacique ordered to be inflicted upon the youth [Juan Ortiz] another torment. . . . This was that day and night he should guard the remains of dead citizens placed in a designated section of a forest that lay at a distance from the town. These bodies had been put above ground in some wooden chests which served as sepulchres. The chests had no hinges and could be closed only by covering them with boards and then placing rocks or beams of wood on top of the board. (Varner and Varner 1951:65)

Archaeological evidence for charnel houses being used in conjunction with burial mounds comes from several Safety Harbor sites. One example is provided by D. L. Reichard's 1934 excavation of Parrish Mound 2, inland in the Circum–Tampa Bay subregion near the Little Manatee River (Willey 1949a:146–152). The low platform mound was sixty-five feet in diameter and six feet high and apparently was flat-topped. The platform had been erected over a large pit one and one-half feet deep filled with charred wood and cremated human bones. This pit, dug through the old ground surface under the mound, seems to have been used to cremate bodies or bones in situ, activities perhaps associated with an early charnel house.

The platform mound built atop the pit was the base for a rectangular or trapezoidal building twenty-five feet on a side. The walls were individual posts five to ten inches in diameter and placed about six inches apart. All were charred. Other charred timbers lay across the top of the mound, just below the surface. They were evidently lying on what had been the floor of the building and may have been fallen roof supports.

One corner of the building was reinforced with a second row of posts abutting the wall posts. This double post row extended six feet along one wall and seven feet along the other. The rectangular area enclosed on two sides by these reinforced walls apparently was used as a place for cremating bodies. Charred wood, ashes, and burned human bones were found there. Under the building floor thirty-two people, all cremated bundled burials, had been interred. Two other bundled burials also were made under the structure, but they were not cremated. Outside the building five cremated bundled burials had been interred along with two cremated primary burials. These latter two individuals had been buried in small, log-lined pits in slightly flexed position. More small logs were placed across the tops of the pits, and then the tombs were ignited, charring both the human bones and the timbers. Chert points and tools and *Busycon* cups accompanied individual interments. Safety Harbor potsherds were found in the mound, as was an owl-effigy water bottle (Willey 1949a:149). European articles also were found, indicating that the upper charnel house in which cremations were carried out was used in the colonial period. After its use as a charnel house was complete, the building was burned.

A contemporary newspaper account of Reichard's excavations says that "numerous pieces of carved woodwork" were found, including a two-inch-diameter circular gorget depicting a "coiled rattlesnake." (This article, labeled "from Newspaper at Bradenton, Fla, Jan. 1934" is titled "Indian Mound Yields Valued Information on Primitive People." A copy of the clipping is on file in the archaeological records of the Florida Park Service curated at the Florida Museum of Natural History.)

The association of charnel houses and bundled secondary burials seems secure. To these two can be added platform mounds, which often serve as the bases for charnel houses, and burial mounds, which are repositories for human interments—bundled burials, mass interments of secondary remains, primary interments, and/or cremations. Platform mounds become burial mounds when the human remains stored in charnel houses are buried in or on the platform mound and the resultant deposit buried under a mound. The result, a burial mound, is actually a more complex structure than the name implies.

Safety Harbor burial mounds containing secondary remains, such as the Tierra Verde Mound in Pinellas County excavated by William Sears (1967b), thus are likely to contain evidence of a platform mound and a charnel structure. A burial mound that covers an earlier platform mound and charnel house remains might also have been reused, serving as the base for construction of another platform mound and charnel house. As Jeffrey Mitchem (1989:592) has pointed out, the

Safety Harbor platform mound excavated by John Griffin and Ripley Bullen (1950) probably was built on top of a burial mound. There is evidence from the mound excavations reported by C. B. Moore (1900) and by Ripley Bullen (1952) that occasionally Safety Harbor platform and burial mounds were built on top of older mounds dating to the Weeden Island period, just as they were built on top of earlier Safety Harbor mounds.

Another mound construction trait is the placement of a ramp up one side or at a corner of a platform mound. Still another trait, known from several mounds, is the presence of a horseshoe-shaped earthen embankment around the mound (e.g., Willey 1949a:478).

One final example of a Safety Harbor mound exhibiting the association of platform mound, charnel house, burial mound, and ramp is Tatham Mound, an isolated mound located just west of the Withlacoochee River in the Northern subregion. The mound was discovered by Brent Weisman and members of the Withlacoochee River Archaeological Council in 1984 during a survey of the Cove of the Withlacoochee. The subsequent excavations were directed by Mitchem and the results reported in his dissertation (Mitchem 1989:306–549). A dissertation by Dale Hutchinson (1991) provides a detailed bioanthropological analysis of the burial population.

Excavations showed that sometime between A.D. 1200 and 1450 (perhaps earlier) Safety Harbor people built a low mound in which nineteen individuals were interred (Hutchinson 1991:96). Most were secondary interments and several were accompanied by shell beads and had crushed galena, a shiny grey mineral, sprinkled on them. The interments were made in a single episode, evidence that a charnel house was present (Mitchem 1989:528).

Four copper objects were placed with individual burials. Such artifacts are rare in Safety Harbor sites. A circular plate or disk about nine inches in diameter lay atop the bones of an infant and a child. The disk has a small central perforation and a row of embossed dots around the edge. Two repaired areas were present, both cracks that had been covered with small pieces of copper held in place with rolled copper rivets (Mitchem 1989:419–422).

Near these two interments was an adult accompanied by galena, a copper plume ornament, and a copper earspool. The plume, ten inches long, is like examples from the Fort Walton Lake Jackson site as well

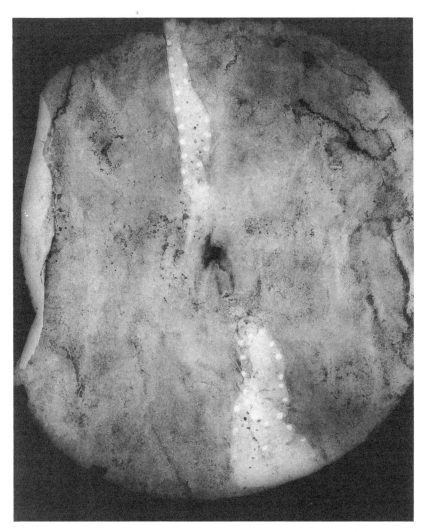

Radiograph of a copper plate 9 inches across, from Tatham Mound. Note the two areas repaired with sheet copper attached with rolled copper rivets. The plate has small embossed dots around its edge, which are not apparent in the radiograph (see Mitchem1989: 419–422; courtesy Jeffrey Mitchem).

as other Mississippian-period sites in the Southeast (Mitchem 1989:420, 423–428). The earspool, a small disk less than two inches across, was perforated in the center and had embossed dots around the edge. It was found on the person's right ear.

An adult woman had been buried with a copper-covered wooden baton or mace on her chest. The wood was identified as cypress.

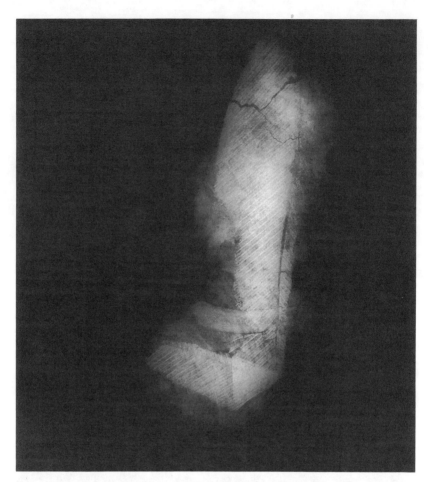

Radiograph of a copper feather plume ornament 9 inches long from Tatham Mound. Both ends have been broken off (see Mitchem 1989:420, 423, 427–428; courtesy Jeffrey Mitchem).

Together these copper objects suggest that the Safety Harbor people in the cove were a part of the Mississippian trade systems that must have spanned the Southeast. The objects also suggest that the individuals buried in the mound may have held high rank. Copper and objects made of copper were among the most valued resources in the precolumbian Southeast.

Although the Tatham Mound copper artifacts are spectacular, especially in a Safety Harbor context where such objects are rare, they do not match the array of Southeastern Ceremonial Complex symbols found at Lake Jackson and among other Mississippian farming populations to the north. Safety Harbor leaders had neither the political power of the Fort Walton elites nor its associated paraphernalia.

After the Tatham Mound interments were made, an earthen ramp was constructed on the east side of the low platform mound and the mound was either left unused or a charnel structure was constructed on its surface. A thick, distinctive layer of black organic soil accumulated on this platform, perhaps on the floor of the charnel structure, if one were present. At one point part of this dark layer was removed, and clean sand was brought in and laid down. Mitchem (1989:529) suggests that this might have been when the charnel structure was refurbished. Afterwards the dark soil continued to accumulate.

Early in the colonial period, perhaps following an epidemic introduced by the Hernando de Soto expedition or another early sixteenth-century Spanish expedition (see Mitchem 1989; also Milanich and Hudson 1993), the charnel house was removed and the top of the platform cleaned. The mound was refurbished with sand added to its top and sides, covering the dark organic soil. Bodies of more than seventy people were then deposited on the clean sand, some laid parallel to one another. On top of and around these people were placed the disarticulated crania and long bones of at least 240 additional people, probably all bundles previously stored in the charnel house.

A shallow sand cap was used to bury the interments, and then a sand ramp was built up the west side of the mound. Finally, what was probably a black drink ceremony was held. Mitchem found a number of *Busycon* cups and broken pottery vessels where they had been left when the ceremony was completed. The site was then abandoned. Over time the cups and pottery vessels left on top of the mound were covered with a thin layer of humus.

Safety Harbor mounds such as the Tatham Mound often contain artifacts deposited with the human interments. Some, like the Tatham shell cups and pottery vessels, were probably used in ceremonies similar to those described in chapters 5 and 6 for Weeden Island cultures. Other artifacts include Safety Harbor vessels and, only occasionally, Weeden Island ceremonial vessels or potsherds. One explanation for the latter is that these were heirlooms or relics retained for generations before finding their way into mounds (Sears 1967b:62, 66).

Safety Harbor Incised water bottle decorated with a Southeastern Ceremonial
Complex hand motif, excavated in 1937 or 1938 from the Picnic Mound as
part of a Works Progress Administration project. The bottle, 10 inches high,
has been partially restored (see Bullen 1952:61–71; courtesy Florida
Museum of Natural History).

Safety Harbor Incised frog-effigy bowl 3½ inches high (head to right), also from Picnic Mound. The bowl has been partially restored (courtesy Florida Museum of Natural History).

Some of the Safety Harbor ceramic vessels in mounds are similar in form to types present in the Fort Walton and other Mississippian cultures. These include open, cazuela, and globular bowls; beakers; jars; and bottles. Some jars and bowls have two or four loop (or strap) handles; others have rim lugs. A few vessels have adornos placed on the rim, usually stylized animal effigies (Luer 1992a). Decorative motifs similar to Fort Walton designs include parallel lines incised in various curvilinear and rectilinear motifs and incised and punctated scrolls and guilloches. Sears (1967b:31–55, 65–70) has compared in detail the form and decorative relationships of the Safety Harbor ceremonial ceramic complex and of the Fort Walton and certain other Mississippian cultures.

Decorated pottery types found in Safety Harbor mounds include Englewood Incised, Sarasota Incised, Safety Harbor Incised, and Pinellas Incised. Southeastern Ceremonial Complex symbols occasionally are incised on Safety Harbor vessels. Undecorated wares are common in mounds. In the Northern subregion—at Tatham Mound,

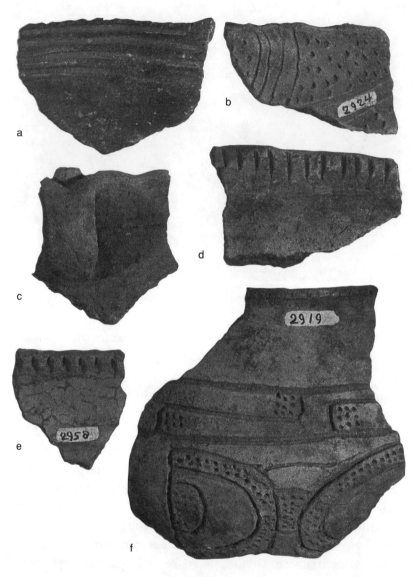

Safety Harbor pottery: *a*, Pinellas Incised, 2 inches high; *b, f*, Safety Harbor Incised; *c–e*, Pinellas Plain (*c* has a handle).

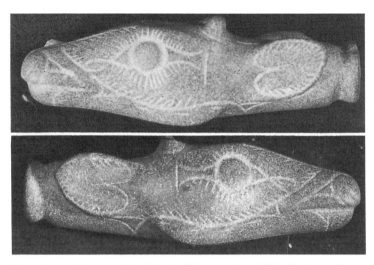

Two views of a stone deer-head effigy pendant 3½ inches long from
Jones Mound (see Bullen 1952: fig. 15).

Quartz crystals modified for hafting, the smaller ¾ inch
long, both from Tatham Mound (see Mitchem
1989:399–402; courtesy Jeffrey Mitchem).

for example—many of these are Pasco Plain limestone-tempered wares.

Other objects found in mounds include the shell beads, *Busycon* cups, galena, and copper artifacts already described from the Tatham Mound, along with finely made celts of ground and polished greenstone and a variety of stone and shell plummets and pendants. Some of these are carved to depict animals, especially birds (e.g., Bullen 1952: figure 16). Quartz crystal pendants also are known (Mitchem 1989:399–402, 580).

The Safety Harbor culture bears many resemblances to the Weeden Island period cultures that preceded it. But other aspects of the culture, such as the platform mound-village complexes around Tampa Bay and the Southeastern Ceremonial Complex symbols on pottery vessels, indicate new settlement complexities and new beliefs added to the old ones. In some ways it appears that Safety Harbor peoples borrowed ideas and practices that helped them to adjust to larger populations and to maintain the greater level of political complexity necessary to support stronger territorialism. But other ideas and practices associated with a fully Mississippian way of life were not adopted because the agricultural economic system at the base of the Mississippian way of life was not possible in coastal Florida. Comparisons of the Pensacola and Safety Harbor cultures with the Fort Walton culture provide insights into the contrasting economic systems that helped to shape precolumbian Florida.

 **EPILOGUE**

We have traced the 12,000-year development of the native American Indians who lived in precolumbian Florida from the Paleoindians to the dawn of the coming of Europeans in the early sixteenth century. During those millennia people and cultures adjusted to changing environmental conditions resulting from climatic fluctuations and to larger population levels and developed new economic pursuits. As a result, a number of lifeways evolved, each suited to a different region of the state.

That process of regionalization was in place by 3000 B.C., the beginning of the late Archaic period and the onset of modern climatic and vegetative regimes in Florida. As we saw in chapter 3, archaeologists can define several regional late Archaic cultures, such as the Elliott's Point complex in the western panhandle. But the nature of the currently available archaeological evidence only allows most of the regional cultures to be easily distinguished after 500 B.C. As more research is carried out and archaeologists are able to better differentiate among late Archaic archaeological assemblages, it is likely that we will be able to trace all regional developments back in time into the Archaic period.

Each regional culture continued to occupy a specific area of the state, maintaining a way of life that persisted through time: a cultural tradition (Goggin 1949b). Some of the cultures can be correlated with native American groups documented in the colonial period.

Regional cultures were not isolated. They shared some of their life-ways even while maintaining adaptations well suited to a particular environmental zone. Nor were the precolumbian cultures static and unchanging. As we have seen, they continued to evolve in order to successfully cope with growing populations, innovations, and new ideas resulting from contact with other cultures. These changes are apparent in the archaeological record and allow archaeologists to define sequential cultures in specific regions. An excellent example is the eastern panhandle where a cultural developmental sequence has been defined: Deptford, Swift Creek, early and late Weeden Island, and Fort Walton. Archaeologists also can go well beyond developing tax-onomies. We can describe and explain many aspects of the pre-columbian cultures and their evolution. For some cultures, such as Safety Harbor, we can recognize variants in archaeological assemblages and economic adaptations. The myriad of ethnic groups living in Florida at the time of European contact is reflected in the many archae-ological assemblages that existed in the late precolumbian period.

From this survey of precolumbian Florida several major points have emerged. For instance, when information on the Paleoindians who lived in Florida 12,000 years ago is compared with what is known about the late precolumbian cultures, we cannot help but acknowl-edge that environmental changes and cultural evolution took place in precolumbian Florida. The arid Florida of the Paleoindians was a quite different land from Florida 500 years ago in terms of vegetation, ani-mals, and even geographical area.

Likewise, extraordinary differences are apparent between the cul-tures of northern Florida 12,000 years ago and those that inhabited that portion of the state 500 years ago. When a Paleoindian site like Harney Flats in Hillsborough County is compared with one of the Fort Walton mound and village complex sites near Tallahassee, we begin to realize the tremendous changes that took place between the two periods: larger populations, more complex social and political organi-zation, and different subsistence and settlement systems. Fort Walton people built temples and other structures on pyramidal, flat-topped mounds and maintained a hierarchy of settlements, while Paleoin-dians did not. Fort Walton villagers tilled the soil, producing a portion of their diet, and they used bows and arrows; Paleoindians did not. Beautifully chipped Paleoindian points pale when compared to the

elaborate Southeastern Ceremonial Complex copper and shell paraphernalia from Lake Jackson. A Paleoindian time-traveler to the Lake
Jackson site would probably feel as alien and out of place as a sixteenth-century Spaniard in modern Tampa.

Another point that becomes apparent is the significance of water.
Marine and freshwater habitats provided important foods for every
precolumbian culture. The distribution of wetlands profoundly affected precolumbian societies. In areas of extensive wetlands—often
the same parts of the state where less fertile agricultural soils are
found—regional native cultures continued to focus on wild resources
for their sustenance rather than adopting intensive agriculture. It was
only in regions where extensive wetlands are not present and where
the more fertile soils are found—parts of northern Florida—that precolumbian peoples became farmers. Indeed, Mississippian-style intensive farming, associated with a host of social and ideological practices,
only developed and persisted in the eastern panhandle, the region of
the Fort Walton culture.

We have also seen that the question of agriculture in precolumbian
Florida is controversial. One example of that controversy concerns
maize cultivation in the Okeechobee Basin. If maize were being grown
in the savanna surrounding Lake Okeechobee shortly after 500 B.C., it
would be the earliest use of that plant in the eastern United States (the
earliest well documented maize is from the Icehouse Bottom site in
Tennessee; Chapman and Keel 1979). There is ample evidence in the
archaeological record for maize farming among the Fort Walton peoples, and maize kernels have been found at a ninth century A.D.
Wakulla culture site. But evidence for maize cultivation in precolumbian Florida before that date is less certain.

Gourds, both bottle gourds and squash gourds, are known to have
been present in Florida at least as long as humans have lived there. But
exactly when those plants were cultivated, as opposed to being
encouraged, also is uncertain. Other wild plants may similarly have
been encouraged by precolumbian peoples, but such a practice is quite
different from the cleared-field, intensive farming of the Fort Walton
people.

If changes in the archaeological record in northern Florida at about
A.D. 750 correlate with the adoption of agriculture, we would expect to
find evidence that plants were being grown. Perhaps the reason such

evidence has not been forthcoming is that the type of agriculture practiced was not as intensive as that in the Fort Walton culture. There may have been a developmental continuum between encouraging wild plants, to casually growing them in gardens near human settlements, to planting cleared fields of corn and other crops.

Another consideration is that to find remains of cultigens in the archaeological record, we must look for them. With archaeobotanical studies becoming a standard part of research strategies, perhaps definitive evidence for the cultivation of plants in Florida prior to the ninth century will be forthcoming. Certainly, as demonstrated at Hontoon Island, Florida's wet sites can provide ample evidence of plant use.

Several other points should be emphasized. One is that the precolumbian cultures of south Florida were not as unique as once was thought. Dividing Florida into northern agriculturists and southern hunter-gatherers-fishers is not an accurate depiction. We can instead differentiate the late precolumbian agricultural groups found in portions of northern Florida from the nonagricultural groups found in many parts of the state. The archaeological assemblages and ways of life associated with the agricultural Fort Walton and Alachua cultures were quite different from those of the many nonagricultural cultures, whether in the Indian River region or on the north peninsular Gulf coast.

Past taxonomies have heavily influenced the ways we classify the precolumbian cultures. It is not easy to change those taxonomies, but that is what is happening as the archaeological record receives closer scrutiny. One example is the area from Tampa Bay south into southwest Florida. Along that coastal area archaeologists are finding it increasingly difficult to differentiate the respective late Archaic period cultures. Likewise, we now must explain the presence of Safety Harbor pottery in mound contexts in both regions. The trend is to look for similarities among the coastal cultures below Tampa Bay, rather than to look for differences in the cultures living north and south of Charlotte Harbor. At various times in the past, the cultures of those two regions may have been more alike than our present taxonomy allows us to articulate.

New data bring both blessings and taxonomic revision. Early taxonomies were based on a smaller database than is available today. As more information is produced, we must alter our taxonomies to reflect new understanding.

Another point that has emerged as a result of increased research in coastal areas is that Florida's archaeological record is incomplete. Many sites have been inundated by the rising sea. But enough coastal Archaic sites remain and have now been studied for archaeologists to realize that, by or shortly after 3000 B.C., year-round occupation of coastal zones took place. As technologies to locate and excavate inundated Archaic-period or even Paleoindian-period sites in the Gulf of Mexico are developed, our knowledge of pre–3000 B.C. coastal cultures will certainly increase.

Still another point is this: Florida provides an excellent laboratory to study the evolution of precolumbian cultures and their interactions with past and present environments. Comparisons of Fort Walton, Pensacola, and Safety Harbor, for instance, allow us to begin to understand the nature of the Mississippian way of life and the importance of a certain constellation of environmental and geographical conditions in the development of that way of life (e.g., conditions suitable for intensive agriculture, a location near other Mississippian societies). Comparisons among Florida's precolumbian cultures also can provide insights into how chiefdom societies can evolve in the absence of intensive agriculture. In the Caloosahatchee region, harvesting marine resources from shallow, grassy tropical coastal waters provided the economic base for such complex political developments.

We also can learn a great deal about past environments through archaeological studies of Florida's precolumbian cultures. As we have seen, archaeological investigations provide information on groundwater levels, sea-level fluctuations, and the plants and animals that once lived in the area.

A final point that is made abundantly clear from this review of precolumbian Florida is that archaeology can inform us about the past. The story of the native American Indians related here comes from archaeological research. It does not come from oral traditions or written records. All we know about precolumbian Florida is the fruit of archaeological investigations, the bulk of which have been carried out in the last fifty years. Archaeologists in Florida, and the people who support their work, deserve accolades for their success.

In a sense, archaeology and the application of archaeobiological and similar scientific methods enable native societies that existed in Florida thousands of years ago to speak to us today. Their worlds are an important part of our cultural and environmental heritage. I hope that this book has made you more aware of those worlds and helped you to hear the native voices from the precolumbian past.

 **REFERENCES**

The following abbreviations are used in the references:

AHRM   Division of Archives, History, and Records Management, Florida Department of State, Tallahassee

BHSP   Bureau of Historic Sites and Properties, Division of Archives, History, and Records Management, Florida Department of State, Tallahassee

FMNH   Florida Museum of Natural History, Gainesville (formerly Florida State Museum)

DA   Department of Anthropology, Florida Museum of Natural History, Gainesville

HR   Division of Historical Resources, Florida Department of State, Tallahassee

SEAC   Southeast Archeological Center, National Park Service, Tallahassee

UWFCA   Office of Cultural and Archeological Research, University of West Florida, Pensacola

Abshire, A.E., Alden L. Potter, Allen R. Taylor, Clyde H. Neel, Walter H. Anderson, John I. Rutledge, and Stevenson B. Johnson

1935   Some Further Papers on Aboriginal Man in the Neighborhood of the Ocala National Forest. [Research reports prepared by the Archaeological Research Group of Co. 1420, Civilian Conservation Corps, Ocala, Florida.] Mimeo. On file, DA.

Adams, Grey L., and William C. Lazarus

1960   Two Skulls from a Fort Walton Period Cemetery Site (OK-35), Okaloosa County, Florida. *Florida Anthropologist* 13:109-114.

Alexander, Michelle
    1984   Analysis of Plant Materials from Three Fort Walton Sites: High
            Ridge, Velda, and Lake Jackson Sites. Paper presented at the 41st
            Southeastern Archaeological Conference, Pensacola.
Allen, Ross
    1948   The Big Circle Mounds. *Florida Anthropologist* 1:17–21.
Allerton, David, George M. Luer, and Robert S. Carr
    1984   Ceremonial Tablets and Related Objects from Florida. *Florida
            Anthropologist* 37:5–54.
Almy, Marion M.
    n.d.   Salvage Excavations at Curiosity Creek. Manuscript. On file,
            Bureau of Archaeological Research, HR.
    1978   The Archaeological Potential of Soil Survey Reports. *Florida
            Anthropologist* 31:75–91.
Anonymous
    1933   Totem Pole from Florida. *Scientific American* 148:292–293.
Anonymous [Alden L. Potter]
    n.d.   Archaeological Reports, Co. 140, C.C.C., Ocala, Florida. [Bound
            photographs, correspondence, and reports.] On file, DA.
Ashley, Keith H.
    1992   Swift Creek Manifestations along the Lower St. Johns River.
            Florida Anthropologist 45:127–138.
Athens, William P.
    1983   The Spatial Distribution of Glades Period Sites within the Big
            Cypress National Preserve, Florida. Master's thesis, Florida State
            University, Tallahassee.
Austin, Robert J.
    1987a   An Archaeological Site Inventory and Zone Management Plan for
            Lee County, Florida. Performed for the Lee County Department
            of Community Development, Division of Planning. On file, BHSP.
    1987b   Prehistoric and Early Historic Settlement in the Kissimmee River
            Basin: An Archaeological Survey of the Avon Park Air Force
            Range. *Florida Anthropologist* 40:287–300.
    1992   A Review of Archaeological Research in the Kissimmee River Re-
            gion of Florida. Manuscript. On file, Archaeology Range, FMNH.
Austin, Robert J., and H. Hansen
    1988   Cultural Resource Assessment Survey of the Walker Ranch DRI
            Development Site, Polk and Osceola Counties, Florida. Report
            submitted by Piper Archaeological Research, Inc., to Fisher and
            Associates, Inc., Kissimmee, Florida. On file, BHSP.
Austin, Robert J., and Michael Russo
    1989   Limited Excavations at the Catfish Creek Site (8So608), Sarasota
            County, Florida. Piper Archaeological Research, Inc., St. Peters-
            burg. On file, BHSP.

Bartram, William
1928   *Travels of William Bartram.* Edited by M. Van Doren. New York: Dover.

Bell, James
1883   Mounds in Alachua County, Florida. *Annual Report of the Smithsonian Institution, 1880–1881*, pp. 635–637, Washington, D.C.

Belmont, John S., and Stephen Williams
1981   Painted Pottery Horizons in the Southern Mississippi Valley. *Geoscience and Man* 22:19–42.

Bense, Judith A.
1969   Excavations at the Bird Hammock Site (8Wa30), Wakulla County, Florida. Master's thesis, Florida State University, Tallahassee.
1985   *Hawkshaw: Prehistory and History in an Urban Neighborhood in Pensacola, Florida.* Report of Investigations 7 . UWFCA.
1992   Santa Rosa–Swift Creek in Northwest Florida. Paper presented at the 49th Southeastern Archaeological Conference, Little Rock.

Bense, Judith A., and John C. Phillips
1990   *Archaeological Assessment of Six Selected Areas in Brevard County: A First Generation Site Location Model.* Report of Investigations 32. Institute of West Florida Archaeology, University of West Florida. Pensacola.

Bense, Judith A., and Thomas C. Watson
1979   A Swift Creek and Weeden Island "Ring Midden" in the St. Andrews Bay Drainage System on the Northwest Florida Gulf Coast. *Journal of Alabama Archaeology* 25:85–137.

Benson, Carl A.
1959   Some Pottery Contributions to the Early Fabric Techniques. *Florida Anthropologist* 12:65–70.
1967   The Philip Mound: A Historic Site. *Florida Anthropologist* 20:118–132.

Beriault, John, Robert Carr, Jerry Stipp, Richard Johnson, and Jack Meeder
1981   The Archeological Salvage of the Bay West Site, Collier County, Florida. *Florida Anthropologist* 34:39–58.

Bond, Stanley C., Jr.
1992   Archaeological Excavations at 8SJ42, the Crescent Beach Site, St. Johns County, Florida. *Florida Anthropologist* 45:148–161.

Borremans, Nina T.
1991   North Peninsular Gulf Coast, 500 B.C.–A.D. 1600. In *Florida's Comprehensive Historic Preservation Plan* (draft, 18 March 1991), pp. 81–88. HR.

Borremans, Nina T., and Michael E. Moseley
1990   A Prehistoric Site Survey of the Cedar Keys Region, Coastal Levy County, Florida. Report submitted to HR.

Bourne, Edward G., trans.
  1904   A Narrative of de Soto's Expedition Based on the Diary of Rodrigo
          Ranjel, his Private Secretary, by Gonzalo de Oviedo y Valdés. In
          Narratives of the Career of Hernando de Soto in the Conquest of Florida,
          Vol. 2, pp. 47–149. New York: A.S. Barnes and Co.
Boyd, Mark F., Hale G. Smith, and John W. Griffin
  1951   *Here They Once Stood: The Tragic End of the Apalachee Missions.*
          Gainesville: University of Florida Press.
Brinton, Daniel G.
  1859   *Florida Peninsula, Its Literary History, Indian Tribes, and Antiquities.*
          Philadelphia: J. Sabin.
Brooks, Mark
  1974   Two Weeden Island Archaeological Sites: Sacred vs. Secular Levels
          of Culture. Honors thesis, University of Florida, Gainesville.
Brose, David S.
  1979   An Interpretation of the Hopewellian Traits in Florida. In *Hopewell
          Archaeology: The Chillicothe Conference,* edited by David S. Brose and
          N'omi Greber, pp. 141–149. Kent, Ohio: Kent State University
          Press.
  1984   Mississippian Period Cultures in Northwestern Florida. In *Perspec-
          tives on Gulf Coast Prehistory,* edited by Dave D. Davis, pp. 165–197.
          Gainesville: University of Florida Press/FMNH.
Brose, David S., and George W. Percy
  1974   Weeden Island Settlement—Subsistence and Ceremonialism: A
          Reappraisal in Systemic Terms. Paper presented at the 37th
          Annual Meeting of the Society for American Archaeology, Wash-
          ington, D.C.
  1978   Fort Walton Settlement Patterns. In *Mississippian Settlement Pat-
          terns,* edited by Bruce D. Smith, pp. 81–114. New York: Academic
          Press.
Brown, James A.
  1985   The Mississippian Period. In *Ancient Art of the American Woodland
          Indians,* pp. 93–145. New York: Harry N. Abrams.
Bullen, Adelaide K.
  1972   Paleoepidemiology and Distribution of Prehistoric Treponemiasis
          (Syphilis) in Florida. *Florida Anthropologist* 25:133–174.
Bullen, Adelaide K., and Ripley P. Bullen
  1950   The Johns Island Site, Hernando County, Florida. *American Antiq-
          uity* 16:23–45.
  1953   The Battery Point Site, Bayport, Hernando County, Florida.
          Florida Anthropologist 6:85–92.
  1954   Further Notes on the Battery Point Site, Bayport, Hernando
          County, Florida. *Florida Anthropologist* 7:103–108.
  1961a   The Summer Haven Site. *Florida Anthropologist* 14:1–16.

1961b   Wash Island in Crystal River. *Florida Anthropologist* 14:69–73.

1963   The Wash Island Site, Crystal River, Florida. *Florida Anthropologist* 16:81–92.

Bullen, Ripley P.

1949   The Woodward Site. *Florida Anthropologist* 2:49–64.

1950   Perico Island: 1950. *Florida Anthropologist* 3:40–44.

1951a   The Enigmatic Crystal River Site. *American Antiquity* 17:142–143.

1951b   *The Terra Ceia Site, Manatee County, Florida.* Florida Anthropological Society Publications 3. Gainesville.

1952   *Eleven Archaeological Sites in Hillsborough County, Florida.* Florida Geological Survey, Report of Investigations 8. Tallahassee.

1953a   Excavations at Manatee Spring. *Florida Anthropologist* 6:53–67.

1953b   The Famous Crystal River Site. *Florida Anthropologist* 6:9–37.

1955a   Archaeology of the Tampa Bay Area. *Florida Historical Quarterly* 34:51–63.

1955b   Carved Owl Totem, Deland, Florida. *Florida Anthropologist* 8:61–73.

1955c   Stratigraphic Tests at Bluffton, Volusia County, Florida. *Florida Anthropologist* 8:1–16.

1958   Six Sites Near the Chattahoochee River in the Jim Woodruff Reservoir Area, Florida. In *River Basin Survey Papers,* edited by Frank H. H. Roberts, Jr., pp. 315–357. Bureau of American Ethnology Bulletin 169. Washington, D.C.: Smithsonian Institution.

1959   The Transitional Period of Florida. *Southeastern Archaeological Conference Newsletter* 6(1):43–53.

1962   Indian Burials at Tick Island. *American Philosophical Society Yearbook 1961,* pp. 477–480.

1965   Crystal River Indian Mound Museum. [Condensed version of Bullen 1953b with additional information on his 1960, 1964, and 1965 excavations.] On file, FMNH.

1966a   *Burtine Island, Citrus County, Florida.* Contributions of the Florida State Museum, Social Sciences 14. Gainesville.

1966b   Stelae at the Crystal River Site, Florida. *American Antiquity* 31:861–865.

1969   *Excavations at Sunday Bluff, Florida.* Contributions of the Florida State Museum, Social Sciences 15. Gainesville.

1971   The Sarasota County Mound, Englewood, Florida. *Florida Anthropologist* 24:1–30.

1972   The Orange Period of Peninsular Florida. In *Fiber-tempered Pottery in Southeastern United States and Northern Colombia: Its Origins, Context, and Significance,* edited by Ripley P. Bullen and James B. Stoltman, pp. 9–33. Florida Anthropological Society Publications 6. Gainesville.

1975   *A Guide to the Identification of Florida Projectile Points.* Gainesville, Fla.: Kendall Books.

Bullen, Ripley P., and Laurence E. Beilman

1973   The Nalcrest Site, Lake Weohyakapka, Florida. *Florida Anthropologist* 26:1–22.

Bullen, Ripley P., and Carl A. Benson

1964   Dixie Lime Caves Numbers 1 and 2, a Preliminary Report. *Florida Anthropologist* 17:153–164.

Bullen, Ripley P., and W. J. Bryant

1965   *Three Archaic Sites in the Ocala National Forest, Florida.* William L. Bryant Foundation, American Studies Report 6. Orlando.

Bullen, Ripley P., and Adelaide K. Bullen

1976   *The Palmer Site.* Florida Anthropological Society Publications 8. Gainesville.

Bullen, Ripley P., and Edward M. Dolan

1959   The Johnson Lake Site, Marion County, Florida. *Florida Anthropologist* 12:77–94.

1960   Shell Mound, Levy County, Florida. *Florida Anthropologist* 13:17–24.

Bullen, Ripley P. and John W. Griffin

1952   An Archaeological Survey of Amelia Island, Florida. *Florida Anthropologist* 5:37–64.

Bullen, Ripley P., and Frederick W. Sleight

1959   *Archaeological Investigations of the Castle Windy Midden, Florida.* William L. Bryant Foundation, American Studies Report 1. Orlando.

1960   *Archaeological Investigations of Green Mound, Florida.* William L. Bryant Foundation, American Studies Report 2. Orlando.

Bullen, Ripley P., Adelaide K. Bullen, and W. J. Bryant

1967   *Archaeological Investigations at the Ross Hammock Site, Florida.* William L. Bryant Foundation, American Studies Report 7.

Bullen, Ripley P., William L. Partridge, and Donald A. Harris

1970   The Safford Burial Mound, Tarpon Springs, Florida. *Florida Anthropologist* 23:81–118.

Bullen, Ripley P., David S. Webb, and Benjamin I. Waller

1970   A Worked Mammoth Bone from Florida. *American Antiquity* 35:203–205.

Bullen, Ripley P., Walter Askew, Lee M. Feder, and Richard McDonnell

1978   *The Canton Street Site, St. Petersburg, Florida.* Florida Anthropological Society Publications 9. Gainesville.

Caldwell, Joseph R.

1971   Chronology of the Georgia Coast. *Southeastern Archaeological Conference Bulletin* 13:88–92.

1978   Report of Excavations at Fairchild's Landing and Harel's Landing, Seminole County, Georgia. Edited by Betty A. Smith. Report submitted to SEAC.

Caldwell, Joseph R., and A. J. Waring, Jr.

1939a   Pottery Type Descriptions. *Southeastern Archaeological Conference Newsletter* 1(5): 4–12.

1939b   Pottery Type Descriptions. *Southeastern Archaeological Conference Newsletter* 1(6): 1–9.

1939c   The Use of a Ceramic Sequence in the Classification of Aboriginal Sites in Chatham County, Georgia. *Southeastern Archaeological Conference Newsletter* 2(1): 6–7.

Carr, Robert S.

1975   *An Archaeological and Historical Survey of Lake Okeechobee.* Miscellaneous Project Report Series 22. BHSP.

1981   Dade County Historic Survey Final Report: The Archaelogical Survey. On file, Historic Preservation Division, Metro-Dade Office of Community and Economic Development. Miami.

1985   Prehistoric Circular Earthworks in South Florida. *Florida Anthropologist* 38:288–301.

1986   Preliminary Report of Archaeological Excavations at the Cutler Fossil Site in Southern Florida. Paper presented at the 51st Annual Meeting of the Society for American Archaeology, New Orleans.

1990   Archaeological Investigations at Pine Island, Broward County. *Florida Anthropologist* 43:249–261.

Carr, Robert S. and John G. Beriault

1984   Prehistoric Man in South Florida. In *Environments of South Florida: Present and Past,* edited by P. J. Gleason, pp. 1–14. 2d ed. Coral Gables: Miami Geological Society.

Carr, Robert S., and B. Calvin Jones

1981   *Florida Anthropologist* Interview with Calvin Jones, Part II: Excavations of an Archaic Cemetery in Cocoa Beach, Florida. *Florida Anthropologist* 34:81–89.

Chance, Marsha A.

1981   Investigations at Wetherington Island: An Archaic Lithic Procurement Site in Hillsborough County. *Florida Anthropologist* 34:109–119.

1982   *Phase II Investigations at Wetherington Island: A Lithic Procurement Site in Hillsborough County, Florida.* Interstate 75 Highway Phase II Archaeological Reports 3. BHSP.

Chapman, Jefferson, and Bennie C. Keel

1979   Candy Creek–Connestee Components in Eastern Tennessee and Western North Carolina and Their Relationship with Adena-Hopewell. In *Hopewell Archaeology: The Chillicothe Conference,* edited by David S. Brose and N'omi Greber, pp. 157–161. Kent, Ohio: Kent State University Press

Claassen, Cheryl

1985   Shellfish Utilization during Deptford and Mississippian Times in Escambia Bay, Florida. *Florida Anthropologist* 38:124–135.

Clausen, Carl J.
  1964   The A–356 Site and the Florida Archaic. Master's thesis, University of Florida, Gainesville.
Clausen, Carl J., H. K. Brooks, and A. B. Wesolowsky
  1975   *Florida Spring Confirmed as 10,000-Year-Old Early Man Site.* Florida Anthropological Society Publications 7. Gainesville.
Clausen, Carl J., A.D. Cohen, Cesare Emiliani, J. A. Holman, and J.J. Stipp
  1979   Little Salt Spring, Florida: A Unique Underwater Site. *Science* 203:609–614.
Cockrell, Wilburn A.
  1970   Glades I and Pre–Glades Settlement and Subsistence Patterns on Marco Island (Collier County, Florida). Master's thesis, Florida State University, Tallahassee.
Cockrell, Wilburn A., and Larry Murphy
  1978   Pleistocene Man in Florida. *Archaeology of Eastern North America* 6:1–13.
Collins, Henry B.
  1928   Burial of Calusa Indians. *El Palacio* 24:223–224.
  1929   The "Lost" Calusa Indians of Florida. *Explorations and Field Work of the Smithsonian Institution* 1928:151–156. Washington, D.C.: Smithsonian Institution.
Cordell, Ann S.
  1984   *Ceramic Technology at a Weeden Island Period Archaeological Site in North Florida.* Ceramic Notes No. 2. Occasional Publications of the Ceramic Technology Laboratory, Gainesville: Florida State Museum.
  1992   Technological Investigation of Pottery Variability in Southwest Florida. In *Culture and Environment in the Domain of the Calusa,* edited by William H. Marquardt, pp. 105–190. Institute of Archaeology and Paleoenvironmental Studies, Monograph 1, DA.
Cumbaa, Stephen L.
  1972   An Intensive Harvest Economy in North-central Florida. Master's thesis, University of Florida, Gainesville.
  1973   Aboriginal Use of Marine Mammals in the Southeastern United States. Paper presented at the 30th Southeastern Archaeological Conference, Memphis.
  1976   A Reconsideration of Freshwater Shellfish Exploitation in the Florida Archaic. *Florida Anthropologist* 29:49–59.
Cumbaa, Stephen L., and Thomas H. Gouchnour
  1970   The Colby Site, Marion County, Florida. *Florida Anthropologist* 23:43–56.
Curren, Caleb
  1987   *Archaeology at Bluewater Bay (8Ok102), a Late Archaic Period Site in Northwest Florida.* Report of Investigations 9. UWFCA.

Cushing, Frank H,
  1897   Exploration of Ancient Key-Dweller Remains on the Gulf Coast of
          Florida. *Proceedings of the American Philosophical Society* 25(153):
          329–448.
Daniel, Randy [I. Randolph, Jr.]
  1982   *Test Excavations at the Deerstand Site (8Hi483A) in Hillsborough County,
          Florida*. Interstate 75 Highway Phase II Archaeological Reports 2.
          BHSP.
Daniel, I. Randolph, Jr., and Michael Wisenbaker
  1981   *Test Excavations at 8Hi450(D): An Inland Archaic Occupation in Hills-
          borough County, Florida*. Interstate 75 Highway Phase II Archaeo-
          logical Reports 1. BHSP.
  1987   *Harney Flats: A Florida Paleo-Indian Site*. Farmingdale, N.Y.: Bay-
          wood.
Davis, Mary B., comp.
  1987   Field Notes of Clarence B. Moore's Southeastern Archaeological
          Expeditions, 1891–1918: A Guide to the Microfilm Edition. New
          York: Huntington Free Library, Museum of the American Indian.
Deagan, Kathleen A.
  1974   Sex, Status, and Role in the *Mestizaje* of Spanish Colonial Florida.
          Ph.D. diss., University of Florida, Gainesville.
  1983   *Spanish St. Augustine: The Archaeology of a Colonial Creole Community*.
          New York: Academic Press.
  1987   *Artifacts of the Spanish Colonies of Florida and the Caribbean,
          1500–1800*. Vol. 1. Washington, D.C.: Smithsonian Institution
          Press.
Deming, Joan
  1980   The Cultural Resources of Hillsborough County: An Assessment of
          Prehistoric Resources. Report submitted to the Historic
          Tampa/Hillsborough County Preservation Board, Tampa.
Denevan, W. D.
  1970   Aboriginal Drained-Field Cultivation in the Americas. *Science*
          169:647–654.
DePratter, Chester B.
  1979   Ceramics. In *The Anthropology of St. Catherines Island 2. The Refuge-
          Deptford Mortuary Complex*, by David Hurst Thomas and Clark
          Spencer Larsen, pp. 109–132. Anthropological Papers of the
          American Museum of Natural History, vol. 56, pt. 1. New York.
DePratter, Chester B., and James D. Howard
  1980   Indian Occupation and Geologic History of the Georgia Coast: A
          5000–Year Summary. In *Excursions in Southeastern Geology, the
          Archaeology-Geology of the Georgia Coast*, edited by James D. Howard,
          Chester B. DePratter, and R. W. Frey, pp. 1–65.Guidebook 20,
          1980 Annual Meeting of the Geological Society of America.

1981   Evidence for a Sea Level Lowstand between 4500 and 2400 Years B.P. on the Southeast Coast of the United States. *Journal of Sedimentary Petrology* 51:1287–1295.

Dickel, D.N. and G.H. Doran

1989   Severe Neural Tube Defect Syndrome from the Early Archaic of Florida. *American Journal of Physical Anthropology* 80:325–344.

Dickens, Roy S.

1971   Archaeology in the Jones Bluff Reservoir of Central Alabama. *Journal of Alabama Archaeology* 17:1–107.

Dickinson, Martin F., and Lucy B. Wayne

1985   Archaeological Mitigation of Two Seminole Sites in Marion County, Florida. Manuscript. On file, Water and Air Research, Inc., Gainesville.

Division of Archives, History, and Records Management

1970   Key Marco Reveals Early Florida Life. *Archives and History News* 1(1): 1, 3–4. Tallahassee: Florida Department of State.

Doran, Glen H.

1992   Problems and Potential of Wet Sites in North America: The Example of Windover. In *The Wetland Revolution in Prehistory,* edited by Bryony Coles, pp. 125–134. Exeter, England: The Prehistoric Society and Wetland Archaeology Research Project, University of Exeter.

Doran, Glen H., and David N. Dickel

1988a   Multidisciplinary Investigations at the Windover Site. In *Wet Site Archaeology,* edited by Barbara Purdy, pp. 263–289. Caldwell, N.J.: Telford Press.

1988b   Radiometric Chronology of the Archaic Windover Archaeological Site (8Br246). *Florida Anthropologist* 41:365–380.

Doran, Glen H., David N. Dickel, William E. Ballinger, Jr., O. Frank Agee, Phillip J. Laipis, and William W. Hauswirth

1986   Anatomical, Cellular, and Molecular Analysis of 8,000-yr-old Human Brain Tissue from the Windover Archaeological Site. *Nature* 323:803–806.

Douglass, Andrew E.

1884   Some Characteristics of the Indian Earth and Shell Mounds of the Atlantic Coast of Florida. *American Association for the Advancement of Science Proceedings* 33:599–601.

1885a   Ancient Canals on the Southwest Coast of Florida. *American Antiquarian and Oriental Journal* 7:277–285.

1885b   Some Characteristics of the Indian Earth and Shell Mounds on the Atlantic Coast of Florida. *American Antiquarian* 7:74–82, 140–147.

Dunbar, James S.

1981   *The Effect of Geohydrology and Natural Resource Availability on Site Utilization at the Fowler Bridge Mastodon Site (8Hi393c/uw) in Hillsbor-*

ough County, Florida. In Interstate 75 Highway Phase II Archaeological Report 5, pp. 63–106. BHSP.

1983   A Model for the Predictability of Clovis/Suwannee Paleo Indian Site Clusters in Florida—A Revival of W. T. Neill's Oasis Hypothesis. Paper presented at the 35th Annual Meeting of the Florida Anthropological Society, Tallahassee.

1991   Resource Orientation of Clovis and Suwannee Age Paleoindian Sites in Florida. In *Clovis: Origins and Adaptations*, edited by R. Bonnichsen and K. Turnmier, pp. 185–213. Corvallis: Center for the First Americans, Oregon State University.

Dunbar, James S., and B.I. Waller

1983   A Distribution Analysis of the Clovis/Suwannee Paleo-Indian Sites of Florida: A Geographic Approach. *Florida Anthropologist* 36:18–30.

Dunbar, James S., Michael K. Faught, and S. David Webb

1988   An Underwater Paleo–Indian Site in Northwestern Florida. *Florida Anthropologist* 41:442–453.

Dunbar, James S., S. David Webb, and Dan Cring

1989   Culturally and Naturally Modified Bones from a Paleoindian Site in the Aucilla River, North Florida. In *First International Bone Modification Conference*, edited by R. Bonnichsen, pp. 473–497. Orono: Center for the Study of the First Americans, University of Maine.

Dunbar, James S., S. David Webb, and Michael Faught

1991   Inundated Prehistoric Sites in Apalachee Bay, Florida, and the Search for the Clovis Shoreline. In *Paleoshorelines and Prehistory: An Investigation of Method*, edited by Lucille Lewis Johnson, pp. 117–146. Boca Raton, Fla.: CRC Press.

Dunbar, James S., S. David Webb, Michael Faught, Richard J. Anuskiewicz, and Melanie J. Stright

1989   Archaeological Sites in the Drowned Tertiary Karst Region of the Eastern Gulf of Mexico. *Underwater Archaeology Proceedings from the Society for Historical Archaeology Conference*, edited by J. Barto Arnold III, pp. 25–31. Baltimore.

Dunn, Mary E.

1981   Botanical Remains from the Cemochechobee Site. In *Cemochechobee, Archaeology of a Mississippian Ceremonial Center on the Chattahoochee River*, by Frank T. Schnell, Vernon J. Knight, and Gail S. Schnell, pp. 252–255. Gainesville: University of Florida Press/FMNH.

du Toit, Brian M.

1986   *Anthropology in Florida: The History of a Discipline*. Florida Journal of Anthropology, Special Publication 5. Gainesville.

Ehrenhard, John E., Robert S. Carr, and Robert C. Taylor

1978   *The Archeological Survey of the Big Cypress National Preserve, Phase I*. SEAC.

1979   *The Big Cypress National Preserve: Archeological Survey Season 2*. SEAC.

Ehrenhard, John E., Gregory Komara, and Robert C. Taylor

1982   *Everglades National Park: Cultural Resource Inventory Interim Report Season 1*. SEAC.

Ehrenhard, John E. and Robert C. Taylor

1980   *The Big Cypress National Preserve: Archeological Survey Season 3*. Southeast Archeological Center, National Park Service, Tallahassee.

Ehrenhard, John E., Robert C. Taylor, and Gregory Komara

1980   *The Big Cypress National Preserve: Cultural Resource Inventory Season 4*. SEAC.

Espenshade, Christopher T.

1983   Ceramic Ecology and Aboriginal Household Pottery Production at the Gauthier Site, Florida. Master's thesis, University of Florida, Gainesville.

Estabrook, Richard W., and Christine Newman

1984   *Archaeological Investigations at the Marita and Ranch House Sites, Hillsborough County, Florida*. Archaeological Report 15. Department of Anthropology, University of South Florida, Tampa.

Estabrook, Richard W., and J. Raymond Williams

1992   Analysis of Lithic Materials from the Rattlesnake Midden Site (8Hi980), Tampa Bay, Florida. *Florida Anthropologist* 45:39–51.

Fagan, Brian M.

1987   *The Great Journey: The Peopling of Ancient America*. New York: Thames and Hudson.

Fairbanks, Charles H.

1959   Additional Elliott's Point Complex Sites. *Florida Anthropologist* 12:95–100.

1965   Excavations at the Fort Walton Temple Mound, 1960. *Florida Anthropologist* 18: 239–264.

1971   The Apalachicola River Area of Florida. *Southeastern Archaeological Conference Newsletter* 10(2):38–40.

1974   The Kingsley Slave Cabins in Duval County, Florida, 1968. *Conference on Historic Site Archaeology Papers 1972* 7:62–93.

Fairbridge, Rhodes W.

1960   The Changing Level of the Sea. *Scientific American* 202(5): 70.

Farrington, Ian

1985   *Prehistoric Intensive Agriculture in the Tropics, Vols. 1, 2*. British Archaeological Reports, International Series 232. Oxford.

Faught, Michael

1988   Inundated Sites in the Apalachee Bay Area of the Eastern Gulf of Mexico. *Florida Anthropologist* 41:185–190.

Faulkner, Charles H.

1977   The Winter House: An Early Southeast Tradition. *Midcontinental Journal of Archaeology* 2:141–159.

Featherstonhaugh, Thomas
1897   [Untitled.] *American Anthropologist* 10:200.
1899   The Mound-Builders of Central Florida. *Publications of the Southern History Association* 3(1): 1–14.
Felmley, Amy
1990   Osteological Analysis of the Pine Island Site Human Remains. *Florida Anthropologist* 43:262–274.
Ferguson, Vera M.
1951   *Chronology at South Indian Field, Florida.* Yale University Publications in Anthropology 45. New Haven.
Fewkes, Jesse W.
1924   Preliminary Archeological Investigations at Weeden Island, Florida. *Smithsonian Miscellaneous Collections* 76(13) :1–26.
1928   Aboriginal Wooden Objects from Southern Florida. *Smithsonian Miscellaneous Collections* 80(9):1–2.
Fitzgerald, Cherry
1987   Analysis of the Faunal Remains at the Bayonet Field Site (8Ci197), Citrus County, Florida. On file, Zooarchaeology Range, FMNH.
Forry, Samuel
1928   Letters of Samuel Forry, Surgeon U.S. Army, 1937–1938. Part III. *Florida Historical Quarterly* 7:88–105.
Fradkin, Arlene
1976   The Wightman Site: A Study of Prehistoric Culture and Environment on Sanibel Island, Lee County, Florida. Master's thesis, University of Florida, Gainesville.
Fradkin, Arlene, and Jerald T. Milanich
1977   Salvage Excavations at the Law School Mound, Alachua County, Florida. *Florida Anthropologist* 30:166–178.
Fraser, Linda
1980   Faunal Analysis of the Venice Site. *Florida Bureau of Historic Sites and Properties Bulletin* 6:77–80.
Fryman, Frank B., Jr,
1971a   Highway Salvage Archaeology in Florida. *Archives and History News* 2(1) :1–4. Tallahassee: Florida Department of State.
1971b   Tallahassee's Prehistoric Political Center. *Archives and History News* 2(3) :2–4. Tallahassee: Florida Department of State.
Fuller, Richard S.
1985   The Bear Point Phase of the Pensacola Variant: The Protohistoric Period in Southwest Alabama. *Florida Anthropologist* 38:150–155.
Fury, John E., Jr.
1972   The Spanish River Complex: Archaeological Settlement Patterning in Eastern Okeechobee Sub–Area. Master's thesis, Florida Atlantic University, Boca Raton.

Gagel, Katherine

1981   *Archaeological Excavations at Site 8Hi483(B): An Archaic Habitation Site in Hillsborough County, Florida.* Interstate 75 Highway Phase II Archaeological Reports 6. BHSP.

Gardner, William M.

1966   The Waddells Mill Pond Site. *Florida Anthropologist* 19:43–64.

Garrison, Ervan G.

1991   Recent Archaeogeophysical Studies of Paleoshorelines of the Gulf of Mexico. In *Paleoshorelines and Prehistory: An Investigation of Method,* edited by Lucille Lewis Johnson, pp. 103–116. Boca Raton: CRC Press.

Gilliland, Marion S.

1975   *The Material Culture of Key Marco, Florida.* Gainesville: University of Florida Press.

1989   *Key Marco's Buried Treasure: Archaeology and Adventure in the Nineteenth Century.* Gainesville: University of Florida Press/FMNH.

Gluckman, Stephen J., and Christopher S. Peebles

1974   Oven Hill (Di-15), a Refuge Site in the Suwannee River. *Florida Anthropologist* 27:21–30.

Goggin, John M.

1939   A Ceramic Sequence in South Florida. *New Mexico Anthropologist* 3:35–40.

1940   The Distribution of Pottery Wares in the Glades Archaeological Area of South Florida. *New Mexico Anthropologist* 4:22–33.

1947   A Preliminary Definition of Archaeological Areas and Periods in Florida. *American Antiquity* 13:114–127.

1948a   A Revised Temporal Chart of Florida Archeology. *Florida Anthropologist* 1:57–60.

1948b   Some Pottery Types from Central Florida. *Gainesville Anthropological Association, Bulletin 1.*

1949a   Cultural Occupation at Goodland Point, Florida. *Florida Anthropologist* 2(3–4):65–90.

1949b   Cultural Traditions in Florida Prehistory. In *The Florida Indian and His Neighbors,* edited by John W. Griffin, pp. 13–44. Winter Park, Fl.: Rollins College Inter–American Center.

1950a   The Indians and History of the Matecumbe Region. *Tequesta* 10:13–24.

1950b   Stratigraphic Tests in the Everglades National Park. *American Antiquity* 15:228–246.

1951   The Snapper Creek Site. *Florida Anthropologist* 3:50–64.

1952a   Archaeological Notes on Lower Fisheating Creek. *Florida Anthropologist* 4:50–66.

1952b   Archaeological Sites in the Everglades National Park, Florida. *Lab Notes,* Laboratory of Anthropology, University of Florida. Gainesville.

1952c   *Space and Time Perspectives in Northern St. Johns Archeology, Florida.* Yale University Publications in Anthropology 47.

1953   An Introductory Outline of Timucuan Archaeology. *Southeastern Archaeological Conference Newsletter* 3(3) :4–17.

1960   *The Spanish Olive Jar, an Introductory Study.* Yale University Publications in Anthropology 62.

1968   *Spanish Majolica in the New World, Types of the Sixteenth to Eighteenth Centuries.* Yale University Publications in Anthropology 72.

n.d.   The Archeology of the Glades Area, Southern Florida. [Written about 1949, with additions in subsequent years into the 1950s.] Typescript. On file, FMNH.

Goggin, John M., and Frank H. Sommer III

1949   *Excavations on Upper Matecumbe Key, Florida.* Yale University Publications in Anthropology 41.

Goggin, John M., and William C. Sturtevant

1964   The Calusa: A Stratified, Non–Agricultural Society (with notes on sibling marriage). In *Explorations in Cultural Anthropology: Essays in Honor of George Peter Murdock*, edited by W. H. Goodenough. New York: McGraw–Hill.

Goldburt, Jules S.

1966   The Archeology of Shired Island. Master's thesis, University of Florida. Gainesville.

Goodyear, Albert C., and Lyman O. Warren

1972   Further Observations on the Submarine Oyster Shell Deposits of Tampa Bay. *Florida Anthropologist* 25:52–66.

Goodyear, Albert C., Sam B. Upchurch, and Mark J. Brooks

1980   Turtlecrawl Point: An Inundated Early Holocene Archeological Site on the West Coast of Florida. In *Southeastern Geological Society Guidebook* 22, edited by Sam B. Upchurch, pp. 24–33. Tallahassee.

Goodyear, Albert C., Sam B. Upchurch, Mark J. Brooks, and Nancy N. Goodyear

1983   Paleoindian Manifestations in the Tampa Bay Region, Florida. *Florida Anthropologist* 36:40–66.

Griffin, John W.

1946   Historic Artifacts and the "Buzzard Cult" in Florida. *Florida Historical Quarterly* 24:295–301.

1947   Comments on a Site in the St. Marks National Wildlife Refuge, Wakulla County, Florida. *American Antiquity* 13:182–183.

1948a   Green Mound, a Chronological Yardstick. *Florida Naturalist* 22(1): 1–8.

1948b   Toward Chronology in Coastal Volusia County. *Florida Anthropologist* 1:49–56.

1949a   The Historic Archaeology of Florida. In *The Florida Indian and His Neighbors*, edited by John W. Griffin, pp. 45–54. Winter Park, Fla.: Rollins College Inter-American Center.

1949b   Notes on the Archaeology of Useppa Island. *Florida Anthropologist* 2:92–93.

1950   Test Excavations at the Lake Jackson Site. *American Antiquity* 16:99–112.

1951   Madira Bickel Mound State Monument. Reprint. *Florida Highways,* May, n.p.

1974   Archaeology and Environment in South Florida. In *Environments of South Florida: Present and Past,* edited by Patrick J. Gleason, pp. 342–346. Coral Gables: Miami Geological Survey.

1988   *The Archeology of Everglades National Park: A Synthesis.* Contract CX 5000–5–0049. SEAC.

Griffin, John W., ed.

1949   *The Florida Indian and His Neighbors.* Winter Park, Fla.: Rollins College Inter-American Center.

Griffin, John W., and Ripley P. Bullen

1950   *The Safety Harbor Site, Pinellas County, Florida.* Florida Anthropological Society Publications 2. Gainesville.

Griffin, John W., and Hale G. Smith

1948   *The Goodnow Mound, Highlands County, Florida.* Contributions to the Archaeology of Florida 1. Florida Board of Forestry and Parks, Florida Park Service. Tallahassee.

1949   Nocoroco, a Timucuan Village of 1605 Now in Tomoka State Park. *Florida Historical Quarterly* 27:340–361.

1954   *The Cotton Site: An Archaeological Site of Early Ceramic Times in Volusia County, Florida.* Florida State University Studies 16. Tallahassee.

Griffin, John W., Sue B. Richardson, Mary Pohl, Carl D. McMurray, C. Margaret Scarry, Suzanne K. Fish, Elizabeth S. Wing, L. Jill Loucks, and Marcia K. Welch

1985   *Excavations at the Granada Site. Archaeology and History of the Granada Site.* Vol 1. AHRM.

Hale, Stephen H.

1984   Environmental Exploitation around Lake Okeechobee. *Southeastern Archaeology* 3:173–187.

1989   Prehistoric Subsistence Strategies and Settlement Patterns in the Lake Okeechobee Basin of the South Florida Peninsula. Ph.D. diss., University of Florida, Gainesville.

Hann, John H.

1988   *Apalachee: The Land between the Rivers.* Gainesville: University of Florida Press/FMNH.

1990   Summary Guide to Spanish Florida Missions and *Visitas* with Churches in the Sixteenth and Seventeenth Centuries. *Americas* 46:417–513.

1991   *Missions to the Calusa.* Gainesville: University of Florida Press/FMNH.

Hauswirth, William W., Cynthia D. Dickel, Glen H. Doran, Philip J. Laipis, and David N. Dickel

1988   8000-Year-Old Brain Tissue from the Windover Site: Anatomical, Cellular, and Molecular Analysis. In *Human Paleopathology: Current Syntheses and Future Options,* edited by Donald J. Ortner and A.C. Aufderheide, pp. 60–72. Washington, D.C.: Smithsonian Institution Press.

Hemmings, E. Thomas

1975   An Archaeological Survey of the South Prong of the Alafia River, Florida. *Florida Anthropologist* 28:41–51.

1978   Cades Pond Subsistence, Settlement, and Ceremonialism. *Florida Anthropologist* 31:141–150.

Hemmings, E. Thomas, and Kathleen A. Deagan

1973   *Excavations on Amelia Island in Northeast Florida.* Contributions of the Florida State Museum, Anthropology and History 18. Gainesville.

Hemmings, E. Thomas, and Tim A. Kohler

1974   The Lake Kanapaha Site in North Central Florida. *Florida Bureau of Historic Sites and Properties Bulletin* 4: 45–64.

Hoffecker, John F., W. Roger Powers, and Ted Goebel

1993   The Colonization of Beringia and the Peopling of the New World. *Science* 259:46–52.

Holmes, William H.

1903   Aboriginal Pottery of the Eastern United States. *Bureau of American Ethnology Annual Report* 20:1–237.

Hoole, W. Stanley

1974   East Florida in 1834: Letters of Dr. John Durkee. *Florida Historical Quarterly* 52:294–308.

Hoshower, Lisa M.

1992   Bioanthropological Analysis of a Seventeenth-Century Native American–Spanish Mission Population: Biocultural Impacts on the Northern Utina. Ph.D. diss. University of Florida, Gainesville.

Hudson, Charles

1976   *The Southeastern Indians.* Knoxville: University of Tennessee Press.

Hudson, Charles, ed.

1979   *Black Drink, a Native American Tea.* Athens: University of Georgia Press.

Hutchinson, Dale L.

1991   Postcontact Native American Health and Adaptation: Assessing the Impact of Introduced Diseases in Sixteenth-Century Gulf Coast Florida. Ph.D. diss. University of Illinois, Urbana-Champaign.

Hutchinson, Dale L., and Lynette Norr

1991   Corn and Dietary Importance: A View from Gulf Coast Florida.

Paper presented at the 56th Annual Meeting of the Society for American Archaeology, New Orleans.

Isçan, M. Yasar

1983   Skeletal Biology of the Margate–Blount Population. *Florida Anthropologist* 36:154–168.

Jaffee, Howard

1976   Preliminary Report on a Midden Mound and Burial Mound of the Boynton Mound Complex (8PB56). *Florida Anthropologist* 29: 145–152.

Jahn, Otto L., and Ripley P. Bullen

1978   *The Tick Island Site, St. Johns River, Florida.* Florida Anthropological Society Publications 10. Gainesville.

Jenks, A.E., and Mrs. H.H. Simpson, Sr.

1941   Beveled Bone Artifacts in Florida of the Same Type as Artifacts Found near Clovis, New Mexico. *American Antiquity* 6:314–319.

Jennings, Jesse, Gordon Willey, and Marshall Newman

1957   *The Ormond Beach Mound, East Central Florida.* Bureau of American Ethnology Bulletin 164, Anthropological Papers No. 49. Washington, D.C.: Smithsonian Institution.

Jeter, Marvin D.

1977   Late Woodland Chronology and Change in Central Alabama. *Journal of Alabama Archaeology* 23:112–136.

Johnson, G. Michael

1985   Lithic Technology and Social Complexity at a North Florida Weeden Island Period Site. Master's thesis, Washington State University, Pullman.

Johnson, G. Michael, and Timothy A. Kohler

1987   Toward a Better Understanding of North Peninsular Gulf Coast Florida Prehistory: Archaeological Reconnaissance in Dixie County. *Florida Anthropologist* 40:275–286.

Johnson, Kenneth W.

1986   *Archaeological Survey of Contact and Mission Period Sites in Northern Peninsular Florida.* Miscellaneous Project Report 37. DA.

1987   *The Search for Aguacaleyquen and Cali.* Miscellaneous Project Report 33. DA.

1991   The Utina and the Potano Peoples of Northern Florida: Changing Settlement Systems in the Spanish Colonial Period. Ph.D. diss. University of Florida, Gainesville.

Johnson, Kenneth W., and Bruce C. Nelson

1990   The Utina: Seriations and Chronology. *Florida Anthropologist* 43:48–62.

1992   *High Plain Swamps and Flatwoods: Archaeological Survey of Portions of Baker, Columbia, and Union Counties in North Florida.* Miscellaneous Project Report 49. DA.

Johnson, Kenneth W., Bruce C. Nelson, and Keith A. Terry
    1988   *The Search for Early Spanish–Indian Sites in North Florida: Archaeological Survey of Portions of Columbia, Suwannee, Union, and Adjacent Counties, Season II.* Miscellaneous Project Report 38. DA.

Johnson, William G.
    1991   Remote Sensing and Soil Science Applications to Understanding Belle Glade Cultural Adaptations in the Okeechobee Basin. Ph.D. diss. University of Florida, Gainesville.

Jones, B. Calvin
    1982   Southern Cult Manifestations at the Lake Jackson Site, Leon County, Florida: Salvage Excavation of Mound 3. *Midcontinental Journal of Archaeology* 7:3–44.

Jones, B. Calvin, and John T. Penman
    1973   Winewood: An Inland Ft. Walton Site in Tallahassee, Florida. *Florida Bureau of Historic Sites and Properties Bulletin* 3: 65–90.

Jones, Paul L., and Nina T. Borremans
    1991   An Archaeological Survey of the Gulf Hammock, Florida. Report of investigations submitted to HR.

Jordan, Douglas F., Elizabeth E. Wing, and Adelaide K. Bullen
    1963   *Papers on the Jungerman and Goodman Sites, Florida.* Contributions of the Florida State Museum, Social Sciences 10. Gainesville.

Kelly, Arthur R.
    n.d.   [1953] *A Weeden Island Burial Mound in Decatur County, Georgia, and Related Rites on the Lower Flint River.* Report 1. Laboratory of Archaeology Series. Report 1. University of Georgia, Athens.

Kennedy, William J.
    1978   A Cultural Resource Reconnaissance of the J. N. "Ding" Darling National Wildlife Refuge, Sanibel, Florida. Manuscript. On file, SEAC.

Kenworthy, Charles J.
    1883   Ancient Canals in Florida. *Annual Report of the Smithsonian Institution* 1881:631–635.

Knight, Vernon J., Jr.
    1984   Late Prehistoric Adaptation in the Mobile Bay Region. In *Perspectives on Gulf Coast Prehistory,* edited by David D. Davis, pp. 198–215. Gainesville: University of Florida Press/FMNH.

Knoderer, C.F.
    1972   The Duda Ranch Shell Mound, Brevard County, Florida. *Florida Anthropologist* 25:101–106.

Kohler, Timothy A.
    1975   The Garden Patch Site: A Minor Weeden Island Ceremonial Center on the North Peninsular Florida Gulf Coast. Master's thesis, University of Florida, Gainesville.

1978   The Social and Chronological Dimensions of Village Occupation at a North Florida Weeden Island Period Site. Ph.D. diss. University of Florida, Gainesville.

1979   Corn, Indians, and Spaniards in North-central Florida: A Technique for Measuring Evolutionary Changes in Corn. *Florida Anthropologist* 32:1–17.

1980   The Social Dimensions of Village Occupation of the McKeithen Site, North Florida. *Southeastern Archaeological Conference Bulletin* 22:5–10.

1991   The Demise of Weeden Island, and Post–Weeden Island Cultural Stability in Non-Mississippianized Northern Florida. In *Stability, Transformation, and Variations: The Late Woodland Southeast*, edited by M. S. Nassaney and C. R. Cobb, pp. 91–110. New York: Plenum.

Kohler, Timothy A., and G. Michael Johnson

1986   Dixie County Archaeological Reconnaissance, Winter 1985–86. Report submitted to HR.

Kozuch, Laura

1986   An Overview of Faunal Lists from Selected Safety Harbor Sites. On file, Zooarchaeology Range, FMNH.

1991   The Everglades Region, A.D. 1 to Contact. In *Florida's Comprehensive Historic Preservation Plan* (draft, 18 March 1991), pp. 119–126. HR.

1993   *Sharks and Shark Products in Prehistoric South Florida.* Institute of Archaeology and Paleoenvironmental Studies, Monograph 2, DA.

LaFond, Arthur A.

1972   A Unique Zoomorphic Effigy from the Queen Mound, Jacksonville, Florida. *Florida Anthropologist* 25:81–86.

1983   The Queen Mound, Jacksonville, Florida. Manuscript. On file, Anthropology Range, FMNH.

Larson, Lewis H.

1958   Cultural Relationships between the Northern St. Johns Area and the Georgia Coast. *Florida Anthropologist* 11:11–21.

Laudonnière, René de

1975   *Three Voyages.* Translated by C. Bennett. Gainesville: University of Florida Press.

Lawlor, David A., Cynthia D. Dickel, William W. Hauswirth, and Peter Parham

1991   Ancient *HLA* from 7,500-Year-Old Archeological Remains. *Nature* 349 (February 28): 785–787.

Laxson, Dan D.

1970   Seven Saw Grass Middens in Dade and Broward Counties. *Florida Anthropologist* 23:151–158.

Lazarus, William C.

1958   A Poverty Point Complex in Florida. *Florida Anthropologist* 11:23–32.

1961   Ten Middens on the Navy Live Oak Reservation. *Florida Anthropologist* 14:49–64.

1965   Effects of Land Subsidence and Sea Level Changes on Elevation of Archaeological Sites on the Florida Gulf Coast. *Florida Anthropologist* 18:49–58.

1971   The Fort Walton Culture West of the Apalachicola River. *Southeastern Archaeological Conference Newsletter* 10(2) :40–48.

Lazarus, Yulee W.

1979   *The Buck Burial Mound, a Mound of the Weeden Island Culture.* Fort Walton Beach, Fla.: Temple Mound Museum.

Lazarus, Yulee W., and Robert J. Fornano

1975   Fort Walton Temple Mound, Further Test Excavations, DePaux 1973. *Florida Anthropologist* 28:159–177

Lazarus, Yulee W., and Carolyn B. Hawkins

1976   *Pottery of the Fort Walton Period.* Fort Walton Beach, Fla.: Temple Mound Museum.

Lazarus, Yulee W., William C. Lazarus, and Donald W. Sharon

1967   The Navy Live Oak Reservation Cemetery Site (8SR36). *Florida Anthropologist* 20:103.

Lee, Arthur R., and John Beriault (with Walter Buschelamn and Jean Belknap)

1993   A Small Site—Mulberry Midden, 8Cr697—Contributes to Knowledge of Transitional Period. *Florida Anthropologist* 46:43–52.

Lee, Chung Ho, Irvy R. Quitmyer, Christopher T. Espenshade, and Robert E. Johnson

1984   *Estuarine Adaptations during the Late Prehistoric Period: Archaeology of Two Shell Midden Sites on the St. Johns River.* Report of Investigations 5. UWFCA.

Little, Keith J., Caleb Curren, and Lee McKenzie

1988   *A Preliminary Archaeological Survey of the Blackwater Drainage, Santa Rosa County, Florida.* Report of Investigations 13. Institute of West Florida Archaeology, University of West Florida.

Little, Keith J., Caleb Curren, Lee McKenzie, and Janet Lloyd

1988   *A Preliminary Archaeological Survey of the Perdido Drainage, Baldwin and Escambia Counties, Alabama* Technical Report 2. Alabama-Tombigbee Regional Commission.

Lorant, Stefan

1946   *The New World: The First Pictures of America.* New York: Duell, Sloan & Pearce.

Loucks, L. Jill

1976   Early Alachua Tradition Burial Ceremonialism: The Henderson Mound, Alachua County, Florida. Master's thesis, University of Florida, Gainesville.

1978   Suwannee County Survey Report, Fall 1977: An Account of Sites on Property Owned by Owens-Illinois, Inc. Manuscript. On file, DA.

Luer, George M.

1977a   Excavations at the Old Oak Site, Sarasota, Florida: A Late Weeden Island–Safety Harbor Period Site. *Florida Anthropologist* 30:37–55.

1977b   The Roberts Bay Site, Sarasota, Florida. *Florida Anthropologist* 30:121–133.

1980   The Aqui Esta Site at Charlotte Harbor: A Safety Harbor–Influenced Prehistoric Site. Paper presented at the 32d Annual Meeting of the Florida Anthropological Society, Winter Park.

1985   An Update on Some Ceremonial Tablets. *Florida Anthropologist* 38:273–274, 281.

1989   Calusa Canals in Southwestern Florida: Routes of Tribute and Exchange. *Florida Anthropologist* 42:89–130.

1992a   Mississippian-Period Pop-Eyed Bird-Head Effigies from West-Central and Southern Florida. *Florida Anthropologist* 45:52–62.

1992b   The Boylston Mound: A Safety Harbor Period Shell Midden; with Notes on the Paleoenvironment of Southern Sarasota Bay. *Florida Anthropologist* 45:266–279.

Luer, George M., ed.

1986   *Shells and Archaeology in Southern Florida.* Florida Anthropological Society Publications No. 12. Tallahassee.

Luer, George M., and Marion M. Almy

1979   Three Aboriginal Shell Middens on Longboat Key, Florida: Manasota Period Sites of Barrier Island Exploitation. *Florida Anthropologist* 32:33–45.

1980   The Development of Some Aboriginal Pottery of the Central Gulf Coast of Florida. *Florida Anthropologist* 33:207–225.

1981   Temple Mounds of the Tampa Bay Area. *Florida Anthropologist* 34:127–155.

1982   A Definition of the Manasota Culture. *Florida Anthropologist* 35:34–58.

1987   The Laurel Mound (8So98) and Radial Burials with Comments on the Safety Harbor Period. *Florida Anthropologist* 40:301–320.

Luer, George M., Marion M. Almy, Dana Ste. Claire, and Robert Austin

1987   The Myakkahatchee Site (8So397), A Large Multi-Period Inland from the Shore Site in Sarasota County, Florida. *Florida Anthropologist* 40:137–153.

Maples, William R.

1987   *Analysis of Skeletal Remains Recovered at the Gauthier Site, Brevard County, Florida.* Miscellaneous Project Report 31. DA.

Marquardt, William H.

1984   *The Josslyn Island Mound and Its Role in the Investigation of Southwest Florida's Past.* Miscellaneous Project Report 22. DA.

1992a   Calusa Culture and Environment: What Have We Learned? In *Culture and Environment in the Domain of the Calusa,* edited by

William M. Marquardt, pp. 423–436. Institute of Archaeology and Paleoenvironmental Studies, Monograph 1.DA.

1992b   Shell Artifacts from the Caloosahatchee Area. In *Culture and Environment in the Domain of the Calusa,* edited by William M. Marquardt, pp. 191–228. Institute of Archaeology and Paleoenvironmental Studies, Monograph 1. DA.

Marquardt, William H., ed.

1992   *Culture and Environment in the Domain of the Calusa.* Institute of Archaeology and Paleoenvironmental Studies, Monograph 1. DA.

Marrinan, Rochelle A.

1985   The Archaeology of the Spanish Missions of Florida: 1565–1704. In *Indians, Colonists, and Slaves: Essays in Memory of Charles H. Fairbanks,* edited by K. W. Johnson, J. M. Leader, and R. C. Wilson, pp. 241–252. *Florida Journal of Anthropology Special Publication* 4. Gainesville.

Martin, Robert A., and S. David Webb

1974   Late Pleistocene Mammals from the Devil's Den Fauna, Levy County. In *Pleistocene Mammals of Florida,* edited by S. David Webb, pp. 114–145. Gainesville: University of Florida Press.

Masson, Marilyn A., and C. Margaret Scarry

n.d.   Carbonized Seeds and Corn Cobs from the Honey Hill Site (8Da411): A Diachronic Glimpse of Plant Use in Everglades Subsistence. In *Historical and Archaeological Investigations at the Honey Hill Site, Dade County, Florida,* by Robert Carr, A. Felmley, and Patsy West. Report 25, Archaeological and Historical Conservancy. Miami. [In preparation; report prepared in 1991.]

McCane-O'Conner, Mallory

1979   *A Comparative Study of Design Motifs Found on Weeden Island and Fort Walton Ceramics.* Fort Walton Beach, Fla.: Temple Mound Museum.

McEwan, Bonnie, ed.

1991   The Missions of Spanish Florida [Special Issue]. *Florida Anthropologist* 44:104–330.

McGoun, William E.

1981   Medals of Conquest in Calusa Florida. Master's thesis, Florida Atlantic University, Boca Raton.

McMichael, Alan E.

1982   A Cultural Resource Assessment of Horr's Island, Collier County, Florida. Master's thesis, University of Florida, Gainesville.

Meadows, Richard, and Nancy M. White

1992   Sam's Creek Cutoff Shell Mound, an Oyster Midden in the Lower Apalachicola Valley, Estuarine Wetlands of Northwest Florida. Paper presented at the 44th Annual Meeting of the Florida Anthropological Society, St. Augustine.

Mikell, Gregory A.

1990   The Sheephead Bayou Site (8By150): A Single Component Fort Walton Hamlet Site in Northwest Florida. *Florida Anthropologist* 43:198–208.

1993   The Little's Bayou West Site: Evidence of the Late Weeden Island-Fort Walton Transition in Northwest Florida. *Florida Anthropologist* 46:12–19.

Milanich, Jerald T.

1968   Excavations on the Fort Center Great Circle Ditches, Glades County, Florida. Paper presented at the 20th Annual Meeting of the Florida Anthropological Society, Crystal River.

1971   *The Alachua Tradition of North-central Florida.* Contributions of the Florida State Museum, Anthropology and History 17. Gainesville.

1972   Excavations at the Richardson Site, Alachua County, Florida: An Early 17th-Century Potano Indian Village (with Notes on Potano Culture Change). *Florida Bureau of Historic Sites and Properties Bulletin* 2: 35–61.

1973   The Southeastern Deptford Culture: A Preliminary Definition. *Florida Bureau of Historic Sites and Properties, Bulletin 3*: 51–63.

1974   Life in a 9th Century Indian Household, a Weeden Island Fall-Winter Site on the Upper Apalachicola River, Florida. *Florida Bureau of Historic Sites and Properties Bulletin* 4: 1–44.

1978   Two Cades Pond Sites in North-central Florida: The Occupational Nexus as a Model of Settlement. *Florida Anthropologist* 31:151–173.

1980   Coastal Georgia Deptford Culture: Growth of a Concept. In *Excursions in Southeastern Geology: The Archaeology-Geology of the Georgia Coast*, edited by James D. Howard, Chester B. DePratter, and R. W. Frey, pp. 170–178. Guidebook 20, 1980 Annual Meeting of the Geological Society of America.

Milanich, Jerald T., and Charles H. Fairbanks

1980   *Florida Archaeology.* New York: Academic Press.

Milanich, Jerald T., and Charles Hudson

1993   *Hernando de Soto and the Indians of Florida.* Gainesville: University Press of Florida/FMNH.

Milanich, Jerald T., and Donna L. Ruhl

1986   *Fort Center and the Belle Glade Culture, Florida.* Weston Conn.: Pictures of Record.

Milanich, Jerald T., and William C. Sturtevant

1972   *Francisco Pareja's 1613* Confessionario: *A Documentary Source for Timucuan Ethnography.* Tallahassee: Florida Department of State.

Milanich, Jerald T., Jefferson Chapman, Ann S. Cordell, Stephen Hale, and Rochelle A. Marrinan

1984   Prehistoric Development of Calusa Society in Southwest Florida: Excavations on Useppa Island. In *Perspectives on Gulf Coast Prehis-*

tory, edited by David D. Davis, pp. 258–314. Gainesville: University of Florida Press/ FMNH.

Milanich, Jerald T., Ann S. Cordell, Vernon J. Knight, Jr., Timothy A. Kohler, and Brenda J. Sigler-Lavelle

1984   *McKeithen Weeden Island: The Culture of Northern Florida, A.D. 200-900.* Orlando: Academic Press.

Milanich, Jerald T., Carlos A. Martinez, Karl T. Steinen, and Ronald L. Wallace

1976   Georgia Origins of the Alachua Tradition. *Florida Bureau of Historic Sites and Properties Bulletin* 5: 47–56.

Miller, James J.

1980   Coquina Middens on the Florida East Coast. *Florida Anthropologist* 32:2–16.

1991   The Fairest, Frutefullest and Pleasantest of all the World: An Environmental History of the Northeast Part of Florida. Ph.D. diss., University of Pennsylvania, Philadelphia.

1992   Effects of Environmental Changes on Later Archaic People of Northeast Florida. *Florida Anthropologist* 45:100–106.

Mitchem, Jeffrey M.

1986   Comments on Some Ceramic Pastes of the Central Peninsular Gulf Coast. *Florida Anthropologist* 39:68–74.

1988   Some Alternative Interpretations of Safety Harbor Burial Mounds. *Florida Scientist* 51:100–107.

1989   Redefining Safety Harbor: Late Prehistoric/ Protohistoric Archaeology in West Peninsular Florida. Ph.D. diss., University of Florida, Gainesville.

1990   The Contribution of Nels C. Nelson to Florida Archaeology. *Florida Anthropologist* 43:156–163.

1991   The Safety Harbor Culture. *In Florida's Comprehensive Historic Preservation Plan* (draft, 18 March, 1991), pp. 140–147. HR.

Mitchem, Jeffrey M., and Brent R. Weisman

1987   Changing Settlement Patterns and Pottery Types in the Withlacoochee Cove. *Florida Anthropologist* 40:154–166.

Moore, Clarence B.

1892–   Certain Shell Heaps of the St. John's River, Florida, hitherto Un-
1894   explored. Reprint. *American Naturalist,* November 1892, pp. 912–922; January 1893, pp. 8–13; February 1893, pp. 113–117; July 1893, pp. 605–624; August 1893, pp. 709–733; January 1894, pp. 15–26.

1894a   Certain Sand Mounds of the St. John's River, Florida, Part I. *Journal of the Academy of Natural Sciences of Philadelphia* 10:5–128.

1894b   Certain Sand Mounds of the St. John's River, Florida, Part II. *Journal of the Academy of Natural Sciences of Philadelphia* 10:129–246.

1896a   Certain River Mounds of Duval County, Florida. *Journal of the Academy of Natural Sciences of Philadelphia* 10:448–502.

1896b   Two Sand Mounds on Murphy Island, Florida. *Journal of the Academy of Natural Sciences of Philadelphia* 10:503–517.

1896c   Certain Sand Mounds of the Ocklawaha River, Florida. *Journal of the Academy of Natural Sciences of Philadelphia* 10:518–543.

1900   Certain Antiquities of the Florida West Coast. *Journal of the Academy of Natural Sciences of Philadelphia* 11:349–394.

1901   Certain Aboriginal Remains of the Northwest Florida Coast, Part I. *Journal of the Academy of Natural Sciences of Philadelphia* 11:419–497.

1902   Certain Aboriginal Remains of the Northwest Florida Coast, Part II. *Journal of the Academy of Natural Sciences of Philadelphia* 12:127–358.

1903a   Certain Aboriginal Mounds of the Apalachicola River. *Journal of the Academy of Natural Sciences of Philadelphia* 12:439–492.

1903b   Certain Aboriginal Mounds of the Florida Central West Coast. *Journal of the Academy of Natural Sciences of Philadelphia* 12:361–439.

1905   Miscellaneous Investigations in Florida. *Journal of the Academy of Natural Sciences of Philadelphia* 13:298–325.

1907   Crystal River Revisited. *Journal of the Academy of Natural Sciences of Philadelphia* 13:406–425.

1918   The Northwestern Florida Coast Revisited. *Journal of the Academy of Natural Sciences of Philadelphia* 16:513–581.

Morlot, A. von

1861   General Views of Anthropology. *Annual Report of the Smithsonian Institution,* 1860, pp. 284–343.

Murphy, Larry E.

1990   *8SL17: Natural Site-Formation Processes of a Multiple Component Underwater Site in Florida.* Southwest Cultural Resources Center Professional Papers No. 39, National Park Service, Santa Fe, New Mexico.

Nance, C. Roger

1976   *The Archaeological Sequence at Durant Bend, Dallas County, Alabama.* Special Publications of the Alabama Archaeological Society 2. Orange Beach, Alabama.

Neill, Wilfred T.

1958   A Stratified Early Site at Silver Springs, Florida. *Florida Anthropologist* 11:33–48.

1964   Trilisa Pond, an Early Site in Marion County, Florida. *Florida Anthropologist* 17:187–200.

1971   A Florida Paleoindian Implement of Ground Stone. *Florida Anthropologist* 24:61–70.

Nelson, Nels C.

1918   Chronology in Florida. *American Museum of Natural History Anthropological Papers* 22 (2) :75–103.

Neuman, Robert W.
1961   Domesticated Corn from a Fort Walton Mound Site in Houston County, Alabama. *Florida Anthropologist* 14:75–80.

Newman, Christine L.
1993   The Cheetum Site: An Archaic Burial Site in Dade County, Florida. *Florida Anthropologist* 46:37–42.

Newman, Christine L., and Brent R. Weisman
1992   Prehistoric and Historic Settlement in the Guana Tract, St. Johns County, Florida. *Florida Anthropologist* 45:162–171.

Newsom, Lee A.
1986   Plants, Human Subsistence, and Environment: A Case Study from Hontoon Island (8Vo202), Florida. Master's thesis, University of Florida, Gainesville.

1987   Analysis of Botanical Remains from Hontoon Island (8VO202), Florida: 1980–1985 Excavations. *Florida Anthropologist* 40:47–84.

Newsom, Lee A., and Barbara A. Purdy
1990   Florida Canoes: A Maritime Heritage from the Past. *Florida Anthropologist* 43:164–180.

Newsom, Lee A., S. David Webb, and James S. Dunbar
1992   History and Geographic Distribution of *Cucurbita pepo* Gourds in Florida. Manuscript. On file, Environmental Archaeology Laboratory, FMNH.

Padgett, Thomas J.
1976   Hinderland Exploitation in the Central Gulf Coast–Manatee Region during the Safety Harbor Period. *Florida Anthropologist* 29:39–48.

Parsons, J.J., and W.D. Denevan
1967   Precolumbian Ridged Fields. *Scientific American* 217:93–100.

Payne, Claudine
1981   A Preliminary Investigation of Fort Walton Settlement Patterns in the Tallahassee Red Hills. *Southeastern Archaeological Conference Bulletin* 24:29–31.

1982   Farmsteads and Districts: A Model of Fort Walton Settlement Patterns in the Tallahassee Hills. Paper presented at the 39th Southeastern Archaeological Conference, Memphis.

1991a   Fort Walton Culture. In *Florida's Comprehensive Historic Preservation Plan* (draft,18 March 1991), pp. 133–139. HR.

1991b   The Pensacola Culture. In *Florida's Comprehensive Historic Preservation Plan* (draft, 18 March 1991), pp. 127–132. HR.

1994   Mississippian Capitals: An Archaeological Investigation of Precolumbian Political Structure. Ph.D. diss., University of Florida, Gainesville. In preparation.

Penton, Daniel T.
  1970   Excavations in the Early Swift Creek Component at Bird Ham-
          mock (8–Wa–30). Master's thesis, Florida State University, Talla-
          hassee.

Percy, George W.
  1971a   Current Research: Florida. *Southeastern Archaeological Conference
          Newsletter* 15(1):7–8.
  1971b   Preliminary report to the Division of Recreation and Parks,
          Department of Natural Resources, State of Florida, on Archaeo-
          logical Work in the Torreya State Park during the Year of 1971 by
          the Department of Anthropology at Florida State University. Man-
          uscript. On file, Florida Department of Natural Resources, Talla-
          hassee.
  1974   A Review of Evidence for Prehistoric Indian Use of Animals in
          Northwest Florida. *Florida Bureau of Historic Sites and Properties Bul-
          letin* 4:65–93.

Percy, George W., and David S. Brose
  1974   Weeden Island Ecology, Subsistence, and Village Life in North-
          west Florida. Paper presented at the 39th Annual Meeting of the
          Society for American Archaeology, Washington, D.C.

Percy, George W., and M. Katherine Jones
  1976   An Archaeological Survey of Upland Locales in Gadsden and Lib-
          erty Counties, Florida. *Florida Anthropologist* 29:105–125.

Phelps, David S.
  1965   The Norwood Series of Fiber–tempered Ceramics. *Southeastern
          Archaeological Conference Bulletin* 2:65–69.
  1969   Swift Creek and Santa Rosa in Northwest Florida. *Institute of Arche-
          ology and Anthropology, University of South Carolina, Notebook* 1(6–9)
          :14–24.

Phillips, John C.
  1989   Hickory Ridge: A Mississippian Cemetery in Northwest Florida.
          Paper presented at the 46th Southeastern Archaeological Confer-
          ence, Tampa.
  1992   Bernath Place (8SR986), A Santa Rosa–Swift Creek Site on
          Mulatto Bayou in Northwest Florida. Paper presented at the 49th
          Southeastern Archaeological Conference, Little Rock.

Potter, Alden L., and Allen R. Taylor
  1937   A Summary of Reports Dealing with the Archaeology of the Ocala
          National Forest and Vicinity—Florida. With Map. Co. 1420,
          C.C.C., Fla. F-5, Ocala, Florida. Mimeo. On file, DA.

Purdy, Barbara A.
  1971   Investigation Concerning the Thermal Alteration of Silica Min-
          erals: An Archaeological Approach. Ph.D. diss. University of
          Florida, Gainesville.

| 1973 | The Temporal and Spatial Distribution of Bone Points in the State of Florida. *Florida Anthropologist* 26:143–152. |

1973   The Temporal and Spatial Distribution of Bone Points in the State of Florida. *Florida Anthropologist* 26:143–152.

1975   The Senator Edwards Chipped Stone Workshop Site (Mr-122), Marion County, Florida: A Preliminary Report of Investigations. *Florida Anthropologist* 28:178–189.

1981   *Florida's Prehistoric Stone Tool Technology.* Gainesville: University of Florida Press.

1987a   Hontoon Island, Florida (8Vo202) Artifacts. *Florida Anthropologist* 40:27–39.

1987b   Investigations at Hontoon Island (8Vo202), An Archaeological Wetsite in Volusia County, Florida. *Florida Anthropologist* 40:4–12.

1991   *The Art and Archaeology of Florida's Wetlands.* Boca Raton, Fla.: CRC Press.

Purdy, Barbara A., ed.

1988   *Wet Site Archaeology.* Caldwell, N.J.: Telford.

Purdy, Barbara A., and Laurie M. Beach

1980   The Chipped Stone Tool Industry of Florida's Preceramic Archaic. *Archaeology of Eastern North America* 8:105–124.

Reiger, John F.

1981   An Analysis of Four Types of Shell Artifacts from South Florida. *Florida Anthropologist* 34:4–20.

1990   "Plummets"—An Analysis of a Mysterious Florida Artifact. *Florida Anthropologist* 43:227–239.

Rouse, Irving

1951   *A Survey of Indian River Archeology, Florida.* Yale University Publications in Anthropology 44.

Royal, William D., and E. Clark

1960   Natural Preservation of Human Brain, Warm Springs, Florida. *American Antiquity* 26:285–287.

Ruppé, Reynold J.

1980   The Archaeology of Drowned Terrestrial Sites: A Preliminary Report. *Florida Bureau of Historic Sites and Properties Bulletin* 6:35–45.

Russo, Michael

1985   *Zaremba: A Short-term Use Malabar II Site.* Miscellaneous Project Report 25. DA.

1986   The Coevolution of Environment and Human Exploitation of Faunal Resources in the Upper St. Johns River Basin. Master's thesis, University of Florida, Gainesville.

1988   Excavations at the Palm Bay Development, Brevard County, Florida: Subsistence and Settlement Pattern. Report submitted to General Development Corporation, Inc. On file, HR.

1991   Archaic Sedentism on the Florida Coast: A Case Study from Horr's Island. Ph.D. diss. University of Florida, Gainesville.

1992a   Chronologies and Cultures of the St. Marys Region of Northeast Florida and Southeast Georgia. *Florida Anthropologist* 45:107–126.

1992b   Subsistence, Seasonality, and Settlement at Futch Cove. Report submitted to Florida Archaeological Services, Inc. On file, HR.

Russo, Michael, Ann S. Cordell, and Donna L. Ruhl

1992   *The Timucuan Ecological and Historic Preserve, Phase III Final Report.* SEAC.

Russo, Michael, Ann S. Cordell, Lee A. Newsom, and Robert Austin

1989   Phase III Archaeological Excavations at Edgewater Landing, Volusia County, Florida. Report submitted to Radnor/Edgewater Landing, Inc., by Piper Archaeological Research, Inc. St. Petersburg.

Russo, Michael, Ann S. Cordell, Lee A. Newsom, and Sylvia Scudder

1991   *Final Report on Horr's Island: The Archaeology of Archaic and Glades Settlement and Subsistence Patterns.* Part II. *Glades, Ceramics, Archaeobotanical, and Soils Analysis, Plus Appendices and References from Horr's Island.* Submitted to Key Marco Developments, Marco Island, Florida. On file, DA.

Russo, Michael, Barbara A. Purdy, Lee A. Newsom, and Ray M. McGee

1992   A Reinterpretation of Late Archaic Adaptations in Central-East Florida: Groves' Orange Midden (8Vo2601). *Southeastern Archaeology* 11:95–108.

Ste. Claire, Dana

1990   The Archaic in East Florida: Archaeological Evidence from Early Coastal Adaptations. *Florida Anthropologist* 43:189–197.

Saunders, Lorraine P.

1972   Osteology of the Republic Grove Site. Master's thesis, Florida Atlantic University, Boca Raton.

Saunders, Rebecca

1987   *Excavations at 8Na41: Two Mission Period Sites on Amelia Island, Florida.* Miscellaneous Project Report 35. DA.

Saunders, Rebecca, Thomas DesJean, and Karen Jo Walker

1985   Descriptive Archaeology of the Kings Bay Site (9Cam171). In *Aboriginal Subsistence and Settlement Archaeology of the Kings Bay Locality,* Vol. 1, edited by William H. Adams, pp. 169–293. Reports of Investigations 1. DA.

Scarry, C. Margaret, and Lee A. Newsom

1992   Archaeobotanical Research in the Calusa Heartland. In *Culture and Environment in the Domain of the Calusa,* edited by William H. Marquardt, pp. 375–402. Institute of Archaeology and Paleoenvironmental Studies, Monograph 1. DA.

Scarry, John

1980   The Chronology of Fort Walton Development in the Upper Apalachicola Valley, Florida. *Southeastern Archaeological Conference Bulletin* 22:38–45.

1981a   Fort Walton Culture: A Redefinition. *Southeastern Archaeological Conference Bulletin* 24:18–21.

1981b   Subsistence Costs and Information: A Preliminary Model of Fort Walton Development. *Southeastern Archaeological Conference Bulletin* 24:31–32.

1984   Fort Walton Development: Mississippian Chiefdoms in the Lower Southeast. Ph.D. diss., Case Western Reserve University, Cleveland.

1985   A Proposed Revision of the Fort Walton Ceramic Typology: A Type-Variety System. *Florida Anthropologist* 38:199–233.

1989   Beyond Apalachee Province: Assessing the Evidence for Early European–Indian Contact in West Florida. Paper presented at the 54th Annual Meeting of the Society for American Archaeology, Atlanta.

1990a   Mississippian Emergence in the Fort Walton Area: The Evolution of the Cayson and Lake Jackson Phases. In *Mississippian Emergence: The Evolution of Ranked Agricultural Societies in Eastern North America,* edited by B. D. Smith, pp. 227–250. Washington, D.C.: Smithsonian Institution Press.

1990b   The Rise, Transformation, and Fall of Apalachee: A Case Study of Political Change in a Chiefly Society. In *Lamar Archaeology: Mississippian Chiefdoms in the Deep South,* edited by Mark Williams and Gary Shapiro, pp. 175–186. Tuscaloosa: University of Alabama Press.

Scarry, John, and Claudine Payne

1986   Mississippian Polities in the Fort Walton Area: A Model Generated from the Renfrew-Level XTENT Algorithm. *Southeastern Archaeology* 5:79–90.

Schoolcraft, Henry R.

1854   Antique Pottery from the Minor Mounds Occupied by the Indians in Feasts to the Dead, on the Seacoast of Florida and Georgia. In *Historical and Statistical Information Respecting the History, Conditions, and Prospects of the Indian Tribes of the United States,* vol.3, pp. 75–82. Philadelphia: Lippincott, Grambo.

Sears, Elsie O'R., and William H. Sears

1976   Preliminary Report on Prehistoric Corn Pollen from Fort Center, Florida. *Southeastern Archaeological Conference Bulletin* 19:53–56.

Sears, William H.

1956a   *Excavations at Kolomoki, Final Report.* University of Georgia Series in Anthropology 5. Athens.

1956b   Melton Mound Number 3. *Florida Anthropologist* 9:87–100.

1957   *Excavations on Lower St. Johns River, Florida.* Contributions of the Florida State Museum, Social Sciences 2. Gainesville.

1958   The Maximo Point Site. *Florida Anthropologist* 11:1–10.

1960   *The Bayshore Homes Site, St. Petersburg, Florida.* Contributions of the Florida State Museum, Social Sciences 6. Gainesville.

1962   Hopewellian Affiliations of Certain Sites on the Gulf Coast of Florida. *American Antiquity* 28:5–18.

1963   *The Tucker Site on Alligator Harbor, Franklin County, Florida.* Contributions of the Florida State Museum, Social Sciences 9. Gainesville.

1967a   Archaeological Survey in the Cape Coral Area at the Mouth of the Caloosahatchee River. *Florida Anthropologist* 20:93–102.

1967b   The Tierra Verde Burial Mound. *Florida Anthropologist* 20:25–73.

1971a   Food Production and Village Life in Prehistoric Southeastern United States. *Archaeology* 24:93–102.

1971b   The Weeden Island Site, St. Petersburg, Florida. *Florida Anthropologist* 24:51–60.

1973   The Sacred and the Secular in Prehistoric Ceramics. In *Variation in Anthropology: Essays in Honor of John McGregor,* edited by D. Lathrop and J. Douglas, pp. 31–42. Urbana: Illinois Archaeological Survey.

1974   Archaeological Perspectives on Prehistoric Environment in the Okeechobee Basin Savannah. In *Environments in South Florida: Present and Past,* edited by Patrick J. Gleason, pp. 347–351. Coral Gables: Miami Geological Society.

1977a   Prehistoric Culture Area and Culture Change on the Gulf Coastal Plain. In *For the Director: Research Essays in Honor of James B. Griffin,* edited by Charles E. Cleland, pp. 152–184. Anthropological Papers 61. Ann Arbor: Museum of Anthropology, University of Michigan.

1977b   Seaborne Contacts between Early Cultures in Lower Southeastern United States and Middle through South America. In *The Sea in the Pre-columbian World,* edited by Elizabeth P. Benson, pp. 1–13. Washington, D.C.: Dumbarton Oaks Research Library and Collections.

1982   *Fort Center: An Archeological Site in the Lake Okeechobee Basin.* Gainesville: University of Florida Press/FMNH.

1992   *Mea Culpa. Southeastern Archaeology* 11:66–71.

Shannon, George, Jr.

1986   The Southeastern Fiber–tempered Ceramic Tradition Reconsidered. In *Papers in Ceramic Analysis,* edited by P. M. Rice, pp. 47–80. Ceramic Notes No. 3. Occasional Publications of the Ceramic Technology Laboratory, Gainesville: Florida State Museum.

Siemens, Alfred H., and Dennis E. Puleston

1972   Ridged Fields and Associated Features in Southern Campeche: New Perspectives on the Lowland Maya. *American Antiquity* 37:228–239.

Sigler-Eisenberg, Brenda, and Michael Russo

1986   Seasonality and Function of Small Sites on Florida's Central–East Coast. *Southeastern Archaeology* 5:21–31.

Sigler-Eisenberg, Brenda, Ann Cordell, Richard Estabrook, Elizabeth Horvath, Lee A. Newsom, and Michael Russo

1985   *Archaeological Site Types, Distribution, and Preservation within the Upper St. Johns River Basin, Florida.* Miscellaneous Project Report 27.DA.

Sigler-Lavelle, Brenda J.

1980a   On the Non-random Distribution of Weeden Island Period Sites in North Florida. *Southeastern Archaeological Conference Bulletin* 22: 22–29.

1980b   The Political and Economic Implications of the Distribution of Weeden Island Period Sites in North Florida. Ph.D. diss., New School for Social Research, New York City.

Simons, M.H.

1884   Shell Heaps of Charlotte Harbor, Florida. *Smithsonian Institution Annual Report* 1882, pp. 794–796.

Simpson, J. Clarence

1948   Folsom-like Points from Florida. *Florida Anthropologist* 1:11–15.

Simpson, Mrs. H.H., Sr.

1935   Mementoes of the Past—In Florida. *Hobbies* 40(4) :93–94.

Smith, Bruce

1986   The Archaeology of the Southeastern United States: From Dalton to de Soto, 10,500–500 B.P. *Advances in World Archaeology* 5:1–92.

Bruce, Robin L., Chad O. Braley, Nina T. Borremans, and Elizabeth J. Reitz

1981   Coastal Adaptions in Southwest Georgia: Ten Archaeological Sites at Kings Bay. Final Report on Secondary Testing at Kings Bay, Camden County, Georgia. On file, DA.

Smith, Samuel D.

1971a   A Reinterpretation of the Cades Pond Archeological Period. Unpublished M.A. thesis, Department of Anthropology, University of Florida. Gainesville.

1971b   Excavations at the Hope Mound with an Addendum to the Safford Mound Report. *Florida Anthropologist* 24:107–134.

Snow, Frankie

1978   *An Archeological Survey of the Ocmulgee Big Bend Region.* Occasional Papers from South Georgia, Number 3. Douglas: South Georgia College.

Steinen, Karl T.

1971   Analysis of the Non–ceramic Artifacts from a Hopewellian Affiliated Site in Glades County, Florida. Master's thesis, Florida Atlantic University, Boca Raton.

1976   The Weeden Island Ceramic Complex: An Analysis of Distribution. Ph.D. diss., University of Florida, Gainesville.

Stewart, T. Dale

1946   A Re–examination of the Fossil Human Skeletal Remains from Melbourne, Florida, with Further Data on the Vero Skull. *Smithsonian Miscellaneous Collections* 106(10):1–28.

Stirling, Matthew W.

1935   Smithsonian Archeological Projects Conducted under the Federal Emergency Relief Administration, 1933–1934. *Annual Report of the Smithsonian Institution* 1934:371–400.

1936   Florida Cultural Affiliations in Relation to Adjacent Areas. In *Essays in Anthropology in Honor of Alfred Louis Kroeber*, pp. 351–357. Berkeley: University of California Press.

Stone, Tammy T., David N. Dickel, and Glen H. Doran

1990   The Preservation and Conservation of Waterlogged Bone from the Windover Site, Florida: A Comparison of Methods. *Journal of Field Archaeology* 17:177–186.

Stowe, Noel R.

1985   The Pensacola Variant and the Bottle Creek Phase. *Florida Anthropologist* 38:144–149.

Stright, Melanie J.

1987   *Inundated Archaeological Sites of the Florida Coastal Region: A Regional Overview.* Proceedings: Eighth Annual Gulf of Mexico Information Transfer Meeting. OCS–MMS 88–0035. New Orleans, Minerals Management Service.

Swanton, John R.

1946   The Indians of the Southeastern United States. *Bureau of American Ethnology Bulletin* 137. Washington, D.C.: Smithsonian Institution.

Taylor, Robert C.

1984   *Everglades National Park: Archeological Inventory and Assessment Season* 2.SEAC.

1985   *Everglades National Park Archeological Inventory and Assessment Interim Report Season* 3. SEAC.

Taylor, Robert C., and Gregory Komara

1983   *The Big Cypress National Preserve: Archeological Survey Season* 5. SEAC.

Tesar, Louis D.

1976   Site Survey Success "Super." *Archives and History News* 6(6):1–3. Tallahassee: Florida Department of State.

1980   *The Leon County Bicentennial Survey Report: An Archaeological Survey of Selected Portions of Leon County, Florida.* Miscellaneous Project Report Series 49. BHSP.

1981   Fort Walton and Leon-Jefferson Cultural Development in the Tal-
        lahassee Red Hills Area of Florida: A Brief Summary. *Southeastern
        Archaeological Conference Bulletin* 24:27–29.

Thomas, Cyrus
1894   Report on the Mound Explorations of the Bureau of Ethnology.
        Twelfth Annual Report of the Bureau of American Ethnology, pp. 3–730.
        Washington, D.C.: Smithsonian Institution.

Thomas, David Hurst
1989   *Archaeology.* Orlando: Holt, Rinehart and Winston.

Thomas, Prentice M., and L. Janice Campbell
1985a   Cultural Resources Investigation at Tyndall Air Force Base, Bay
        County, Florida. *New World Research, Inc., Report of Investigations*
        84–4.

1985b   The Deptford to Santa Rosa/Swift Creek Transition in the Florida
        Panhandle. *Florida Anthropologist* 38:110–1 19.

1990   The Santa Rosa/Swift Creek Culture on the Northwest Florida
        Gulf Coast: The Horseshoe Bayou Phase. Paper presented at the
        47th Southeastern Archaeological Conference, Mobile.

1991   The Elliott's Point Complex: New Data Regarding the Localized
        Poverty Point Expression on the Northwest Florida Gulf Coast,
        2000 B.C.–500 B.C. In *The Poverty Point Culture, Local Manifestation,
        Subsistence Practices, and Trade Networks,* edited by Kathleen M.
        Byrd, pp. 103–119. *Geoscience & Man* 29. Baton Rouge: School of
        Geoscience, Louisiana State University.

1993   Eglin Air Force Base Historic Preservation Plan: Technical Syn-
        thesis of Cultural Resources Investigations at Eglin; Santa Rosa,
        Okaloosa, and Walton Counties, Florida. 2 vols. *New World
        Research, Inc., Report of Investigations* 192.

Turner, Victor
1969   *The Ritual Process: Structure and Anti-Structure.* Ithaca, N.Y.: Cornell
        University Press.

Varner, John G., and Jeanette J. Varner, trans. and eds.
1951   *The Florida of the Inca.* Austin: University of Texas Press.

Walker, Karen Jo
1989   Artifacts of a Fishy Nature: Charlotte Harbor's Prehistoric Estu-
        arine Fishing Technology. Paper presented at the 46th South-
        eastern Archaeological Conference, Tampa.

1992a   Bone Artifacts from Josslyn Island, Buck Key Shell Midden, and
        Cash Mound: A Preliminary Assessment for the Caloosahatchee
        Area. In *Culture and Environment in the Domain of the Calusa,* edited
        by William H. Marquardt, pp. 229–246. Institute of Archaeology
        and Paleoenvironmental Studies, Monograph 1. DA.

1992b   The Zooarchaeology of Charlotte Harbor's Prehistoric Maritime Adaptation: Spatial and Temporal Perspectives. Ph.D. diss., University of Florida, Gainesville.

Walker, S. T.
1880   Report on the Shell Heaps of Tampa Bay, Florida. *Annual Report of the Smithsonian Institution* 1879:413–422.
1883   The Aborigines of Florida. *Annual Report of the Smithsonian Institution* 1881:677–680.
1885   Mounds and Shell Heaps on the West Coast of Florida. *Annual Report of the Smithsonian Institution* 1883:854–868.

Waller, Benjamin I.
1970   Some Occurrences of Paleoindian Projectile Points in Florida Waters. *Florida Anthropologist* 23:129–134.
1971   Hafted Flake Knives. *Florida Anthropologist* 24:173–174.
1976   Paleo–associated Bone Tools, Florida. Paper presented at the 28th Annual Meeting of the Florida Anthropological Society, Fort Lauderdale.

Waller, Benjamin I., and James Dunbar
1977   Distribution of Paleo–Indian Projectiles in Florida. *Florida Anthropologist* 30:79–80.

Walthall, John A.
1975   Ceramic Figurines, Porter Hopewell, and Middle Woodland Interaction. *Florida Anthropologist* 28:125–140.
1980   *Prehistoric Indians of the Southeast: Archaeology of Alabama and the Middle South.* Tuscaloosa: The University of Alabama Press.

Warren, Lyman 0.
1964   Possible Submerged Oyster Shell Middens of Upper Tampa Bay. *Florida Anthropologist* 17:227–230.
1968   The Apollo Beach Site, Hillsborough County. *Florida Anthropologist* 21:83–88.
1970   The Kellog Fill from Boca Ciega Bay, Pinellas County, Florida. *Florida Anthropologist* 23:163–167.

Warren, Lyman O., and Ripley P. Bullen
1965   A Dalton Complex from Florida. *Florida Anthropologist* 18:29–32.

Warren, Lyman O., William Thompson, and Ripley P. Bullen
1967   The Culbreath Bayou Site, Hillsborough County, Florida. *Florida Anthropologist* 20:146–163.

Watts, William A.
1969   A Pollen Diagram from Mud Lake, Marion County, North-central Florida. *Geological Society of America, Bulletin* 80:631–642.
1971   Post-Glacial and Interglacial Vegetation History of Southern Georgia and Central Florida. *Ecology* 52:676–689.

Watts, William A., and Barbara C. S. Hansen

1988   Environments of Florida in the Late Wisconsin and Holocene. In *Wet Site Archaeology,* edited by Barbara A. Purdy, pp. 307–323. Caldwell, N.J.: Telford.

Wayne, Lucy B., and Martin F, Dickinson (with contributions by Randy Bellomo, Ann Cordell, Michael Gardner, and Elizabeth Sheldon)

1993   Archaeological Excavations, Lake Jesup South Site (8Se580), Seminole County, Florida. Report prepared for Breedlove, Dennis & Associates, Inc. SouthArc, Inc., Gainesville. On File, SouthArc, Gainesville.

Webb, S. David, James Dunbar, and Lee Newsom

1992   Mastodon Digesta from North Florida. *Current Research in the Pleistocene* 9:114–116.

Webb, Clarence H.

1977   *The Poverty Point Culture.* Geoscience and Man 17. Baton Rouge: School of Geoscience, Louisiana State University,

Webb, S. David, Jerald T. Milanich, Roger Alexon, and James S. Dunbar

1984   A *Bison Antiquus* Kill Site, Wacissa River, Jefferson County, Florida. *American Antiquity* 49:384–392.

Weisman, Brent R.

1986   The Cove of the Withlacoochee: A First Look at the Archaeology of an Interior Florida Wetland. *Florida Anthropologist* 39:4–23.

1987   A Cultural Resource Inventory of the Crystal River Archaeological Site (8CI1), Citrus County, Florida. Submitted to the Florida Department of Natural Resources, Bureau of Land and Aquatic Resource Management, Tallahassee.

1989   *Like Beads on a String: A Culture History of the Seminole Indians in North Peninsular Florida.* Tuscaloosa: University of Alabama Press.

1992   *Excavations of the Franciscan Frontier, Archaeology of the Fig Springs Mission.* Gainesville: University Press of Florida/FMNH.

1993   An Overview of the Prehistory of the Wekiva River Basin. *Florida Anthropologist* 46:20–36.

Welch, James M.

1983   *Mitigative Excavations of the South Prong I Site, 8-Hi-418, and the Cates Site, 8-Hi-425, Hillsborough County, Florida.* Archaeological Report 13 , Department of Anthropology, University of South Florida.

Wharton, Barry, and J. Raymond Williams

1980   An Appraisal of Hardee County Archaeology: Hinterland or Heartland? *Florida Scientist* 43:215–220.

Wharton, Barry, George Ballo, and Mitchell Hope

1981   The Republic Groves Site, Hardee County, Florida. *Florida Anthropologist* 34:59–80.

White, Nancy M.

1981a   Archaeological Survey at Lake Seminole, Jackson and Gadsden Counties, Florida, Seminole and Decatur Counties, Georgia. Final Report Submitted to the U.S. Army Corps of Engineers, Mobile District, in Fulfillment of Contract No. DACW01–78–C–0163. Cleveland Museum of Natural History Archaeological Research Report.

1981b   The Curlee Site (8Ja7) and Fort Walton Development in the Upper Apalachicola–Lower Chattahoochee Valley in Florida. *Southeastern Archaeological Conference Bulletin* 24:24–27.

1982   The Curlee Site (8Ja7) and Fort Walton Development in the Upper Apalachicola–Lower Chattahoochee Valley. Ph.D. diss., Case Western Reserve University, Cleveland.

1986   Prehistoric Cultural Chronology in the Apalachicola Valley: The Evolution of Native Chiefdoms in Northwest Florida. In *Threads of Tradition and Culture along the Gulf Coast,* edited by R. V. Evans, pp. 194–215. Pensacola: Gulf Coast History and Humanities Conference.

White, Nancy M., and Audrey M. Trauner

1987   Archaeological Survey of the Chipola River Valley, Northwest Florida. Manuscript submitted to the Bureau of Historic Preservation, Tallahassee.

Widmer, Randolph E.

1974   *A Survey and Assessment of Archaeological Resource on Marco Island, Colleir County, Florida.* Miscellaneous Project Report Series 19. BHSP.

1978   The Structure of Late Prehistoric Adaptation on the Southwest Florida Coast. Master's thesis, Pennsylvania State University, College Park.

1984   The Evolution of the Calusa, a Non–agricultural Chiefdom on the Southwest Florida Coast. Ph.D. diss. Pennsylvania State University, College Park.

1986   Prehistoric Estuarine Adaptation at the Solana Site, Charlotte County, Florida. Report submitted to the Florida Department of Transportation and Federal Highway Administration. On file, BHSP.

1988   *The Evolution of the Calusa: A Nonagricultural Chiefdom on the Southwest Florida Coast.* Tuscaloosa: University of Alabama Press.

Willey, Gordon R.

1945   The Weeden Island Culture: A Preliminary Definition. *American Antiquity* 10:225–254.

1948   Culture Sequence in the Manatee Region of West Florida. *American Antiquity* 13:209–218.

1949a   *Archeology of the Florida Gulf Coast.* Smithsonian Miscellaneous Collections 113. Washington, D.C.: Smithsonian Institution.

1949b   *Excavations in Southeast Florida.* Yale University Publications in Anthropology 42.

Willey, Gordon R., and Jeremy A. Sabloff

1974   *A History of American Archaeology.* San Francisco: W. H. Freeman.

Willey, Gordon R., and Richard B. Woodbury

1942   A Chronological Outline for the Northwest Florida Coast. *American Antiquity* 7:232–254.

Williams, Wilma B.

1983   Bridge to the Past: Excavations at the Margate–Blount Site. *Florida Anthropologist* 36:142–153.

Wilson, Charles J.

1982   *The Indian Presence: Archeology of Sanibel, Captiva, and Adjacent Islands in Pine Island Sound.* Sanibel–Captiva Conservation Foundation, Sanibel, Florida.

Wing, Elizabeth

1965   Animal Bones Associated with Two Indian Sites on Marco Island, Florida. *Florida Anthropologist* 18:21–28.

1984   Faunal Remains from Seven Sites in the Big Cypress National Preserve. *CNRS Notes et Monographies Techniques* 16:169–181. Paris.

Wing, Elizabeth, and L. McKean

1987   Preliminary Study of the Animal Remains Excavated from the Hontoon Island Site. *Florida Anthropologist* 40:40–46.

Worth, John E.

1992   The Timucuan Missions of Spanish Florida and the Rebellion of 1656. Ph.D. diss. Department of Anthropology, University of Florida. Gainesville.

Wyman, Jeffries

1867   Florida Shell Mounds. *Boston Society of Natural History Proceedings* 11:158–159.

1868   An Account of the Fresh–water Shell Heaps of the St. Johns River, East Florida. *American Naturalist* 2:393–403, 440–463.

1875   Fresh–water Shell Mounds of the St. Johns River, Florida. *Peabody Academy of Science Memoir* 4:3–94. Salem, Mass.

Zubillaga, Felix, ed.

1946   *Monumenta Antiquae Floridae* (1566–1572). Monumenta Historica Societatis Iesu 69, Monumenta Missionum Societatis Iesu 3. Rome.

 **INDEX**

Page numbers given in italics indicate that the reference is to a figure or table on that page.

Tick Island site, *62*, 76, 107, *259*; burials
at, 82–84, 88
Tierra Verde site, *395*, *397*, 399, 403
Timucua Indians, 2, 165, 243, *247*,
249
Timucua Preserve sites, *62*, 89. *See also*
specific sites
Tomoka River site, 254
Tony's Mound, *280*, 281–82, *282*, 297
Torrence, Corbett, 102
Torreya Ravines, 197
Torreya Ravines State Park sites, 95,
197–98, *200*
Tortoise, 46–47, 117, 266
Transitional period, 35, 88
Trilisa Pond site, *62*, 64
Troyville culture, 160
Tucker Ridge-pinched pottery, 262
Tucker site, *165*
Turner River site, *280*, 308
Turtle, 47, 74, 92, 117, 119–20, 179, 200,
214, 231, 251, 266, 272, 291, 338–39,
364, 395
Turtle Mound, 257

Underwater archaeology, 20–23, *21–22*,
46–47. *See also* specific sites
Union County, 349
United States Department of Agriculture,
Forestry Service, 24
United States National Museum, 8.
See also Smithsonian Institution
University of Central Florida, 24
University of Florida, 12, 14, 16, *17*,
18–19, 21–22, 24, 31, 208, 229, 239
University of Miami, 24
University of North Florida, 24
University of South Florida, 24–25
University of West Florida, 24
Useppa Island sites, *62*, 84–85, 101–2, *280*,
313–14, 319
Uzita Indians, 397, 401–2

Velda site, 365
Vero Beach, 252

Vero Beach site, 7, 9
Volusia County, 7, 9, 76, 84, 88–89, *90*,
245, 261, 269
Von Morlot, A., 4

Wacasassa River, 208
Wacissa point, 63–64
Wacissa River, 41, 43, 46
Waddell's Mill Pond site, *361*, 363
Wakulla Check Stamped pottery, 157,
159, 194, 202, 224, 227
Wakulla Weeden Island culture, 108,
160, 163–64, 194–204, 326, 348, 350,
355, 362, 364; agriculture in, 194, 196,
200; ceramics in, 194, 202, 204; ceremonialism in, 197; chronology of, 194,
197–98, 202, *203*; earspool in, 204;
households in, 198–202; lithic artifacts
in, 202–4; mounds in, 197; pipes in,
204; plant use in, 194, 196, 200–201;
region of, *195*; shell artifacts in, 204;
site types and locations of, 195–97;
social organization of, 197; subsistence
in, 194, 196, 198–201
Walker, Karen, 315, 319, 322
Walker, S.T., 4–5
Walker Point Mound, 269
Waller, Benjamin, 42
Walton County, 98, 384
Waring, Antonio, 13, *15*
Warm Mineral Spring site, 44, *45*, 47, 52,
58, *62*, 64
Warren, Lyman O., 100
Washington State University, 208
Wash Island site, 116, *209*, 211
Watson, Thomas, 145, 151
Webb, Clarence, 107
Webb, S. David, 21, 33, 40–41
Weeden Island cultures, 27, 133, 141,
145, 155–204, 205–41, 228, 326, 349,
364–65, 389, 407, 412, 414; ceramics
in, 4, 142, 146, 155–57, 159–63,
220–21, 227–28, 238, 241, *247*, 248,
260, 262, 313, 319–20, 356, 365, 378;
ceremonialism in, 149, 164, 221–22;
chronology of, 144, 157–59, 161–63,